Crafting identities

MANCHESTER
1824
Manchester University Press

To buy or to find out more about the books currently available in this series, please go to: https://manchesteruniversitypress.co.uk/series/studies-in-design-and-material-culture/

STUDIES IN DESIGN & MATERIAL CULTURE

general editors
Elizabeth Currie
Sally-Anne Huxtable
and
James Ryan

founding editor
Paul Greenhalgh

Crafting identities

Artisan culture in London, *c.* 1550–1640

Jasmine Kilburn-Toppin

Manchester University Press

Published by Manchester University Press
Altrincham Street, Manchester M1 7JA
www.manchesteruniversitypress.co.uk

British Library Cataloguing-in-Publication Data
A catalogue record for this book is available from the British Library

ISBN 978 1 526 14770 7 hardback

First published 2021

Typeset
by New Best-set Typesetters Ltd

For my parents

Contents

Plates

Figures

Acknowledgements

This book would not have been written without the generous support of the Arts and Humanities Research Council and the Paul Mellon Centre for Studies in British Art. I am grateful also to the archivists and librarians at Guildhall Library, where much of the research for this project took place. I spent many a happy research day at the Goldsmiths' Hall Library – there are few more splendid settings for carrying out archival work – and I am especially thankful to David Beasley, Eleni Bide, and Sophia Tobin for sharing their expertise and knowledge of the collection. In the final stages of book writing, Murray Edwards College, Cambridge, and Cardiff University were very supportive and stimulating places to work; I am grateful to all History colleagues and students at these institutions. I am thankful also to Emma Brennan at MUP for her help and patience in bringing the book into being, and to the two anonymous reviewers whose remarks sharpened the text.

Angela McShane has been there from the start of this book project, and I am indebted to her for so much of her time, expertise, and enthusiasm for historical research. She has been an inspiration to work with. I have a great debt of gratitude also to Bernard Capp for generously reading and commenting on many book chapters, and for sharing his extensive knowledge of all themes and sources early modern. I so value his friendship and sage advice, and I count myself very fortunate to be an honorary 'Cappite'. Rebekah Higgitt and Keir Waddington read various draft chapters over the years, and their recommendations have certainly improved the end product. Additionally, I am grateful to them for being such supportive managers of my early research and teaching career.

I am very appreciative of brilliant friends who have provided encouragement and distraction, and occasional, gentle enquiries into the progress of the book. Special thanks to Ben Barrat, Jess Fogarty, Madeleine Patston,

Charlotte Merry, Rosie Sharkey, Jonny Austin, Thomasin Summerford, Alice Dolan, Jenny Saunt, Elaine Tierney, Deborah Barton, Bronach Kane, and Georgina Martin. Over the years, Tess, Finn, and Juno have truly been the sheepdog dream team – I am grateful for their wonderful companionship and our diverting walks.

Finally, I cannot thank my family enough. Fleur has been an endless source of encouragement and is a role model of intellectual achievement. James has read every page of this book and provided so much emotional and practical sustenance, not least some excellent chocolate cakes. I am lucky to have met such a brilliant partner and historian. I am very sorry that Phillipa did not live to see this book published – I have fond memories of our mutual enthusiasm looking at museums and churches together in Switzerland. This volume is dedicated with love to my parents, Nicola and John, who have always fostered my historical interests, and whose ceaseless support and enthusiasm has made everything else possible.

Abbreviations

BL	British Library
GHA	Goldsmiths' Hall Archive, London
GL	Guildhall Library, City of London
LMA	London Metropolitan Archive
TNA	The National Archives, Kew

Note on spellings and dates

Original spellings from manuscript sources have been retained and abbreviations expanded. Quotations from printed primary sources are cited verbatim.

Until 1752 the year officially began on 25 March in England. Hence, any manuscript dated between January and 24 March is referenced using both Old and New Style calendars (e.g. January 1572/3).

1

Introduction: crafting identities

In a detailed inventory of the company hall on Lime Street, in the City of London, dated 1490, the Pewterers' Company clerk listed all the material possessions owned by the guild, and the various rooms in which these objects and fixtures were located. An inventory taken a century and a half later, in 1640, shows that in this intervening period the guild had substantially enlarged their hall, creating new chambers and additional storeys, and had also accumulated a far larger collection of material culture. This included textiles and soft furnishings, furniture, plate, cooking apparatus, armour, books, and manuscripts.[1] Examination of the Pewterers' Company court records reveals a particularly intense period of rebuilding and decorative improvement to their livery hall between the early 1550s and late 1580s, including the construction of a new parlour, gallery, and court chamber.[2]

The example of Pewterers' Hall, though unusually well-documented, was far from unique. It speaks to a broader pattern of structural and material change to guild buildings across early modern London. During the 1560s, for example, the governors of the Tallow Chandlers' Company decided that their parlour 'shalbe raysed higher and buylded of new ageyne'.[3] Similarly, between 1572 and 1614 the Carpenters' Company transformed their hall, building a new parlour, counting house, gallery, staircase, and stables. The Carpenters also enlarged their internal hall chamber and commissioned a new decorative scheme for the high end of the hall to represent the biblical and historic ancestry of their craft.[4] The Armourers' Company erected a new gallery, from which their extensive collection of full suits of armour, gifted by makers and patrons, could be viewed by all visitors to the company building.[5] These examples of adaptation and material enhancement could be multiplied many times over. Furthermore, we are dealing not just with alterations to existing built fabrics. Between 1549 and 1638 the Cordwainers', Clothworkers', Goldsmiths', and Ironmongers'

Companies demolished their halls, and constructed entirely new institutional buildings on the same sites. The assistants of the Goldsmiths' Company declared in 1635 that the new Goldsmiths' Hall, which took half a decade to complete and involved intensive, sometimes fraught negotiations with civic and royal authorities, was 'a publique work for a never dyeing body'.[6] The degree to which the 'publique' nature of this project infringed upon the Goldsmiths' autonomy was a matter which preoccupied the guild for the remainder of the 1630s.

This book explores artisanal identity and culture in early modern London. Craftsmen were integral to the social, political, and economic organisation of the city, and thus played an essential role in the meteoric rise of London's status in Europe and the wider world. Yet there is a surprising absence of literature on artisanal cultural practices. This book argues that the social and intellectual status of London's crafts and craftsmen was embedded in particular material and spatial contexts. The focus of this study is the institutional buildings and material cultures of London's craft companies. Artisans physically shaped the built environment of the city, but the experience of negotiating urban space also impacted directly upon their own distinctive identities. In the pages that follow we take seriously the perspectives and voices of London's artisans, rather than simply reiterating what was said about craftsmen by those with greater economic and social capital. *Crafting Identities* recaptures the social experiences and knowledge cultures of artisans in England's early modern metropolis.

Crafting identities

A major aim of this book is to identify and examine a significant cultural development hitherto overlooked by social and architectural historians: a City-wide movement to enlarge, beautify, and rebuild company halls from the mid-sixteenth century to the start of the English civil wars. These were expensive, highly visible, and time-consuming projects in which London's leading artisans played key roles as commissioners, advisors, and practitioners. The period witnessed a substantial expansion in the number, size, and complexity of guild structures. But the book also has a larger ambition and a far wider scope. By exploring these re-building projects in depth – including design processes, construction works, and the multifarious spatial practices which took place within and around these architectures – it throws new light on artisanal cultural production and self-presentation in England's most diverse and challenging urban environment. The book's novel focus on artisanal spaces and material collections reveals a culture that was undergoing re-definition and change from the mid-sixteenth century, while still retaining important links to its late medieval heritage. Moreover, the spatial framework of analysis exposes a number of shared trends across London's artisanal communities concerning knowledge cultures and the representation of expertise, the organisation of social relations, the negotiation of identity and status, and the establishment of distinctive memorial cultures.

The first common theme across London's artisanal population relates to building sites and their knowledge cultures. Establishing the parameters and depth of artisanal epistemologies is especially important against a historical (and historiographical) backdrop in which craftsmen were frequently reduced by their social superiors to no more than unthinking operators.[7] Historians have often been guilty of repeating the same prejudices.[8] Skilled craftsmen were central to all building schemes throughout the city and its growing suburbs. But uniquely in the case of these hall rebuilding projects, artisans were patrons, designers, material suppliers, and construction workers. The interactions between craftsmen on these sites, recorded in great depth in company court minutes, reveal how knowledge of the 'mind' and skills of the 'hand' were perceived to be mutually reinforcing. Knowledge was understood to be a combination of propositional, embodied, and instrumental expertise.[9] Building 'plots' or plans drawn up by masons with experience in building design were regarded by guildsmen as works-in-progress to be negotiated on-site, in consultation with construction workers. Moreover, disagreements over the design and construction of artisanal buildings reveal the fundamentally collaborative nature of artisanal knowledge production and assessment. No decision was made unilaterally by company master or wardens; proposed 'surveyors' and designs of building projects were put to the vote by (and among) guild governors. This collaborative dimension is further reinforced when we step inside livery company halls and explore the spatial practices which defined guild life. Assessments about the design and workmanship of masterpieces, for instance, or the material quality of objects brought back for evaluation following the search, were always made collaboratively, and were typically based upon wide-ranging experiential, sensory, and technical understandings.

This leads us to the second shared theme to emerge from a focused study of the material conditions of artisanal lives: artisanal architectures served to articulate and define changing social relationships within craft companies, and political relations between citizens and the Crown. *Crafting Identities* thus redresses the impression in the existing literature on guilds that artisanal social relations simply took place *in* company architectures, building sites, streets, or workshops. It suggests instead that identities and social interactions were shaped *within* and *through* these built environments. The experience of the physical built environment served to construct an (often uneasy) sense of artisanal community.[10] This is evidenced, for example, in the prestigious routes constructed within company buildings, including new staircases and doorways to provide artisanal elites with direct and exclusive access to new or rebuilt, high-status upper-floor rooms, such as dining chambers, galleries, and parlours. By the late sixteenth century, journeymen were almost universally excluded from these spaces, further reinforcing their subordinate status. Foreign, or, as they were known, 'alien' craftsmen, might receive an invitation to dine with guild elites in the company hall, but they were effectively barred from parlours and treasuries. Through this reconfigured architecture, the social boundaries of belonging were materially articulated and reinforced. Identities and relationships were also constituted in relation to exterior architectural boundaries and designs. By the early seventeenth century, disagreements over where the external walls of company halls ended and public streets began were both a symptom of, and came to symbolically define, souring relations between the City's most influential artisans and retailers, and agents of royal authority.[11] A parallel tension was also erupting over the appropriate location of the most prestigious workshops and shops in the City (and suburbs). Contested interpretations over the 'public' nature of artisanal spaces, in workshops and city streets, as within company halls, came to define an artisan's place within the body of the guild and civic society, or his exclusion from it.

Finally, focusing attention upon the buildings designed and inhabited by London's leading craftsmen reveals the significance of material cultures in forging individual and collective artisanal reputations. Life-writings are an insufficient pool of evidence for exploring a group whose commercial success depended upon the skilled manipulation of tools, designs, and materials. Artisanal reputations were, for example, established and upheld through the gifting of carefully selected material gifts to the 'house' (the craftsman's company hall).[12] Close analysis of the rites of object-exchange reveals how master artisans negotiated civic status, authority, and memory through the presentation of a wide range of gifted artefacts for display and ritual use in London's livery halls. Such gifts included hand-wrought textiles, furniture, armour, plate, manuscripts, and decorative material fixtures such as wainscot (some of which still survive within company collections). Moreover, this culture of material gift-giving was so deep-rooted that it survived the Reformation upheavals largely intact. Material collections in guild buildings were viewed by a broad civic audience, and they served to promote distinctive themes of craft antiquity and workshop-based skills and knowledge. In short, artisanal identities and post-mortem reputations were fashioned through things. And to comprehend artisanal culture we must pay close attention to the designs, materialities, and iconography of the material cultures that craftsmen recorded and left behind.

This study enriches our understanding of the cultural and social lives of craft guilds, but it also illuminates broader themes about early modern urban space, 'civic' and 'urban' renaissances, and artisanal and metropolitan knowledge cultures. The enhanced visibility of artisanal buildings proposed here has implications for customary accounts about the transformation and experience of urban space. Showing how artisans and merchants fashioned their collective spaces decentres narratives about changes to the built environment of early modern London that are usually framed solely from the perspective of aristocratic, gentlemanly, and royal activity.[13] Artisans were active participants in the design and subsequent use and social negotiation of urban space. Crucially, this study also offers a new chronology of urban reconstruction and rebuilding. Whereas existing research has been almost exclusively focused upon the political and cultural reconstruction of the Restoration city (post-1660), *Crafting Identities* locates this activity firmly in the sixteenth and early seventeenth centuries.[14]

Aside from the physical transformation of the built environment, an enhanced awareness of artisanal spaces has implications for understanding how contemporaries experienced, navigated, and imagined their city. Recovering these hitherto forgotten sites further reveals the dense networks of social, political, and cultural exchange that were characteristic of metropolitan life. It is evident from the available urban sources that London's leading artisans repeatedly traced routes between domestic residences, workshops, retail spaces, taverns, parish churches, Guildhall, and livery halls, on personal and official business, communicating news, gossip, and trade secrets, conveying tools, gifts, masterpieces, and building plans. Company buildings were also central to the topography of civic processions, the rituals through which citizens displayed and performed their values and physically marked out the boundaries of their communities. Even for urban inhabitants who were not deeply invested in the day-to-day governance or administration of the guilds, these spaces still featured strongly in their 'imagined' urban geographies. For example, artisanal company halls were key sites in the unique autobiographical survivals of the Puritan turner and chronicler, Nehemiah Wallington (1598–1658), lifelong inhabitant of the parish of St. Leonard Eastcheap.[15] In an account of Whitsun Tuesday in May 1640, for instance, he writes that 'many youths and prentiesses did meete at Deyars Hall [Dyers' Hall, near Thames Street] in fasting and prayr on that day'.[16] Reflecting upon the subject of death, Wallington relates the tale of a neighbour and fellow turner, Master Bartlet, who on 4 May 1654 'was at Turners Hall [in Smithers Lane] (very brisk and in helth) chusing of Master and wardens ... and the next day ... he was dead'.[17] Institutional artisanal spaces were firmly integrated into Wallington's mental map of the city. In a far from complimentary vein, customs official and antiquarian Thomas Milles imagined company halls at the confluence not just of metropolitan life, but of national commerce. Writing in 1608, he reflected:

> Our *Trades* doe meete in *Companies*, our *Companies* at *Halls*, and our *Halls* become *Monopolies* of Freedome, tyde to *London:* where all our *Crafts* & *Mysteries* are so layd vp together ... By meanes whereof, all our Creekes seeke to one Riuer, all our Riuers run to one Port, all our Ports ioyne to one Towne, all our Townes make but one Citty, and all our Citties but Suburbes to one vast, vnweldy, and disorderlie *Babell* of buildings, which the worlde calls *London.*[18]

The placing of London's livery halls at the centre of the 'disorderlie *Babell* of buildings' that together constituted the metropolis is suggestive of their perceived and symbolic significance to contemporaries. In recovering institutional artisanal sites this book thus recaptures valuable experiences and imaginings about urban space.

Through exploration of the intersection of artisanal and civic cultures, this study also speaks to a broader historiographical debate about the nature and timing of English 'civic' and 'urban' renaissances in the sixteenth and seventeenth centuries, and the social groups participating in this cultural resurgence.[19] For example, the elaboration of gift-giving rituals within guild communities, underlining the reciprocal relationship between citizen and company, provides further evidence for the rise of an associational 'bourgeois' culture in this period.[20] Moreover, the synchronisation of gifting and feasting rites within company halls from the mid-sixteenth century – both practices intended to reinforce bonds between citizens – suggests the increasing linguistic, institutional, and cultural importance of civic sociability or 'company' in early modern urban England.[21]

The present volume makes two key interventions in this debate. First, it brings to light the importance of the subjective notion of skill, or expertise, to London's citizens.[22] The historiographic focus upon the political dimensions of urban freedom has led to a representation of London's leading artisans and retailers solely as political agents.[23] In the chapters which follow, it is argued that workshop-based expertise had strong cultural valence, alongside other commonly cited values such as philanthropy. Considering that the great majority of London's sixteenth- and early seventeenth-century citizens were educated in the workshop or retail space, and their reputations and livelihoods depended upon embodied skills, we should take seriously their interest in demonstrating, assessing, and proving expertise. This is not to affirm an old-fashioned economic functionalism,[24] but rather to suggest that the assertion of craft knowledge and technical ability was a form of cultural capital, and a way of furthering one's status within urban institutions and society.

Crafting Identities also has something to say about the pace of change within urban culture across the early modern period. While work on English provincial towns and the urban renaissance has stressed a starkly 'secularized' post-Reformation culture, this book comes to very different conclusions.[25] Late sixteenth- and early seventeenth-century craft guilds deployed religious symbolism, especially the figure of the patron saint as renowned craft expert, to draw attention to the association between artisanal skill and the historic origins of the guild fraternity. This imagery of antique expertise in exclusive spaces and during public ceremonies was especially pertinent during an era in which the ability of guilds to regulate craft production was under increasing strain, due to rapid demographic growth and the physical expansion of the city.[26] In the metropolis, religious iconography persisted alongside civic motifs in artisanal spaces.

Finally, looking beyond England, this work contributes to a contemporary Europe-wide debate on the meaning of 'expertise', and the role of artisans in shaping early modern 'knowledge cultures'.[27] Long-standing hierarchies of knowledge were becoming unstable, and were being renegotiated in this period. The Aristotelian dichotomy between knowledge of the 'mind' and of the 'hand', or theory and practical knowledge, was beginning to break down against the backdrop of growing literacy, an expanding print culture, increasing urban wealth, commerce and trade, and enhanced rivalry between nascent nation states.[28] There was thus a heated contemporary argument over the nature of true 'knowledge': was practical experience, technical proficiency, or book-based learning sufficient? Was an individual truly knowledgeable if he could undertake a process – for example the construction of a fortification – but did not understand the theoretical principles behind his work? It is frequently asserted that humanist scholars, gentlemen, merchants, and craftsmen played mutually significant roles in blurring the boundaries between 'theory' and 'practice'. But while in the English context the part of 'expert mediators' and gentlemen conducting investigations into the natural world are well known, the viewpoints of London's sixteenth- and early seventeenth-century artisans remain largely concealed.[29] The present study recovers long-obscured artisanal perspectives. Chapters 2 and 3 examine trends and tensions within London's artisanal knowledge cultures, and the ways in which artisans articulated, contested, and disseminated their epistemologies. Moreover, rather than focusing upon individual, exceptional artisans and their engagement with knowledge cultures, as has been the case in European literature on craftsmen, this study uncovers the broader social and institutional networks within and through which artisanal practices were embedded and perpetuated.

The spatial focus of the present volume is artisanal company halls and their immediate environs. A more expansive analysis of artisanal spaces and cultures might also ideally include the large number of artisanal houses, shops, workshops, and warehouses in the City and suburbs. Very broadly, we know that living and working spaces for early modern artisans were frequently coterminous; craftsmen typically lived behind or above workshops and commercial spaces which fronted the street.[30] Thus, in a will of 1618, London citizen and armourer Edward Langton made a direct provision for his wife Elizabeth, who was to inherit his 'dwelling house' after his death, to have 'free way and passage throughe my sayd shopp [which had been left to their son Edward to operate as a commercial premises] at all convenient tymes into out of and from my house'.[31] The lack of substantial direct surviving evidence for these sites in sixteenth- and early seventeenth-century London – such as probate inventories – precludes a comprehensive parallel analysis of artisanal homes and workshops. But these significant urban spaces do feature in this book. Chapters 2 and 3 explore a prominent mason's workshop, and consider how an urban building site, a hive of artisanal expertise, operated like a craft workshop writ large. In Chapter 5 we repeatedly encounter material cultures which originated from London artisanal workshops and homes. Moreover, the penultimate chapter of this study examines the well-documented campaign to return all 'remote' goldsmiths (with retail premises and workshops located in western suburbs) to Cheapside (their customary City location).

Artisans in early modern London: definitions and diversity

In early modern London an artisan was an individual who exercised a craft or trade and belonged to an occupational guild, also known as a 'livery company'. Membership of a guild was essential not just for legitimately operating a business, but also for establishing and maintaining status within civic society.[32] London's artisans produced, assembled, and often marketed a vast range of material products which were eagerly consumed by expanding urban, provincial, and international markets. Craftsmen who were engaged in construction work, such as masons, plasterers, and carpenters, played essential roles in the design, rebuilding, and expansion of the city and its surrounding environs. Workshop practitioners were also fundamental to the operation of a number of state institutions, including the Royal Mint at the Tower, the armouries at Greenwich, and the Woolwich Dockyard. Furthermore, London's late sixteenth- and seventeenth-century artisans, particularly highly skilled instrument makers, were central participants in the development of natural philosophy.[33]

Contemporaries employed a varied terminology for workshop practitioners, including labourer,[34] craftsman,[35] craftsmaster,[36] artificer,[37] artisan,[38] handicraftsman,[39] and mechanick.[40] 'Labourer' indicated unskilled manual work, and 'mechanick' was frequently pejorative in tone; but 'craftsmaster' and 'artisan' had more positive connotations, suggesting an experienced workshop practitioner and householder.[41] Rare accounts of artisanal self-description also betray a keen awareness of distinctions between craftsmen. The author of an early seventeenth-century English manuscript on metallurgy, whom we will encounter again in the next chapter, claimed that 'a complete Goldesmythe' is 'a workeman bothe in golde and sylver' whereas an artisan who 'is but parte of a gouldsmythe is skilled but in one of these'.[42] This subtle distinction was overlooked by the prominent sixteenth-century English social theorist, William Harrison, who grouped all craftsmen or 'artificers' together in the lowest social category: the 'fourth sort people … have neither voice nor authority … but are to be ruled and not to rule other'.[43] This blanket categorisation by a gentleman with a disdain for all manual work, and no interest in the multiplicity of distinctions below the level of the yeomanry, misses the lived reality, the wide variations among urban artisans in terms of wealth, skill, and political authority.[44] Moreover, since in London a householder was typically both a citizen (a social category which Harrison ranked second only to gentlemen) and an 'artificer', these neat boundaries quickly dissolve.[45]

Scholars working on early modern urban culture and society have stressed the diversity of artisanal products and working practices.[46] In London, the artisanal social grouping was especially broad, and, indeed, becoming more diverse over time.[47] The extraordinary size and wealth of London's population created a huge market for consumable, semi-durable and durable goods, and for innovative products.[48] It is well established that early modern London experienced vast demographic growth, from *c.* 75,000 inhabitants in 1550 to *c.* 575,000 by 1700. This huge population growth was sustained by high levels of in-migration to the city. Across the sixteenth century the population at least quadrupled in size, with the last few decades seeing particular growth. By 1600 there were approximately 200,000 Londoners.[49] Urban workshops were often highly specialised and interconnected to other sites of manufacture and retail through networks of credit and subcontracting relations.[50] In the late sixteenth-century City there were up to seventy craft and mercantile guilds, and this number grew in the 1600s, as groups working in novel and highly specialised trades, such as lens grinding and clock making, were newly incorporated (to the considerable chagrin of existing companies).[51] Tellingly, as Alexandra Shepard's research has shown, artisanal witnesses in courts also used a growing variety of occupational titles across the seventeenth and early eighteenth centuries.[52] To do justice to this broad range of expertise, this book examines archival materials from a wide variety of London's craft practitioners and livery companies, across the spectrum or hierarchy of crafts and trades. Case studies are drawn from among the Armourers', Bakers', Barber Surgeons', Blacksmiths', Carpenters', Clockmakers', Coopers', Cutlers', Drapers', Founders', Girdlers', Goldsmiths', Ironmongers', Pewterers', Tallow Chandlers', Tylers', Wax Chandlers', and Weavers' Companies. This array of guild archives – including those relating to the metallurgy, building, chandlers, and textile trades – offers considerable scope for comparison of civic status, company size, affluence, expertise, and material production. These companies ranged from highly prestigious and skilled luxury crafts (such as goldsmithing), with members who were also engaged in City governance at the highest level, to the more humble craft and social aspirations of guilds such as the Tallow Chandlers' Company.

Artisanal identities

Despite the diversity of artisanal experiences and perspectives, there were significant common threads running throughout and sustaining craft culture. Closer attention to the spatial and material dimensions of artisanal lives is essential for gaining insight into shared epistemological, social, political, and memorial cultures. In other words, an examination of artisanal spaces and things in the following chapters can shed light upon complex craft-based identities. Before attempting such a task it is necessary to delineate here the broad contours of artisanal identity and status. Identity in the early modern period, especially in urban areas, was strongly shaped by association with, or membership of, multiple 'overlapping groupings', including household, parish, guild, confraternity, and civic government.[53] Contrary to the Burckhardtian thesis – that individual subjectivity was only achieved by the shedding of medieval collective associations and consciousness – these 'elaborate networks of communal relations' have now taken centre stage in scholarly understandings of the formation of identity in the early modern era.[54] The importance of these collective networks to the construction and experience of identity comes through even in relatively traditional 'ego-documents' such as diaries and chronicles. In an exploration of artisan 'autobiographies', historian James Amelang found that 'their assumption of voice rested to a large degree on earlier experience of participation ... in ordering their trade, neighbourhood, church, and local government'.[55] Moreover, Judith Pollmann's work on pre-modern memorialists has shown how personal identity was about 'performing the identities for which one was born or trained'. She suggests that there were 'social and cultural scripts for being a child, a man, a father, an artisan ... an identity as a citizen of a particular city', and yet, crucially, historical actors 'followed such scripts as individuals ... that is why personal experiences mattered'.[56]

Artisanal identities in London, individual and collective, were hugely complex. Associational and institutional belonging were perhaps especially significant in an urban environment as large, challenging, and often bewildering as late sixteenth- and seventeenth- century London.[57] Artisans typically fashioned a distinctive sense of self through a multitude of occupational, associational, familial, religious, and social networks. To present and identify as a reputable artisan, and to be perceived by others as such, depended especially upon guild membership, familial networks, and masculine status. London's most successful artisans oversaw independent workshops, businesses, and households, held property at a prestigious address, had a substantial quantity of moveable goods, extensive credit networks, and exercised considerable authority through guild, ward, and parish office-holding. As Margaret Pappano and Nicole Rice argue, 'an artisan was not simply someone who possessed skill but also someone with authority to exercise that skill'.[58] These relatively prosperous and privileged artificers, who also made the key decisions concerning the designs, materials, uses, and maintenance of company halls, are the main subjects of this study. These are men like citizen and pewterer Edward Ketchre, whose will of December 1562 reveals a dense network of familial, parish, and corporate responsibilities and loyalties. In addition to making financial and material provisions for his wife, six children, siblings, godchildren, wider kin, and several household servants, Ketchre left 'a black coote [coat]' and 10s to his two apprentices, to be received upon completion of their service. The will also stipulated that rents from his four tenements in the parish of St. Peter le Poer in the ward of Bread Street were to fund quarter day feasts at Pewterers' Hall, and annual payments to five poor men of the guild.[59]

Individual and collective identities, or the 'internal' and the 'external' self, so far as we can speak of these categories, are best understood as relational and highly dynamic.[60] The subjective voice is repeatedly negotiated in relation to collective institutions. We perceive this relational force in the construction and experience of craft identities in the artisanal-authored (or directed) texts of Chapters 2 and 3. The master mason Nicholas Stone, who chronicled his material production and witnessing of the major events of the civil war in London, did so within documents rooted in the collaborative workshop environment. Likewise, the goldsmiths who authored a book of craft secrets did so self-consciously as part of a broader manuscript and workshop tradition of epistemological revelation. Chapters 4 and 5 show how the symbol of the craft mark, the ultimate sign of an individual skilled artisan or workshop, was inserted into corporate archives and inscribed onto gifted objects and built interiors. In so doing the identity of both craftsman and guild collective was altered; the expertise and honour of the artisan was immortalised, and his status among fellow craftsmen was heightened. And the collective ritual and material memorial culture of a craft company, particularly in relation to other artisanal corporations, was enhanced.

Guild membership

We cannot speak of artisanal identities in London without acknowledging the importance of occupational guilds. The various economic, political, social, and religious features of these institutions offered numerous compelling possibilities for urban dwellers to identify their interests with those of the guild. It is a central thesis of the book that institutional artisanal spaces were critical sites for demonstrating particular behaviours, and articulating skills and knowledge that marked a man out as a respectable artisan. To appreciate the centrality of guild membership to artisanal identity we must further examine the multifunctional nature of craft companies.

The guild was the fundamental institution for the organisation and regulation of artisanal labour across urbanised late medieval and early modern Europe. Guilds varied widely in size, status, and the financial resources at their disposal, but nearly all attempted, through legal means, to ensure that their members held the exclusive rights to undertake particular economic activities (including manufacturing specific products).[61] In addition, craft guilds typically controlled the process of transmission of specific workshop skills and craft 'secrets' through indenturing apprentices to experienced master craftsmen.[62] Through the authority of royal charter, London's livery companies were also invested with the responsibility to search periodically the city workshops and retail spaces of all craftsmen and retailers engaged in the associated craft or trade. For some guilds this task was metropolitan in scope, and went well beyond the ancient City walls. The purpose of the search, which took the form of a perambulation of the city streets and inspection of goods by company officials, often accompanied by craft experts, was ostensibly to ensure that all products conformed to a standard material quality. Faulty goods were ritualistically destroyed in shops or workshops, or in the associated company hall, and wrong-doers punished and then ideally brought back quickly within the corporate fold.[63] No doubt the search also had a broader symbolic importance in terms of 'collectively protecting the exercise of skilled labour', and of visibly marking out the geography of company authority.[64] The walk of the searchers linked urban workshops and retail spaces to the company hall, the site from which guild officials conspicuously departed and returned at the start and close of business.

The latest literature on the economic role of livery companies suggests that we should be sceptical about the long-standing theory of 'guild decline' across the early modern period.[65] Despite the rapid physical growth of London's suburbs and liberties beyond the City walls and the lord mayor's jurisdiction, and notwithstanding the expansion of London's 'unfree' population, many guilds were still central to the city's economic growth and regulation well into the late seventeenth century, and, in some cases, beyond. A number of companies appear, indeed, to have spurred artisanal innovation.[66] Joseph Ward's account of guilds as dynamic and flexible institutions suggests that there was no simple antagonistic relationship between the City of London and its suburbs and liberties. Instead, notions of community, and opportunities for profit and regulation could be metropolitan in scope.[67]

The right of a freeman to practice any trade or craft in the City, known as the custom of London, meant that in some instances associational and occupational identities did not correlate. By-employment was also a common feature of working lives.[68] The custom of London impacted upon occupational homogeneity primarily in the 'great twelve' livery companies however, rather than the 'minor' craft guilds. London's guilds were ranked in order of precedence, with the 'great twelve' mercantile companies foremost in status, wealth, and authority.[69] Even among the ruling bodies of craft companies, a strong majority of members were artisans practising the associated craft. In any case a disjuncture between craft practice and guild membership was also largely a feature of the late seventeenth and eighteenth centuries.[70] This book is primarily interested in what we might meaningfully say about trends across artisanal culture.[71] The existence of occupational fluidity and by-employment do not therefore present a particular problem in identifying shared cultural features.

Guilds had a central economic role within the urban environment, but their significance to members (and indeed, to those excluded from corporate privilege) was also political, social, and religious. In the City of London, a charter of 1319 made freedom of a guild a prerequisite for citizenship. Only citizens could participate fully in urban life. Freedom was necessary legitimately to carry out a trade (including the establishment and maintenance of a shop), to nominate aldermen or elect common councilmen, or serve in relation to either office.[72] The status of different occupations – usually linked to the value of the materials with which guildsmen worked or sold – was demonstrated, and reinforced, through a strict hierarchy of guild participation in civic ceremonial, including feasts at Guildhall, and processions and pageantry at midsummer and on lord mayor's day. The account by clothier and chronicler Henry Machyn of the inauguration of Sir Thomas White in 1553, for instance, records the ordered hierarchy of 'waytyng of my lord mayre('s) barge unto Westmynster [and] all the craftes bargers with stremars and banars [of every] craft'.[73]

A number of the craftsmen and retailers who feature in these pages also participated in parish administration as members of vestries, and, more rarely, in civic governance as common councillors and aldermen. These roles might have heavily shaped their personal and collective social and political identities. Mindful of these connections, I broadly trace influences and parallels between adaptations to the built environment at Guildhall, the site of greatest civic significance, and associated spatial and ceremonial practices (at events such as election ceremonies and feasting rites), and the use of space and ritual practices within individual company properties.

In the late medieval urban environment, craft guilds and religious fraternities were often inextricably entwined. In London, craft fraternities provided lights in honour of patron saints, and in memory of departed members. They organised prayers, alms, and funerals, and on significant days in the ritual calendar they hosted feasts for the advancement of commensality and charity amongst living brethren. Religious guilds and fraternities were suppressed by Edwardian injunctions in 1547, but London's craft and mercantile institutions persisted, and continued to celebrate significant ritual festivities, manage charitable bequests, and supply welfare (alongside their economic roles).[74] While land held for chantry purposes was lost by many guilds in the mid-sixteenth century, crucially companies 'continued to build up their estates hereafter'.[75] Indeed, the practice of giving land or property to corporations – as a gift or as a bequest to finance charitable activities – gained momentum in the 1500s. As a consequence, the most prestigious and affluent guilds, such as the Clothworkers' and Drapers' Companies, accumulated large swathes of London estate in the sixteenth century. In addition to their economic, political, and social roles, some City companies were thus property managers on a large scale, actively involved in leasing, inspecting, and ensuring the material upkeep of their estates. City guilds engaged in regular 'views' of their property, and some corporations, such as the Goldsmiths' Company, employed an official carpenter to supervise maintenance and repairs.[76]

By the late sixteenth century, London possessed a distinct civic culture in which mercantile elites, chiefly those associated with the 'great twelve' companies, established perpetual gifts and charitable trusts in addition to one-time gifts administered on their behalf by fellow guild members.[77] As Matthew Davies writes of the Clothworkers' Company, 'most of the properties were granted to the Company with clauses attached to use defined amounts from the rental income to provide and monitor charity'.[78] The direct beneficiaries were the 'deserving' urban poor (including company widows and orphans), university scholars, godly parish preachers, inhabitants of hospitals, prisons and almshouses, and impoverished, or 'decayed', company members. Charity (and notions of godliness) was also extended beyond the City walls to the benefactor's county of origin, to include provincial preaching lectureships, grammar schools, and almshouses.[79] This book explores a significant but overlooked culture of material gift-giving within London craft companies, beyond the grand philanthropic gestures on which so much historiographical attention has been focused. It argues that the material cultures of craft guilds provide a valuable (and hitherto unrecognised) source through which to assess how Londoners negotiated religious and civic identities in the post-Reformation era.

London's guilds were structured according to hierarchies of status, 'with men in one estate possessing more wealth, political power, and prestige than men in inferior estates'.[80] At the pinnacle of the institutional hierarchy was the master of the company, who was customarily elected on an annual basis. The master was closely supported in his governing duties by three wardens. Among other responsibilities, the wardens searched workshops and collected rents from guild-owned properties. The master was also sustained by a group of ex-wardens known as the assistants. Collectively the wardens and ex-wardens constituted the court of assistants, which exercised almost total authority over all decisions concerning the governance of the guild and the regulation of the craft or trade.[81] Voting rights and responsibilities, as concerning the election of the master and the wardens, were almost always restricted to the assistants or the livery.[82] The liverymen were senior guildsmen who were physically distinguished from the rest of the company by their ceremonial liveries: fur-lined cloaks with satin hoods. The livery served as stewards on quarter days and at feasts, and participated in the administrative and judicial work of the guilds, including oversight of lawsuits and appeals to the Crown or parliament.[83]

The livery also enjoyed trade privileges, such as the right to take on more apprentices than most ordinary freemen.[84] Admission into the livery was (relatively) expensive and controlled by the company's assistants.[85] Those guildsmen – the majority – who were not members of the livery were known as the yeomanry. This group tended to be socioeconomically heterogeneous, consisting of a range of retailers, master craftsmen (who typically ran a shop), householders, and journeymen. The latter were effectively wage or day labourers who had not established their own workshops.[86] In many companies the yeomanry had their own regulations, officers, and revenue and would organise their own formal and informal social gatherings, memorials, and dinners. In Cutlers' Hall the yeomanry even had their own separate hall chamber.[87]

The numerical size of London's early modern guilds varied considerably. The wealthiest mercantile companies were also the largest: the Grocers' Company constituted around 1,000 guildsmen by 1595; the Drapers' Company was 2,000 strong by 1600. The largest guild was the Merchant Taylor's Company, with a total membership of 2,673 by 1595, according to Ian Archer's estimate.[88] By 1640, the chronological end point of this book, the Goldsmiths' Company had at least 400 members.[89] Craft guilds were considerably smaller than their mercantile counterparts, but the overall pattern across the sixteenth and early seventeenth centuries was one of growth. The Carpenters' Company had about 130 freemen in 1500, between 130 and 300 from 1546 to 1573, and between 250 and 300 freemen from 1573 until 1600. Out of a guild of 250–300, around 40 were liverymen, and on average 8 freemen formed the court of assistants.[90] The Cutlers' Company had about 65 members in 1537–38 and about 120 guildsmen by the early 1600s.[91]

Most livery companies included merchants, retailers, master craftsmen, and journeymen. At the highest levels, the boundaries between a manufacturer, a retailer, and a merchant could be somewhat hazy, since artisans with sufficient capital were also directly engaged with retail, occupying premises from which material things were sold, as well as produced. The relative balance of mercantile and craft members depended upon the nature, wealth, and prestige of a particular company. In the 'great twelve', the livery was largely composed of merchants, while in the less prestigious crafts, which are the primary focus of this study, such as the Carpenters', Pewterers', and Tallow Chandlers' Companies, almost all members of the guild were practising craftsmen.[92] The vast majority of sixteenth-century citizens, regardless of their position in the company estate hierarchy, also had the shared experience of apprenticeship.[93]

Evidently some craftsmen and retailers were much more invested in guild life than others, and played a greater role in formal corporate sociability, administration, and ceremony.[94] The livery estate of London's guilds almost certainly had a greater sense of institutional loyalty and affinity through virtue of their decision-making responsibilities, and engagement in the social and ceremonial round, than those lower down the estate hierarchy.[95] This is amply demonstrated again by the experiences of Nehemiah Wallington. Nehemiah's membership of the Turners' Company did not have a profound impact upon his cultural and social life, though it did play a major role in the lives of his father and brother, both also practising turners. John Wallington Sr., and his son John Wallington Jr., were liverymen of the Turners' Company, and both served as master of the guild.[96]

An early twentieth-century historiography, which presented a picture of sustained internal conflict within guilds – between economically conservative governors, and their wilful artisanal subordinates – has been replaced by a much more subtle reading of the internal social relations within companies.[97] The work of Steve Rappaport and Ian Archer has demonstrated that London's livery companies were still essential in maintaining social stability, particularly during the tumultuous 'crisis decade' of the 1590s. Archer presents a picture of urban society that is less cohesive and stable than that proposed by Rappaport, but both suggest that through responsive courts, charitable largesse, and opportunities for social mobility, livery companies served to reduce tensions within guilds and in urban society at large.[98] Companies' courts of assistants, which typically met monthly or weekly, were 'courts of first and usually last instance' for Londoners, 'settling a range of civil disputes and quasi-criminal offences'. As well as dealing with economic violations of guild ordinances, courts of assistants dealt with the recovery of debt, family disputes, and the resolution of interpersonal conflict between guildsmen.[99]

A man's position in the guild was not fixed. Social and economic status might shift throughout the life-cycle of an individual artisan.[100] The boundary between the estates was porous for some; the most ambitious and successful members of the yeomanry – known as wardens of the yeomanry, or the bachelors in the 'great twelve' companies – had reason to be optimistic that they would become liverymen. Upward mobility was a 'more realistic prospect' in relatively small craft guilds such as the Pewterers' or Armourers' Companies, where the liverymen accounted for a comparatively high proportion of members.[101] In the competitive and uncertain environment of early modern London, clearly downward social mobility was also a perennial feature, and fear, of urban life. Creditors breaking their promises, a workplace accident, or simply old age and associated infirmities, might impact severely upon the prospects and work-based identity of a craftsman. Guild charities and patronage were in part intended to alleviate personal misfortune and the general vicissitudes of urban life. Goldsmith Robert Hooke, for example, who in prosperous middle-age had been employed by the Goldsmiths' Company in the 1630s as supervisor 'about the new building of the Hall, wherein he spent his time daily for the space of about four years both faithfully and carefully', successfully petitioned the guild for a pension twenty years later, at the venerable age of seventy-nine.[102]

Family, social networks, and gendered status

The discussion so far concerning company membership should not be taken to imply that artisanal lives were shaped solely by the regulations, duties, and diversions of their guilds. Guild membership was one (albeit often a significant) feature of diverse experiences and associations.[103] Artisanal life-writings, such as the chronicle of seventeenth-century Barcelonan master tanner Miquel Parets, show that identity was also shaped by familial responsibilities and allegiances, and by kinship networks.[104] Sandra Cavallo's work on barber surgeons and other associated 'artisans of the body' in seventeenth- and early eighteenth-century Turin argues for the significance of family and kinship ties for professional identity and advancement.[105] Material gifts and bequests in surviving artisan wills from London also speak of the strong obligations and bonds of affection between craftsmen and their family, kin, working associates, and friends. Post-mortem gifts had a variety of social, economic, and emotive meanings and significances. In addition to remembering his guild – 'to the Armourers' [Company] hall one cup', worth £5 – armourer Thomas Rigge left, in 1570, his 'best livery coat' to his brother, 'a joyned bedsted, standing in the chamber where I use to lye' to his daughter Joan, a silver pot to his cousin Elizabeth, and 'my best vyce' to his workshop assistant. A female relative was given 'my wife's best gown'. All of the 'tools and ymplements belonging to my shop', objects with both a substantial monetary value, and things that symbolically represented embodied skills, were equally divided between Rigge's brother William and his daughter Joan.[106] The distribution of material gifts in citizen wills also shows how bonds were sustained with kin who lived at considerable distances from London, frequently from the testator's parish of origin. The reflections of Nehemiah Wallington further reveal how the identity of a craftsman could be moulded by membership of a particular religious community. As Paul Seaver has shown, this turner's spiritual endeavours were at the root of his identity, and 'patterns of work and consumption and the ethics of getting and spending were subordinate to Wallington's major concerns with personal salvation and the fate of the godly community'.[107]

Artisan status was also inherently gendered; to be an artificer was to be male. Indeed, the ideal career progression for an artisan – from apprentice to journeyman to master craftsman – was centred on the male life-cycle.[108] Full civic status, though, was reserved for adult men. Apprentices lived and worked in their master's household, under his authority, and were not permitted to get married.[109] These youthful men were thus kept in an economically and socially dependent state and prohibited from setting up an independent household, a key element of full patriarchal manhood.[110] Apprenticeship was intended to be an extended period of skill acquisition, free labour for the master, and a means of socialising London's young men according to civic customs and values.[111] This was clearly the ideal, but apprenticeship contracts frequently went unfulfilled; approximately 50 per cent of London's sixteenth- and seventeenth-century apprentices left their training before the end of their formal contract (of at least seven years).[112]

A significant minority of the adult male population in the City of London was also denied full artisanal status. London inhabitants born elsewhere in England who did not acquire citizenship (referred to as 'foreigners'), and emigrants, predominantly French and Dutch Protestants (termed 'aliens' or 'strangers' by native Londoners and civic and royal authorities alike), were largely excluded from the economic, social, and political benefits of guild membership. The sons and grandsons of continental immigrants were debarred also. The consequences were serious even for the minority of aliens admitted into guilds; among other deprivations, strangers could not keep open shops, or train apprentices (including their own sons and male relatives).[113] Unlike native English, aliens who joined guilds did not automatically receive the freedom of the City.[114] Citizenship was acquired by some foreigners by redemption – on payment of a fee – often with patronage from the royal court, but this was a rare course of action; no stranger goldsmiths, for example, obtained citizenship through redemption during Elizabeth I's reign.[115] Active across a broad range of crafts and trades, strangers were proportionally most significant (and visible) in the clothing industry, metalwork, and trade.[116] In the sixteenth century many aliens settled in the liberty of St. Martin le Grand, a precinct within the walls at the west end of the City. As a liberty this area was excluded from the City companies' regulatory authority over the manufacture and retail of goods.[117] The numerical proportion of aliens relative to the native London population peaked in the late sixteenth century, but began to decline in the early seventeenth century; numbers began to increase again in the mid-seventeenth century. Broadly, these fluctuations map onto periods of relative calm, and political and religious upheaval in continental Europe.[118] Historiographical discussion on the relationship between alien and citizen craftsmen in London has 'focussed on moments of crisis'.[119] However, a more representative overview suggests that the response of native craftsmen to these groups of immigrants varied according to a man's estate and craft, and the economic climate of the capital in a particular season or year. At times of economic hardship, the yeomanry repeatedly petitioned company courts about the unwelcome economic competition posed by aliens; more substantial craftsmen frequently took a more opportunistic approach to pools of (often highly skilled) available labour.[120]

This book shows how artisan identities in London were shaped in response to the skilled alien presence. Chapter 2 shows how the wardens of the Goldsmiths' Company reinstated the custom of the masterpiece, to be undertaken by apprentices at the end of their training, or journeymen, within a workshop at Goldsmiths' Hall, in part because they feared that specialisation within the domestic trade was bringing 'aliens and straingers workemanshipp in better reputac[i]on'. It was well known that the masterpiece was a standard practice within guilds in the Low Countries and France.[121] In so doing the masters of the trade augmented their efforts in marking out Goldsmiths' Hall as a preeminent site of craft knowledge and innovation. Chapter 5 includes case-studies of newly naturalised alien craftsmen (with royal support) presenting material gifts, in effect masterpieces, to the associated London guild as a means of smoothing their passage into the corporation, and demonstrating their unquestionable expertise. Tracing networks of things here elucidates previously unmapped interactions between 'native' and 'alien' artisanal communities.

Overall, women's labour, at all stages of the life-cycle, was hugely important to the growth of the early modern English economy.[122] Women were working in great numbers in the metropolis, primarily in low-status and poorly paid roles, such as needlework, weaving, spinning, washing, laundering, and 'body work'. Others worked as servants, laboured in victualling houses, sold produce in markets, or on city streets as hucksters.[123] Significantly, 'domestic work' tasks such as cooking, cleaning, textile production, and care work 'were not separate from the market economy but were highly commercialized'.[124] However, single women were effectively barred from the legitimate exercise of a craft or trade. 'Whatever their rights in common or customary law … in practice single women who never married were all but excluded from formal participation in the economy.'[125] The vast majority of women were denied the occupational identities and formal training available to many of their male counterparts through guild membership. More rarely, citizen wives and widows ran workshops and retail businesses, and some of these women took on their own – male and female – apprentices.[126] These women also contributed skills, brokered credit, and brought patronage links through marriage.[127] In London companies, 'widows were the only women who in practice possessed the economic rights of companymen' and might, thus, legitimately undertake a craft or trade 'with some degree of institutional freedom'. However, these rights were removed if a widow married a man from another guild.[128] Whatever their stage of the life-cycle, all women were, however – and this is the crucial point – fundamentally excluded from the governance and administration of London's livery companies. Women could not hold office or vote on guild issues, nor did they speak at guild assemblies.[129] More broadly, participation in civic ceremony was a masculine privilege, and women were thus visibly excluded from the symbolic civic community.[130] Whereas institutional belonging and office-holding were central to middling urban masculinity, female identities were rooted in the neighbourhood.

City women observed and intervened in household disputes; they upheld and denigrated reputations through talk, gossip, and litigation; and female neighbours, friends, and kin provided practical and emotional support for each other at childbed.[131]

As the role of women in particular neighbourhoods suggests, gendered identities were in part constituted through uses and negotiations of urban space.[132] Artisanal company halls were primarily masculine spaces, and gendered prescriptions around access and use reinforced the status and privilege of honourable artisans. Since admission to guild buildings could be closely monitored through central gates, artisanal and mercantile halls were among the most intensely male-dominated spaces in the city. Women were not entirely absent from company halls, but they were present only in prescribed circumstances, and their access was then restricted to particular rooms. Guild court minutes and accounts show that the wives of company beadles were routinely paid for undertaking washing and laundering tasks, following company dinners and feasts. At the opposite end of the social spectrum, citizen wives would occasionally be invited to dine with their husbands in company halls. But even at these rarefied events, women were typically seated on separate tables from their husbands, or even in different rooms of the hall to the freemen.[133]

Approaching artisanal culture: methodologies and primary sources

The institutional spaces and material cultures of London's foremost artisans have not hitherto attracted the attention of historians. This neglect is surprising, given both the acknowledged political, social, and economic significance of sixteenth- and seventeenth-century livery companies, and the recent surge of research into London's spaces, places, and sites of exchange. Theatres,[134] inns and taverns,[135] domestic lodgings,[136] sites of scientific experimentation,[137] the Inns of Court,[138] and urban streets, squares, shops, and marketplaces, have all been subject to fruitful spatial analysis.[139] A number of studies have also examined ritual movement,[140] or personal journeys through the city's geographical and symbolic spaces,[141] while others have explored the sensory dimensions of urban space.[142] Collectively this important new research has demonstrated, first, the variegated spatial experiences of Londoners; second, the rapidity of physical change in the urban fabric; and third, the enduring importance of historic associations of sites in the generation of contemporary (early modern) meanings. It is thus a timely moment for us to consider the spatial dimensions of artisanal culture and society.

Crafting Identities draws upon spatial theory and material culture studies to examine artisanal cultures. It brings together all the available evidence (manuscript, printed, visual and material) from numerous City archives and collections, to build a comprehensive picture of the changing built environments and conditions of London's early modern craftsmen. An interdisciplinary methodology is particularly appropriate in exploring an artisanal culture which recognised no distinct boundaries between propositional (theoretical) knowledge and embodied skills typically gained through observation and practice in the workshop. Only an approach sensitive to the spatial and material aspects of past lives, making full use of the visual evidence of guild halls as well as the surviving material gifts and products of the workshop, can hope to provide an informed analysis of skilled craft practitioners, who communicated chiefly through visual and material media rather than through print.

Since the early 2000s, historians of early modern urban culture have meaningfully engaged with the theoretical concept of 'space'. Scholars have drawn heavily on Henri Lefebvre's conceptualisation of space as an active framework, simultaneously produced by spatial practices, representations of space, and representational spaces.[143] This spatial approach encourages a multifaceted exploration of the complexity of urban experience 'at the physical, the ideological, and the symbolic levels'.[144] Crucially, social and cultural historians have been concerned not simply with describing the built environment, or the designs which informed its construction, but with examining the ways in which these sites were variously appropriated by urban inhabitants (through, for instance, their patterns of work, socialisation, and consumption) and made meaningful through symbolic associations over time (such as customary sites of execution, or civic ritual).[145] Latterly there has also been an emphasis upon the materiality of physical space in influencing human behaviour, thought, and identity.[146]

Crafting Identities exposes the material, social, and symbolic meanings of institutional artisanal spaces in order to deepen our understanding of urban culture and society. We face an immediate challenge: the physical structures which are the key sites of analysis do not survive. The majority of sixteenth-century livery halls, an estimated forty-four out of sixty company buildings, were destroyed by the Great Fire.[147] Those that escaped ruin in September 1666 were destroyed by subsequent fires, or else demolished and replaced with new institutional buildings. Despite the loss of the guild buildings, by piecing together the surviving manuscript and material evidence we can build up a reliable picture of how these buildings were designed and constructed, the ways in which they were used, and their representational meanings for London's artisanal community and wider civic audiences. A close reading of company court minutes in dialogue with surviving visual plans of guild buildings, for example, allows us to chart changes in the organisation and meaning of ritualised practices, such as feasting, and the testing or assessment of workshop products. This methodology also uncovers complex attitudes to the notion of 'private' and 'public' spaces, seen, for example, in how guild office-holders made a distinction during rebuilding projects between 'inward' works, over which they exercised close control, and the 'outward' walls, where responsibility was largely delegated to those with architectural expertise and royal connections.[148]

This book reinforces the idea that the materiality of space is integral to its social and conceptual meanings, and we are dealing here with historical agents who were especially sensitive to the designs, materials, and techniques embodied in artefacts.[149] Material cultures can be interpreted as cultural signs that reveal identities, systems of belief or knowledge.[150] Where physical objects survive, or we have documented details of gifted artefacts from guild collections, the plate, paintings, textiles, sculpture, and workshop tools provide a visual imagery and materiality that is complex and often intriguing. Visual references to company, City, and Crown abound; so too do the craft marks of particular artisans and workshops, and the late medieval iconography of guild patron saints. The sign of the craft mark was reproduced on company records, on the walls and ceilings of company halls, and on moveable gifted artefacts. It emerges as a charged symbol of ownership, status, and expertise. A 'parcel' of artisanal material gifts often reveals multiple loyalties and cultural identities. In 1559, for instance, the tallow chandler John Mery donated two green streamers for display in his company's court house, 'the one of the picture of Seynt Peter and the other of the Armys of London'. In the Pewterers' mid-sixteenth-century hall we find the two 'scowchyns [painted wooden shields] of the gyfte of Robert Taylor one with our Lady Assumptyon and one with ye kynges [Edwards'] armes'.[151] Moreover, beyond their symbolic functions, objects or commodities, like people, can be said to have 'social lives' and culturally embedded biographies. Objects do not just represent identities or values, but act to create them. It is only by tracing the 'trajectory' of the life of the 'thing' that we begin to comprehend the shifting associations between artefacts, human agents, and spatial and temporal contexts.[152] Analysing guild inventories together with citizen wills and surviving artefacts enables us to chart the original location of objects and their subsequent movement (and changing meanings) between the rooms of the company hall, private residences, civic buildings, and the city streets.

The present volume explores artisanal identity and culture through a variety of primary sources, reflecting the diversity of artisanal experiences and the complexities of urban identities. Guild records feature heavily in this book. Where they survive, the archival records of London's craft guilds are exceptionally rich primary materials; they are certainly the most extensive source base for approaching London's artisans. Guild archives include court minutes and accounts, and also maps and plans, inventories, and books of wills and gifts. They are unique in their variety and depth of detail concerning the governance of companies; the role of guilds in craft and trade regulation, and in binding apprentices; and their engagement with civic philanthropy – themes which have been effectively examined by historians. However these archives also provide valuable insight into artisanal cultural practices and productions. Moreover, whereas previous studies have been principally concerned with the guilds' economic dimensions, and the connections between institutional membership and urban political stability, I read these craft company archives through spatial and material lenses. The abundance of guild sources, from a wide range of City guilds over considerable periods, enables us to construct a dynamic picture of cultural change and continuity. Examining the archives of a variety of craft workers, from coopers to goldsmiths, enables the delineation of cultural practices – in this case the appropriation of buildings and material artefacts – that were common across craft lines. My approach thus breaks with a long-standing tradition of writing single-company histories. Such works, while often providing a great deal of detail about a particular guild, have tended to romanticise past guild communities. Their singular focus has also meant that some company histories contribute little to a wider understanding of urban society.[153]

The archives of craft guilds are not without their challenges. The language of livery company court minutes was deliberately framed by clerks to emphasise fellowship and company and diminish division and conflict, real and threatened.[154] Further, on the basis of guild documents, we know much more about the attitudes and activities of the livery than the yeomanry. Uncovering the voices of the yeomanry is a challenge when faced with records almost always compiled from the perspective of the company elite. The assistants in particular, the most privileged among the livery, closely controlled the content of company archives, their storage, and access to them.[155] In the chapters which follow, every effort has been made to include the viewpoints of the yeomanry, though we should certainly not assume that their attitudes were uniform or necessarily opposed to those of the livery and assistants.[156] The means by which many householders and journeymen were increasingly excluded from company spaces and formal sociability is elucidated in Chapters 4 and 6 of this book. Conversely, the active role of 'the yo[u]nger sort or yeomanry' in gifting cultures comes clearly into view in Chapter 5.[157] Inevitably the nature of the archive means that this study is largely an account of the most successful and (often) affluent householders, that is, those who operated as master craftsmen with independent businesses, were frequently engaged in retail, and who also rose to positions of authority within their companies.

In contrast to the abundant institutional sources, primary evidence from London, which might allow greater insight into the particular experiences of urban craftsmen, such as patterns of informal sociability outside of the guild context, is relatively thin. The practice of producing chronicles, autobiographies or 'life writings', from the artisanal perspective, was apparently stronger in continental Europe than in English towns and cities.[158] Wallington's account, from the viewpoint of a humble turner, is a highly atypical survival. Furthermore, very few early modern account books survive from English workshops to reveal work patterns, including female labour and practices of subcontracting. Wherever possible, my examination of artisanal culture goes beyond the records of the craft guilds to include manuscript materials presenting individual artisanal perspectives. These sources include wills and probate inventories, rare workshop account books, and treatises on the mechanical arts authored by craftsmen. Chapters 2 and 3 explore the connection between artisanal identities and knowledge production, through analysis of a mason's account book, a goldsmith's treatise, printed accounts by carpenters of practical mathematics, the City Viewers' reports, and oral disputes between master craftsmen about the evaluation of skill on building sites. Chapter 5 brings together personal and institutional sources (wills, inventories, and material cultures) to uncover the relationships between urban identities and hand-wrought gifts. Sixteenth- and seventeenth-century artisanal culture was heterogeneous, and is most profitably interpreted through productive, social, intellectual, and political frameworks. An examination of craft culture through the archives of craft companies, but in close dialogue with sources from individual urban dwellers, thus enables us to explore the multifaceted nature of artisanal identity.

Book structure

The structure of this book reflects the complexities and richness of artisanal culture, and its rootedness in particular urban spaces. Broadly we begin with the theme of artisanal knowledge cultures and spaces of craft production, including domestic and institutional workshops and urban building sites. From the construction site of Goldsmiths' Hall on Foster Lane in the mid-1630s we move squarely into the interior of London's early modern craft company halls, first taking into consideration changes and continuities in their spatial and material organisation, then moving on to explore the spatial practices through which these sites were made meaningful to contemporary artisans, such as material gifting, testing, and feasting. Having attended to interiors and internal guild hierarchies, our discussion then broadens outward to examine exterior walls and architectural designs of early seventeenth-century livery halls. Specifically, we will see how these external features of the corporate built environment mediated guild, civic, and royal – that is, political – relationships. Each chapter engages with different bodies or combinations of primary evidence (manuscript, printed, visual, and material). But a central analytical thread running throughout is the strong imbrication of artisanal knowledge cultures, the spatial dimensions of craft identity, and the material aspects of artisanal experience.

Chapters 2 and 3 uncover the interrelationship between practical and theoretical knowledge and artisanal identity in early modern London. They examine the contested meaning of true 'knowledge' of craftsmanship and how these understandings were articulated and disseminated in manuscript, print, and orally in company halls, on streets, and on construction sites throughout the city. These chapters interrogate which groups in English society had cultural and intellectual ownership of the mechanical arts, and who could legitimately 'read' and evaluate artisanal expertise. Chapter 2, 'Artisanal identities and cultures of knowledge', takes as its focus rare artisan-authored texts produced by masons, goldsmiths, and carpenters. We find that when artisans wrote about their experiences they repeatedly stressed the collaborative dimension, and the broader spatial and material cultures and networks of knowledge production. These emerging themes are the broad contours of the craft culture which are examined in greater depth in subsequent chapters. Chapter 3, 'The view from the building site', takes us out of the bounded workshop and onto urban construction sites, including the livery hall building site owned and managed by the early seventeenth-century Goldsmiths' Company. Through consideration of the practices and interactions of artisanal agents on the ground engaged in design and construction, we explore the dynamic between propositional and embodied knowledge cultures, and the collective dimensions of craft assessment and social identities.

Having established the basic groundwork of artisanal identities and knowledge cultures, Chapters 4, 5, and 6 examine in much greater depth changes and continuities to the interior architectural and material organisation of London's livery halls. Drawing on a wide variety of archival sources, including inventories, company court minutes, maps and plans, these chapters reconstruct for the first time the material, social, and symbolic meanings of guild architectures, and assert the significance of buildings and material cultures in the articulation of artisanal identities. Chapter 4, 'Rebuilding and adaptation', establishes the multifunctional nature of craft guild halls, buildings in which guild members and officers lived, governed, worked, and socialised. Additionally, it shows how property ownership became embedded in collective understandings of guild customs and histories. Significantly, this chapter also uncovers distinctive patterns in the changing physical layout and material organisation of craft company halls – including the development of new chambers, novel routes through buildings, and enhanced material cultures and building fixtures – and considers the implications of this for individual and collective identities. It shows that these improvements were shaped, both conceptually and materially, by a considerable range of established and aspirational guildsmen. The status of a master craftsman within the guild hierarchy depended in part on his personal contribution to the material and structural organisation of company buildings. Architectural adaptations and rebuilding also generated a competitive dynamic between City guilds.

Using company gift books, inventories, and material survivals from guild and civic collections, Chapter 5, 'Material gifting: artisanal virtuosity and material memorialisation', explores the deep-rooted custom of material gift-giving by artisans to their guild, as a means of advancing the individual's reputation and authority within the company. I demonstrate how the materiality, design, and iconography of the hand-wrought guild gift, in a multitude of different forms, were very significant in craft companies highly attuned to skill, technique, and material properties. From this close analysis of guild gifting cultures, the livery hall emerges as the primary location for the memorialisation of eminent master craftsmen, the construction of a symbolic historic community, and the display of artisanal skills and craft networks. Chapter 6, 'Shaping artisanal and civic identities', takes as its focus the mutually constitutive relationship between guild buildings and their artisanal communities. Through consideration of particular rooms within company halls, such as domestic institutional spaces and institutional workshops, as well as spatial practices – namely material testing and feasting – this chapter explores issues of openness and secrecy, inclusion and exclusion. It shows how the architectural and material organisation, and ritualised uses of craft company halls, reinforced social, gendered, and generational hierarchies. Redrawing the boundaries of company halls resulted in a growing exclusion of journeyman craftsmen, women, and alien workers from the social and political life of craft companies and knowledge-making practices, such as testing the material qualities of products.

Moving from the internal structure and organisation of buildings and guild communities, Chapter 7, '"Outward walls" and "publique works"', examines external walls and civic relationships. Fundamentally, this chapter locates 'improvements' to guild halls within a broader political and cultural programme to refashion the urban fabric of the City and its environs, a movement driven by both citizens and the Crown. We see here how discussions over the 'publique' nature of institutional architectures were linked in the early seventeenth century to wider concerns about the locations of artisanal workshops and retail spaces within the metropolis, and the spatial and political conformity of its citizens. The book concludes with reflections upon the interrelationship of skilled identities, urban space, and material cultures.

Notes

1 Guildhall Library, City of London [hereafter GL], MS 7110, fos 1r–2v, 72v–74r.
2 GL, MSS 7090/1–2.
3 GL, MS 6152/1, fo. 156r.
4 GL, MS 4326/6, fo. 39r.
5 GL, MS 12107, fo. 6r.

6 Goldsmiths' Hall Archive, London [hereafter GHA], W[ardens] A[ccounts] and C[ourt] M[inutes], S1, fo. 56v.

7 There are many examples of gentlemen showing appreciation for the significance of workshop knowledge in general, while concurrently denigrating the (allegedly) meagre abilities and aspirations of artisans. For example, Francis Bacon praised the potential of 'experiments in the mechanical arts' for the development of experimental science, while simultaneously disparaging the artisan labouring 'with feeble effort and slight success'. See *Novum Organum: with other parts of the great instauration*, translated and edited by Peter Urbach and John Gibson (Chicago, IL: Open Court, 1994), pp. 26, 44.

8 For instance, Eric Ash repeats the derogatory language of contemporaries – 'unlearned' (pp. 11, 153, 169), 'mere practitioners' (p. 134) – when talking about craftsmen, as compared to 'expert mediators'. See *Power, Knowledge and Expertise in Elizabethan England* (Baltimore, MD; London: Johns Hopkins University Press, 2004). For the attitudes of early modern gentlemen to knowledge production and social status, see Steven Shapin, *A Social History of Truth: Civility and Science in Seventeenth-Century England* (Chicago, IL: University of Chicago Press, 1994).

9 In notable contrast, Robert Tittler writes that provincial town halls in England 'exhibit an emphasis on utility rather than aesthetic considerations, they reflect practical rather than theoretical training on the part of their designers'. See *Architecture and Power: The Town Hall and the English Urban Community c. 1500–1640* (Oxford: Clarendon Press, 1991), p. 42.

10 Exclusion and conflict were 'intrinsic to … the precepts and practices of community'. See Alexandra Shepard and Phil Withington (eds), *Communities in Early Modern England* (Manchester: Manchester University Press, 2000), 'Introduction', pp. 1–15, at p. 6.

11 The gradual alienation of the City from the royal court is explored in Robert Ashton, *The City and the Court, 1603–1643* (Cambridge: Cambridge University Press, 1979).

12 In guild gift-giving culture, a citizen 'gave unto this house', not an individual. See GL, MS 5817, fos 7–8.

13 Norman Brett-James, *The Growth of Stuart London* (London: Allen & Unwin, 1935); Malcolm R. Smuts, 'The court and its neighbourhood: royal policy and urban growth in the early Stuart West End', *The Journal of British Studies*, 30:2 (1991), 117–49; Paul Griffiths, 'Politics made visible: order, residence and uniformity in Cheapside, 1558–1645', in Paul Griffiths and Mark Jenner (eds), *Londinopolis: Essays in the Social and Cultural History of Early Modern London* (Manchester: Manchester University Press, 2000), pp. 176–96; Linda Levy Peck, *Consuming Splendor: Society and Culture in Seventeenth-Century England* (Cambridge: Cambridge University Press, 2005), ch. 5; Christine Stevenson, *The City and the King: Architecture and Politics in Restoration London* (New Haven, CT: Yale University Press, 2013), ch. 2.

14 Miles Ogborn, *Spaces of Modernity: London Geographies 1680–1780* (New York; London: Guilford Press, 1998); Cynthia Wall, *The Literary and Cultural Spaces of Restoration London* (Cambridge: Cambridge University Press, 1998); Elizabeth McKellar, *The Birth of Modern London: The Development and Design of the City, 1660–1720* (Manchester: Manchester University Press, 1999); Stevenson, *The City and the King*. Anya Lucas's research on mercantile livery halls has focused largely on post-Fire rebuilding projects, see 'With honour yet frugality: the rebuilding of the livery company halls after the Great Fire', in Mark Hallett, Nigel Llewllyn, and Martin Myrone (eds), *Court, Country, City: British Art and Architecture, 1660–1735* (New Haven, CT: Yale Centre for British Art, 2016); 'The lost halls', in Anya Lucas and Henry Russell, *The Livery Halls of the City of London* (London: Merrell in association with the Worshipful Company of Chartered Architects, 2018), pp. 225–57.

15 Seven of Nehemiah Wallington's notebooks have survived, out of a total of fifty. See Paul S. Seaver, *Wallington's World: A Puritan Artisan in Seventeenth-Century London*

(Stanford, CA: Stanford University Press, 1985), pp. 199–202; *The Notebooks of Nehemiah Wallington, 1618–1654*, ed. by David Booy (Aldershot: Ashgate, 2007), pp. 7–8.

16 Nehemiah Wallington, *A bundel of marcys*, British Library, Additional Manuscript 21 935, fo. 96v; in *The Notebooks of Nehemiah Wallington*, ed. by Booy, p. 127.

17 Nehemiah Wallington, *An extract of the passages of my life or the booke of all my writting books*, Folger Shakespeare Library, Manuscript V.a.436, pp. 213–14; in *The notebooks of Nehemiah Wallington*, ed. by Booy, p. 301.

18 Thomas Milles, *The custumers alphabet and primer* (London, 1608), sig. L1v.

19 Phil Withington, 'Two renaissances: urban political culture in post-Reformation England reconsidered', *Historical Journal*, 44:1 (2001), 239–67.

20 Jonathan Barry, 'Bourgeois collectivism? Urban association and the middling sort', in Jonathan Barry and Christopher Brooks (eds), *The Middling Sort of People: Culture, Society and Politics in England, 1550–1800* (London: Macmillan, 1994), pp. 84–112.

21 Phil Withington, *The Politics of Commonwealth: Citizens and Freemen in Early Modern England* (Cambridge: Cambridge University Press, 2005), pp. 129–37; Phil Withington, 'Company and sociability in early modern England', *Social History*, 32:3 (2007), 291–307, at pp. 297–300; Phil Withington, *Society in Early Modern England: The Vernacular Origins of Some Powerful Ideas* (Cambridge: Polity, 2010), pp. 102–33.

22 Notably, valuable connections between the meanings of citizenship and artisanal skill have recently been made by scholars working on early modern urban culture in the Southern Netherlands and Germany. See Bert De Munck, 'Dissembling the city: a historical and an epistemological view on the agency of cities', *Journal of Urban History*, 43:5 (2017), 811–29; Hannah Murphy, 'Artisanal "histories" in early modern Nuremberg', in Bert De Munck and Antonella Romano (eds), *Knowledge and the Early Modern City: A History of Entanglements* (London: Routledge, 2020), pp. 58–78.

23 Jonathan Barry, 'Civility and civic culture in early modern England: the meanings of urban freedom', in Peter Burke, Brian Harrison, and Paul Slack (eds), *Civil Histories: Essays Presented to Sir Keith Thomas* (Oxford: Oxford University Press, 2000), pp. 181–96.

24 James Farr, *Artisans in Europe, 1300–1914* (Cambridge: Cambridge University Press, 2000), p. 3.

25 Tittler, *Architecture and Power*, pp. 92–3; *The Reformation and the Towns in England: Politics and Political Culture, c.1540–1640* (Oxford: Clarendon, 1998).

26 On the growth of London, see Vanessa Harding, 'City, capital, and metropolis: the changing shape of seventeenth-century London', in J. F. Merritt (ed.), *Imagining Early Modern London: Perceptions and Portrayals of the City from Stow to Strype, 1598–1720* (Cambridge: Cambridge University Press, 2001), pp. 117–43.

27 Pamela O. Long, *Openness, Secrecy, Authorship: Technical Arts and the Culture of Knowledge from Antiquity to the Renaissance* (Baltimore, MD: Johns Hopkins University Press, 2001); Pamela H. Smith, *The Body of the Artisan: Art and Experience in the Scientific Revolution* (Chicago, IL: Chicago University Press, 2004); Ursula Klein and E. C. Spary, *Materials and Expertise in Early Modern Europe: Between Market and Laboratory* (Chicago, IL; London: University of Chicago Press, 2009); Pamela O. Long, *Artisan/Practitioners and the Rise of the New Sciences, 1400–1600* (Corvallis, OR: Oregon State University Press, 2011); Pamela H. Smith, Amy R. W. Meyers, and Harold J. Cook (eds), *Ways of Making and Knowing: The Material Culture of Empirical Knowledge* (Ann Arbor: The University of Michigan Press, 2014); Paola Bertucci, *Artisanal Enlightenment: Science and the Mechanical Arts in Old Regime France* (New Haven, CT: Yale University Press, 2017).

28 Long, *Openness, Secrecy, Authorship*, pp. 1–15; Elspeth Whitney, 'Paradise restored: the mechanical arts from antiquity through the thirteenth century', *Transactions of the American Philosophical Society*, 80 (1990), pp. 1–169.
29 Deborah E. Harkness's discussion of artisanal involvement in the social and intellectual foundations of the scientific revolution is largely confined to instrument makers, see *The Jewel House: Elizabethan London and the Scientific Revolution* (New Haven, CT; London: Yale University Press, 2007), pp. 97–141.
30 *The London Surveys of Ralph Treswell*, ed. by John Schofield (London: London Topographical Society, 1987), p. 22.
31 The National Archives, Kew [hereafter TNA], PROB 11/132/202.
32 Steve Rappaport, *Worlds within Worlds: Structures of Life in Sixteenth-Century London* (Cambridge: Cambridge University Press, 1989), pp. 29–30.
33 Steven Shapin, 'The house of experiment in seventeenth-century England', *Isis*, 79:3 (1988), 373–404; Stephen Pumfrey, 'Who did the work? Experimental philosophers and public demonstrators in Augustan England', *British Journal for the History of Science*, 28:2 (1995), 131–56; Gloria Clifton (ed.), *Directory of British Scientific Instrument Makers, 1550–1851* (London: Zwemmer in association with the National Maritime Museum, 1995); Larry Stewart, 'Science, instruments, and guilds in early modern Britain', *Early Science and Medicine*, 10:3 (2005), 392–410.
34 'labourer | laborer, n.' *OED Online*. Oxford University Press, September 2016. Web. 2 October 2016.
35 'craftsman, n.' *OED Online*. Oxford University Press, September 2016. Web. 2 October 2016.
36 'craftsmaster, n.' *OED Online*. Oxford University Press, September 2016. Web. 2 October 2016.
37 'artificer, n.' *OED Online*. Oxford University Press, September 2016. Web. 2 October 2016.
38 'artisan, n.' *OED Online*. Oxford University Press, September 2016. Web. 2 October 2016.
39 'handicraftsman, n. *OED Online*. Oxford University Press, September 2016. Web. 2 October 2016.
40 'mechanic, adj. and n.' *OED Online*. Oxford University Press, September 2016. Web. 2 October 2016.
41 For the strong associations between urban freedom and householder status, see Barry, 'Civility and civic culture', pp. 191–2.
42 GHA, MS C II.2.1, fo. 32v.
43 William Harrison, *The description of England*, ed. by George Edelen (Washington, DC: Folger Shakespeare Library, and Dover; London: Constable, 1994), p. 118.
44 For the lack of engagement with social distinctions below the level of the yeomanry, see Keith Wrightson, *English Society, 1580–1680* (London: Routledge, 2003), pp. 28, 38–9, 45.
45 Harrison, *The description of England*, p. 115.
46 James R. Farr, 'On the shop floor: guilds, artisans and the European market economy, 1350–1750', *Journal of Early Modern History*, 1:1 (1997), 24–54; Margaret A. Pappano and Nicole R. Rice, 'Medieval and early modern artisan culture', *The Journal of Medieval and Early Modern Studies*, 43:3 (2013), 473–85.
47 A. L. Beier, 'Engines of manufacture: the trades of London', in A. L. Beier and Roger Finlay (eds), *London 1500–1700: The Making of the Metropolis* (London: Longman, 1986), pp. 141–67, at pp. 147–9.
48 John Styles, 'Product innovation in early modern London', *Past and Present*, 168:1 (2000), 124–69, at pp. 128–9; Ian Archer, 'Material Londoners?', in Lena Cowen Orlin (ed.), *Material London, ca. 1600* (Philadelphia, PA: University of Pennsylvania Press, 2000), pp. 174–92; Peck, *Consuming Splendor*, ch. 1.

49 Vanessa Harding, 'The population of London, 1550–1700: a review of the published evidence', *The London Journal*, 15:2 (1990), 111–28.
50 Farr, 'On the shop floor', p. 26.
51 Ian Anders Gadd and Patrick Wallis (eds), *Guilds, Society and Economy in London 1450–1800* (London: Centre for Metropolitan History, Institute of Historical Research in association with Guildhall Library, 2002), 'Introduction', pp. 1–14, at p. 5; Michael Berlin, 'Guilds in decline? London livery companies and the rise of a liberal economy, 1600–1800', in S. R. Epstein and Maarten Prak (eds), *Guilds, Innovation and the European Economy, 1400–1800* (Cambridge: Cambridge University Press, 2008), pp. 316–41, at pp. 328–30.
52 Alexandra Shepard, *Accounting for Oneself: Worth, Status, and the Social Order in Early Modern England* (Oxford: Oxford University Press, 2015), pp. 268–9.
53 John Jeffries Martin, *Myths of Renaissance Individualism* (Basingstoke: Palgrave Macmillan, 2004), pp. 17, 22, 27.
54 Hannah Wojciehowski, *Group Identity in the Renaissance World* (New York, 2011), p. 9. See also Gervase Rosser, *The Art of Solidarity in the Middle Ages: Guilds in England 1250–1550* (Oxford: Oxford University Press, 2015).
55 James S. Amelang, *The Flight of Icarus: Artisan Autobiography in Early Modern Europe* (Stanford, CA: Stanford University Press, 1998), p. 229.
56 Judith Pollmann, *Memory in Early Modern Europe, 1500–1800* (Oxford: Oxford University Press, 2017), p. 38.
57 Vanessa Harding, 'Memory, history, and the individual in the civic context in early modern London', in Vanessa Harding and Koichi Watanabe (eds), *Memory, History, and Autobiography in Early Modern Towns in East and West* (Newcastle-Upon-Tyne: Cambridge Scholars Publishing, 2015), pp. 109–20, at p. 109.
58 Pappano and Rice, 'Medieval and early modern artisanal culture', p. 478.
59 TNA, PROB/11/46/67.
60 Martin, *Myths of Renaissance Individualism*, pp. 14, 17.
61 Sheilagh Ogilvie, 'The economics of guilds', *The Journal of Economic Perspectives*, 28:4 (2014), 169–92, at p. 174.
62 S. R. Epstein, 'Craft guilds, apprenticeship, and technological change in pre-industrial Europe', *The Journal of Economic History*, 58:3 (1998), 684–713; Patrick Wallis, 'Apprenticeship and training in premodern England', *The Journal of Economic History*, 68:3 (2008), 832–61; Burt De Munck, Steven L. Kaplan and Hugo Soly (eds), *Learning on the Shop Floor: Historical Perspectives on Apprenticeship* (New York; Oxford: Berghahn Books, 2007).
63 Michael Berlin, '"Broken all in pieces": artisans and the regulation of workmanship in early modern London', in Geoffrey Crossick (ed.), *The Artisan and the European Town, 1500–1900* (Aldershot: Scolar, 1997), pp. 75–91; Patrick Wallis, 'Controlling commodities: search and reconciliation in the early modern livery companies', in Gadd and Wallis (eds), *Guilds, Society and Economy*, pp. 85–100.
64 Berlin, "Broken all in pieces", p. 79.
65 On guild decline, see George Unwin, *The Gilds and Companies of London*, 4th edn (London: Cass, 1963).
66 Berlin, 'Guilds in decline?', pp. 325–30. Though the relationship between early modern European guilds and economic growth (and innovation) is still very contentious, see Sheilagh Ogilvie, 'Rehabilitating the guilds: a reply', *Economic History Review*, 61:1 (2008), 175–82.
67 Joseph Ward, *Metropolitan Communities: Trade Guilds, Identity, and Change in Early Modern London* (Stanford, CA: Stanford University Press, 1997).
68 Shepard, *Accounting for Oneself*, pp. 249–55; K. Tawny Paul, 'Accounting for men's work: multiple employments and occupational identities in early modern England', *History Workshop Journal*, 85 (2018), 26–46.
69 William Herbert, *The History of the Great Twelve Livery Companies of London*, 2 vols (London, 1837), I, pp. 101–2.

70 Ian Archer, *The Pursuit of Stability: Social Relations in Elizabethan London* (Cambridge: Cambridge University Press, 1991), pp. 104–5; Giorgio Riello, 'The shaping of a family trade: the Cordwainers Company in eighteenth-century London', in Gadd and Wallis (eds), *Guilds, Society and Economy*, pp. 141–59; Jasper Ridley, *A History of the Carpenters' Company* (London: Carpenters' Hall, 1995), p. 29. Though a member of the great twelve, the Goldsmiths' Company also had a relatively strong affiliation between craft and trade, 'with most of the Company concerned in some way with the goldsmiths' trade'. See David Mitchell, *Silversmiths in Elizabethan and Stuart London: Their Lives and their Marks* (Woodbridge: The Boydell Press, 2017), p. 11.

71 James Farr has argued for a shared 'artisan mentality' based on a keen sense of social differentiation (between master craftsmen and subordinate journeymen) in early modern Dijon. However, Farr does not exactly clarify how the values and honour codes of artisans differed from other social groups. See *Hands of Honor: Artisans and Their World in Dijon, 1550–1650* (Ithaca, NY; London: Cornell University Press, 1988). Based upon a study of printed broadside ballads, Mark Hailwood suggests that 'it may be more appropriate to think of occupational identity in terms of broader 'work-based' rather than the narrower 'craft-specific' identities.' See 'The honest tradesman's honour': occupational and social identity in seventeenth-century England', *Transactions of the Royal Historical Society*, 6th ser., 24 (2014), 79–103, at p. 82.

72 Rappaport, *Worlds within Worlds*, pp. 29–31, 188.

73 Henry Machyn, *The Diary of Henry Machyn, Citizen and Merchant-Taylor of London, from A.D. 1550 to A.D. 1563*, ed. by John Gough (London, 1848), p. 47.

74 Susan Brigden, 'Religion and social obligation in early sixteenth-century London', *Past and Present*, 103:1 (1984), 67–112, at pp. 94–102.

75 *A Survey of Documentary Sources for Property Holding before the Great Fire*, ed. by Derek Keene and Vanessa Harding (London, 1985), British History Online, www.british-history.ac.uk/london-record-soc/vol22 [accessed 14 July 2020].

76 John Schofield, *The Building of London: From the Conquest to the Great Fire*, 3rd rev. edn (Stroud: Sutton, 1999), p. 12.

77 Ian Archer, 'The livery companies and charity in the sixteenth and seventeenth centuries', in Gadd and Wallis (eds), *Guilds, Society and Economy*, pp. 15–28, at p. 15; Archer, *The Pursuit of Stability*, pp. 120–23; Rappaport, *Worlds within Worlds*, pp. 195–201; Ilana Krausman Ben-Amos, *The Culture of Giving: Informal Support and Gift-Exchange in Early Modern England* (Cambridge: Cambridge University Press, 2008), pp. 95–104.

78 *People, Property and Charity: The Clothworkers' Company, 1500–1688*, http://history.ac.uk/cmh/ppc-clothworkers [accessed 14 July 2020].

79 Joseph Ward, 'Godliness, commemoration, and community: the management of provincial schools by London trade guilds', in Muriel McClendon, Joseph Ward, and Michael MacDonald (eds), *Protestant Identities: Religion, Society and Self-Fashioning in Post-Reformation England* (Stanford, CA: Stanford University Press, 1999), pp. 141–57; Joseph Ward, *Culture, Faith and Philanthropy: London and Provincial Reform in Early Modern England* (New York: Palgrave Macmillan, 2013).

80 Rappaport, *Worlds within Worlds*, p. 218.

81 *Ibid.*, p. 250.

82 *Ibid.*, pp. 252–3; Archer, *The Pursuit of Stability*, pp. 103–4.

83 Rappaport, *Worlds within Worlds*, p. 255.

84 *Ibid.*, pp. 250–73.

85 *Ibid.*, pp. 256–7.

86 *Ibid.*, pp. 219–32; Archer, *The Pursuit of Stability*, pp. 106–11.

87 GL, MS 7164, fo. 8r.

88 Archer, *The Pursuit of Stability*, pp. 114, 123.

89 Walter Sherburne Prideaux, *Memorials of the Goldsmiths' Company*, 2 vols (London: Eyre and Spottiswoode, 1896–97), I, pp. 341–52.
90 B. Alford and T. C. Barker, *A History of the Carpenters' Company* (London: Allen and Unwin, 1968), pp. 24–5.
91 Charles Welch, *History of the Cutlers' Company of London and of Minor Cutlery Crafts*, 2 vols (London: Privately printed for the Cutlers' Company, 1916–22), I, pp. 351–2; Thomas Girtin, *The Mark of the Sword: A Narrative History of the Cutlers' Company, 1189–1975* (London: Hutchinson, 1975), p. 158.
92 Archer, *The Pursuit of Stability*, pp. 102–6.
93 Steve Rappaport's quantitative analysis of surviving mid-sixteenth-century freedom registers shows that for nine out of every ten citizens, apprenticeship was the route through which they gained the freedom. See *Worlds within Worlds*, p. 24.
94 Joseph Ward suggests that the 'extent to which Londoners considered companies to be meaningful associations' was ultimately personal and individual. See *Metropolitan Communities*, p. 6.
95 Archer, *The Pursuit of Stability*, pp. 111–24.
96 Seaver, *Wallington's World*, pp. 113–16.
97 Unwin, *The Gilds and Companies of London*, p. 224.
98 Rappaport, *Worlds within Worlds*; Archer, *The Pursuit of Stability.*
99 Rappaport, *Worlds within Worlds*, pp. 201–9.
100 Henry French and Jonathan Barry, "Identity and agency in English society, 1500–1800' – Introduction', in *Identity and Agency in England, 1500–1800* (Basingstoke: Palgrave Macmillan, 2004), pp. 1–37, at pp. 10, 25; Peter Earle, 'The middling sort in London', in Barry and Brooks (eds), *The Middling Sort of People*, pp. 141–58, at pp. 143–5, 148, 155.
101 Archer, *The Pursuit of Stability*, pp. 109–10, 114.
102 Prideaux, *Memorials of the Goldsmiths' Company*, II, p. 120.
103 Gervase Rosser, 'Crafts, guilds and the negotiation of work in the medieval town', *Past and Present*, 154:1 (1997), 3–31, at pp. 7–8; Barry, 'Bourgeois collectivism?'
104 Amelang, *The Flight of Icarus*, ch. 4.
105 Sandra Cavallo, *Artisans of the Body in Early Modern Italy* (Manchester: Manchester University Press, 2007), ch. 5.
106 TNA, PROB/11/53/33.
107 Seaver, *Wallington's World*, p. 112.
108 Geoffrey Crossick, 'Past masters: in search of the artisan in European history', in Crossick, *The Artisan and the European Town*, pp. 1–40, at p. 13.
109 Rappaport, *Worlds within Worlds*, pp. 236–7. London apprentices typically started their training in their mid-to-late teens.
110 Alexandra Shepard, *Meanings of Manhood in Early Modern England* (Cambridge: Cambridge University Press, 2003), ch. 3.
111 Archer, *The Pursuit of Stability*, p. 216. See also Maarten Prak and Patrick Wallis (eds), 'Introduction', in *Apprenticeship in Early Modern Europe* (Cambridge: Cambridge University Press, 2020), pp. 1–19, at p. 7, 'on one side sustaining social order, on the other increasing productivity'.
112 Ilana Krausman Ben-Amos, 'Failure to become freemen: urban apprentices in early modern England', *Social History*, 16:2 (1991), 155–72, at p. 155.
113 Lien Bich Luu, *Immigrants and the Industries of London* (Aldershot; Burlington, VT: Ashgate, 2005), pp. 234–5; Jacob Selwood, *Diversity and Difference in Early Modern London* (Farnham: Ashgate, 2010), pp. 41–2.
114 Selwood, *Diversity and Difference*, p. 43.
115 Luu, *Immigrants and the Industries*, p. 235.
116 *Ibid.*, p. 120, table 4.7.
117 Shannon McSheffrey, 'Stranger artisans and the London sanctuary of St. Martin le Grand in the reign of Henry VIII', *Journal of Medieval and Early Modern Studies*, 43:3 (2013), 545–71.

118 Luu, *Immigrants and the Industries*, p. 227; Selwood, *Diversity and Difference*, p. 27. Calculating a precise figure of numbers of aliens is not possible based on the surviving evidence.
119 Matthew Davies, 'Aliens, crafts and guilds in late medieval London', in Elizabeth A. New and Christian Steer (eds), *Medieval Londoners: Essays to Mark the Eighteenth Birthday of Caroline M. Barron* (London: University of London Press, 2019), pp. 119–47, at p. 121.
120 Rappaport, *Worlds within Worlds*, p. 60; Archer, *The Pursuit of Stability*, pp. 131–3.
121 GHA, WA/CM, 03, fo. 552.
122 Alexandra Shepard, 'Crediting women in the early modern English economy', *HWJ*, 79:1 (2015), 1–24.
123 Eleanor Hubbard, *City Women: Money, Sex, and the Social Order in Early Modern London* (Oxford: Oxford University Press, 2012), pp. 196–7.
124 Jane Whittle, 'A critique of approaches to "domestic work": women, work and the pre-industrial economy', *Past and Present*, 243:1 (2019), 35–70, at p. 60.
125 Rappaport, *Worlds within Worlds*, pp. 37–8.
126 Amy Erickson has calculated that in the first half of the eighteenth century, 1 per cent of London's apprentices were female [an equivalent calculation has not been made for the sixteenth or seventeenth centuries]. See 'Eleanor Mosley and other milliners in the City of London companies 1700–1750', *HWJ*, 71:1 (2011), 147–72, at p. 150. Laura Gowing suggests that 'in the first half of the seventeenth century, very few companies seem to have apprenticed any girls at all', though there was a 'small influx of young women into late seventeenth-century London companies'. See 'Girls on forms: apprenticing young women in seventeenth-century London', *Journal of British Studies*, 55:3 (2016), 447–73, at pp. 449–50.
127 Amy Erickson, 'Married women's occupations in eighteenth-century London', *Continuity and Change*, 23:2 (2008), 267–307.
128 Rappaport, *Worlds within Worlds*, pp. 39–40.
129 This exclusion was typical across Europe. See Sheilagh Ogilvie, *The European Guilds: An Economic Analysis* (Princeton, NJ: Princeton University Press, 2019), pp. 248, 260–1.
130 Laura Gowing, '"The freedom of the streets": women and social space, 1560–1640', in Griffiths and Jenner (eds), *Londinopolis*, pp. 130–51, at p. 131.
131 Hubbard, *City Women*, ch. 5.
132 Gowing, '"The freedom of the streets"'.
133 In mercantile company halls, such as those belonging to the Drapers' and Clothworkers' Companies, citizen wives had separate chambers.
134 Janette Dillon, *Theatre, Court, and City, 1595–1610: Drama and Social Space in London* (Cambridge: Cambridge University Press, 2000); Anne Lancashire, *London Civic Theatre: City Drama and Pageantry from Roman times to 1558* (Cambridge: Cambridge University Press, 2002); Jean E. Howard, *Theatre of a City: The Places of London Comedy, 1598–1642* (Philadelphia, PA: University of Pennsylvania Press, 2007).
135 Alan Everitt, 'The English urban inn 1560–1760', in Everitt (ed.), *Perspectives in English Urban History* (London: Macmillan, 1973), pp. 91–137; Peter Clark, *The English Alehouse: A Social History 1200–1830* (London: Longman, 1983); Michelle O'Callaghan, 'Tavern societies, the Inns of Court, and the culture of conviviality in early seventeenth-century London', in Adam Smyth (ed.), *A Pleasing Sinne: Drink and Conviviality in Seventeenth-Century England* (Cambridge: D. S. Brewer, 2004), pp. 37–51.
136 John Schofield, *Medieval London Houses* (New Haven, CT; London: Yale University Press for the Paul Mellon Centre for Studies in British Art, 1995); Lena Cowen Orlin, *Locating Privacy in Tudor London* (Oxford: Oxford University Press, 2007).

137 Shapin, 'The house of experiment', pp. 373–404; Shapin, *A Social History of Truth*; Robert Iliffe, 'Material doubts: Hooke, artisan culture and the exchange of information in 1670s London', *The British Journal for the History of Science*, 28:3 (1995), 285–318.

138 *Records of Early English Drama: Inns of Court*, ed. by Alan H. Nelson and John R. Elliott (Cambridge: D. S. Brewer, 2010); Jayne E. Archer, Elizabeth Goldring, and Sarah Knight (eds), *The Intellectual and Cultural World of the Early Modern Inns of Court* (Manchester; New York: Manchester University Press, 2011).

139 Peck, *Consuming Splendor*; Vanessa Harding, 'Cheapside: commerce and commemoration', *Huntingdon Library Quarterly*, 71:1 (2008), 77–96; Patrick Wallis, 'Consumption, retailing, and medicine in early-modern London', *Economic History Review*, 61:1 (2008), 26–53.

140 Michael Berlin, 'Civic ceremony in early modern London', *Urban History Yearbook*, 13 (1986), 15–27; David M. Bergeron, *English Civic Pageantry, 1558–1642*, rev. edn (Tempe, AZ: Arizona State University, 2003); Tracey Hill, *Pageantry and Power: A Cultural History of the Early Modern Lord Mayor's Show, 1585–1639* (Manchester: Manchester University Press, 2010).

141 Ian W. Archer, 'Social networks in Restoration London: the evidence in Samuel Pepys's diary', in Shepard and Withington (eds), *Communities in Early Modern England*, pp. 76–94; Gowing, '"The freedom of the streets"'.

142 Bruce R. Smith, *The Acoustic World of Early Modern England: Attending to the O-Factor* (Chicago, IL; London: University of Chicago Press, 1999); Alexander Cowan and Jill Steward (eds), *The City and the Senses: Urban Culture Since 1500* (Aldershot: Ashgate, 2007); Karen Newman, *Cultural Capitals: Early Modern London and Paris* (Princeton NJ; Oxford: Princeton University Press, 2007), pp. 76–91.

143 Henri Lefebvre, *The Production of Space*, trans. by Donald Nicholson-Smith (Oxford: Blackwell Publishing, 1991).

144 Peter Arnade, Martha Howell, and Walter Simons, 'Fertile spaces: the productivity of urban space in northern Europe', *The Journal of Interdisciplinary History*, 32:4 (2002), 515–48, at p. 541.

145 Fabrizio Nevola, 'Street life in early modern Europe', *Renaissance Quarterly*, 66:4 (2013), 1332–45, at p. 1334.

146 Leif Jerram, 'Space: a useless category for historical analysis?', *History and Theory*, 52:3 (2013), 400–19, at p. 411. See also Ralph Kingston, 'Mind over matter?', *Cultural and Social History*, 7:1 (2010), 111–21, at p. 114.

147 Thomas F. Reddaway, *The Rebuilding of London after the Great Fire* (London: Arnold, 1951), p. 26.

148 GHA, WA/CM, S1, fo. 39r.

149 This argument concerning 'the integral connectivity of the material and immaterial' is effectively made in: Riitta Laitinen and Thomas V. Cohen (eds), *Cultural History of Early Modern Streets* (Leiden; Boston, MA: Brill, 2009), 'An Introduction', pp. 1–10, at p. 3.

150 John Dixon Hunt, 'The sign of the object', in Steven Lubar and W. David Kingery (eds), *History From Things: Essays on Material Culture* (Washington, DC: Smithsonian Institution Press, 1993), pp. 293–8; Richard Grassby, 'Material culture and cultural history', *The Journal of Interdisciplinary History*, 35:4 (2005), 591–603, at pp. 592–4.

151 GL, MSS 6152/1, fo. 70r; 7110, fo. 20v.

152 Arjun Appadurai, 'Introduction: commodities and the politics of value', in Appadurai (ed.), *The Social Life of Things: Commodities in Cultural Perspective* (Cambridge: Cambridge University Press, 1986), pp. 3–63; Igor Kopytoff, 'The cultural biography of things: commoditization as process', in *The Social Life of Things*, pp. 64–91.

153 On 'single-company histories', see Gadd and Wallis (eds), *Guilds, Society and Economy in London*, pp. 1–14, at pp. 3–4.

154 For clerks and the potential manipulation of archival materials, see Jennifer Bishop, 'The clerk's tale: civic writing in sixteenth-century London', in Liesbeth Corens, Kate Peters, and Alexandra Walsham (eds), *The Social History of the Archive: Record Keeping in Early Modern Europe*, Past and Present Supplement 11 (Oxford, 2016), pp. 112–30.
155 Paul Griffiths, 'Secrecy and authority in late sixteenth- and seventeenth-century London', *The Historical Journal*, 40 (1997), 925–51.
156 Rosser, 'Crafts, guilds and the negotiation of work', pp. 4–5.
157 GL, MS 6163/1, fo. 29v.
158 For a rich discussion of (predominantly) European artisanal 'autobiographic' writings, see Amelang, *The Flight of Icarus*.

2

Artisanal identities and cultures of knowledge

This chapter explores the interrelationship between knowledge, text, and artisanal identity in early modern London. The focus here, unusually, is not on literary representations of craftsmen, or the archives produced by craft companies, but on materials that were independently authored by artisans. This examination of early seventeenth-century artisanal writings includes a variety of sources: a master mason's account book and notebook composed for his immediate workshop and household; a manuscript treatise on metallurgy written by goldsmiths for a select civic audience; and a printed text of practical mathematics authored by a carpenter for a far-reaching commercial public. These texts might be broadly categorised as, respectively, an account book, memoir, book of craft secrets, and how-to manual; such writings are usually viewed by historians as discrete genres.[1] Here they are examined in dialogue, and the analysis uncovers several trends and tensions within artisanal knowledge cultures. This chapter asks why London's artisans wrote about their embodied practices and lived experiences, and what their central priorities and themes were when they did so.

The *artes mechanicae* in early modern England are usually scrutinised solely within the framework of natural philosophy, with a specific focus upon what these craft recipes and technological treatises might tell us about the development of 'observational' and 'experimental' science.[2] The chapter seeks to illuminate the wider workshop, guild, and commercial contexts within which craftsmen articulated their practices. The aim is to elucidate the artisanal perspective for its own sake, rather than simply the 'craftsman's' contribution to the 'gentleman's' natural philosophy.

Why are these eclectic writings by masons, goldsmiths, and a carpenter the starting-point for our broader exploration of artisanal identities and knowledge cultures? We open with these sources because they offer more 'individual' or subjective artisanal perspectives than guild records. The latter were explicitly constructed as a collective record of corporate activity, and thus identities are necessarily represented through this institutional lens. By contrast, the accounting of master mason Nicholas Stone, for instance, allows us to view the working practices, social and commercial networks, and strategies for memorialisation of a single, ambitious, artisanal dynasty. We begin with these artisanal-authored texts because in their discussions of household, commercial, and civic activities, they illuminate key features of a broader epistemological culture and network of metropolitan spaces, which will be examined in greater depth in subsequent chapters.

This discussion thus attends to a range of contemporary texts on the mechanical arts from the artisanal perspective. Despite the diversity of their form, intended purpose, and audience, they reveal a number of common themes. First, they show experiential knowledge and propositional knowledge, or the labour of the 'hand' and the 'mind', to be fundamentally interlinked. The ideal master craftsman had both extensive practical experience and an understanding of the theoretical principles underpinning his labour. As argued in the goldsmiths' manuscript, workshop activities 'are not eselie reduced to matter of Argument, unlesse Exercise [practice] be joyned w[i]th speche'.[3]

Second, the epistemological value of workshop expertise, and the question of who exactly possesses authentic skill and 'knowledge' of craftsmanship, emerge as contested cultural issues. Expertise in early modern London was a charged concept, intersecting with social and political stratifications within civic culture. There is a tendency in the historiography to see tensions over the social ownership of knowledge as exposed by the establishment of the Royal Society in the latter half of the seventeenth century, and founded on the notion of gentility.[4] However this study shows that questions of epistemological authority were pertinent to citizens too, and at an earlier date than is generally acknowledged.

A third shared theme is that workshop production and assessment of material quality are represented by artisans as collaborative processes, subject to social negotiation.[5] Individual master craftsmen accumulated considerable expertise over the duration of their working lives, but legitimate judgements about material quality and craftsmanship were made collectively, within select civic spaces, such as the assay house or company parlour. Texts on the mechanical arts were themselves typically collaborative enterprises, both in the social sense of multiple practitioners contributing to the finished written product, and intellectually, with authors liberally borrowing from existing commentaries on their theme or subject.[6]

A fourth shared element is that none of these artisanal texts was meant to be understood in isolation; they all point towards corresponding material cultures and urban spaces. The mason's account book and notebook are textual records of his physical funerary monuments, located in the most prestigious ecclesiastical and domestic spaces in early seventeenth-century England. The goldsmith's manuscript, a product of urban workshops of metallurgical testing and regulation, proposes the material masterpiece as the ultimate proof of artisanal accomplishment. And works of practical mathematics (as texts of applied theory) point their readers towards new instruments and sites of learning, and direct engagement with their immediate physical environment.

Artisan authors

By their very nature as artisanal-authored texts, these accounts of the mechanical arts are all unusual. Any first-hand accounts authored by artisans are rare. Craftsmen did not routinely articulate their understanding of materials, or the working of their instruments, through manuscript or print. There are several possible explanations for this general reticence. Primarily, there were practical limitations on the reproduction of technical knowledge in sixteenth- and early seventeenth-century London, namely reading and writing skills. David Cressy's now classic study of social degrees and literacy demonstrates that: 'Illiteracy was stratified by occupation and trade as well as by general social categories.'[7] Artisan-retailers who were engaged in relatively prestigious trades, such as goldsmiths, apothecaries, and drapers, enjoyed much higher literacy rates than weavers, blacksmiths, or carpenters.[8] Cressy's findings indicate that the 'more specialized, complex, refined or expensive the business the more likely was its practitioner to be able to sign his name'.[9] But this was also a fluid picture, and whereas in mid-sixteenth-century London full literacy was perhaps the preserve of the artisanal and mercantile elite, by the 1640s approximately 70 per cent of London's male inhabitants enjoyed 'signature literacy' – the highest national level.[10] No doubt the city had 'an elaborate hierarchy of literacy skills', and a greater proportion of the urban population had some reading ability.[11]

In addition, guild culture privileged secrecy, a significant barrier to the codification of workshop knowledge.[12] The London Goldsmiths' Company's first extensive book of Ordinances and Statutes, compiled in September 1478, included appropriate penalties 'if any man reveals the secrets of his craft'.[13] All City companies had such regulations. In effect, propriety attitudes over the craft 'mystery' – the collective embodied skills and techniques of craftsmen – were an attempt to protect the economic interests of members. As William Eamon has argued, particularly 'in specialized and highly skilled crafts ... success depended upon precise and detailed knowledge of the kind and quality of materials for a process, the manner and proportions of combining them, and the often subtle effects of temperature on the materials. Such "trade secrets" were valuable intellectual property.'[14] And thus the wardens of the Pewterers' Company, concerned about the revelation of trade secrets and technologies warned that it was forbidden for men to 'worketh openly in the shopes w[i]th ther great wheles w[hi]ch is ane occasion that pewterers of the country [non-citizens] & others shall come to great lyght of farther knowleg to the great hindraunce of the company'.[15] From the perspective of guild governors, knowledge and skills transfer was expected to take place within the particular setting of the artisanal workshop. Learning a craft involved a series of oral and observational exchanges between master, journeyman, and apprentice, and the precise nature of this unrecorded exchange has inevitably proved frustratingly elusive for historians of pre-modern apprenticeship.[16] By taking craft processes as their subject matter, the texts discussed in this chapter – particularly *The Gouldesmythes' Storehowse*, which details the activities of the master assayer – threatened to undermine the orderly corporate notion of knowledge transfer taking place within the confines of the craftsman's workshop, beyond the public gaze.

Finally, there is a self-conscious irony running throughout artisanal-authored texts: the written word alone is an inadequate form of communication for explaining practices which are primarily unspoken. The degree to which *The Gouldesmythes' Storehowse*, for instance, genuinely reveals the artisan's working practices is somewhat doubtful. By its very nature artisanal knowledge was largely embodied and experiential.[17] The difficulty of capturing tacit knowledge was, later in the century, a major thorn in the side of the Royal Society's (failed) attempts to compile a comprehensive History of Trades.[18] In his *Mechanick exercises or the doctrine of handy-works* – a series of fourteen printed and richly illustrated accounts of the work of the smith, joiner, carpenter, and turner – Joseph Moxon, the author, who was a prominent printer, globe, map, and instrument maker at the Sign of Atlas at Ludgate Hill, explained that:

> I thought to have given these Exercises the Title of The Doctrine of Handy-Crafts; But ... I found the Doctrine would not bear it: because Handy-Craft signifies Cunning, or Sleight, or Craft of the Hand, which cannot be taught by Words, but is only gain'd by Practice and Exercise: therefore I shall not undertake that with the bare reading of these Exercises any shall be able to perform these Handy-Works; but I may safely tell you, that these are the Rules that every one that will endeavour to perform them must follow ....[19]

Similarly, modern theorists of craft and expertise have stressed that artisanal skills are learned by observation and hands-on experience.[20]

In the face of these challenges, the question thus remains, why did artisans write about their workshop experiences at all? I argue here that the rationale for artisanal writings – so far as we can ascertain motivations – was diverse. Craftsmen engaged in relatively prestigious trades might be fully literate, and an ability to both read and write, and considerable numerical dexterity, was becoming increasingly important for keeping workshop accounts.[21] Full literacy was a requirement for all young men indentured to the Goldsmiths' Company as apprentices, for example.[22] The master mason's workshop account book, discussed presently, was used to keep track of complex projects involving a wide network of skilled practitioners, materials, and credit. This multi-authored document was also a means of training the master's sons in the workings of the trade. Artisanal writings could also have a commercial motivation. Carpenters and joiners authored texts of practical mathematics as a means of pointing readers towards new instruments, makers, shops, and profitable spaces of learning.[23]

Authorship was certainly also a strategy for enhancing the craftsman's social and intellectual prestige, particularly within a cultural landscape in which manual work was generally disparaged. The mason's notebook, recording his lifetime's work of designing and producing funerary monuments, reads like a directory of the early Stuart court; the goldsmith's manuscript is self-consciously dedicated as a learned gift to the Goldsmiths' Company, and printed works by self-proclaimed 'mathematical practitioners' were in part a strategy to establish their expertise as a legitimate field of knowledge, and raise the status of their artisanal authors. The demonstration of expertise in text and sketches, and repeated intertextual references, elevated the artisan-author's status above the general mass of urban mechanicians.[24]

This discussion of artisanal writings is not ordered by date of authorship, but according to urban spaces of production, consumption, and regulation. We thus move from workshops, to institutions, to the broader commercial locations within which these materials were read and consumed. We begin with the workshop account book and notebook of master mason Nicholas Stone, who executed funeral monuments and designed houses for the most eminent families in early seventeenth-century England. Nicholas Stone will also be a central figure in Chapter 3, through his role as designer and project manager for the Goldsmiths' Company's livery hall rebuilding scheme of the mid-1630s. While Stone's influence and expertise have long been acknowledged by architectural historians and scholars researching funerary monuments, his rich archival 'life-writings' have been overlooked by social and cultural historians.[25] We turn next to *The Gouldesmythes' Storehowse* (1604), a manuscript on the 'many hidden secrets of that Ingenious Misterie', in the style of European treatises on the mechanical arts.[26] This book demonstrates how notions of expertise intersected with hierarchical civic authority and institutional spaces (including Goldsmiths' Hall and the Tower mint). Finally, we consider a printed text on the geometric basis of carpentry, authored by a practitioner with mathematical aspirations. This work takes us out of company buildings, towards alternative sites of urban learning, commerce, and construction. Collectively these texts demonstrate how craft knowledge and workshop expertise were integral to artisanal identity, and also had a bearing upon wider epistemic debates in early modern England.

A mason's workshop in St. Martin-in-the-Fields

The notebook and account book of Nicholas Stone (1585/6?–1647), detailing the material production and professional networks of this exceptionally skilled and highly successful master mason, provide unusual written evidence of artisanal working practices and the commemoration of labour. Taken together, Stone's manuscripts are the most detailed archival evidence for the workshop practices of an early modern English mason, or for that matter (probably) any artisan practitioner in seventeenth-century England. They can be read as autobiographical documents, a form of artisanal 'life-writing', combining workshop activities, political events, and personal recollections.[27] Stone's surviving documents were never intended to be public handbooks of technical knowledge, and they do not include specific details of his working techniques. These writings do, however, shed light upon the collaborative nature of artisanal practice, both within a single workshop in St. Martin-in-the-Fields, Westminster, and more broadly between masters of different crafts on construction sites. Stone's notebook and account book also show that from the perspective of those tasked with organising production – such as the construction of a funeral monument, or the erection of a house – propositional and experiential knowledge were interlinked.

Between 1631 and 1642 Nicholas Stone kept a workshop account book recording private commissions and work undertaken in his capacity as master mason to the Crown, a position he held from 1632.[28] In 1633 and 1634 Stone was also master of the London Masons' Company. This document details contracts negotiated with clients and the materials used, rates charged, and craftsmen hired for specialist piecework. The account book reveals some very illustrious patrons, from among the most politically influential families at the royal court. This is indicative of Stone's status as England's leading sculptor and master mason by the 1630s.[29] These clients include King Charles and Henrietta Maria, the Paston family, Lord Clifford, and Lord and Lady Arundel.[30] In April 1635, for example, Stone's account book includes a series of completed works which had been sculpted in his workshop on Long Acre, St. Martin-in-the-Fields, and were presently to be 'sent don to Norfolk for the Right Worshipful William Patson [sic]'. These diverse sculptural works – which amply show off Stone's ability to cater to elite interests in the 'antique' – included: 'On[e] Tombe for Sir Edward Paston'; 'On[e] statua of Jupeter of portland stone biger than the life'; 'On[e] Cerbros of portland stone with a pedestall', and 'On[e] sheld of Armes'.[31] In July and August 1640, Stone was paid £7 by Sir Christopher Hatton, 'For 6 Emperours heads, with there Pedestalles cast in Plaister, molded from the Antiques, for basketts, and straw and packing of them up, and sending of them away' [to Kirby Hall in Gretton, Northamptonshire].[32]

Aside from the social 'quality' of his patrons, the account book also reveals the multiplicity of Nicholas Stone's artisanal skills.[33] It is evident that Stone was being employed both to design and execute a wide variety of stone and marble sculptures, including chimneypieces, busts and full length figures for the interior and exterior of domestic and institutional buildings, garden statuary, and memorials to the dead in churches (see figure 2.1).

Stone was also contracted to supply building plans and oversee building projects. In 1631, for example, it was 'Agreed with the Right Hon. Lord Earell of Dareby for to mak 3 ston gates in to the phiseck garden Oxford: and to desine a new Hows for him at Corenbury in Oxfordsheer and to dereckt the workemen and mak all thar moldes, I was thar in 2 years 33 times and my covenant of accord with his lord. Was 1000£.'[34] Here Stone was designer, technical supervisor of construction, and provider of moulds for all masons working on the project. Most of the sculptures recorded in the account book are memorials to the dead, such as the black-and-white marble monument 'agreed with my Lord Clifford' in 1632, which was to have the familial arms 'carved in bost with the coronett and fairly polished and glased in white marble'.[35] In his work as a master mason, Stone also

Figure 2.1 Nicholas Stone, monument to Sir Moyle Finch and Elizabeth, Countess of Winchilsea, from the ruined church of St. Mary, Eastwell, Kent. Carved marble and alabaster, c. 1630.

directed teams of craftsmen and organised production, as at the Arundels' impressive property, Tart Hall, on the west side of St. James's Park, during the 1630s.[36] From 1635 to 1638, Stone was also contracted as the 'surveyor' for the rebuilding of Goldsmiths' Hall on Foster Lane.[37] For this extensive architectural project, Nicholas Stone produced the external plans and interior designs for the new building, employed specialist craftsmen of his choosing, and acted as director of works on site. Stone's great nephew, Charles Stoakes, added a coda to the account book from 1669 to 1676, listing 'some of the most Eminentt Workes that my Uncle Mr Nickcolas Stone Senior did in England in Holland and Scottland'; the emphasis here is on architectural projects. First mentioned is 'the Banqueting Roome att Whitehall'. Stoakes also itemised works undertaken at Somerset House, the Queen's House at Greenwich, 'the Curious Phisicke Garden' in Oxford, and 'Gould Smithes hall in Foster Lane hee desind & built, it stands betweene 4 streetes & never a Right angle without side & yet al square Roomes Within side, with a Noble Entrance of the Doricke Order'.[38]

The account book locates Stone within a network of extremely ambitious and prosperous craftsmen, and highlights the collaborative nature of artisanal endeavours. These were artisans who were paid for undertaking whole schemes of work, not by the measure, as was customary.[39] A number of these master craftsmen, such as carpenter Anthony Jerman and joiner Jeremy Kellet, were, like the master mason, employed by the Royal Works, and served as masters of their respective companies.[40] The account book also shows how, beyond England, Stone was maintaining close professional and personal contacts with the prominent Netherlandish de Keyser family, with whom he was directly related through his Dutch wife Mayken (Mary), the daughter of Amsterdam sculptor and architect Hendrick de Keyser (1565–1621). As a young man, Nicholas Stone might have been trained as an assistant within Hendrick's workshop in Amsterdam.[41] An entry from June 1632 records the receipt of stone and marble shipped from Amsterdam by Peter and Thomas de Keyser (sons of Hendrick), and Nicholas Stone's dispatch of alabaster (and gifts of clothes) to them.[42] A letter in Dutch from Thomas de Keyser to Nicholas Stone, dated December 1639, and pasted into the St. Martin-in-the-Fields' account book, records complex credit networks between the two families, and the exchange of personal news, including the good health of Stone's sons, Henry and Nicholas, who were visiting Rome on their Grand Tour of Europe. As an aside, Thomas thanks his brother-in-law Nicholas for 'the beaver hat; it suits me very well'.[43] The families also shared skills training; Henry Stone was apprenticed to painter Thomas de Keyser, his maternal uncle, in Amsterdam, and two of Hendrick de Keyser's sons were probably apprenticed to Nicholas Stone in Westminster.[44] The account book is further revealing of the artisanal dynasty which Stone attempted to build through the transmission of his own expertise, and (tacit and propositional) knowledge. Multiple entries in the account book have been written in the hands of his sons Nicholas and John, who were both trained for a short time in their father's workshop, and went on to become sculptors in adult life, as did their eldest brother, Henry. Nicholas Stone the younger's diary of his Grand Tour experience records how he studied sculpture with great masters like Gianlorenzo Bernini, and also purchased books, prints, models, drawings, and casts, including 'the booke of Archytecture of Domenico Fontana to be sent for England for Mr Kinsman being very scarsly to be found', and '113 small peeces of seuerall sorts of marbles to send for England according to my fathers command'.[45] Ultimately though, none of the sons was to achieve the success of his father.

Nicholas Stone's account book looks to be a continual work in progress, updated from his workshop as projects were negotiated with clients. It is probable that there were other workshop account books, pre-1631, which have not survived. Stone's notebook was probably composed in the last decade of his life, and retrospectively acknowledges some of the major projects, predominately funerary monuments, crafted and erected between 1614 and 1641.[46] This document is a rare artisanal record of material production. Stone provides details of the client, the location of the material memorial, and the sum paid for the commission. Personal features are woven into this narrative too. Regarding a tomb constructed in 1615 'for my lord of North hamton [Northampton] and to set it up in Dover Castell', Stone added that 'I mad Mr Isak James a partner with me in cortisay be case he was my master 3 years that was 2 years of my prentes and on year journiman'.[47] He proudly recalls how in 1619 'I was sent for to the ofisor of his Ma[jesty's] works to under take the charges of the plas of Mast[er] mason for the new Banking hows [Banqueting House] at Whithall'.[48] In a more frivolous tone, Nicholas Stone remembers how 'very extreordenerly entertayned' he had been on the occasion of setting up a tomb for 'my lady Paston of Norfolk' in 1629.[49]

The order in which Stone accounted for these commissions in the notebook is particularly intriguing. It is not organised in a straightforward chronological fashion, instead many of Stone's works are grouped in this document according to spatial location (and sometimes familial context). All the monuments executed within a single church, for instance, regardless of date of completion, are itemised together. This is evidenced in a note detailing three separate monuments to the Bacon family, erected at different dates in St. Mary's Church, Redgrave, Suffolk: 'In Sofolke I mad a tombe for Ser Edmond Bacons lady and in the sam Chearch of Redgrave I mad an other for his sister my lady Gady … and in the sam plas I mad 2 pectors of whitt marbl of Ser Nicholas Bakon and his lady and the war layed upon the tombe that Barnard Jansen had mad thar …'.[50] The sculptor Bernard Janssen (or Janson) was a neighbour of Nicholas Stone the Elder in St. Martin-in-the-Fields, and collaborated with him.[51] Likewise, five separate monuments located in Westminster Abbey, including that for the poet Edmund Spenser (1620), and for Sir George Villiers and his wife, Mary, Countess of Buckingham (1631–32), are grouped together in his notebook.[52] This account of his material production indicates that recording spaces of display was more significant than a precise chronological description of workshop production. This method of recounting work was probably also a reflection of contemporary practices of mnemotechnics, whereby things or words might be recalled through their imagined location in particular architectures.[53] The youngest son, John Stone, also contributed to his father's notebook, after Nicholas Stone's death in August 1647. Following Nicholas's account of major commissions completed between 1614 and 1641, John added a list of sixteen church monuments which he executed between 1650 and 1657.[54] There is a clear sense that this manuscript, for both father and son, was a written memorial of material production, a statement of dynastic artisanal accomplishment.

As well as this process of material recollection, Nicholas Stone's notebook contains a short chronicle of significant personal and political events occurring within London and its hinterlands between 3rd November 1640 and 23rd October 1642.[55] Stone recorded, for example, that 'The 11 of February 1641 I fel sick of a fever and kept my chamber 12 weeks'. Such a narrating of bodily distress and subsequent recovery was typical of early modern life-writings.[56] Of wider public significance, on 'the 12 of May 1641 my lord of Straford was beheaded; and my lord of Canterbury thine being commited to the Tower'. On 'the 21 of June 1641 Mr Balwing [Baldwin] Controler of his M[ajesty's] works [a working associate of Stone] died and was bured at Barcamsted Midsomerday' (Stone would later design his monument, the last job mentioned in the account book). On 16 July 'I had a trial att Gield hall London Befor my lord Chef Justes of the Comon Pees Lord Bankes; between Wattes the Admensterator of Mrs Van de Stane [an agent through whom Stone obtained black marble from Holland] for 200£ that shee oedd me'.[57] Attending to royal and civic ceremony, Stone wrote how on 25 November 1641 'his Ma[jesty] Returned from Scotland and was Entertayened by the Cetyzons and fested at Gild Hall the maner was this … the lord mare and Aldermen of London war thar atend his Ma[jesty] … then all the companys in order rood on befor all cloed in velvet and plesh with gold chenes and very well horsed …'. A number of Stone's recollections of critical events in the build-up to civil war are eye-witness accounts. This includes a disturbing encounter in January 1641/2, during which he personally witnessed, from the building site of an architectural project, the Court of Guard at Whitehall Palace: 'som[e] rued multetud of Cetezones and prenteses cam[e] in tumultes man[n]er to the parlement Hows with lowe out cries saing no Bishepts no papes lords to have foot in parlement … I saw it all and mad[e] as much hast[e] from the Courtt of gard of [thatt thin was in bilding] to be out of harmes waye'.[58] Considering Stone's intimate connections with Charles I and the royal court, these major political events were of considerable personal consequence. Nicholas Stone's career ended with the outbreak of civil war; shortly after he penned this recollection and journal, he was 'sequestered, plundered and imprisoned', allegedly on account of his loyalty to the Crown.[59]

At his death in 1647, Nicholas Stone bequeathed to his three sons 'all my books manuscripts draughts designes instruments and other thinges thereunto belonginge, which nowe remayne in my studie in my nowe dwelling howse to be equally divided amongst theme share and share alike'.[60] Having apprenticed his descendants within his own workshop, Stone finally passed on the instruments of his trade – those varied media which both constituted and embodied a lifetime of accumulated artisanal knowledge, experience, and skill. The significance of these objects as symbols of craft identity and epistemological status is heightened since they were the only moveable possessions specifically itemised in his last will and testament. These material remains of Stone's working life thus appear to have been his most precious belongings. The easy juxtaposition of texts, designs, and physical tools in this will demonstrates that Nicholas Stone understood his labours to have been both 'theoretical' and 'practical'. This master mason would have had little appreciation for the classically inherited distinction between 'liberal' (intellectual) and 'mechanical' (manual) arts. The material bequests of other master masons betray a similar desire to perpetuate the hereditary skills connection through tools, drawings, and books.[61] In 1579 the Dutch mason and naturalised London citizen William Cure the elder left to his son Cornelius his best (civic) gown and 'my books paternes tooles and other necessaryes belonging to my occupacon excepting those paternes which I have already bestowed and appointed for my son in law Robert Sturdye'.[62] Cornelius Cure went on to become master mason of the royal works in 1596 (to be succeeded by Nicholas Stone in 1632).

The notebook and account book of Nicholas Stone are a highly personal reflection of a working life. Unlike the goldsmith's manuscript and texts of practical mathematics, which had – to a lesser or greater extent – 'public' audiences, Stone's writings were probably never intended to be seen beyond the confines of the workshop and immediate household. Workshop account books must have been maintained by other substantial English master craftsmen for the effective operation of their businesses, but these documents have simply not survived. This textual articulation and commemoration of workshop labours demonstrates how artisanal expertise and material production were inextricably linked to Stone's social identity. His notebook of funerary monuments reads like a 'who's who' of the early seventeenth-century royal court, and Stone's elevated social status was such that two of his sons went on the Grand Tour, and styled themselves as young gentlemen.[63] A sketchbook belonging to Henry Stone, which provides a visual record of key sites of the continental tour, is archived along with his father's

Figure 2.2 Henry Stone, sketchbook of landscape and figure studies, and drawings after Italian masters and the antique made during Italian sojourn, *c.* 1638–42, vol. 92/17.

life-writings in Sir John Soane's Museum, London (see figure 2.2). Aside from social identity, Nicholas Stone's workshop documents point to their corresponding material cultures, particularly the monuments to the dead in churches across England, for which Stone's expertise was especially sought-after. Ultimately these monuments did not merely commemorate their noble subjects; they served as the most significant material markers of their maker's artisanal legacy.

The Gouldesmythes' Storehowse

On 20 June 1606, the wardens of the Goldsmiths' Company were presented at Goldsmiths' Hall with the gift of a manuscript whose author 'had taken greate paines in translat[i]on'.[64] The work was entitled *The Gouldesmythes' Storehowse. Wherein is layde up many hidden secrets of that Ingenious Misterie* (see figure 2.3). The text had been presented, 'compiled, made, and drawen into this Method by H-G. Citizen and Gouldsmythe of London', and is dated 1604.[65] As is typical of books of craft secrets and technological treatises, the *Storehowse* explores a wide variety of subject matter, including the social and institutional organisation of the Mint, translations of late medieval lapidaries, and alchemical experiments and formulas.[66] The manuscript consists of eighty-three quarto leaves, and is divided into three

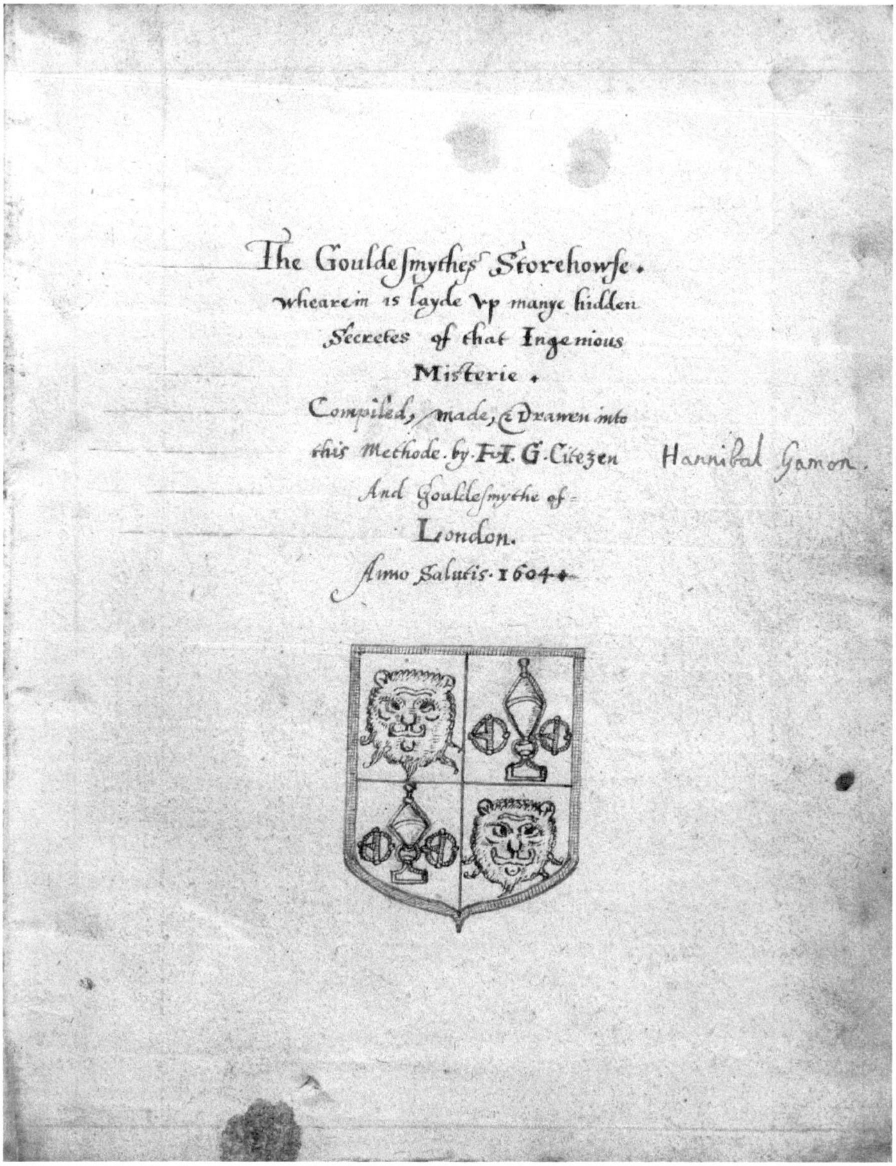

Figure 2.3 Hannibal Gamon, title page of *The Gouldesmythes' Storehowse*, 1604, GHA, MS C II.2.1.

books, containing multiple short chapters.[67] Thematically, the overall focus of the work is on the activities of assaying, refining, and monetary circulation. Manuscripts and printed texts on craft mysteries, including metallurgy, were produced and circulated in ever greater numbers in sixteenth- and seventeenth-century Europe, and allegedly revealed to literate audiences 'the secrets of the arts' which had formerly been hidden within artisanal workshops.[68] *The Gouldesmythes' Storehowse* is particularly intriguing, as it combines this secrets tradition with contemporary civic concerns about hierarchies of skill and knowledge acquisition.

Assayers were responsible for testing the precious metal content of ores, bullion, coinage, and plate. This was a hugely significant role. As merchant and natural philosopher Clement Draper (*c.* 1542–1620) wrote from his cell in the King's Bench prison, Southwark, where he was imprisoned for debt: without the practice of assay 'no man can justlye sell or buy or receave gold or silver or other metals', and no 'myne master or goldsmythe or gold fyner or gold beatter can well exersyse their artts'.[69] The principal institutional assay workshops were situated in Goldsmiths' Hall on Foster Lane, in the heart of the City, and at the Royal Mint in the Tower, on its far eastern boundary (see figure 2.4). It was at these sites that trials were made of precious metals. The Goldsmiths' Company's assayer was, by authority of royal charter, tasked with carrying out the assay of all precious metals worked by the city's goldsmiths, both the raw materials (the ingot) and the fashioned articles. If judged to be of the correct standard by the assayer, then items would be marked by the touch warden and thus deemed authentic and suitable for sale. Faulty wares were broken up in ritualistic fashion, in the artisan's shop, or in Goldsmiths' Hall. Assayers tested the purity of precious metals through two principal methods: 'the one by sighte upon the Touchstone: the other by tryall at the Assaye'.[70]

It is probable that *The Gouldesmythes' Storehowse* was a collaboration between a father and son, both named Hannibal Gamon, and both members of the Goldsmiths' Company. The son, Hannibal Gamon the younger (bap. 1582), graduated from Broadgates Hall, Oxford with a BA degree in 1603, and an MA in 1606.[71] He was a company exhibitioner, meaning that he received financial support from the Goldsmiths' Company towards his university education. In 1603 the company gave him £5 'toward his grace in the universitie and the charges of his com[m]encement', and on receipt of the manuscript in 1606, the guild gave him £10 towards his commencement 'to be Master of artes'.[72] *The Gouldesmythes' Storehowse* thus appears to have been a learned gift in return for the Goldsmiths' Company's patronage of Gamon's higher education; indeed the company's arms feature prominently on the title page of the manuscript, and the wardens were pleased that he 'shewed A thankfull minde to the Company in the dedicat[i]on' of the book.[73] Hannibal Gamon senior gained his freedom in 1575, and was a practising goldsmith with premises on Cheapside. Multiple members of the Gamon family also belonged to the Goldsmiths' Company, including Henry Gamon, brother of Hannibal Gamon the younger (who gained his freedom through apprenticeship in 1604), and Richard Gamon, son of Hannibal Gamon the younger (who gained his freedom through patrimony in 1626).[74]

Figure 2.4 William Badcock, *A Touchstone for Gold and Silver Wares* (London, 1677). Frontispiece showing the interior of a goldsmith's shop (top) and the assay workshop at Goldsmiths' Hall (bottom).

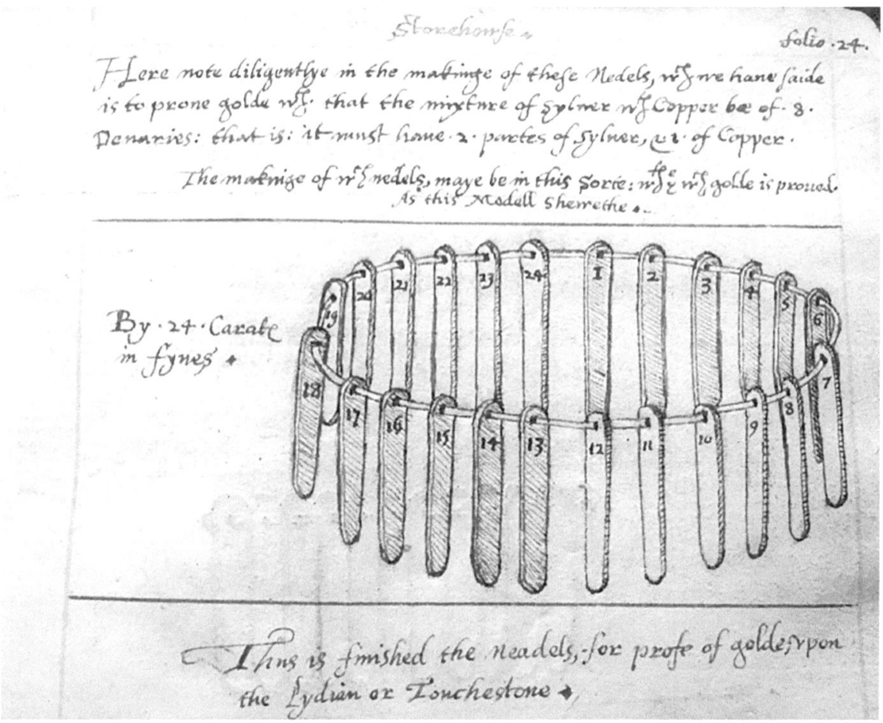

Figure 2.5 Hannibal Gamon, *The Gouldesmythes' Storehowse*, 1604, GHA, MS C II.2.1, fo. 24r. Illustration showing touch needles.

The Gouldesmythes' Storehowse contains many references to ancient and contemporary sources, including Aristotle's *Ethics*, Pliny the Elder's *Naturalis Historia*, and Agricola's *de re Metallica*.[75] In chapter sixteen of the first book, Agricola is recognised as being the authority on 'the makinge of those [touch] Ne[e]dels bothe for the Tryall of golde and sylver'.[76] Illustrations are also included of these important assay tools, which were employed to test the purity of precious metals (figure 2.5). Each made of a particular alloy of gold or silver, touch needles would be struck upon a dark touch stone and the resulting mark, representing a particular fineness, would be compared to the metal object under scrutiny. It is also evident that the authors of the *Storehowse* had read a copy of Thomas Aunsham's early sixteenth-century manuscript on minting and assaying. As deputy to the comptroller of the Tower mint, Sir Henry Wyatt, Aunsham was ideally placed to write about institutional knowledge cultures.[77] Hannibal Gamon the younger was evidently well-positioned to compile a treatise that included scholarly references, and details about contemporary craft practices and controversies. There are, though, certain particulars about workshop practices which could only have been known by the elder Hannibal Gamon. These details include a first-hand account of the outcome of the trial of the pyx in 1600 and 1601, for which Gamon senior had served on the jury.[78] This annual ceremonial testing process undertaken at the court of Star Chamber at Westminster involved the assay of a sample of coins produced at the Mint by a jury of experienced goldsmiths, to ensure the coinage met the standards set by the Crown. The likely circumstances behind the composition of the *Storehowse* – of a university-educated author in dialogue with workshop-based artisanal practitioners – are similar to the 'collaboration and communication' between different cultures of learning and knowledge that Pamela Long has identified in southern Germany and northern and central Italy from the early fifteenth century.[79] Authors of early modern technical treatises often originated from an artisanal family. Georgius Agricola (1494–1555), for instance, was a university educated humanist, but came from a dynasty of practising craftsmen in Saxony. These familial connections were 'central to his [Agricola's] appreciation for empirical knowledge and practical techniques'.[80]

For the purposes of this exploration of craft knowledge and artisanal identities, the *Storehowse* reveals three significant themes. First, the manuscript emphasises the importance of both experiential and propositional knowledge. Goldsmiths are said to assess the value of materials and craftsmanship not simply from a mathematical understanding of metallic compositions, or a book-based humanist education, but also through experience gained by years of toil in the workshop, and acutely trained sensory faculties. There is no clear distinction made here between the activities of the 'mind' and those of the 'hand'. Second, the *Storehowse* draws parallels between a citizen's status within his guild, and the depth of his authentic 'knowledge' of craftsmanship. Skill and expertise are thus mapped onto pre-existing civic hierarchies, and in the process craft knowledge is imbued with political and social distinction. Third, the goldsmiths argue that the production of knowledge about craft products – an assessment of intrinsic material, as well as technical and aesthetic qualities – was a collective social process, which ideally took place in particular locales, with select groups of guild-trained master craftsmen.[81] It is well-established that the experimental activities of gentlemen natural philosophers had definite spatial and social dimensions; so too did artisanal knowledge-making.[82]

Experiential and propositional knowledge

In a chapter on the philosophy of money, in the first book of the *Storehowse*, Gamon claims that whereas 'everye man knowethe' by sight the basic distinction between bullion and money, 'tryall at the Assaye', by a 'man experte and skilful throwe practize in the Arte of Assaye Makinge', is required for 'the perfit knowledge of Golde and Sylver'.[83] For fire assay, also called cupellation assay, the practitioner took a sample of precious

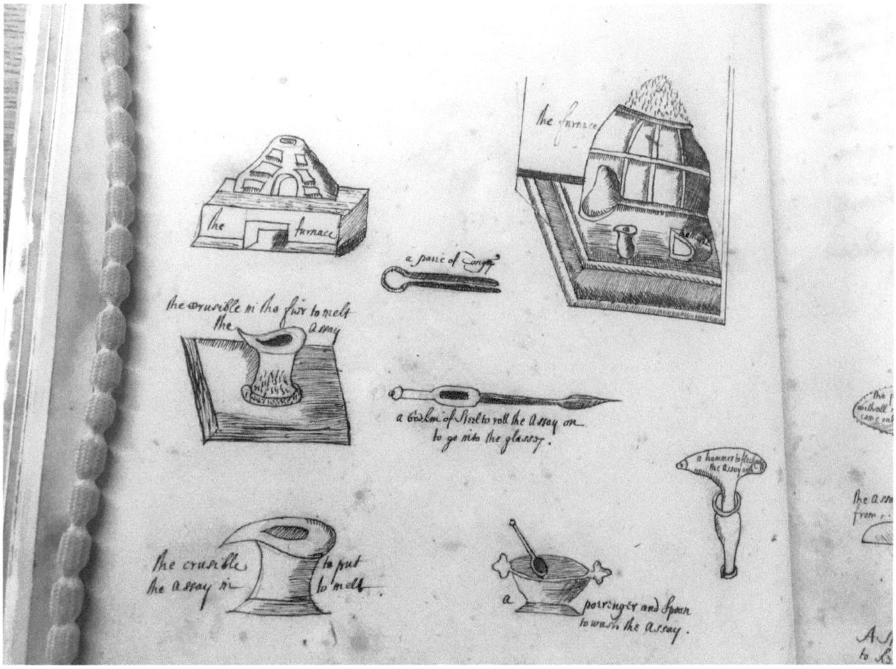

Figure 2.6 *Mint and Moneta*, TNA, MS T 48/92, fo. 12v. Illustration of equipment and instruments used for assay, including furnaces.

metal from the article to be tested, which was weighed, and then melted down multiple times in a cupel (cup of bone ash) with lead until the base metals in the sample were absorbed into the cupel. Base and precious metals thus separated, the fineness of the pure sample, or bead, was then weighed and calculated.[84] Assay by fire involved an experiential understanding of many workshop variables, including furnace temperatures, and the malleability of metals (see figures 2.6 and 2.7). It was said by Gamon that this complex process, through which the material purity of a metallic sample is tested, 'Requyrethe a p[er]fit Assaye man, whose p[er]fection must be grounded upon Artificiall Exercise; for these things doe rather consist in doinge, then in Resoninge, for they are not eselie reduced to matter of Argument, unlesse Exercise be joyned w[i]th speche'.[85] It was thus not enough for a man to have read about the craft process of assaying; textual learning was no substitute for first-hand manual practice, or 'Exercise'.

The *Storehowse* acknowledges the difficulty, and ultimately the irony, of expressing non-discursive practices through the written word. After claiming that the work of the assayer is not 'eselie reduced to matter of Argument', Gamon announces, somewhat defensively, 'Notwythestyandinge the said Triall of Assaies of Golde and Sylver is made w[i]th these communications

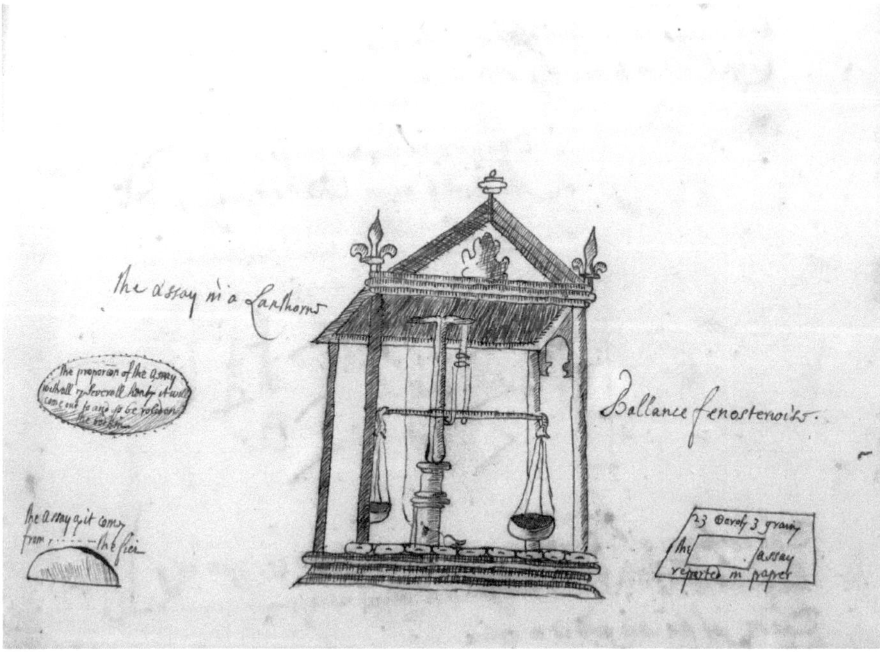

Figure 2.7 *Mint and Moneta*, TNA, MS T 48/92, fo. 13r. Illustration of a set of balances used for cupellation assay.

herafter followinge'.[86] Through this emphasis placed upon the embodied elements of artisanal expertise, Gamon reiterates the counsel of contemporary authorities on assaying. The German metallurgist and mining and assaying practitioner Lazarus Ercker (*c.* 1530–94) stated in his *Treatise on Ores and Assaying* (1580), which was inspired by Agricola's *De re metallica*, that 'These things cannot be pictured on paper in such a way that they can be understood and judged merely by reading about them. Reading shows you the way, but the work of your own hands gives you the experience.'[87] The personal qualities of the 'perfect' assayer, who must be acutely aware of 'anye defecte' which would make the assay 'uncertaine and not reportable', are further developed within the *Storehowse*. Assaying, it was said, 'askethe a good Judgement, gotten rather by yeares and experience, then by speculation and dispute … [further] that besydes his grownded experience in this scyence or mysterye [the artisan] should have a perfit eie to vewe [or "discerne"], and as stedye a hande to waye for other mens senses cannot serve him'.[88] In the third book on recipes for the assaying of gold and silver, Gamon writes of the importance of hearing: 'to have surer knowledge therof laye your eare unto the saide glasse and yf it be full laden and charged w[i]th sylver it will sounde in this wise. bott, bott, bott'.[89] The metallurgical expert should thus combine extensive workshop experience and uniquely attuned sensory perceptions. He must also have a thorough knowledge and understanding of his workshop tools; Gamon asserts that 'w[i]thowte knowledge therin, the worke master shall goe blindlye to worke'.[90] This is a combination of expertise for the production of knowledge with which supporters of the 'new method of philosophizing' would have been wholly in sympathy; it is (only) the assayer's social status which makes him an unreliable participant.[91]

The complexity and experiential nature of the assayer's work – one could not merely read about how to react to the temperature of the fire, or the smell of molten metal – means that the *Storehowse* did not genuinely equip the reader with sufficient knowledge to carry out the workshop practices it describes; it was not a true 'instruction' manual.[92] But the work of the assayer was also socially and politically sensitive. The results of their metallurgical experiments directly impacted upon the reputations and livelihoods of London's goldsmiths and merchants, the credit of their institutions (the Goldsmiths' Company and the Tower mint), and the fineness of coin and bullion. Within the Goldsmiths' Company the position of the assay master was said to be 'a place of great trust to be supplied by men of skill and integrity', and his precise technical knowledge was a closely guarded secret.[93] Chapter 6 addresses the difficulty of policing, or physically containing this knowledge within the Assay Office at Goldsmiths' Hall.

A hierarchy of skill and knowledge

If the perfect assay master was a man of applied experience, heightened sensory discernment, and textual learning, then what of the other practising goldsmiths in London, those who bought, sold, and produced material products? Members of the Goldsmiths' Company in the early seventeenth century included plateworkers, wiredrawers, jewellers, engravers, refiners, and shop-keeping goldsmiths.[94] In the final chapter of the first book of *The Gouldesmythes' Storehowse*, Gamon considers the social distribution of artisanal knowledge within the Goldsmiths' Company. He turns his attention to 'other particuler partes of this Arte, more knowen and used by everye particuler gouldesmythe, as of consequence being trayned up therin, it followethe by Tradition from one to another'. 'Tradition' here clearly refers to guild-controlled apprenticeship. Gamon starts by setting up a distinction between 'a complete Goldesmythe', and a citizen who 'is but p[ar]te of a gouldsmythe'. The former is 'a workeman bothe in golde and sylver', the latter 'is skilled but in one of these'. The further specialisation of workshop skills had allegedly resulted in a situation in which few individual artisans could undertake every technique and process required for the production of a single piece of plate; that the silver worker 'can onlye nayle it, and fashion it and can goe no farther, so that then for the graving and chasinge, an other w[hi]ch can doe no other worke, must finyshe that worke'. Likewise, the gilding of silver was said to be, 'an arte of singuler skill, and fewe can doe it, as it oughte to be, and as it hathe bene donne in tymes paste'. Many workers in gold are said to be similarly singular or incomplete: 'For wheras his skill oughte to doe anything pertinent to a golde worker, it is devided into severall mens skils, As one to make Jewels onlye, an other Ringes, others Borders, others Chaines brasletts, others wyer worke ... And so no generall golde worker, but a parte of one.'[95]

Aside from those who were practising artisans, Gamon dedicates a final paragraph to 'the Marchant goldesmythe, otherwise termed the Buyer and Seller'. By contrast to the workmen, it is said that these retailers 'must have skill and knowledge, in all these aforesaide severall knowledges. Or els he cannot be estemed in this function a perfitt Artiste'. The merchants, who also typically held the most prestigious and authoritative offices within the livery company, were thus said to be the citizens with the broadest range of practical skills, and deepest theoretical understanding of the craft. Contrary to his previous assessment in favour of the embodied knowledge of the assayer, Gamon claims here that ultimate 'skill and knowledge', 'cannot in manye yeares be attayned unto only by Tradition; Unles le[a] rninge; which is gotten by Readinge severall Authors, be joyned therto'.[96] Apprenticeship is allegedly insufficient if a man aspires to 'completeness', or to be 'synguler in the arte'.[97] The experiential features of workshop training were thus ideally to be combined with theoretical book-learning. Within a treatise which attempted to mediate the tacit and propositional knowledge(s) of the goldsmith, it is unsurprising that Gamon placed emphasis upon the textual basis of the 'marchant' goldsmith's education. This weighting must in part have been a rhetorical tool of self-promotion.

Collective assessment of artisanal expertise

As a corrective to the specialisation of corporate knowledge, Gamon argued that it was imperative that 'everye workman ... wilbe accounted a perfit worke mayster, to labour w[i]th all his Industrie, and dilligence, to gaine to be synguler in the arte, which he professethe'.[98] There is clearly an inherent irony here, in that Hannibal Gamon the younger himself would have lacked the manifold skills and experience necessary to produce a goldsmith's masterpiece. Gamon's (scholarly) masterpiece is instead the *Storehowse* manuscript itself.[99] The degree to which Gamon's criticisms echoed the concerns of the Goldsmiths' Company, and in a timely fashion, is, however, revealed in a declaration by the wardens, 'read openly in the hall to all the company', in November 1607, concerning 'the arte and misterie of Goldsmithrie ... dispersed into many partes'. As claimed in the *Storehowse*, the wardens were deeply troubled that 'now very fewe workeman are able to finishe and p[er]fecte A piece of plate singularly with all the garnishinges and partes thereof withoute the helpe of many and severall hands'. Furthermore, individual workshops had taken to specialising in their production: 'onely Bell saltes or onely belles or onely casting bottles ... some others to be spoone makers and some to be badge makers'. Additional concern was raised about goldsmiths seeking 'the use and helpe of sundry inferior handy craftes as pewterers founders and turners for the p[er]fecting of divers workes to the great scandall and disgrace of this misterie'.[100] Such a statement is indicative of the company's proprietorial attitude towards the particular technical skills and knowledge of the goldsmiths. The concern over 'the helpe of many and severall hands', like Gamon's reflections upon those who are 'no general golde worker, but a part of one', also speak to widespread and intensifying practices of subcontracting and specialisation within the trade.[101] The company assistants were frustrated at the symbolic loss of skill that the dispersal of 'the arte and misterie' represented, and, though unspoken, of the challenge to guild regulation that such a complex craft economy presented. For many working goldsmiths, however, subcontracting was a dynamic and flexible response to consumer demand and dense credit networks.[102]

The solution to this 'negligence', which the assistants feared might 'bring aliens and straingers workemanshipp in better reputac[i]on' and 'decay the whole mistery', was to re-establish the custom of the masterpiece.[103] Journeymen, or apprentices towards the end of their training, would have to produce a masterpiece as a condition of the freedom (and the right to set up as an independent master craftsman).[104] The court minutes state in 1607 that:

> no workman, foreigner, nor son of any freeman of this City ... nor no workman's apprentice of this Mystery ... shalbe allowed to have assaye and tutche within Goldsmithes hall or shalbe suffred to keepe open shoppe wherein to worke for himself as A workmaister before such tyme ... he have made and wroughte within the workehowse newly erected in Goldsmithes hall ... such A compleate peece of worke commonly called a m[aste]rpiece (to bee begonne and finished by him self) withoute the helpe or instruct[i]on of any other.[105]

The guild archive gives no further precise detail of the techniques and skills which were to be tested through a trial piece, or of the physical dimensions or precise location of the 'workehouse' built especially for the restoration of the 'complete' goldsmith. Broadly, the purpose of the task was evidently to show off the widest range of processes and expertise necessary to fashion a 'compleate peece of worke'. The court minutes do, however, articulate the broader social practices through which goldsmiths established epistemological authority. The final masterpiece of the goldsmith was to be subject to the collective 'viewe and Judgement of the fowre wardens ... and 2 skillfull workemen of the same misterie to be by the said wardens yearly nominated and chosen for that purpose adjudged and declared to be A p[er]fecte and skill full workeman and soe recorded'.[106] Similarly, masterpieces were brought to Armourers' Hall by aspiring master armourers for display and collective judgement by the court. Journeymen who presented pieces considered 'to be workmanly done', were 'alowde to kepe shope'.[107] Pewterers were likewise expected to submit 'a proofe peece of his owne makinge' to be examined by the master, wardens, and assistants, before setting up as an independent artisan.[108]

Since the wardens at Goldsmiths' Hall employed 'workemen' for arbitrating on artisanal expertise, we might question Gamon's claim that the 'marchant' goldsmiths had 'skill and knowledge, in all these aforesaide severall knowledges'.[109] Whatever the precise dynamic between the wardens and the '2 skillfull workemen', it is telling that the ideal scenario for assessing the artisanal masterpiece was within a group of knowledgeable and authoritative guild members. Similarly, when hiring a new assay master, the short-listed applicants would demonstrate their practical skills in front of select groups of goldsmiths at the assay house in Goldsmiths' Hall.[110] The description in *The Gouldesmythes' Storehowse* of the trial of the pyx, undertaken 'in one parte of ye Inner Chamber in ye Starre Chamber' at Westminster, further affirms the collective nature of artisanal knowledge-making.[111] The text reveals that fifteen 'Ancient and skilfullest goldsmythes' were chosen for the jury, and 'thyther they all resorte, [to the court] w[i] th their glasse, waightes, stronge water, and all other things necessarye pertinent to asaye makinge'. It is indicative of the structure of London society, and the perceived need to ritually perform social difference, that 'the Lordes goe to dynner in the nexte Roomthe, and so the Jurie goe to worke, that they maye be redie w[i]th their verdict against the nobell men have dyned'.[112] In 1601, however, a year in which Hannibal Gamon senior was serving on the jury, 'This Tryall being thus made, and findinge the furnace for want of use not agreable … we departed, to make farther Tryall at the Goldesmythes Hale'.[113] The work of Patrick Wallis and Catherine Wright on guild searches of artisanal shops and work spaces throughout the early modern metropolis also stresses the importance of this collective decision-making dimension. Groups of three of four citizens would apply their full range of senses and technical abilities when making judgements about material quality.[114]

We cannot know how widely *The Gouldesmythes' Storehowse* was circulated, or indeed read, within the Goldsmiths' Company, or civic society at large. The text might have been deliberately left in manuscript form to preserve the notion that Gamon was revealing 'secrets' to a select group of trustworthy intimates. Customarily the 'property in a [gifted] book was as much collective as private', and here the author(s) of this manuscript present collective secrets, techniques, and traditions to the very institution that embodied the craft mystery.[115] In early seventeenth-century London a manuscript on the literatures and practices of assay might have had a dual didactic purpose for goldsmith readers, worthwhile both for youthful assayers in the process of learning the craft, and for mercantile members of the guild. A text on assay would be useful for men somewhat detached from the production side of the trade, but interested in being able to speak knowledgably and authoritatively about workshop matters. The flattery of the retailers within the guild, who were said to have ultimate 'skill and knowledge', including experiential and book-based learning, was likely a reflection of his readers' expectations; presumably many were rooted in the upper echelons of the guild. This praise also reflects the wider textual culture of *artes mechanicae*, in which patrons were routinely lauded and complimented.[116]

The intended effect of codifying the customs and recipes of goldsmiths was surely also to elevate the social value of their shared knowledge cultures. The Gamons were further reinforcing the epistemological claim of metallurgy, in general, as a legitimate field of knowledge, that could be theorized and categorized. In this respect it is telling that Gamon repeatedly refers to practitioners of the craft, particularly assayers, as experts 'in this scyence or mysterye', or 'masters of this science'.[117]

Gamon's exploration of the processes through which experienced master goldsmiths collectively ensured the material quality of silver, gold, and precious stones, may have also been intended to reassure the consumers of these products. It is pertinent that the first printed text in English on 'The Rules belonging to that [the goldsmiths'] Mystery', *A Touch-Stone for Gold and Silver Wares* (1677), was published precisely to make assaying and marking practices transparent for 'the Publique Good', 'whether Buyers, Sellers, or Wearers of any manner of Goldsmiths Work'.[118] Likewise, the Goldsmiths' Company's decision to reinstate the trial of the masterpiece, within their institutional space, perhaps reflected both an ambition to raise technical standards among apprentices and journeymen, and also to legitimise these skills and symbolically reassure consumers of a standard level of quality. Bert De Munck's research on woodworkers' guilds in sixteenth- and seventeenth-century Antwerp has shown that the masterpiece was important among these artisans to 'preserve the image and prestige of the masters and their products'.[119]

If the unmediated views of the 'working goldsmiths' had been similarly preserved for posterity, they might well have contested the notion that their guild governors were superior to them 'in all these aforesaid severall knowledges'.[120] It is telling that when a controversy erupted in the 1580s between the company's assayers and a group of working goldsmiths, over the breaking of faulty plate, it was decided that the matter was to be considered by five liverymen 'and men skilful in making assays'.[121] The latter group were brought in to arbitrate precisely because the court of assistants was unable to reach a satisfactory decision on the basis of its own expertise and political subjectivity. Though unlikely to be representative of the views of all goldsmiths, the *Storehowse* is highly revealing in its allusions to the contested nature of artisanal knowledge in early modern guilds. The balance between 'good Judgement, gotten rather by yeares and experience in this scyence or mysterye' and 'le[a]rninge; whiche is gotten by Readinge severall Authors', is never fully resolved within Gamon's text.[122] The assertion that artisanal knowledge is an essential component of status within the guild – distinguishing between 'everye particuler gouldesmythe' and 'the Marchant goldesmythe' – suggests that, for contemporaries, civic hierarches were a complex blend of social, political, and epistemological prestige.[123]

The Carpenters Rule: mathematical practitioners and instrument makers

> If any man of knowledge shall expect against me, for my rude writing and grosse demonstrations: I pray them to understand, that I writ not for them, but for the simple; and therefore I demonstrate grossely, not being able to do better: Also, that I am not a scholler but a Carpenter, and therefore could not but write rudely.[124]

The final part of this chapter examines a printed text authored by Richard More, *The Carpenters Rule; or, a book shewing many plain waies, truly to measure ordinarie timber* (1602). Positioned at the interface between guild, commercial, and mathematical cultures, this case-study comes at the end of this discussion of artisanal-authored writings. Whereas Nicholas Stone's account book was rooted in the workshop/household, and *The Gouldesmythes' Storehowse* was a product of the institutional cultures of the guild, university, and Mint, Richard More is here explicitly encouraging his readers to engage with the shops, instruments, texts, and sites of learning associated with the mathematical sciences.[125]

We know very few personal details about Richard More, only that he was a member of the Carpenters' Company, and a practitioner of this craft.[126] But *The Carpenters Rule* is self-consciously a product of a lively metropolitan culture of practical, applied mathematics. For mathematical practitioners, knowledge was fundamentally a combination of theoretical, experiential, and instrumental learning.[127] The book is an interesting example of a craft practitioner claiming allegiance to the mathematical sciences, and, in the process, critiquing customary artisanal practices. It is also a very rare instance of an English carpenter attempting to craft an intellectual and commercial identity through print.

The central purpose of this 'how-to' book is to instruct its readers on the fundamentals of measurement. *The Carpenters Rule* was the second printed text in Britain on the subject of mensuration for carpenters; it was the first such publication, though, to be authored by a working practitioner.[128]

It was to act as 'a remedie' for erroneous craft practice by introducing readers to the basic principles of geometry and arithmetic. More's ambition was to have 'the common errors plainly laid open to the capacitie of the simplist; so that all men might take knowledge thereof'. The key message of the text is that in order to work efficiently, accurately, and in a trustworthy manner, an artisan must possess theoretical (mathematical) knowledge:

> Onely let me put you in minde of this one thinge: That in as much as nothing is more fit for Carpenters to make them readie, not only in measure but also in other things, then Geometrie: that therefore such as are of reasonable capacitie, would spend some part of their spare times to studie the same, in some measure at the least.[129]

Richard More anticipates a range of readers who might benefit from the lessons contained in this didactic book. First, traders and merchants (and perhaps gentlemen), who might be cheated by inaccurate techniques of measuring timber: 'These errors are such … I would they might not bee said to be a great cause … of the impairing of some mens estates.'[130] Second, practising carpenters: 'the ordinarie and common sort of men'. Third, a wider range of artisanal practitioners, for whom 'accurate' measurement was (said to be) central to their labour: 'For besides that the Carpenter may measure hereby any canted peece of timber, as steps for staires, and … the plaisterer also, who often worketh by the yard, may hereby measure gable-ends … and also it may stand the Mason oft in stead.'[131] Aside from these acknowledged readers, who might find a 'how to' book on measuring to be of genuine applied use, there is evidently also an expectation that this text will be recognised by fellow practitioners of the mathematical sciences, and thus form part of a broader canon of vernacular literature on mathematics.

Organised into three parts, each with multiple short chapters, *The Carpenters Rule* explores how practitioners err as a consequence of their lack of understanding of the geometrical principles underlying their labour. And thus the first part demonstrates 'the errors most commonly committed, and taken for truth, in measuring of timber', second, 'how ordinarie timber may be measured, both by sundrie plaine waies, as also by waies more artificiall', and finally, 'how extraordinarie timber and sollid formes may be measured'.[132] The common habit of carpenters simply copying division markings from one rule to another also comes under criticism from More, for the inevitable inaccuracy that results: 'Yea hardly shall you see two Rules that do euery where agree.'[133] The carpenter instead encourages the use of new instruments for solving practical problems. In the preface, More specifically recommends the rule designed by the late Thomas Bedwell, former Keeper of Ordinance Stores at the Tower of London: 'While this booke was in printing I came to the sight of a Ruler, sometimes inuented by one Master *Bedwel*; which as it is easie, so it is most speedie, and not lesse certaine (being truly made) for the measuring of timber and boord; which I expect and hope will be shortly published for the common good.'[134] To further facilitate understanding of geometry, the book is richly illustrated with diagrams of geometric shapes, geometric solids, a carpenter's rule, and a table of board measure. At the start of the third section of the book, More also includes a glossary of useful geometric terms translated into a craft vernacular, for instance: 'An oblique Angle (which we call beuell or skew) is euery angle not being a right angle, whether it be greater or lesse, or (as we say) whether it spread or clitch.'[135] Aside from potentially enhancing the reader's understanding of the text, the inclusion of this glossary is evidently an opportunity for More to present himself as a cultural translator – and dual expert – between the worlds of craft practice and mathematical knowledge.

The themes of More's publication – the identification and correction of artisanal 'error' – are typical of the production of self-styled Elizabethan 'mathematical practitioners'. This was a heterogeneous group of craftsmen, merchants, technicians, engineers, and gentlemen, who promoted the study of the mathematical arts and sciences for private and public profit.[136] Knowledge was said to be a blend of theory and experiential understanding, and thus the making, study, and use of instruments for exploring the natural and built environment, was key. In the words of mathematical practitioner Leonard Digges, whose work aimed at reforming the 'vulgar errors' of practitioners, 'oft diligent reading, joyned with ingenious practise, causeth profitable laboure'.[137] Digges's *A Boke named Tectonicon* (1556), the very first in Britain on the subject of the practical application of the mathematical sciences – ostensibly for the benefit of 'surveyors, landemeaters, joyners, carpenters, and masons' – in 'our tongue', whetted the public appetite for vernacular books of instrumentation for generations to come.[138]

The dedication and preface to *The Carpenters Rule* betray a direct allegiance to fellow advocates of the mathematical sciences. The book is dedicated to the merchant and alderman Sir Henry Billingsley, whose translation and publication of Euclid's *Elements of Geometrie* in English, in 1570, was fundamental to the flowering of the mathematical sciences in England. John Dee's preface to Billingsley's translation achieved perhaps even greater fame as a statement of mathematics as fundamental to all knowledge, the basis of universal wisdom. Dee presented a visual plot of a 'Mathematical Tree' with 'chief armes and second (grafted) branches' which represent the twenty-seven applied mathematical arts and sciences, including astronomy, architecture, music, and navigation.[139] In rooting all these (seemingly) disparate bodies of knowledge and practice in arithmetic and geometry, Dee makes the compelling claim that all human knowledge is essentially mathematical.[140] Richard More asserts that his book is 'to testifie my dutifull thankfulnes for your great paines and no small cost, in publishing in our English ... *Euclide Elements of Geometrie.* A booke, from which ... I haue receiued all that little insight in Geometry, which I haue attained vnto.'[141] In the spirit of the public utility of the mathematical sciences, More also encourages readers of his text to further their learning through attendance at 'the Lecture at Gresham Colledge every Thursday in the Terme times'.[142] Established in 1597 through provisions made in the will of Mercer Sir Thomas Gresham, the innovative institution and lectures, including the subjects of astronomy and geometry, were intended to further the learning of London's inhabitants, particularly those involved in trade and commerce.[143] Members of the Carpenters' Company did not have far to travel if they wished to attend lectures at Gresham College; Gresham House on Bishopsgate was in very close proximity to Carpenters' Hall (both buildings were located within Broad Street Ward). The final passage of *The Carpenters Rule* also encourages further independent reading of vernacular texts of geometry: 'There are many other kinds of plaines and sollids, but I may not stand to write of them. If any man, either for pleasure or profit, shall desire to know them, or their measure, let him looke into *Euclides* Elements, Master *Digs* his Pantametria, Master *Lucars* Solace, and other good books of Geometrie, which are extant in English.'[144] Aside from enriching his readers' understanding of geometry, there is perhaps a further agenda at work here through inclusion of these intertextual references. Richard More, an obscure London carpenter, is positioning his work as a starting-point for a wide-ranging dialogue with the most well-known mathematical writers of his day.

Whereas practitioners of the mathematical sciences are praised in *The Carpenters Rule*, Richard More is somewhat disingenuous in his claim that the work is also dedicated to the master, wardens, and assistants of the Carpenters' Company. In reality, *The Carpenters Rule* is intended as a critique of contemporary craft practice and those who regulate the labour of London's carpenters. More asserts in the preface to the text that he had initially thought to privately discuss with the governors of the guild 'what errors I had observed in our ordinarie measure, and so to have desired you in all dutie to have provided a remedie'. But instead More decides to take an altogether more public course of action, through publication, because he recognised that flawed practice was endemic to the Carpenters' system of learning through apprenticeship: 'I perceived, that custome had caused error to be received as a truth, and that therefore men would not forsake them, unless they were plainly convinced to have erred'.[145]

Richard More asserts that the purpose of his writing is to improve the theoretical knowledge, and thus working practices, of craftsmen, and so protect the interests and profits of all those engaged with artisans. But we can speculate that for this unusually well-educated and articulate carpenter, authorship of a publication went beyond these simple didactic aims. First, this humble text on mensuration was a means of staking his claim to expertise, and thus enhancing his social reputation. Positioning himself as a 'cultural amphibian' – a mathematical expert, who also has vernacular knowledge of carpentry – has the effect of elevating More above 'the simple' mass of London's labourers and craftsmen.[146] Second, by 'revealing' geometry as the basis of carpentry, and thus rooting the labour of woodworkers within a broader culture of mathematical science, More is inferring that humble construction work might also be raised beyond the mechanical and classed as one of the liberal arts. Similarly, in their treatises on pyrotechnic knowledge sixteenth- and seventeenth-century gunners emphasised the mathematical basis of the crafts of making, designing, and deploying fireworks.[147] This was part of a broader strategy that 'exploited the language of geometry, natural philosophy, and the notion of ingenious invention to express and lend credit to their labours'.[148] Third, in addition to presenting himself as an expert through authorship of this book, Richard More is also further reinforcing the epistemological claim of practical mathematics, in general, as a legitimate field of knowledge.[149] Lastly, More might also have hoped to gain some financial profit from authorship, though in the event the text does not appear to have been a huge commercial success; it was republished once in 1616.

Conclusion

For mason Nicholas Stone, the Gamon goldsmith dynasty, and carpenter Richard More, writing about their working practices was a means of articulating identity, accounting for their lives, and perhaps facilitating social mobility. Either implicitly or directly, each of these texts shows that artisanal knowledge was multifaceted and ideally based upon a blend of experiential, theoretical, and instrumental understanding. These writings on workshop labour also demonstrate that ascertaining expertise might be complex and contested. The seemingly straightforward instrumental precision set out by Richard More does not account for the varied sensory, personal, and institutional variables laid out by the Gamons.

Each of these sources acknowledges that text alone is an insufficient basis for understanding a culture which was largely tacit, embodied, and based on accumulated lived experience. Our textual case-studies have repeatedly directed us away from their singular perspective and outward towards the wider familial, social, institutional, material, and spatial contexts within and through which craftsmen established and upheld their reputations. These artisanal accounts are rooted in and speak of a diverse metropolitan network of spaces of cultural production, regulation, and exchange, including homes, workshops, company halls, royal and civic institutions (such as the Royal Mint or Gresham College), retail spaces, and building sites. Accordingly, the next chapter takes us out of the first-person text and onto a construction site at the heart of the City. We explore an urban space within and through which London's craftsmen negotiated expertise, epistemological status, and the social dimensions of artisanal decision-making.

Notes

1 See James Amelang's focus on memoirs, diaries, and chronicles as forms of artisanal autobiography in *The Flight of Icarus.* See also William Eamon's examination of 'books of secrets' as a discrete genre in *Science and the Secrets of Nature: Books of Secrets in Medieval and Early Modern Culture* (Princeton, NJ: Princeton University Press, 1994).
2 Edgar Zilsel, 'The sociological roots of science', *The American Journal of Sociology*, 47:4 (1942), 544–62; Eamon, *Science and the Secrets of Nature*; Harkness, *The Jewel House*.
3 GHA, MS C II.2.1, fo. 4v.
4 Shapin, 'The house of experiment'; Shapin, *A Social History of Truth*.
5 For a broader European dimension to collaborative artisanal practices, see Pamela Smith, 'Making and knowing in a sixteenth-century goldsmith's workshop', in L. Roberts, S. Shaffer, and P. Dear (eds), *The Mindful Hand: Inquiry and Invention from the Late Renaissance to Early Industrialisation* (Amsterdam: Koninkliijke Nederlandse Akademie van Wetenschappen, 2007), pp. 33–57, at pp. 38–9.
6 Pamela Smith, 'Why write a book? From lived experience to the written word in early modern Europe', *West 86th: A Journal of Decorative Arts, Design History, and Material Culture*, 19 (2012), 25–50, at pp. 32–3, 39.
7 David Cressy, *Literacy and the Social Order: Reading and Writing in Tudor and Stuart England* (Cambridge: Cambridge University Press, 1980), p. 129.
8 *Ibid*., pp. 134–5.
9 *Ibid*., p. 136.
10 *Ibid*., p. 73.
11 Keith Thomas, 'The meaning of literacy in early modern England', in Gerd Baumann (ed.), *The Written Word: Literacy in Translation* (Oxford: Clarendon Press, 1986), pp. 97–131, at p. 101; Margaret Spufford, *Small Books and Pleasant Histories: Popular Fiction and its Readership in Seventeenth-Century England* (London: Methuen, 1981), p. 27; Barry Reay, *Popular Cultures in England 1550–1750* (London: Longman, 1998), pp. 39–47.
12 For craft guilds and secrecy, see Long, *Openness, Secrecy, Authorship*, pp. 3–4, 6–7, 13–14, 72–101; Karel Davids, 'Craft secrecy in Europe in the early modern period: a comparative view', *Early Science and Medicine*, 10:3 (2005), 341–8.
13 GHA, MS 2524, fo. 55v. This ordinance states that if any man 'reveals the secrets and good regulations of the craft to him, [a stranger] he shall be deprived of all the benefits of St Dunstan until in the presence of the whole livery he acknowledges his misdeeds or else he shall pay a fine of 40s'.
14 Eamon, *Science and the Secrets of Nature*, p. 81.
15 Charles Welch, *History of the Worshipful Company of Pewterers: Based Upon Their Own Records*, 2 vols (London: Blades, East & Blades, 1902), II, pp. 34–5. This comment raises the intriguing question of how shops and workshops were spatially organised. It is possible that there were relatively 'open' and also 'secret' areas (less exposed to public view).
16 Bert De Munck and Hugo Soly, '"Learning on the shop floor" in historical perspective', in Munck, Kaplan, and Soly (eds), *Learning on the Shop Floor*, pp. 3–32, at p. 7; Wallis, 'Apprenticeship and training in premodern England', pp. 847–8.
17 Smith, *The Body of the Artisan*, pp. 80–2. See also Eric H. Ash, 'Introduction: expertise and the early modern state', in *Expertise: Practical Knowledge and the*

Early Modern State (Chicago, IL: University of Chicago Press, 2010), pp. 1–24, at p. 9.

18 Kathleen H. Ochs, 'The Royal Society of London's history of trades programme: an early episode in applied science', *Notes and Records*, 39:2 (1985), 129–58, at 130–1.

19 Joseph Moxon, *Mechanick exercises: or, the doctrine of handy-works* (London, 1677), sig. A4r. Moxon's *Mechanick exercises* were probably intended as a contribution to the Royal Society's 'history of trades' project; Moxon was the first tradesman elected to the Royal Society (1678). See Graham Jagger, 'Joseph Moxon, F. R. S., and the Royal Society', *Notes and Records of the Royal Society of London*, 49:2 (1995), 193–208, at pp. 199–200.

20 Richard Sennett, *The Craftsman* (London: Penguin, 2008), ch. 5.

21 Keith Thomas, 'Numeracy in early modern England'. The Prothero Lecture, *TRHS*, 37 (1987), 103–32, at pp. 106, 111,

22 Rappaport, *Worlds within Worlds*, p. 298.

23 D. J. Bryden, 'Evidence from advertising for mathematical instrument making in London, 1556–1714', *Annals of Science*, 49:4 (1992), 301–36, at pp. 304–17.

24 Stephen Johnston, 'Mathematical practitioners and instruments in Elizabethan England', *Annals of Science*, 48:4 (1991), 319–44, at pp. 326–7; William Eamon, 'How to read a book of secrets', in Elaine Leong and Alisha Rankin (eds), *Secrets and Knowledge in Medicine and Science, 1500–1800* (Burlington, VT: Ashgate, 2011), pp. 23–46, at p. 30. See also Bertucci, *Artisanal Enlightenment*, ch. 5, esp. pp. 147, 153–5.

25 For Nicholas Stone's contribution as master mason to royal building projects, including Bagshot Lodge (Surrey), the Queen's House (Greenwich), Oatlands (Surrey), St. James's Palace, Somerset House, and Whitehall Palace, see H. M. Colvin (ed.), *The History of the King's Works*, vol. IV 1485–1660 (Part II) (London: H. M. S. O., 1982), pp. 37, 49, 119, 121, 216, 248, 266, 269, 332, 342. For Stone's work in funerary monuments, see Adam White, 'A biographical dictionary of London tomb sculptors, c. 1560–c. 1660', *The Volume of the Walpole Society*, 61 (1999), pp. 1–162, at pp. 118–38.

26 GHA, MS C II.2.1.

27 I have found Adam Smyth's discussion of a broad 'culture of innovation and adaptation' in relation to 'life-writing' very helpful here. Crucially, Smyth argues for a strong 'relationship between financial accounting and accounting for life'. See *Autobiography in Early Modern England* (Cambridge: Cambridge University Press, 2010), pp. 2–3, 57–122. Smyth's exploration of the practice of 'shunting' records 'from text to text' as part of the practice of life-writing (pp. 2, 59–60) is also pertinent to a full understanding of Nicolas Stone's use of his notebook and account book; there are repetitions, elaborations, and connections between these texts.

28 Adam White, 'Stone, Nicholas (1585x8–1647)'. *Oxford Dictionary of National Biography*. 23 September 2004. Oxford University Press [accessed 28 July 2020].

29 White, 'A biographical dictionary of London tomb sculptors', p. 119.

30 Sir John Soane's Museum, London [hereafter JSM], MS 22, fos 3r, 11r, 12r, 34r.

31 Walter Lewis Spiers, 'The note-book and account book of Nicholas Stone', *The Volume of the Walpole Society*, 7 (1918–19), pp. 1–200, at p. 102.

32 *Ibid.*, p. 129.

33 Master masons had always undertaken very varied tasks. See L. R. Shelby, 'The role of the master mason in medieval English building', *Speculum*, 39:3 (1964), 387–403, at pp. 387–8.

34 Spiers, 'The note-book and account book', p. 70.

35 JSM, MS 22, fo. 12r.

36 JSM, MS 22, fo. 34r.

37 This project is recorded in meticulous detail in the Goldsmiths' Company's wardens' accounts and court minutes, but is not mentioned by Stone in his notebook or account book. This omission indicates that the surviving account book (1631–42) under-represents the number of projects undertaken by Nicholas Stone's workshop.
38 JSM, MS 22, fos 43v–44r.
39 For the distinction between contracts 'by the measure' and 'by the great' see McKellar, *The Birth of Modern London*, p. 86.
40 JSM, MS 22, fo. 10v.
41 White, 'A biographical dictionary of London tomb sculptors', pp. 118–19.
42 Spiers, 'The note-book and account book', p. 93.
43 *Ibid.*, pp. 116–17. The brothers were in Italy between 1638 and 1642.
44 H. J. Louw, 'Anglo-Netherlandish architectural interchange c.1600–c.1660', *Architectural History*, 24 (1981), 1–23, at p. 2.
45 Spiers, 'The note-book and account book', pp. 193, 197.
46 JSM, MS 23.
47 JSM, MS 23, fo. 1.
48 Spiers, 'The note-book and account book', p. 49.
49 *Ibid.*, p. 58.
50 JSM, MS 23, fo. 11.
51 White, 'A biographical dictionary of London tomb sculptors', p. 63. For the westward move of prominent master masons from the City of London to the suburban parishes of St. Martin-in-the-Fields and St. Giles-in-the-Fields, see Nigel Llewellyn, *Funeral Monuments in Post-Reformation England* (Cambridge: Cambridge University Press, 2000), p. 193.
52 Spiers, 'The note-book and account book', p. 53.
53 Mary Carruthers, *The Book of Memory: A Study of Memory in Medieval Culture*, 2nd edn (Cambridge: Cambridge University Press, 2008), pp. 89–98.
54 JSM, MS 23, fos 22v–24r.
55 The combination of intensely personal and public and civic events is typical of autobiographical writing in this period. See Amelang, *The flight of Icarus*, pp. 31–2; Smyth, *Autobiography in Early Modern England*, p. 11.
56 Pollmann, *Memory in Early Modern Europe*, pp. 27–9.
57 Spiers, 'The note-book and account book', p. 81.
58 JSM, MS 23 [this section of the manuscript is not foliated].
59 White, 'A biographical dictionary of London tomb sculptors', p. 119.
60 TNA, PROB 11/203/300. The reference to Stone's 'studie' is surely indicative of his elevated social status.
61 John Summerson, 'Three Elizabethan architects', *Bulletin of the John Rylands Library*, 40:1 (1957), 202–28, at pp. 212, 219; Christy Anderson, *Inigo Jones and the Classical Tradition* (Cambridge: Cambridge University Press, 2007), p. 53.
62 TNA, PROB 11/61/343.
63 'His [Henry Stone's] epitaph praised his "Excellency in Artes & Languages" … and the church burial register distinguishes him by the title of gentleman.' See White, 'A biographical dictionary of London tomb sculptors', p. 113.
64 GHA, WA/CM, O3, fo. 454.
65 GHA, MS C II.2.1.
66 For the breadth of subject matter in books of secrets, see Eamon, *Science and the Secrets of Nature*, pp. 112–20.
67 There are two manuscript versions of *The Gouldesmythes' Storehowse*, and five known copies. The copy owned by the Goldsmiths' Company is the longer version, and contains a discussion of the specialisation of the trade. See Janelle Jenstad, '"The Gouldesmythes Storehowse": early evidence for specialisation', *The Silver Society Journal*, 10 (1998), 40–3, at p. 40.

68 William Eamon, 'Arcana disclosed: the advent of printing, the books of secrets tradition and the development of science in the sixteenth century', *History of Science*, 22:2 (1984), 111–50.
69 British Library [hereafter BL], Sloane MS 1423. And for a broader discussion of Clement Draper and his writings and experimental practices, see Harkness, *The Jewel House*, ch. 5.
70 GHA, MS C II.2.1, fo. 4v.
71 Duffin, Anne. 'Gamon, Hannibal (bap. 1582, d. 1650/51)'. *Oxford Dictionary of National Biography*. 3 January 2008. Oxford University Press. [accessed 28 July 2020].
72 GHA, WA/CM, O2, fo. 313; O3, fo. 454.
73 GHA, WA/CM, O3, fo. 454.
74 See Records of London's Livery Companies Online: Apprentices and Freemen 1400–1900 (ROLLCO) www.londonroll.org [accessed 20 October 2012].
75 GHA, MS C II.2.1, fos 23r–v, 33v.
76 GHA, MS C II.2.1, fos 23r–v.
77 BL, Harley MS 38.
78 GHA, MS C II.2.1, fos 28r, 30r.
79 Long, *Openness, Secrecy, Authorship*, p. 246.
80 Pamela Long, 'The openness of knowledge: an ideal and its context in sixteenth-century writings on mining and metallurgy', *Technology and Culture*, 32:2 (1991), 318–55, at pp. 334–5, 355.
81 For an overview of 'the situated character of our most highly valued forms of knowledge, especially of science', see Adi Ophir and Steven Shapin, 'The place of knowledge: a methodological survey', *Science in Context*, 4:1 (1991), 3–21, at p. 4.
82 Shapin, 'The house of experiment', pp. 68–71.
83 GHA, MS C II.2.1, fo. 4v.
84 John S. Forbes, *Hallmark: A History of the London Assay Office* (London: Unicorn, 1999), p. 21.
85 GHA, MS C II.2.1, fo. 4v.
86 *Ibid.*
87 Long, 'The openness of knowledge', p. 350; Lazarus Ercker, *Treatise on Ores and Assaying*, trans. by Anneliese Grünhaldt Sisco and Cyril Stanley Smith (Chicago, IL: University of Chicago Press, 1951), p. 194.
88 GHA, MS C II.2.1, fo. 5v.
89 GHA, MS C II.2.1, fo. 76v.
90 GHA, MS C II.2.1, fo. 6r.
91 Pamela Smith and Benjamin Schmidt, 'Introduction: knowledge and its making in early modern Europe', in Smith and Schmidt (eds), *Making Knowledge in Early Modern Europe: Practices, Objects, and Texts, 1400–1800* (Chicago, IL; London: University of Chicago Press, 2007), pp. 1–16, at p. 13.
92 Eamon, *Science and the Secrets of Nature*, pp. 4–5.
93 GHA, WA/CM, P2, fo. 15v.
94 Mitchell, *Silversmiths in Elizabethan and Stuart London*, pp. 12–13.
95 GHA, MS C II.2.1, fo. 31v.
96 GHA, MS C II.2.1, fo. 32r.
97 GHA, MS C II.2.1, fos 31v–32r.
98 GHA, MS C II.2.1, fo. 31v.
99 For the early modern 'book-as-gift' as a means of self-fashioning, see Jason Scott-Warren, *Sir John Harrington and the Book as Gift* (Oxford: Oxford University Press, 2001), pp. 12, 17.
100 GHA, WA/CM, O3, fo. 551–2.
101 This growth of subcontracting and specialisation was part of a broader trend among luxury crafts and trades. See John Styles, 'The goldsmiths and the London luxury

trades, 1550 to 1750', in David Mitchell (ed.), *Goldsmiths, Silversmiths and Bankers: Innovation and the Transfer of Skill, 1550 to 1750* (Stroud: A. Sutton, 1995), pp. 112–20, at pp. 113–15. This heightened specialisation was not unique to London. See Michèle Bimbenet-Privat, 'Goldsmiths' apprenticeship during the first half of the seventeenth century: the situation in Paris', in Mitchell (ed.), *Goldsmiths, Silversmiths and Bankers*, pp. 23–31, at p. 28.

102 Styles, 'The goldsmiths and the London luxury trades', pp. 114–15.

103 Proportionally, alien goldsmiths may have constituted up to 36 per cent of active goldsmiths in London in the 1570s. See Bich Luu, *Immigrants and the Industries of London*, pp. 226–7. In 1571, and again in 1574, the company court had announced that young men were 'not to be set up for themselves until they have made their master-piece'. See Prideaux, *Memorials of the Goldsmiths' Company*, I, pp. 75, 78.

104 Maarten Prak and Patrick Wallis have stressed that 'importantly, the masterpiece was *not* an examination to test what had been learned during apprenticeship. It usually followed several years in which the aspiring master had been working as a journeyman' (Introduction to *Apprenticeship in Early Modern Europe*, p. 17). In the case of the London Goldsmiths' Company, though, the likely candidate for presenting a masterpiece appears to be an apprentice *or* a journeyman.

105 GHA, WA/CM, 03, fo. 552.

106 *Ibid.*

107 GL, MS 12071/2, fos 305–6.

108 Welch, *History of the Worshipful Company of Pewterers*, II, p. 77.

109 GHA, MS C II.2.1, fo. 32r.

110 Prideaux, *Memorials of the Goldsmiths' Company* I, p. 139.

111 GHA, MS C II.2.1, fo. 27r–v.

112 GHA, MS C II.2.1, fo. 27v.

113 GHA, MS C II.2.1, fo. 28v.

114 Patrick Wallis and Catherine Wright, 'Evidence, artisan experience, and authority in early modern England', in Smith, Meyers, and Cook (eds), *Ways of Making and Knowing*, pp. 138–63.

115 Natalie Zemon Smith, 'Beyond the market: books as gifts in sixteenth-century France', *Transactions of the Royal Historical Society*, 33 (1983), 69–88, at p. 72.

116 Pamela Long, 'Power, patronage, and the authorship of the ars: from mechanical know-how to mechanical knowledge in the last scribal age', *Isis*, 88:1 (1997), 1–41.

117 GHA, MS C II.2.1, fos 5v, 74v, 76r.

118 W. B., *A touch-stone for gold and silver wares; or, a manual for goldsmiths and all other persons, whether buyers, sellers, or wearers of any manner of goldsmiths work* (London, 1677).

119 Bert De Munck, 'Construction and reproduction: the training and skills of Antwerp cabinetmakers in the sixteenth and seventeenth centuries', in De Munck, Kaplan, and Soly (eds), *Learning on the Shop Floor*, pp. 85–110, at p. 87.

120 GHA, MS C II.2.1, fo. 32r.

121 Prideaux, *Memorials of the Goldsmiths' Company*, I, p. 81.

122 GHA, MS C II.2.1, fos 5v, 32r.

123 GHA, MS C II.2.1, fos 31v–32r.

124 Richard More, *The carpenters rule; or, a book shewing many plain waies, truly to measure ordinarie timber* (London, 1602), sig. A4v.

125 For a broader discussion of the diverse commercial mathematical culture of sixteenth- and early seventeenth-century London, see Harkness, *The Jewel House*, ch. 3.

126 He is indexed as Richard More in *Records of the Worshipful Company of Carpenters*, ed. by B. Marsh, J. Ainsworth, and A. M. Millard, 7 vols (Oxford University Press, 1914–68), VII.

127 Jim Bennett, 'The mechanics' philosophy and the mechanical philosophy', *History of Science*, 24:1 (1986), 1–28, at p. 2; Johnston, 'Mathematical practitioners and instruments', pp. 320, 324–5, 329–30, 334–5; Katherine Hill, '"Juglers or Schollers?" Negotiating the role of a mathematical practitioner', *The British Journal for the History of Science*, 31:3 (1998), 253–74.
128 Eileen Harris, *British Architectural Books and Writers 1556–1785* (Cambridge: Cambridge University Press, 1990), p. 317.
129 More, *The Carpenters Rule*, sig. A4v.
130 More, *The Carpenters Rule*, sig. A3v.
131 More, *The Carpenters Rule*, sig. G2r.
132 More, *The Carpenters Rule*, sig. A3v.
133 More, *The Carpenters Rule*, sig. B1v. The custom of creation by copying 'was still drawing the fire of mathematical authors more than half a century later [after More]'. See Stephen Johnston, 'Reading rules: artefactual evidence for mathematics and craft in early modern England', in Liba Taub and Frances Willmoth (eds), *The Whipple Museum of the History of Science: Instruments and Interpretations* (Cambridge: Cambridge University Press, 2006), pp. 233–53, at p. 247.
134 E. G. Taylor, *The Mathematical Practitioners of Tudor and Stuart England* (Cambridge: Cambridge University Press, 1954), p. 177; Johnston, 'Mathematical practitioners and instruments', pp. 321–7; More, *The Carpenters Rule*, A4v.
135 More, *The Carpenters Rule*, F4v.
136 Taylor, *The Mathematical Practitioners.*
137 Leonard Digges, *A boke named tectonicon briefelye shewynge the exacte measurynge, and speady rekenynge all maner lande, squared timber, stone, steaples, pyllers, globes* (London, 1556), sig. Ar.
138 Harris, *British Architectural Books*, p. 41, 'The rules of measuring were "lock'd up in strange tongues" until 1556 when Leonard Digges made them available to English artisans for the first time in their own language in his *Boke named Tectonicon*.' See also Anthony Gerbino and Stephen Johnston, *Compass and Rule: Architecture as Mathematical Practice in England, 1500–1750* (New Haven, CT; London: Yale University Press, 2009), p. 46. Reprinted at least twenty times between the mid-sixteenth and late seventeenth centuries, *Tectonicon's* 'sheer quantitative dominance is hard to overstate: it had more editions in its first century than all the more strictly architectural books in England put together'.
139 John Dee, *The Mathematicall Preface to the Elements of Geometrie of Euclid of Megara* (London, 1570), sig. A5r.
140 Jennifer Rampling, 'The Elizabethan mathematics of everything: John Dee's 'Mathematicall praeface' to Euclid's Elements', *Journal of the British Society for the History of Mathematics*, 26:3 (2011), 135–46, at pp. 140–1.
141 More, *The Carpenters Rule*, sig. A2r–v.
142 More, *The Carpenters Rule*, sig. A4v.
143 There was said to be poor attendance at these lectures by the 1620s. See Mordechai Feingold, 'Gresham college and London practitioners: the nature of the English mathematical community', in Francis Ames-Lewis (ed.), *Sir Thomas Gresham and Gresham College: Studies in the Intellectual History of London in the Sixteenth and Seventeenth Centuries* (Aldershot: Ashgate, 1999), pp. 174–88, at p. 176.
144 More, *The Carpenters Rule*, sig. H4v.
145 More, *The Carpenters Rule*, sig. A3r.
146 I have taken the phrase 'cultural amphibian' from: Bernard Capp, *The World of John Taylor the Water-Poet* (Oxford: Clarendon, 1994), p. 92.
147 Simon Werrett, *Fireworks: Pyrotechnic Arts and Sciences in European history* (Chicago, IL: University of Chicago Press, 2010), pp. 8–9, 57–9, 171–4.
148 *Ibid.*, p. 38.

149 Bradin Cormack and Carla Mazzio have suggested that a 'how-to' book 'was useful in two ways, instructing individual practitioners and consolidating the claims of the group as a whole to a field of knowledge or expertise'. See *Book Use, Book Theory: 1500–1700* (Chicago, IL: University of Chicago Library, 2005), p. 85. See also Natasha Glaisyer and Sara Pennell, *Didactic Literature in England 1500–1800: Expertise Constructed* (Aldershot: Ashgate, 2003), p. 9, 'A rhetoric of utility went hand in hand with a conception of the authors of these texts as equipped with the expertise to dispense appropriate knowledge.' Literature on modern craft theory suggests too that 'how-to' books have multiple purposes: educative, philosophic, and entertainment. See Glenn Adamson (ed.), *The Craft Reader* (Oxford: Berg, 2010), pp. 9–10.

3

The view from the building site

In one of the first substantial interpretations of architectural theory in English, entitled *The Elements of Architecture* (1624), Sir Henry Wotton made a firm distinction between the role, knowledge, and capabilities of the architect and common artisanal practices. Wotton claimed that whereas artisans – such as master masons and carpenters – busied themselves with material engagement, the architect was instead concerned with the intellectual process of design:

> I must heere remember that to choose and sort the *materials*, for every part of the *Fabrique*, is a Dutie more proper to a second *Superintendent*, over all the Under Artisans … and in that Place expressely distinguished, from the *Architect*, whose glory doth more consist, in the Designement and *Idea* of the whole *Worke*, and his truest ambition should be to make the *Forme*, which is the nobler Part (as it were) triumph over the *Matter*.[1]

Further, the architect's design practice was said to be rooted in mathematical understanding and activity.[2] The architect was said to possess 'a *Philosophical* Spirit; that is, he would have him (as I conceave it) to be no superficiall, and floating *Artificer*; but a *Diver* into *Causes*, and into the *Mysteries* of *Proportion*'.[3] Similarly, in his *Mathematical Preface*, authored over half a century earlier, mathematician and antiquary John Dee had firmly separated theoretical understanding (design) from mechanical practice (construction). In his defence of architecture as a mathematically grounded art, Dee repeatedly distinguished between the status, responsibilities, and intellectual aptitude of the 'architect', and the inferior position of the working artisan on the construction site: 'the Architect … he is neither Smith, not Builder: nor, separately, any Artificer: but the He[a]d, the Provost, the Director, and Judge of all Artificiall workes, and all Artificers … he, onely, searcheth out the causes and reasons of all Artificiall thynes.'[4] The social and intellectual elevation of the figure of the 'architect', said to be rooted in a thorough understanding of geometrical principle, effectively enacted a distancing from the commonplace labour of master mason and carpenter. In architectural treatises, artisans were presented as no more than the mindless hands or tools of the architect. The latter, the designer-in-chief, 'directeth, the *Mechanicien*, to handworke'.[5]

This distinction between embodied and theorised knowledge was a familiar trope of continental architectural treatises from the sixteenth century, in which architecture was presented as a liberal art. Many of these works were directly or indirectly modelled on Vitruvius's *De architectura*, which had emphasised the importance 'of both construction or practice (*fabrica*) and reasoning (*ratiocinatio*)'. According to Vitruvius, the ideal architect possessed both attributes.[6] And yet, with the objective to present 'architecture as a humanist discipline' to educated patrons and readers, early modern architectural theorists such as Leon Battista Alberti, and indeed Sir Henry Wotton, 'forever changed the understanding of architecture as divisible into two realms, one embodied and the other theorised'.[7]

Separation of the cerebral process of design and mechanical construction, promoted in contemporary architectural treatises, is, however, a grossly misleading representation of building practice in sixteenth- and seventeenth-century England. Late medieval and early modern master masons and carpenters often undertook both design and construction activities.[8] A disjuncture between mind and hand is largely a product of humanist texts, intent upon raising the intellectual and social status of architecture. And yet, that disingenuous representation has proved to be highly influential and long-lasting. It is an impression perpetuated by the use and privileging of treatises as the most significant form of evidence for architectural history.[9] It is a notion preserved also by the long-standing trend within English architectural history, particularly, to privilege any conceivable 'Palladian' influence above all other design and craft practices. In short, there has been a strong tendency 'to create a history that defines English architecture in terms of how closely it follows recognisable Italian or other European models and adopts identical designs'.[10] Native or 'vernacular' building styles or techniques have consistently been presented as aesthetically less accomplished, or meaningful, than those directly based upon the classical orders. Central to this perception is the figure of Inigo Jones, Surveyor of the King's Works from 1615 to 1643.[11] Jones very self-consciously constructed a persona at the Stuart Court as an 'architect-scholar'.[12] His practice as surveyor was deeply rooted in his reading and interpretation of continental architectural treatises and direct experience of ancient architecture. In England, no person before Jones had 'so closely linked their activities as designers with reading and the study of books', and Jones 'used every opportunity to contrast his education, training, and skill with other artists at court'.[13] Jones's self-presentation was highly successful, and from his own day to the present he has been much feted by architectural historians as 'the first educated artist, the first classicist, the first Renaissance architect in Britain, and the saviour of British building from the long winter of the Elizabethan style'.[14]

This chapter is not concerned with aesthetic evaluations of architectural style, but instead considers artisanal practices and interactions on the building site. If we broaden our focus from rarefied texts of architectural theory, authored and translated by gentlemen, to evidence of practice and engagement on work sites, then a very different picture of knowledge cultures emerges. Records of contemporary assessments of buildings and the process of work on construction projects shed light upon the range of skills, techniques, and languages employed by master craftsmen in the building trades, including masons, carpenters, joiners, and bricklayers. This discussion of the London building site as a space of *knowledge exchange* thus acts as an important corrective to the dominant theoretical narrative of an epistemological and social separation between 'mind' and 'hand'. This chapter shows that a firm division between propositional and tacit knowledges was not recognised by London's artisanal population.

From the perspective of the building site, we encounter the changing built environment of sixteenth- and early seventeenth-century London, the broad material hinterland against which livery hall rebuilding was taking place. Rare accounts of building works in the city also reveal the outlines of on-site artisanal knowledge cultures. Primarily, artisanal knowledge was communicated through a range of mediums, including the spoken word, written instructions, and visual sources. The legitimate authority of oral, textual, and visual representations varied according to context, including the particular craftsmen and institutions involved. Assessment of the built environment also required a range of expertise and the application of varied sensory perceptions. The four master craftsmen specifically employed by the City to adjudicate upon contentious building projects were said to have 'not only viewed, searched and seen [the built fabric] but also [to have] herd, examined and well considered the depositions, evidence and testymony'.[15] And thus, evaluation of building construction, sustainability, and design was demonstrably a job for (undifferentiated) mind, body, and hand. Similarly, the citizens who were engaged in the major project to rebuild Goldsmiths' Company Hall on Foster Lane from the mid-1630s individually and collectively looked at the site, physically examined the old structure and new building, and repeatedly consulted those with specific building expertise. A series of designs conceived and drawn up by master mason Nicholas Stone (with the advice of Inigo Jones) were essential in the rebuilding of Goldsmiths' Hall. Crucially, however, these drawings were not produced or interpreted in isolation from the material construction site; rather, the 'plots' were read in direct dialogue with the building site as well as the practitioners undertaking the construction work. Finally, accounts from construction sites record how closely craft labour and the assessment of expertise were understood to be collaborative endeavours. The notion of a detached genius designer is simply unsustainable.

In this account of the built fabric from the 'ground up', we first consider the broad range of expertise required for evaluating the urban environment through the records of the City Viewers. To deepen our focus upon the interrelationship between building design, construction, and artisanal status, we then turn to an exceptionally rich case-study: the early seventeenth-century rebuilding of Goldsmiths' Hall.

The London Viewers and artisanal knowledge cultures

The sights, sounds, and inconveniencies of building work were all too familiar to London's sixteenth- and early seventeenth-century inhabitants. From the mid-sixteenth century, London experienced spectacular demographic and physical growth. A fashionable West End area developed outside the walls, centred on the business and culture of the royal court, legal and financial services, and luxury consumption. As Linda Levy Peck writes, 'whether they built great places on the Strand, villas in the suburbs, rented new houses in Covent Garden, or took rooms with the tailor in Fleet Street, the nobility and gentry [of England] were increasingly urban and, in the early seventeenth century, intermingled with the London populace'.[16] To the east of the City walls a growing network of 'industrial activity, warehousing, and maritime activities' was emerging. The dissolution of the monasteries between 1536 and 1540, institutions which predominately lay near the wall (inside and outside), resulted in the substantial release of land and grand properties. John Schofield contends that this was a two-part process of urban re-appropriation. The period 1532 to 1570 was 'the era of the urban mansions and other prestigious uses of the precincts' such as at Charterhouse and Bermondsey Abbey, while from 1560 to 1600 Londoners witnessed 'the succeeding fragmentation of the precincts into many tenancies'.[17] Within the walls, rising population density resulted in the development of 'a bewildering maze of lanes, alleys, and courtyards' between grander streets.[18] These insalubrious lanes and alleys were populated with ramshackle plaster and timber structures. Meanwhile, as the value of ground rents grew on desirable streets such as Cheapside, property boundaries were re-drawn, and tenements were subdivided and extended upwards and outwards at an unparalleled pace. In the 1630s, houses fronting Cheapside were often four or even five storeys high, plus garrets.[19] Seeking to attract and retain desirable tenants 'at the upper end of the market', landlords undertook programmes of building repair and adaptation, with houses on grand streets glazed, wainscoted, and otherwise 'bettered'. The Drapers' and Mercers' Companies were two such institutional landlords who made improvements to their Cheapside property from the 1520s.[20]

Changes to the material fabric of the city were experienced by all social groups, whether as property-owners, tenants, neighbours, or bystanders. The Girdlers' Company reported that 'theare is in the [guild] Chest A deede that no man shall build agaynst our hall wyndowe in the Garden And that our raigne water shall fall of the kytchyn into the same Gardeyn without lett of any person'.[21] In 1630 one Edward Bridgman, citizen and grocer, lessee of a tenement 'adjoyninge to the southend of Clerks Hall', agreed, in return for 20s, that he would permit 'a small light lately stopped upp in the repaireing of the said hall'. Six years later, in return for 30s, Bridgman consented to 'peaceably permit and suffer a post or peice of timber to be sett up in my seller to support the foundacon of Clerks hall and the buildings thereunto belonging'.[22]

None directly witnessed or recorded these changes to the built environment more intimately than the City Viewers. The four London Viewers were among the most experienced and authoritative masons, carpenters, and tilers in the city, entrusted by the City's governors to make assessments of disputed and troubling building works. After all, the aldermen were typically inexpert in assessing the condition or proper direction of walls, or measuring the boundaries between properties.[23] The role of Viewer was a prestigious position and these skilful artisans also held office within craft guilds (as wardens and masters).[24] These men combined substantial institutional and civic authority with artisanal expertise. The Carpenters' Company and Masons' Company customarily presented candidates when a Viewer's post became available, and from 1607 the Carpenters' Company even formally gained the legal right to choose and elect 'such persons as shalbe hable aswell in cunnynge as otherwise' for the office of Viewer. The position of City Viewer was held for life, or until old age or infirmities made it impossible to adequately undertake the considerable responsibilities associated with the role.[25]

The Viewers examined both 'public' and 'private' cases and nuisances. That is to say, both cases initiated by the mayor and aldermen (concerning features of the built environment that encroached upon or endangered public spaces), and matters brought by private petitioners (including religious bodies, guilds, and individuals).[26] The Viewers were informed of alleged encroachments or inconveniences relating to a particular site; they would then visit the location – in their distinctive striped gowns, granted by the Chamber of London – undertake their examinations of the built fabric, and finally report their findings back to the mayor and aldermen.[27] Their assessments of the built environment of London have been preserved in the form of brief reports or certificates; these documents were likely composed by the First Clerk of the Mayor's Court.[28]

The certificates of the London Viewers can be productively mined by historians as evidence of intense urban expansion and the social and environmental nuisances resulting from crowded living conditions.

Complaints from private individuals and from institutions about overflowing gutters, contested party walls, restricted light, and divided tenements are testament to the rapid population expansion and physical growth of the city. These surveys 'register the stresses of life in London as it urbanized'.[29] Guilds feature as both plaintiffs and defendants in these documents. We see glimpses in these records of adaptations and modifications made to company halls, and the wider stock of urban property owned and managed by London's companies. In 1536, for example, a view was taken of 'ground and buildings' belonging to the Mercers' Company, specifically 'the chapel and new building of the Mercers in Westcheap'.[30] The building of a kitchen at Wax Chandlers' Hall in the parish of St. John Zachary in 1544 was alleged to be a 'nuisance' by the parson and churchwardens since it blocked the light of the church.[31] The City Viewers also adjudicated on a case in the same parish involving 'the NE corner principal post' of Goldsmiths' Hall which 'overhangs 4 ½ in. eastward against a new counting house lately set up by the tenant of the Haberdashers'.[32] In the early 1540s, the Viewers investigated a 'variance' between the Fishmongers' Company (the plaintiffs) and the Carpenters' Company (the defendants) concerning ownership of 'a certain piece of garden ground with a pale [a stake, stake fence] thereon'.[33] In 1631 they undertook a view of 'a house of office and a wall lately new erected neare vnto Curriers' Hall' (the Viewers found that there was no offensive 'vent towards the hall' from the privy).[34]

There is, of course, another perspective to be gleaned from the certificates: that of their chief protagonists, the artisanal Viewers. If we adjust our focus from the petitioners and defendants, to the expert practitioners undertaking the viewings, these sources also reveal aspects of the working processes and knowledge cultures of skilled craftsmen. Descriptions of the Viewers' assessments of buildings make frequent reference to a range of evidence, expertise, and sensory knowledge. In the formulation of their judgements, the artisanal Viewers typically inspected the site of contention, undertook measurements, consulted any available written or visual evidence, and heard oral testimonies and histories from local inhabitants. Experiential, technical, and perceptual knowledge were all part of their evaluations of the built environment.

The language of these reports speaks of the application of varied sensory knowledge. A verdict concerning the aforementioned garden contested by the Fishmongers' and Carpenters' Companies, was based 'in the judgement and sight of a man's ie [eye]'.[35] Adjudicating a dispute between a gentleman and the dean and chapter of St. Pauls concerning 'a certain old house end', the Viewers were said 'by all their discretions [to] have viewed, seen and searched by good advisement and ripe deliberation'.[36] This was a common summary of their active process of assessment. On another occasion, 'by all their discretions [they] have serched seen and ripely understond'.[37] A method which involved sight and the more ambiguous verb 'search' was characteristic of these sixteenth-century reports. In contemporary parlance, 'searched' meant to examine thoroughly, including haptic knowledge.[38] Physically examining a stone wall in the parish of St. Benet Fink, the Viewers found 'a truss of stone 10 ft. in length, set to bear a chimney'.[39] The regulatory searches of artisanal shops and workshops undertaken by guild authorities typically involved a full application of sensory perceptions: 'learning about most kinds of commodities meant having a fundamentally physical encounter with the substance. It involved tasting, smelling, and touching as often as looking.'[40]

Experience was also crucial in carrying out views and searches. In the parish of St. Lawrence Jewry the Viewers provided a judgement that seemingly acknowledged a form of ineffable, tacit knowledge, as well as demonstrable written evidence: that they 'can perceyve and knowe aswell by their owne reasons and discrecions as also by good and substanciall evidence in writyng to them shewed and redde'.[41] Asked to comment upon the building of a church in the parish of St. Vedast – specifically on whether the structure had been adapted and extended over time – the Viewers simply responded, in a judgement ostensibly based on experiential understanding of construction, that it was all one building, built in one season.[42] Similarly, considering a variance between two merchant tailors over the location of a warehouse in the ward of Cornhill, the Viewers just asserted that two tenements and the contentious warehouse 'at their first building were framed and built all jointly together'.[43] In a case from the parish of St. John Evangelist concerning access rights on a site where old houses had been taken down the Viewers determined from the evidence of particular doors on the east side of the petitioner's house that 'there hath ben goyng furth that wey in ii places'. Unfortunately, the Viewers could not ascertain precise dimensions because 'every thing is taken downe there that myght lede them to any further knowledge in that behalf'.[44] Occasionally the Viewers articulated the evidential basis on which an expert decision was made, as in July 1631 following the viewing of brew house and stable belonging to St. Bartholomew's Hospital when they found 'two principall posts and a binding joyst' and took this as evidence of a former partition.[45] The assessments of the Viewers were rooted in long-standing experience of construction.

In many cases for which their specialist judgement was sought, the Viewers also undertook careful measurements of the property or its boundaries. They thus applied technical knowledge to the assessment process. Over the course of the sixteenth century, measurement is specifically mentioned more frequently in their reports. The standard description of their activities becomes: 'we the said foure sworne viewers have viewed, serched, sene, and measured'.[46] The reports emphasise the allegedly objective nature of this process: it was said that 'the viewers have indifferently measured'.[47] Particular tools are not mentioned in their statements, though they likely used poles, knotted ropes, and perhaps carpenter's rules to undertake the measurement of property boundaries.[48] On some occasions, having made their measurements, the artisan Viewers set out the correct dimensions of property boundaries precisely, using stakes. Medieval master masons used the same technique for outlining the plan of the structure on the building site.[49] In early modern London, plaintiff and defendant were expected to follow these marked boundaries exactly: 'The stake and three other stakes there likewise driven into the ground by the Viewers stand upon the ground of Duffe, on which ground he may and ought to set and make his defence line right and plumb from stake to stake all length'.[50]

The Viewers additionally made use of visual evidence in the form of plans, or 'plots'. Drawn surveys were very occasionally 'attached to a deed or lease to show what was being transferred'.[51] In January 1553/54 the Viewers visited a contested wall in the parish of St. Sepulchre without Newgate and 'William Collins, carpenter, hath now shewed forth unto us, the said Viewers, a leese made unto hym by the said Maister and Chaplayns of the Savoye dated the xxviith yere of Kinge Henrie Theight with certen platt [a map, design, or plan] indented and annexed unto the same lease'.[52] A carpenter plaintiff was a likely candidate for presenting a plat as a form of evidence (since plans were part of their working practice). In a case from 1631 concerning land use in the parish of St. Botolph Billingsgate, the resident parson desired that 'the forsaid viewers should ... take a plot [a ground plan or map] of the whole ground ... and examine whether the house in question be within the bounds of that ground used for a burial place within the said parishe'. A year later a plaintiff presented the Viewers with 'a plot of all which said sevall buildings have drawen and made'.[53] Unfortunately, no more detail is provided in the reports concerning the nature of the drawings, and the plans do not survive in the archive as separate forms of evidence. Considering the legalistic context in which the drawings were produced – particularly relating to contested boundaries – it is highly likely that the 'plats 'or 'plots' were measured surveys.

Aside from drawn evidence, and their own assessments of the built environment – based upon their 'discretions' and 'ripe examinations' – the Viewers also heard oral testimonies and histories of local inhabitants concerning customary land uses and boundaries. There were said to be many 'liberties, priviledges, and customes' which 'are pertaining to the city of London; whereof no man can remember them all to set them downe in writing being only recorded by mouth'.[54] Custom could be a very powerful resource for lower and middling types of people in early modern society, typically based upon a highly particularised sense of local rights and landscapes. The articulation of popular memory was also crucial to the assertion of custom, and in urban settings customary memory was often rooted in the social organisation of space.[55] And thus the Viewers heard of and inspected a 'certain lane ... whiche lane hath ben used & accustomed over tyme oute of mynde to be a comen wey from the Vyntry down to the waterside of Thamyse' (but which had lately been 'stopped & closed up by Edward Burlace').[56] Settling a variance in the mid-1530s between neighbours in the ward of Cordwainer Street and the ward of the Vintry over 'a certain house and garden set in Turnbaston Lane', the Viewers formed their opinion on the basis of having 'viewed and seen and upon their diligent search, inquisition, and deliberate examination of the oldest men and longest dwellers within the said wards now living'.[57] Likewise, in April 1543, in a case concerning the appropriate course of a brick wall set alongside the east side of St. Paul's Wharf, the expert artisans were reported to have 'not only viewed, serched and seen [the wall] but also have herd, examined and well considered the depositions, evidence and testymony of iiii old inhabitantes and dwellers thereby'. In this instance, the four men giving customary evidence were specifically named as: 'Robert Kytchyn, dyer; John Edsall, Richard Fetford, and Arthure Purseys, watermen, being sworne as afore a judge to give true evidence unto the said viewers in that behalf.'[58] Almost a century later, the Viewers were still hearing from 'anntient neighbours'.[59] Indeed, in an extraordinary case from April 1631, one of the two parties in a dispute, a merchant named Mr Gee, called upon Inigo Jones, the king's surveyor, as a witness to the historic built environment of a house 'neare Pauls wharfe':

> The said Gee did likewise p[ro]duce vnto us a certificate vnder the hand of Mr Inigo Jones his Maj[esties] Surveyor who as wee are informed was borne and lived in the same house w[hi]ch the said Gee now possesseth that hee remembereth ... there were noe shedds built vpon the said wall, and that there was onely a dyhouse in the yard of the said Trice on thother side opposite against the said wall and that the rest of the said Trice's yard was free and open w[i]thout building except one little roome or banquetting house neere to the waters side and a little stable and hay loft on it, And wee are of opinion that the said shedds are an inchroachm[en]t vpon the said Gees wall and ought not to bee suffered.[60]

One could not hope for a more qualified or authoritative expert witness, but as a former inhabitant of the building, Jones's statement and remembrances of the immediate built environment of his childhood home were also deeply personal. Incidentally, this detail provides more context to the architect's early life than has ever previously been known.[61]

Written evidence could also play a significant role in the viewing process, specifically in the form of historic leases and deeds.[62] Examining a variance between the master and wardens of the Goldsmiths' Company and John Olyff, barbersurgeon and tenant on Friday Street in the parish of St. Matthew, the Viewers consulted an old deed 'containing the measure of the tenement that in old time the tenement was divided by its owner'.[63] Many such writings were dated from the late fifteenth and early sixteenth centuries.

Taking the Viewers' reports as a collective body of evidence, it is noticeable that consultations of leases and deeds are mentioned more frequently across the sixteenth and early seventeenth centuries – 'and at the makinge of the said view there was shewed forth unto us a certen lease'.[64] This is undoubtably a reflection of the growth of written legal culture, part of a much broader late medieval and early modern process through which 'the written word extended further into almost every aspect of economic, social, and cultural life'.[65] Manuscripts, though, were but part of the evidence base for the London Viewers; written words were considered alongside experiential encounters. Concerning a variance between a skinner and gentlemen over a brick wall on Fleet Street in the 1550s, a judgement was made 'as farre as we see by experyence and have lerned by profe of certen wrtyngs'.[66]

The City Viewers considered all forms of available evidence and employed a range of expertise and literacies in making their assessments about London's built environment. These respected artisans looked, touched, measured, and interpreted written, material, visual, and oral evidence. Judgements based on their 'discretions' – inexpressible experiential knowledge – sat alongside decisions founded upon precise measurements. Oral testimony was considered to be as significant a form of evidence as plans of buildings and neighbouring lands. The artisan Viewers, and the civic authorities who acted upon their reports, simply did not recognise distinctions between their wide ranging intellectual and manual labours. Having taken a broad survey of London's changing built fabric and artisanal knowledge cultures with the City Viewers, we turn now to one very significant and richly recorded building site: Goldsmiths' Company Hall in the 1630s.

The rebuilding of Goldsmiths' Hall

In 1634 the Goldsmiths' Company demolished their medieval company hall and replaced it, over the next three years, with an enlarged, much more visually striking and materially splendid building. A red brick and stone-clad 'Palladian'-style building was substituted for the original wooden structure, whose chambers and outward boundaries had been adapted piecemeal over centuries (see Plate 1). Goldsmiths' Hall had been located on the same site – on the corner of Foster Lane and Maiden Lane in the parish of St. John Zachary – since the 1330s (see figure 3.1).[67] Company governance, administration, and sociability were all concentrated within this building. As we saw previously, Goldsmiths' Hall also contained the assay office, within which precious metals were tested, and hallmarked. Described by John Stow at the turn of the seventeenth century as 'a proper house, but not large', by the early 1630s, company members were expressing deep concern about 'the great decayes and wante of repayringe this [Goldsmiths'] hall'.[68]

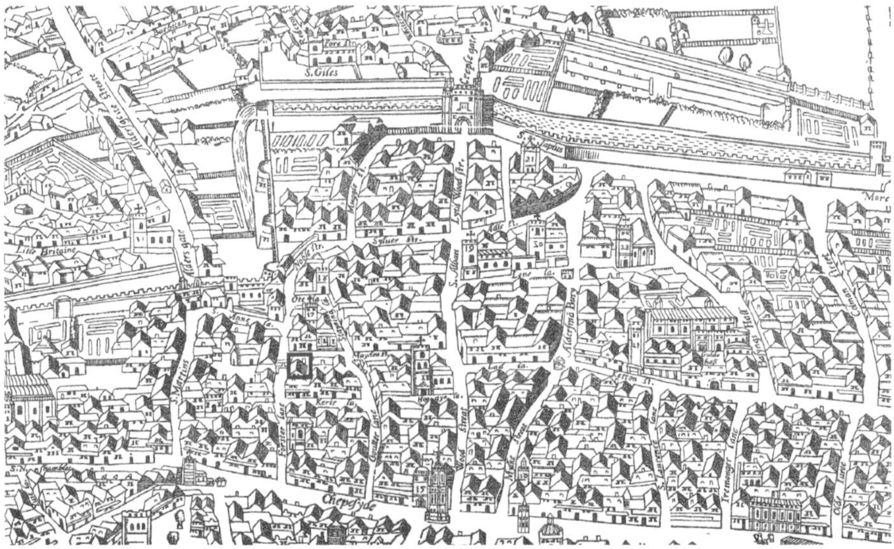

Figure 3.1 *'Agas' Map of London*, c. 1561, this edition published c. 1633, sheet 7. The bold rectangle indicates the original site of Goldsmiths' Hall.

A close reading of company court minutes and accounts suggests that in early discussions, prominent goldsmiths envisioned major repairs (but not a total rebuild): the great kitchen, clerk's house, and part of the assayer's house were to be pulled down and rebuilt, and the interior hall was to be enlarged.[69] The nature and extent of the building project was to change rapidly ('in regard it is all soe much decayed that vpon necessitye all must bee taken downe'). The Goldsmiths reported in July 1634 that Inigo Jones, Surveyor of the King's Works, 'upon some occasion of passing by [Goldsmiths' Hall], did view the same'.[70] Jones was that very month engaged in remodelling the west end of St. Paul's Cathedral, including a vast Corinthian portico, two hundred yards from the Goldsmiths' site. It is thus not inconceivable that, by chance, he passed by. More probably, Jones's viewing of the Goldsmiths' property was highly deliberate; as Surveyor of the King's Works, Jones did not simply concern himself with buildings explicitly associated with the court, 'but also intervened in any building matters that closely concerned royal interests'.[71] It is likely profitable to frame Jones's engagement with Goldsmiths' Hall alongside his involvement with the royal cathedral works, and the Crown's determined plan of action to improve the material fabric, uniformity, and splendour of Cheapside's west end. Coincidental viewing or not, Inigo Jones made direct recommendations to the company wardens as to a competitive process of design for an entirely new, and considerably expanded, Goldsmiths' Hall.[72]

The rebuilding of Goldsmiths' Hall is a highly revealing and unusual case-study of artisanal labour on the building site, the significance of which stems from several different features of the project. Fundamentally, the archival record detailing craft organisation and the progress of the rebuilding is exceptionally rich. The entire site operation was documented in great detail, in an unbroken series of records in the Goldsmiths' Company's wardens' accounts and court minutes. Such meticulous site records very rarely survive for civic building projects in London in this period (certainly pre-1666).[73] The rebuilding of Goldsmiths' Hall is especially intriguing because of the dynamic cast of characters engaged in the project. Goldsmiths were in the role of architectural patrons, many of whom were practising artisans or merchants as well as guild officer-holders. Moreover, the expansion and redesign of Goldsmiths' Hall involved the most eminent building practitioners of the day in the role of designers and construction specialists. This included mason Nicholas Stone, whose life-writings we have previously encountered, and master carpenter Anthony Jerman. The construction site on Foster Lane thus involved interactions and complex negotiations between leading artisans of varied specialisms. Finally, the prestige of the Goldsmiths' Company and the prominent location of its institutional headquarters – in very close proximity to Cheapside and St. Pauls – elicited significant contemporary notice. More particularly, the Goldsmiths' project captured the attention of the royal court, resulting in intricate and lengthy negotiations over the architectural design and materiality of the new building, and ultimately the authority of London's leading artisans. Our focus here is the use, communication, and interpretation of building designs as part of the site operation. A deeper examination of the symbolic meanings of Stone's designs for the new Goldsmiths' Hall is reserved for Chapter 7.

Two central themes emerge from the Goldsmiths' meticulous records of their building site. First, the thorny question of how to communicate artisanal knowledge. We find there was no consensus on this matter. Verbal instructions, on-site demonstrations, written words, and visual aids were all employed to communicate ideas relating to the scale, materiality, and design of the building. The authority of these different mediums of communication fluctuated across the duration of the project. Second, the issue of how to assess artisanal labour. Once construction was underway, appraisals of the value and quality of craft labour were a source of tension and heated debate among the master craftsmen engaged in the rebuilding scheme. Ascertaining the value of workmanship was not presented here as a precise art, but rather as a subjective, social process of arbitration and compromise, which ideally took place within assemblies of similarly skilled and established guildsmen.

'Plots', site operations, and status disputes

The rebuilding of Goldsmiths' Hall in the second half of the 1630s has been narrated as a triumphal story of the 'modern' architect. Writing in

Architectural History in the early 1970s, John Newman hailed the project as 'the first documented example outside the Royal Works of an architect practising in the modern sense of the word'.[74] This argument stemmed from Nicholas Stone's employment as the Goldsmiths' Company surveyor from December 1634. Stone's responsibilities included the provision of building designs, the recommendation of artisans for the project, the overall supervision and assessment of craft labour, and the procurement of building materials. Newman perceived this comprehensive role as a new development; in his words, here we have 'an intermediary between the Company and the workmen, an intermediary who would provide a design for the new building'. The stated desire of this master mason that 'for the directions of the workemen in their proceedings noe perticuler man may intermeddle but himselfe', was taken by Newman to imply 'complete control' over the design and building process.[75] Close reading of the accounts from the building site reveal this to be a problematic assumption.

Contrary to Newman's confident assertions, we should be wary of narrowly framing Nicholas Stone in the mode of a detached and controlling 'architect'. In his search for 'the manner in which Inigo Jones's ideas were disseminated in England', Newman overlooked the nuances within the archive which suggest a complex negotiation between theoretical knowledge and material expertise on the work site.[76] The evidence from the construction site suggests that Stone's 'plots' for Goldsmiths' Hall were not finished blueprints, but rather works in progress, viewed and interpreted in dialogue with the built environment. Furthermore, Stone's designing activities were not his endeavour alone; the plots were repeatedly consulted and commented upon by other building practitioners, and goldsmith patrons, and thus the plans were collaboratively adapted over the life of the project.[77]

In order to fully appreciate the critical role of building plans in the Goldsmiths' project, both as a design tool and as a means of negotiating authority on the work site, it is necessary to take up the story of the rebuilding in June 1634, shortly before Jones and Stone became involved in the scheme. Early in June a 'plott' for the new building, drawn up by John Hawes, a goldsmith, was considered by the four wardens and a newly formed committee for building (consisting of ten goldsmith assistants). In a move which highlights the collaborative way in which designs were critiqued and negotiated, the 'grownde being digged and opened ready for a foundac[i]on', the wardens had direct on-site 'consultac[i]on w[i]th the workemen', and then 'deliv[er]ed [the plott] to the workemen aparte to consider of it by themselves'.[78] The whole scheme proposed by goldsmith Hawes was 'altogether frustrated' though, upon Inigo Jones 'passing by' Goldsmiths' Hall. Having viewed the site and consulted with the workmen, Jones initially encouraged the Goldsmiths to undertake a competitive process of design for the new building. The company court minutes reveal that 'accordinge to the advice of Mr Survayer It is now agreed ... that Mr Wardeins give order for the drawing of 2 or 3 seuerall plotts'.[79] The designs included a new attempt by John Hawes, two plans by 'Mr Burrage and Osbourne the Bricklayers', and another by 'Mr Jerman the carpenter'. We are left ignorant as to the nature of these design drawings. Perhaps they consisted of measured plans and/or summary sketches. The wardens also desired that Jones might 'come hither and to view the grounde and plotts together'.[80] Once it had been 'agreed by most voyces', in October 1634, which of the entries would be considered at the next court of assistants – one of the designs executed by the bricklayers and the 'plott' submitted by Hawes – it was also 'ordered that these two plotts remayne with the Clerke for any of the Assistants to have recourse vnto in the meane time to view them and the ground together the better to informe themselues to deliver their opynion at theire next meetinge'.[81] The design process was evidently understood to be a dynamic dialogue between drawn proposal, practitioners, patrons, and the built fabric of the building site.[82]

In the event, the deliberations of senior goldsmiths over the relative merits of the various designs for their new institutional home proved to be largely inconclusive: 'divers plotts for new building the hall were now viewed and Mr Stone the Kings Mason (beeinge thereto requested) was now present And after much debateinge thereof noethinge was now resolued on'. The impasse was apparently broken by Nicholas Stone. He was invited to a court meeting to judge the entries – most likely on the recommendation of Inigo Jones – and 'was intreated to take some paynes once more to draw an other plot w[i]th what speed hee could'.[83] At the same meeting, it was 'ordered that for the Companyes building they may entertayne an understandinge and skillfull man well experienced in building to bee a surveyor for the worke ... It is generally thought fitt that Mr Stone the King's Mason shall bee the Surveyor in all the building.'[84] Nicholas Stone was to be paid £10 quarterly.[85]

On 8 December 1634, Nicholas Stone was again present at the company court, together with his 'plott for the new buildinge'. It was decided by a close vote at the ballot that his plan rather than a design by Hawes was preferred, and according to which the company would proceed. Despite his status and established expertise, Stone's ideas were still subject to close scrutiny. We can imagine that as England's foremost mason and sculptor, Nicholas Stone's designs were more sophisticated and impressive than those of goldsmith Hawes. Moreover, it is of significance that whereas Hawes's plan 'had the hall gate leading out Mayden Lane', a relatively minor thoroughfare and a positioning that would have resulted in the building facing towards the walls, Stone's design positioned Foster Lane 'for the settinge out of the outward walls'.[86] A main entrance on Foster Lane connected Goldsmiths' Hall directly to Cheapside, the customary location for goldsmiths' shops and retail sites, and the principal ceremonial route through the City. In February 1634/5 Stone was again present at the

Goldsmiths' court, and he 'brought w[i]th him the plotts for the new building w[i]th the severall draughts of the ffronte and sides to the streetside and the patterne of the greate gate to ffoster lane ward as alsoe the ffronte of the hall parlor and dyneinge chamber towards the greate courte All w[hi] ch were well approued of and his care com[m]ended'. Stone also made clear that his drawings had been subject to the personal oversight of Inigo Jones.[87] Stone's original designs for Goldsmiths' Hall do not survive. However, survey drawings of the building executed in 1691–93 suggest that in the preparation of his designs for the façade of Goldsmiths' Hall, Stone was strongly influenced by the works of Italian architect Sebastiano Serlio.[88] Stone's plans for the façade of Goldsmiths' Hall articulated a clear design aesthetic of civic magnificence and order.

Stone's drawings were a means of communicating design ideas to the goldsmith patrons and the artisans directly involved in construction. Stone's 'severall draughts' included façade and side elevations for the new Goldsmiths' Hall (and maybe measured plans too).[89] As the project progressed Stone also supplied sketches of particular building features, such as staircases. Drawings could act as invaluable collaborative tools for dialogue in construction projects. Expertise in design and construction included an ability to adjust proposals flexibly as building proceeded.[90] For the rebuilding of Ironmongers' Hall on Fenchurch Street in the mid-to-late 1580s, specifically the new building of 'the ten[emen]te adioyninge to the hawle', carpenters Edward and Elias Jerman 'were appoynted to drawe a platforme [a design, a pattern] in what sorte it should be made and the same plot to bring to mr wardens. And that therevppon the comp[a]nie wold have further conference w[i]th them'.[91] Evidently the plot was used here to communicate a building design to merchant patrons (a design which was subsequently subject to discussion and amendments). Accordingly in May 1588, following their 'further conference', 'Elias Jerman carpenter brought a draughte in a pap[er] booke' to the assistants of the Ironmongers' Company, 'conteyninge a forme and propor[c]ion of a new frame for the two ten[emen]ts adioyninge to the west ende of the newe hall and made promise to the comp[a]nie to erecte builde and sett vpp the same newe frame … according to the same pap[er] booke'.[92] We see here the gradual process of design dialogue and revision over the course of a corporate rebuilding project.

The 'plotts' presented by Nicholas Stone for the 'ffronte and sides to the streetside' and 'the ffronte of the hall Parlor and dyneinge Chamber towards the greate Courte' were examined by 'workemen and such of the Assistants as wilbee present with them'.[93] Specifically, the artisans Jerman, Burrage, and Osborne, were instructed to 'set downe in writinge' any 'excepc[i]ons [that] shalbee taken to the plot or any parte thereof'.[94] Suggestively, the carpenter and bricklayers insisted that their 'excepc[i] ons' 'cannot bee soe well set downe in writinge as by conferring w[i]th

Mr Stone'.[95] Such an explicit affirmation of their preference for verbal exchange is revealing. Though these authoritative and experienced artisans were fully literate, craft processes were best communicated orally. Textual alterations to the plan of the new building were simply inadequate; not 'soe well' suited as verbal interaction in person and on location. This suggests that there was no fixed hierarchy of communicative methods on this building site.[96]

Even with Nicholas Stone as 'surveyor' for the Goldsmiths' building project, the design process was collaborative and involved the expertise of a range of construction practitioners. As building advanced, the experiential knowledge of artisans engaged on the project was taken fully into account. And thus, deciding upon structural features of the Hall behind the clerk's and assayer's houses, the Goldsmiths' committee for rebuilding was only convinced of Stone's suggestions 'after some conferrence had w[i]th the carpenter mason and bricklayers then and there present and beeing sattisfied by them that it was the best way to bee soe donne'.[97] Likewise, 'concerning the makeinge of the great pairre of staires leading vp into the great chamber', Nicholas Stone's designs were only agreed upon by the Goldsmiths' Company following an inspection of the site and 'some conference had w[i]th very able artists in the like affaires (haveinge noe relac[i]on or dependance vpon the worke or any directinge the same)'.[98] Hence, we cannot view this building project in the mode of a detached theoretical architect figure unilaterally handing down designs to the lowly '*Mechanicien*'.[99]

In the rebuilding of Goldsmiths' Hall, drawn plans were not just a means of communicating design ideas to patrons and construction practitioners. An incident on the worksite in January 1636/7 is highly revealing of how authorship, ownership, and interpretation of designs also intersected with notions of artisanal authority.[100] The dispute was between mason Nicholas Stone and goldsmith Robert Hooke; the latter had been appointed in the early stages of the rebuilding project for 'aydinge and assistinge' the surveyor in his work.[101] Hooke was an assistant of the Goldsmiths' Company and a former prime warden; he thus had considerable status within his guild. Stone and Hooke's disagreement centred upon the visibility of Stone's plans for the new Goldsmiths' Hall, specifically how readily accessible the building designs might be to other artisans working on the project. Whereas Hooke desired to show the drawn plans to craftsmen 'in private', Stone preferred for them to remain with the company clerk. The court minutes relate how:

> Mr Hooke did affirme that a composic[i]on with any workeman might be made better in private then w[i]th soe many and therefore desired that hee might haue the draughts of the plotts to shew vnto other workemen but Mr Stone desired that they might not bee shewed whereby to bee co[m]mon but that

> they might remayne w[i]th John Parker [company clerk] to bee viewed at any time, w[hi]ch the co[m]mittee for the most parte agreed vnto And Mr Hooke was desired to confer w[i]th some workemen against the next Courte of Assistants at w[hi]ch time the co[m]mittee desire It may bee then debated.[102]

The reporting of this episode suggests that Stone would not easily relinquish control over 'the draught of the Plotts' to Hooke. These designs were perhaps too integral to his identity or status as master mason, and role as surveyor. Moreover, Hooke and Stone had conflicting notions of what constituted discretion in relation to the plans. Whereas Stone was content that the designs might reside with the clerk, and thus be 'viewed at any time' by the Goldsmiths' Company's committee for rebuilding, Hooke's suggestion that he personally take custody of the plans and show them to other artisans was simply unacceptable to the master mason.[103] Hooke suggested that this scheme was essentially a move towards privacy, whereas Stone interpreted this plan in quite the opposite manner; there was a risk that his designs would be 'shewed whereby to bee co[m]mon'.[104] At the root of this tense encounter over possession and visibility of building designs was the issue of authority. We can detect here different shades of influence. Whereas Robert Hooke was flexing his political authority as a high-ranking goldsmith supervising the project, Nicholas Stone was asserting his epistemic authority as chief designer for the new Goldsmiths' Hall.[105]

Measurement and expertise

As surveyor for the rebuilding of Goldsmiths' Hall, another key responsibility of Nicholas Stone was the identification and employment of suitably skilled craftsmen for the realisation of his designs, and subsequently the measurement and evaluation of artisanal labour on the building site. Varied contractual agreements with different crafts were required for this complex building project. And thus, while general labourers were employed 'by the day' for the task of demolishing the old Goldsmiths' Hall – 'the foundac[i]on worke shalbe done by day worke and not by greate' – tasks requiring more specialised skills were contracted 'by measure' and 'by the great'.[106] Master plasterer Mr Knifman, and joiner, Mr Kellett, were recruited in January 1636/7 on the basis of payment by the measure, though their perceived skill differential was taken into account and valued separately. The Goldsmiths' court minutes record that 'the plaisterer hee offred to doe the worke for 3£ a yard the company findeinge all materialls the joyner demaunded xv [shillings] the yard and to ffinde nothinge but glue and nayles'.[107]

As the project progressed, certain accomplished artisans were contracted 'by the great'. This was an agreement by which a particular master craftsman was given responsibility to complete a scheme of work, and if necessary, sub-contract elements of the project to other artisans.[108] In October 1638, for example: 'Mr Wardens agreed with Mr Knifman the plaisterer for the plaisteringe and whiteinge the ceeling in the Gallerye and the roome at the staire head goeinge into the great chamber and the ceeling ouer the gate comeinge into the yard all which hee is to doe very well and workeman like and to finde all materialls and to paye all workemens wages and hee to have for the doeing thereof £4'.[109] Likewise, in November 1639, an agreement was made with the joiners John Lane and Edmund Ward for 'wainscotting the greate Chamber and the parlor ... Accordinge to the designes prepared by Mr Nicholas Stone and now shewed unto them consistinge of 9 papers for the doeinge whereof the Companye is to paye £140 in money and finde all the stuffe.'[110]

As isolated pieces of evidence, these contracts give the impression that the assessment of artisanal labour on the building site was a straightforward business, and thus a certain monetary value could be assigned to a set measure or scheme of work. However, the detailed negotiations recorded in the Goldsmiths' Company archive between Nicholas Stone and the artisans employed for the rebuilding project reveal how measuring and evaluating craftsmanship could be a complex process of arbitration. These deliberations show how project manager Nicholas Stone oversaw the process of assessment on behalf of the Goldsmiths, but his personal evaluations were heavily scrutinised and frequently rejected. These accounts ultimately present the measurement of craft work as a heavily subjective process. Assessment was ideally undertaken by a group of specialised craft experts. The artisans contracted for the rebuilding of Goldsmiths' Hall took exception to the evaluation of their work by men who were acknowledged master craftsmen but not experts in their particular trade.

Among the most contentious and extended negotiations were those undertaken with master carpenter Anthony Jerman, and his son, Hugh Jerman. Employed by Nicholas Stone to carry out the major construction work for the new Goldsmiths' Hall, the Jermans were among the most successful and sought-after carpenters in London. Anthony and Hugh Jerman were the third and fourth generations respectively of an eminent family of London carpenters, with a name (variously spelt Germain, Jarman, or Jerman) that is suggestive of Protestant ancestors from the Low Countries. The Jermans held prominent positions within the Carpenters' Company. Anthony Jerman (d. 1650) was elected master of the Carpenters Company for 1633–34, and also held the positions of City Carpenter and Viewer. He took on twelve apprentices across his working life, including his middle son Hugh.[111] Notably, Anthony donated a silver-gilt election cup and cover (the fourth such cup in the collection) to the Carpenters' Company in 1628, a gift which is still within the guild's plate collection. The cup is decorated with engravings of the arms of the company and Jerman's 'mark flanked by his initials and with three compasses below'. And the lip of the cup is pounced with the following inscription, which emphasises his various guild and City roles: 'The guift of Anthony Jarman Yonger Warden of the Carpenters and M^{r} to the Chamber of London and one of the foure vewers of the same Cyttye Aug 12 1628.' In the year following his mastership Jerman also donated a stained glass panel to Carpenters' Hall, dated 1634, and featuring his carpenter's mark.[112] Anthony's eldest son, Edward Jerman (*c.* 1605–88), was a post-Fire City carpenter of considerable significance (he designed the Royal Exchange (1667–71) and eight livery halls), and he acted as one of the three surveyors for the rebuilding of the City.[113] As might be anticipated from such experienced and authoritative artisans, the Jermans were highly assertive about the value of their expert labour. For several years, from the spring of 1635/6 to the late summer of 1639, a dispute ran between these carpenters and master mason Nicholas Stone, which focused precisely on the appropriate method and personnel through which their craftsmanship might be adequately assessed.

The indented articles of agreement, dated 18 July 1635, between Robert Hooke and the Jermans state that the carpenters are responsible for the supply of 'timber, boards, nails, carving, workmanship and materials whatsoever belonging to carpenters work for the erecting, building or fitting up of a Hall … for the said Company of Goldsmiths, London, bounding upon Foster Lane, Gutter Lane and Maiden Lane'. The articles note that 'all and every timber to be of good sound oak, and all the boards of the floors to be of good and well seasoned deal'. Overall it is stressed that the carpenters work 'shall substantially, neatly, artificially well and workmanly be performed', and undertaken 'according to the draft or design thereof drawn'. The Jermans were paid £150 at the sealing of the contract, and the remainder of their payment would be forthcoming 'when the said carpenters' work is set up and fully finished according to the true meaning of the said plott or design drawn … and true admeasurement thereof made'.[114]

The question of measurement first came to the attention of the Goldsmiths' Company court on 5 April 1636, when Anthony Jerman 'desired the company to appoynte one to measure his worke because hee alleageth that hee is a greater some of money out of purse for the companyes building then hee hath receaued'.[115] A year later, in April 1637, Jerman once again 'desired that his worke might bee viewed and measured', on this occasion 'before any more thereof bee hidden by the plaisterer or otherwise hee shalbee a loser by itt'.[116] The Goldsmiths proposed 'Thursdaye Ffrydaye and Satterday in Whitson weeke for measureinge and estimateinge of the carpenters worke', as these were the first days when Nicholas Stone was available 'to bee present at the doeinge therof'.[117] In the event, master carpenter Anthony Jerman was not satisfied with 'the reporte of the view and measuring of his worke', and Stone's evaluating abilities were brought into question.[118] Suggestively, those who had been appointed to carry out the appraisal of the Jermans' workmanship were not trained carpenters:

a goldsmith and a plasterer were assigned to the task.[119] Thus, in January 1637/8, Anthony Jerman once again complained to the Goldsmiths' court of assistants, who granted his request:

> that all his worke about the hall shalbee measured againe by two carpenters to bee brought by himselfe and two other carpenters to bee brought by the companye, to w[hi]ch purpose Mr Stone beeinge now present was requested to bringe two carpenters to joyne w[i]th Mr Jarmans carpenters in the measuringe of his worke … and Mr Marr and Mr Bowen [goldsmiths] or one of them to bee p[re]sent at the said measuring.[120]

Evidently, from the perspective of this master carpenter, the only appropriate context in which his artisanal skills might be adequately evaluated was within an assembly of artisans specifically in possession of carpentry expertise. The presence of goldsmiths Marr and Bowen was clearly to ensure, from the viewpoint of the Goldsmiths, that their corporate interests were also being upheld. This collective dimension to craft assessment was customary. When master carpenters Edward and Elias Jerman were contracted for the rebuilding of Ironmongers' Hall from June 1586, the craftsmen were to be paid 'more money [than had hitherto been agreed] if by the discretion of two indifferent p[er]sons whereof the one to be elected by the comp[a]nie yt shalbe thought meete in equitie'.[121] Elias Jerman was the father of the aforementioned Anthony Jerman, Edward Jerman was Anthony's uncle.[122] Likewise, when the parlour was extensively repanelled at Drapers' Hall in the mid-1570s and there was a disagreement over the charges, four men were responsible for measuring, 'two on behalf of the Drapers and two for the joiners'.[123]

But even once this process of evaluation had been carried out at the site of Goldsmiths' Hall, ascertaining the worth of the Jermans' labour continued to be a controversial issue. In April 1638, three months after the agreement that each party might bring their own experts to the site had been brokered, a petition composed by master carpenter Jerman was read to the Goldsmiths' court: 'wherein hee alleageth many losses … thereby and that his workmanship and timber com[m]eth to £1686 or there aboute and that hee hath receaued but £1200 and therein desireth the companye to make choise of 3 or 4 sufficient carpenters freemen and hee will doe like to mediate the difference betweene them'.[124] Jerman was here proposing that he himself take control of the evaluation process. Having heard this appeal, the wardens of the Goldsmiths' Company asserted the authority of their archival records and 'read to Mr Jarman the carpenters bill of booke of accompt for the carpenters worke accordinge to the measure taken by Mr Marr on the companyes behalf in presence of Mr Jarman and certen others on his behalfe'. According to this official company record, and contrary to the claims of the master carpenter, 'the Totall thereof amounteth vnto the som[m]e of £1217 5s 10d or thereaboute'. Each party seemingly unwilling to compromise and 'the difference beeinge debated on both sides', the wardens of the Goldsmiths' Company finally offered 'to refer the price of all estimate worke vnto two indifferent men or to Mr Surveyor [Nicholas Stone] but Mr Jarman refused soe to doe'. The impasse continued until Nicholas Stone brought political pressure to bear in the form of senior carpenters within the King's Works: 'Mr Stone useinge some speeches of the Kings Majesty M[aste]r Carpenter, Mr Jarman said hee would refer the difference unto M[aste]r Carpenter'.[125] Stone was probably referring here to Ralph Brice, Master Carpenter of the Office of Works.[126] The following spring, 'the kings Majesty Mr Carpenter and Mr Banks of East Smithfield Carpenter' delivered their 'judgement and determinacon' to the company, and not without further dispute, the measuring matter was finally resolved in August 1639.[127]

On the Goldsmiths' Company building site complaints about the measurement and evaluation of artisanal labour were also raised by the master bricklayers commissioned by Nicholas Stone. The disagreement between the guild and the bricklayers Burridge and Osborne reveals how subjective the estimation of skilled craftsmanship might be, even that allegedly agreed 'by the measure'. In April 1638, the bricklayers were in attendance at the company court – the same meeting at which Anthony Jerman's petition had been read to the assembled goldsmiths – 'and demaunded the remaynder of the much money as they pretended to bee due unto them for the bricklayers worke in buildinge of the hall and the Officers houses and tenement adioynenige'. Crucially, the dispute centred on the 'difference betweene them and the Companye for the price of every rodd of brickworke'.[128]

The original terms of the bricklayers' contract had been negotiated by the goldsmith, Robert Hooke, on behalf of the Goldsmiths' Company, the minute details of which 'were to[o] tedious' to relate, according to the commentary of the company clerk. However, the outlines of the court debate in the spring of 1638 reveal that the antagonism between Hooke and the bricklayers was largely based on the goldsmith's insufficient understanding of the bricklayer's craft practices. Though bricklayer 'Osborne confessed the agreement of all the brickwork to bee for 26 [shillings] the rodd runnynge measure as hee termed itt', Hooke had understood 'that they would not demaunde measure for brickwork in vacant places of dores and windowes where noe brick were used there was noe agreement made in writeinge'. The bricklayers took 'exceptons at the omission of the vacuities [the vacant spaces] as they term it'.[129] Moreover, since there was further confusion in the Goldsmiths' Company court as to whether 'the worke of hewinge the bricke for the buildinge was alsoe to be included in the bricklayers worke', it seems that those unfamiliar with the craft had not adequately considered their terms for the preparation of materials.[130] In the initial negotiation between the bricklayers and goldsmith Hooke, verbal and written translations of tacit processes were clearly problematic. The clerk's language, specifically the phase 'hee [or they] term it', is also suggestive of discrete craft vernaculars. Evidently London's master artisans did not all speak the same technical language.[131]

Conclusion

The view from the metropolitan building site has brought into focus a working culture which valued a diverse range of literacies, and which communicated understanding and expertise through word, text, image, and material demonstration. The artisans encountered in this chapter, among the most talented and politically influential in early modern England, did not recognise a fundamental division between propositional and experiential knowledge. Design and construction were not discrete activities. The production of building plans – which involved a working knowledge of geometry, and for Nicholas Stone, a familiarity with continental architectural treatises – and the interpretation and application of designs, were undertaken in dialogue with the built environment. The City Viewers, and the artisans engaged in the rebuilding of Goldsmiths' Hall, communicated on the building site through oral and written instructions, drawn plans, and on-site demonstrations. Designs or plans were means of communicating ideas to building experts, and to patrons, with little working knowledge of construction. But the physical possession of building plans, and the ability to control access to these drawings, were also means of asserting political and epistemic authority.

When it came to the assessment of the built environment, and particular works of craftsmanship, the collective judgement of acknowledged experts was essential. The four City Viewers presented a common recommendation for dealing with nuisance building works. Specialist judgement could also be significant. For the Jermans, one of the leading carpentry dynasties in London, the evaluation of their work by leading experts in other crafts was not acceptable on the Foster Lane site. Further, it is apparent that 'measurement' of artisanal labour was not simply a matter of aesthetics, technical skills, and the use of appropriate precision instruments; social and political influence might also be brought to bear upon evaluations.

Notes

1 Henry Wotton, *The Elements of Architecture, collected by Henry Wotton Knight, from the Best Authors and Examples* (London, 1624), pp. 11–12. Emphasis in original.
2 Gerbino and Johnston, *Compass and Rule*.
3 Wotton, *The Elements of Architecture*, p. 55. Emphasis in original.
4 Dee, *The Mathematicall Preface to the Elements of Geometrie*, sigs. d4r–v.
5 *Ibid.*, sig. d3r.
6 Long, *Artisan/Practitioners and the Rise of the New Sciences*, p. 63; Caroline van Eck (ed.), *British Architectural Theory 1540–1750: An Anthology of Texts* (Aldershot; Burlington, VT: Ashgate, 2003), pp. 1–2, 7–8.

7 Christy Anderson, 'Live words and experience in early modern architecture', in Nebahat Avcioglu and Allison Sherman (eds), *Artistic Practices and Cultural Transfer in Early Modern Italy: Essays in Honour of Deborah Howard* (Farnham: Ashgate, 2015), pp. 77–87, at pp. 81, 85. See also Matthew Walker, *Architects and Intellectual Culture in Post-Restoration England* (Oxford: Oxford University Press, 2017), p. 24, 'Later in the [seventeenth] century, this position was firmly established in English architectural writings, even if it was not necessarily the norm in practice.'

8 The artisans of the King's Works were, for example, responsible for designing and constructing royal buildings. See Colvin (ed.), *The History of the King's Works*, vol. 3, 1485–1660, pt. 1, p. 42.

9 Anderson, 'Live words and experience', p. 81, 'The development of moveable type in the fifteenth century and subsequent emergence of the architectural treatise as a distinct literary genre in the sixteenth century has tended to overshadow the continuing importance of tacit knowledge in architectural production.'

10 McKellar, *The Birth of Modern London*, p. 4.

11 Colvin (ed.), *The History of the King's Works*, vol. 3, 1485–1660, pt. 1, p. 406.

12 Anderson, *Inigo Jones and the Classical Tradition*, pp. 19, 25.

13 *Ibid*., pp. 12–13.

14 *Ibid*., p. 1. See, for example, Howard Colvin (ed.), *A Biographical Dictionary of British Architects, 1600–1840*, 4th edn (New Haven, CT; London: Yale University Press, 2008), p. 28, 'in Britain it was the more sophisticated taste of the Stuart court that first allowed a man of genius to exercise the full functions of an architect in the modern sense. That man was Inigo Jones, and it was he who first imposed Italian discipline on English architecture, taking his ideas direct from the Italian masters … For the Palladian architecture which Inigo Jones introduced into England was based on a highly sophisticated theory of design which could not well be studied outside Italy, and was beyond the intellectual grasp of the average master builder.'

15 *London Viewers and their Certificates, 1508–1558: Certificates of the Sworn Viewers of the City of London*, ed. by Janet Senderowitz Loengard (London: London Record Society, 1989), no. 179. Numbers here relate to the series of bound certificates in the Corporation of London Records Office. Since the publication of Loengard's edition, some of these records (Misc. MSS, Box 91) have been recatalogued; however, for the sake of consistency, I refer here to Loengard's numbering system throughout.

16 Peck, *Consuming Splendor*, p. 205.

17 John Schofield, 'The topography and buildings of London, ca. 1600', in Orlin (ed.), *Material London*, pp. 296–321, at pp. 297, 304.

18 Robert Bucholz and Joseph Ward, *London: A Social and Cultural History, 1550–1750* (Cambridge: Cambridge University Press, 2012), p. 45.

19 Derek Keene, 'Tall buildings in medieval London: precipitation, aspiration and thrills', *The London Journal*, 33:3 (2008), 201–15, at p. 207.

20 Vanessa Harding, 'Houses and households in Cheapside, c.1500–1550', in Matthew Davies and James A. Galloway (eds), *London and Beyond: Essays in Honour of Derek Keene* (London: Institute of Historical Research, 2012), pp. 135–54, at pp. 140–1.

21 GL, MS 5817, fo. 5.

22 GL, MS 4890, fos 2r, 3r.

23 *London Viewers and their Certificates*, xii.

24 *Ibid*., xvi–xvii.

25 *Ibid*., xviii–xx.

26 *Ibid*., xxi–xxiii.

27 *Ibid*., xi, xvi.

28 *Ibid*., xxxii. These reports exist up to 1558, after which the archive is lost, except for a series of certificates for the period 1623–36.

29 Orlin, 'Boundary disputes in early modern London', in Orlin (ed.), *Material London*, pp. 344–76, at p. 349.

30 *London Viewers and their Certificates*, no. 421.
31 *Ibid.*, no. 183.
32 *Ibid.*, no. 178.
33 *Ibid.*, no. 167.
34 London Metropolitan Archive [hereafter LMA], COL/SJ/27/465, fo. 18r.
35 *London Viewers and their Certificates*, no. 167.
36 *Ibid.*, no. 41.
37 *Ibid.*, no. 38.
38 'search, v.' *OED Online*. Oxford University Press, June 2020 [accessed 19 July 2020].
39 *London Viewers and their Certificates*, no. 12.
40 Wallis and Wright, 'Evidence, artisan experience, and authority', p. 146.
41 *London Viewers and their Certificates*, no. 49.
42 *Ibid.*, no. 36.
43 *Ibid.*, no. 135.
44 *Ibid.*, no. 89.
45 LMA, COL/SJ/27/465, fo. 17r.
46 *London Viewers and their Certificates*, no. 356.
47 *Ibid.*, no. 49.
48 Gerbino and Johnston, *Compass and Rule*, pp. 26, 49–53; J. A. Bennett, 'Geometry and surveying in early-seventeenth-century England', *Annals of Science*, 48:4 (1991), 345–54.
49 See Gerbino and Johnston, *Compass and Rule*, p. 24, 'In a sense, the detailed "drawing" of plans took place on site using stakes and string, with many planning issues resolved not by erasing lines on paper but by moving stakes.'
50 *London Viewers and their Certificates*, no. 63.
51 Dorian Gerhold, *London Plotted: Plans of London Buildings c. 1450–1720* (London: London Topographical Society, 2016), p. 1. See also Gerbino and Johnston, *Compass and Rule*, p. 29, medieval surveys 'tended to be written, not drawn'.
52 *London Viewers and their Certificates*, no. 345.
53 LMA, COL/SJ/27/465, fos 18v, 19r.
54 *The City-Law, or, The Course and Practice in all Manner of Juridicall Proceedings in the Hustings in Guild-Hall, London* (1647, London), p. 20.
55 Andy Wood, *The Memory of the People: Custom and Popular Senses of the Past in Early Modern England* (Cambridge: Cambridge University Press, 2013), pp. 10–13, 117–18.
56 *London Viewers and their Certificates*, no. 145. To establish the 'legal validity of custom' it was necessary 'to demonstrate continuity *time out of mind*'. See Andrew Gordon, *Writing Early Modern London: Memory, Text and Community* (New York: Palgrave Macmillan, 2013), p. 122. Emphasis in original.
57 *London Viewers and their Certificates*, no. 121.
58 *Ibid.*, no. 179.
59 LMA, COL/SJ/27/465, fo. 16r.
60 LMA, COL/SJ/27/465, fo. 16v.
61 On the lack of contextual detail concerning Inigo Jones's early life, see Anderson, *Inigo Jones and the Classical Tradition*, p. 26.
62 *London Viewers and their Certificates*, xlv, 'They could and did interpret documents: leases, deeds, earlier views, "other writings", even the Husting Rolls.'
63 *Ibid.*, no. 166.
64 *Ibid.*, no. 345.
65 Adam Fox, *Oral and Literate Culture in England 1500–1700* (Oxford: Clarendon, 2000), p. 12.
66 *London Viewers and their Certificates*, no. 341.
67 Thomas Reddaway and Lorna Walker, *The Early History of the Goldsmiths' Company, 1327–1509* (London: Arnold, 1975), pp. 29–30.

68 *A Survey of London by John Stow; Reprinted from the Text of 1603, with Introduction and Notes by Charles Lethbridge Kingsford*, 2 vols (Oxford: Clarendon Press, 1908), I, p. 305; GHA, WA/CM, R2, fo. 216v.
69 GHA, WA/CM, R2, fos 216v, 218r; S1, fo. 2v.
70 GHA, WA/CM, S1, fo. 9v.
71 Anderson, *Inigo Jones and the Classical Tradition*, p. 45.
72 GHA, WA/CM, S1, fos 9v, 11r.
73 This level of detail is unusual for contemporaneous building projects in general. See Anderson, 'Live words and experience', pp. 81–2. Another rare example of thorough institutional building accounts from London – in this case from the late sixteenth century – is Middle Temple; see Judy Z. Stephenson, '"Real" wages? Contractors, workers, and pay in London building trades, 1650–1800', *Economic History Review*, 71:1 (2018), 106–32, at p. 110.
74 John Newman, 'Nicholas Stone's Goldsmiths' Hall: design and practice in the 1630s', *Architectural History*, 14 (1971), 30–9, at p. 33.
75 *Ibid.*, pp. 32–3.
76 *Ibid.*, p. 30.
77 Perhaps Newman took it as read that plans would be adapted over time according to the requirements of different vested interests; and yet he emphasises the ideal 'complete control' of the surveyor (in the shadow of Inigo Jones) over the building project and makes no mention of the ongoing social process of design, which is detailed so meticulously in the Goldsmiths' Company court minutes. In other words, I contend that Newman exaggerates Stone's complete authority as surveyor and designer.
78 GHA, WA/CM, S1, fos 3v–4r.
79 GHA, WA/CM, S1, fo. 9v.
80 GHA, WA/CM, S1, fo. 11r.
81 GHA, WA/CM, S1, fo. 19v.
82 For Inigo Jones the practice of building was based upon an intense dialogue between architectural treatises and plans, and the physical built environment. See Anderson, *Inigo Jones and the Classical Tradition*, pp. 171, 175.
83 Jones's professional relationship with Stone began when, in his capacity as Surveyor of the King' Works, he employed Stone as master mason for the building of the Banqueting House in Whitehall (1619–22).
84 GHA, WA/CM, S1, fo. 22v.
85 Prideaux, *Memorials of the Goldsmiths' Company*, I, p. 163.
86 GHA, WA/CM, S1, fo. 39r.
87 GHA, WA/CM, S1, fos 56r–v.
88 Newman, 'Nicholas Stone's Goldsmiths' Hall', p. 35.
89 Perhaps – and this can only be speculation – considering the 'especiall care' and advice of Inigo Jones, the plans presented by Stone were orthogonal elevations.
90 Stephan R. Epstein, 'Transferring technical knowledge and innovating in Europe, c.1200–1800', part of the series: *Working Papers on the Nature of Evidence: How Well Do 'Facts' Travel?* No. 01, London: Department of Economic History, London School of Economics, pp. 1–40, at p. 10. This collaborative dimension (involving architects, builders, and patrons) is, of course, also a feature of architectural design today; see Magnus Rönn, 'Quality in architecture – a disputed concept'. *ARCC Conference Repository*, August 2014, doi:10.17831/rep:arcc%y335 [p. 239].
91 GL, MS 16967/1, fo. 176r.
92 GL, MS 16967/1, fo. 182r.
93 GHA, WA/CM, S1, fo. 56r.
94 GHA, WA/CM, S1, fo. 33v.
95 GHA, WA/CM, S1, fo. 38v. Adam Fox, 'Custom, memory and the authority of writing', in Steve Hindle, Adam Fox, and Paul Griffiths (eds), *The Experience of Authority in Early Modern England* (Basingstoke: Macmillan, 1996), pp. 89–166, at

p. 90, writing could be seen as 'a poor substitute for personal contact and verbal exchange'.

96 Adam Fox and Daniel Woolf (eds), *The Spoken Word: Oral Culture in Britain, 1500–1850* (Manchester: Manchester University Press, 2002), p. 7: the relationship between speech, writing, and print 'can be shown to have altered and evolved dynamically at various times, in different regions, and within quite distinct social contexts'. See also Elizabeth Horodowich, 'Introduction: speech and oral culture in early modern Europe and beyond', *Journal of Early Modern History*, 16 (2012), 301–13, at p. 305, 'oral, textual, and visual … At times one form surpassed another in terms of importance, but they never remained in any fixed hierarchy.'

97 GHA, WA/CM, S2, fo. 229v.

98 GHA, WA/CM, T, fo. 31r.

99 Dee, *The Mathematicall Preface to the Elements of Geometrie*, sig. d3r.

100 For the relationship between artisanal authority and drawn designs in general, see Anderson, 'Live words and experience', p. 85, 'Drawing (as well as model making) was a physical act that architects used to claim authority for their ideas.'

101 GHA, WA/CM, S1, fo. 39v. Over twenty years later, as an elderly man of seventy-nine, Robert Hooke requested – and subsequently received – a charitable pension from the Goldsmiths' Company. He pleaded that: 'he was formerly employed by the Company about the new building of the Hall, wherein he spent his time daily for the space of about four years both faithfully and carefully, but never received any recompense for that employment' (Prideaux, *Memorials of the Goldsmiths' Company*, II, p. 120).

102 GHA, WA/CM, S2, fos 235v–236r.

103 Nicholas Stone's suggestion that the plans remain with the company clerk was also consistent with previous practice. In October 1634 the plans were to 'remayne w[i]th the Clerke for any of the Assistants to have recourse vnto' [GHA, WA/CM, S1, fo. 19v].

104 GHA, WA/CM, S2, fo. 236r.

105 I have borrowed the phrase 'epistemic authority' from Chandra Mukerji's excellent discussion of different shades of authority on the extensive seventeenth-century building site of the Canal du Midi. See *Impossible Engineering: Technology and Territoriality on the Canal du Midi* (Princeton, NJ; Oxford: Princeton University Press, 2009), Chapter 3.

106 GHA, WA/CM, S1, fo. 4r. On urban labourers, see Donald Woodward, *Men at Work: Labourers and Building Craftsmen in the Towns of Northern England, 1450–1750* (Cambridge: Cambridge University Press, 1995), pp. 93–4.

107 GHA, WA/CM, S2, fo. 235v.

108 McKellar, *The Birth of Modern London*, p. 86.

109 GHA, WA/CM, T, fo. 125r.

110 GHA, WA/CM, V, fos 21v–22r.

111 Helen Collins, *Edward Jerman 1605–1668: The Metamorphosis of a Master-Craftsman* (Cambridge: Lutterworth Press, 2004), p. 39.

112 Alford and Barker, *A History of the Carpenters' Company*, pp. 207, 213, 232.

113 John Newman, 'Jerman, Edward (c. 1605–1668), carpenter and architect.' *Oxford Dictionary of National Biography*. 4 October 2008. Oxford University Press [accessed 29 July 2018]; James Stevens Curl, 'Jerman, Edward.' Dictionary of Architecture and Landscape Architecture: Oxford University Press, 2006. Oxford Reference [accessed 9 January 2020].

114 Goldsmiths' Company indented articles, transcribed in Collins, *Edward Jerman*, pp. 189–91.

115 GHA, WA/CM, S2, fo. 184v.

116 GHA, WA/CM, S2, fo. 252v.

117 GHA, WA/CM, S2, fo. 261v.

118 GHA, WA/CM, T, fo. 10r.

119 GHA, WA/CM, S2, fo. 255v, 'Alsoe that the carpenters worke shalbee measured as soone as conveniency will p[er]mitt and that Mr Bowen in Philpott Lane neere Ffanchurch Streete and Mr Knifman the plaisterer are nominated to bee measurers for and on the behalfe of the company if it shall not bee otherwise ordered.'

120 GHA, WA/CM, T, fo. 44r.

121 GL, MS 16967/1, fo. 179v.

122 Elias Jerman presented nine apprentices and served as warden of the Carpenters' Company. See Collins, *Edward Jerman 1605–1668*, pp. 36–7.

123 Orlin, *Locating Privacy*, p. 120.

124 GHA, WA/CM, T, fo. 74r.

125 GHA, WA/CM, T, fos 74r–v.

126 Ralph Brice was Master Carpenter from 1629/30 to (after) 1640. See Colvin (ed.), *The History of the King's Works*, vol. 3, 1485–1660, pt. 1, p. 408.

127 GHA, WA/CM, V, fos 6v–7r.

128 GHA, WA/CM, T, fo. 73r.

129 GHA, WA/CM, T, fo. 73r. Henry Wotton used the term 'vacuities' in his *Elements of Architecture* (p. 27).

130 GHA, WA/CM, T, fos 73r–74v.

131 Fox, *Oral and Literate Cultures*, pp. 89–90; Keith Thomas, *The Ends of Life: Roads to Fulfilment in Early Modern England* (Oxford: Oxford University Press, 2009), p. 107, 'Every trade had its technical vocabulary, so bafflingly arcane to the outsider'.

4

Rebuilding and adaptation

A mid-sixteenth-century manuscript composed by London's Girdlers' Company records gifts of land, property, and moveable goods by prominent members of the craft to their guild. It begins with the most substantial and significant gift of all, Andrew Hunt's bequest, in 1431, of 'two tenements and a voyde pece of ground ... with a greate gate and an Entrye under the Solar of Maude Moundevyle. These two tenements are nowe Thalle [the hall] and the voyde grounde is the yarde at the comyng in thereof The Soleir [upper floor chamber] of Maude Moundevyle is the Chamber over the Entrye and gate at the Comyng into Thalle.'[1] This generous bequest was followed by that of Robert Belgrave, who in 1505 'gave unto this Companye ... a Tofte of Lande, a Sollar and garden lyeing w[i]thin an Allye callyd Moundevyle allye ... and thus is comprehendyd the whole hall and every part of the same of many peces made one by us the said Companye'.[2]

This retrospective account of property acquisition, development, and consolidation on Bassinghall Street is a good example of how institutional artisanal narratives of corporate identity and reciprocity were rooted in the built environment of the company hall. Craft guilds in London did not compose formal chronicles, but the guild inventory or gift book often worked to construct a historic narrative of institutional exchange and fraternity. These opening entries in the Girdlers' Company inventory book also neatly encapsulate the typical pattern through which London's guilds acquired their halls; a wealthy and prominent member of the craft bequeathed a building, usually a substantial timber-framed courtyard house, to a cluster of trustees, some of whom were guild members. Subsequently the guild made adaptations to the built fabric.[3] In January 1429/30, two carpenters gained the lease of five cottages and a waste piece of land from the Priory and Convent of St. Mary's Hospital in Brodestreet ward, located between Bishopsgate and Moorgate, which they regranted to twenty-nine fellow carpenters; the guild then demolished the cottages and on the same site constructed a hall and four houses, which faced onto London Wall.[4] In his late sixteenth-century perambulation of the city streets, John Stow reported that Carpenters' Hall was now 'amongest many proper houses'.[5] Many guilds acquired halls very soon after, or even in anticipation of, acquisition of a royal charter of incorporation, the legal requirement for owning communal property.[6] In 1446, less than a decade after securing incorporation, the Vintners' Company was left a site in the Vintry by vintner Guy Shuldham in his will, on which they built their hall and thirteen almshouses 'for poor and needy men and women of the said mistery'.[7] In 1475 the newly incorporated Pewterers' Company acquired a house on Lime Street through a past master and generous benefactor, William Smallwood.[8] The guild had formerly hired the refectory of the Austin Friars for meetings of the craft. The overall pattern is growth. In 1400 six mercantile guilds likely had halls.[9] By 1475 the number had risen to at least twenty-seven, and to forty-seven by 1540.[10] At the turn of the seventeenth century, around sixty London guilds had an institutional home within the ancient City walls.[11]

As in other English cities with a strong guild presence, such as York, London guild halls established in the fourteenth and early fifteenth centuries were usually situated in the midst of their craft or trade cluster. These were increasingly dense networks of workshops, warehouses, retail sites, and domestic residences.[12] Occupational clustering was a consequence of a range of influences, including trade interdependencies (as among the weapons-related crafts), access to raw materials, established social and religious networks, and statutory regulation (as in the cases of the Butchers and Fishmongers).[13] Moreover, 'business convenience and pleasantness set a premium on sites by the river or on the main city thoroughfares'.[14] From the thirteenth century, goldsmiths tended to live and trade at the corner of Cheapside and Friday Street, the cordwainers south of Cheapside, and the vintners 'near the Thames in the Vintry'.[15] For guild authorities with the responsibility to 'search' artisanal workshops and mercantile retail spaces, occupational clustering was a hugely significant feature of guild control over material standards and production; it was also, perhaps, an important factor in the development and dissemination of innovatory craft practices.[16]

For London's late medieval artisanal and mercantile guilds, possession of an institutional building was becoming highly desirable. Ownership of a hall provided a permanent space for guild members to hold court meetings, mediate internal disputes, register apprentices, compile records, manage estates and charities, socialise, feast, and host visiting citizens and dignitaries. Additionally, the company hall was a relatively secure storage facility for growing volumes of guild accounts, funds, and precious plate. Guild buildings also provided a welcome source of rental income. Pewterers' Hall was hired out to guild members for special occasions such as wedding celebrations, and to 'a Spanyarde for kepyng Daunsyng' (hosting dancing lessons).[17] This building was also rented by guilds such as the Coopers and the Glovers who were yet to establish their own institutional homes.[18] The Blacksmiths' Company rented Cutlers' Hall for feasts from 1442–43 to 1464–65.[19]

The craft hall was at the centre of guild activities and had a substantial impact on everyday encounters and exchanges, but this multifunctional space was also fundamental to the collective historic imagination, or memory, of London's craftsmen. Through their designs, materialities, layout, and furnishings, craft halls held great symbolic significance for their artisanal members and the broader urban community. Over time, multiple generations of artisans made their mark on craft halls, inscribing these sites with accumulated weighty meanings and significance.[20] These buildings represented and materialised the antiquity, benevolence, and expertise of the craft or trade. Craft halls were sites through which the skills, generosity, and fraternity of previous generations of eminent craftsmen were memorialised. Through their impressive material collections, such as the assemblage of miniaturised and full-sized suits of armour found in the sixteenth- and seventeenth-century Armourers' Hall on Coleman Street, these buildings could even act as sites of design and technical innovation. We saw in previous discussions of goldsmiths and knowledge cultures how the early seventeenth-century Goldsmiths' Hall contained a (temporary) workshop specifically for signifying the expertise of London's youthful trainee goldsmiths. Looking outwards, company halls were also embedded in the broader urban topography of commerce and ceremony. Highly ritualised searches of artisanal workshops and retail sites, undertaken by senior guild members, began and ended at the associated guild building, and the livery halls of the most eminent mercantile guilds, such as the Mercers' Company, were incorporated into civic and royal processional routes.

The rebuilding of Goldsmiths' Company Hall in the mid-1630s – an undertaking which we encountered in the previous chapter – was an exceptionally elaborate and expensive project. Nevertheless, the impetus to remodel the built fabric of the guild was entirely typical of London's early modern companies. From *c.* 1550 to *c.* 1640, dozens of guild halls across the City were adapted, enlarged, and rebuilt. Artisans were investing significant funds, time, energy, materials, and ingenuity into the institutional built environment of their craft. Expanding on the previous discussion of knowledge cultures on London's construction sites, this chapter turns our attention to artisanal built fabrics. We begin to uncover the spatial dimensions of artisanal identities through a consideration of change and continuity in the physical structure, layout, and material arrangement of craft company halls.

First, the chapter explores the sources and approaches employed in this reconstruction of artisanal built environments, before turning to consider the key features of the late medieval built fabric. This will position us to understand the most fundamental early modern adaptations to artisanal architectures. The chapter demonstrates that while the basic spatial organisation of guild halls, around a courtyard, remained constant over time, the institutional built fabric was also subject to considerable change, particularly from the middle decades of the sixteenth century. These significant modifications included the expansion of buildings, the development of new specialised chambers, and the insertion of structural features, such as staircases, which altered patterns of movement within guild architectures. More elaborate interior decorative schemes involving plaster, paint, and wooden panelling were also added to company halls from *c.* 1560, and these institutional buildings housed and displayed a growing volume and variety of material cultures. We conclude the discussion on rebuilding and adaptation with a reflection upon the likely social, cultural, economic, and political contexts to such significant (re)investments in built environments across this period, and the implications for identities, both individual and collective.

Tracing continuity and change

The sixteenth- and early seventeenth-century built fabric does not survive; the vast majority of London's timber-framed and brick livery halls were destroyed by 'those dreadfull flames' of 1666.[21] This absence certainly adds an extra layer of interpretive challenge to the already substantial task of unearthing 'the complexity of the social, political and economic forces which impacted upon the built environment' of late medieval and early modern towns and cities.[22] However, through close analysis of documentary, visual, and material evidence in dialogue, here a vivid impression of the layout, design, materiality, and manifold spatial practices associated with London's artisanal halls is made possible.

The richest archival evidence for artisanal halls comes from guild inventories. Unlike probate inventories of contemporary domestic interiors, which were, by definition, taken at the end of a person's life and that of the household, and thus depict one fixed moment, guild inventories are representations of a living, dynamic community.[23] Taking an inventory did not signal the demise of the institution but a particular moment in the life of a corporation which expected to exist in perpetuity. Most London guilds made inventories of their corporate possessions at some point, albeit at irregular intervals. These documents uniquely enable us to analyse changes over time in the organisation and use of built environments, patterns of guild 'consumption', and the 'social life' of specific objects.[24] Artisanal companies that did not compile dedicated 'inventory books' sometimes listed the contents of their livery halls within general administrative and court minutes. An inventory of Armourers' Hall from 1585 listed objects according to their location in the hall, buttery, kitchen, harness gallery, parlour, and counting house.[25] It is probable that many more guild inventories once existed but have been lost. A single, damaged folio from 1558 survives, for example, listing part of the Curriers' Company's communal property.[26]

Company court minutes and accounts meticulously detail the collective income and expenditure of the craft guild and, thus, where they survive, they are another highly valuable source material for fleshing out changes and continuities relating to the built fabric. Take the Tallow Chandlers' Company's accounts which record hundreds of minor repairs and adjustments, undertaken by masons, carpenters, smiths, and joiners, in addition to periods of major remodelling of Tallow Chandlers' Hall on Thames Street. The guild's accounts thus include entries reflecting routine maintenance, such as fees 'paide to the masons men for mendyg sondry things', and rather singular events, as when it was decided, in October 1569, 'that the parlour and building next over shalbe taken down from the west syde of the hall … and that the same shalbe raysed higher and buylded of new ageyne'.[27] These records also give insight into status hierarchies within the crafts. Master carpenters, for example, are specifically mentioned by name when the Tallow Chandlers constructed a penthouse in 1563, and master artisans, including joiners, plumbers, masons, and plasterers are specified when the guild commissioned 'the new frame joyninge to our hawle' in 1569; but craftsmen without workshops of their own are referred to generically as 'the masons men' or the 'carvers man'.[28] The accounts of London's artisanal guilds also offer unusual glimpses of the materials involved in craft practice. When engaged in the rebuilding of the hall windows in 1580, for instance, the painter employed by the Tallow Chandlers charged for white lead unground, linseed oil, 'best florry', 'Spanish Browne', and 'Spanish White'.[29] Since workshop inventories or accounts do not survive for this period, these are valuable material insights.

Contemporary visual sources of fifteenth-, sixteenth-, and early seventeenth-century company halls are very limited.[30] The surveys of Ralph Treswell undertaken for the Clothworkers' Company in 1612 include a detailed, measured representation of Clothworkers' Hall on Mincing Lane, and a simple outline of Ironmongers' Hall on Fenchurch Street (see Plate 2).[31] However, plans of company halls undertaken in the later seventeenth century (such as those of Armourers' Hall in 1679 and Goldsmiths' Hall in 1692) can provide valuable insights as to the pre-Fire spatial organisation of the hall; unusually these institutional buildings were not destroyed by the great conflagration (see Plates 3 and 4). The interior view, elevation of Foster Lane front, and bird's eye view of Goldsmiths' Hall by John Ward also demonstrate building style and material furnishings (see Plates 5 and 6, and Plate 1). Together with visual sources, rare contemporary material survivals from halls, including moveable objects, wall paintings, and fixtures such as wainscot panels – as well as textual recordings of material things

– are an invaluable archive. Interpretation of materials, designs, symbolism, colours, and inscriptions, and an understanding of object use and significance within artisanal companies, are crucial in elucidating individual and collective identity formation.

The late medieval plan and built fabric

The surviving documentary and visual evidence indicates that craft company halls in late medieval and early modern London were typically organised according to the courtyard plan. In this spatial formation, a series of interconnected chambers were organised around a central courtyard. This was the usual spatial arrangement for large domestic residences, Inns of Court, and Oxford and Cambridge colleges.[32] The incorporation of courtyard and communal hall with a raised platform or 'dais' end was symbolically significant. This late medieval building design articulated the 'inward-looking' concerns of the particular community, and simultaneously the fundamental socio-political distinctions between different members of the household. As archaeologist Matthew Johnson contends, 'the differing statuses of the groups making up the household were emphasized through their varying positions around the court and signified through architectural detail ... The courtyard plan thus expressed the notion of community to the outside world – in its unity around a central point – while combining this idea with spatial and stylistic expression of social inequality within the household.'[33]

The first records in the book of inventories begun by 'the brethirhode of thassupcion of our blessid lady of the crafte of pewtrer of London' in 1489–90 mention a hall, parlour, counting house, courtyard, bowling alley, and garden (including a vine) in Langbourn Ward.[34] These chambers and leisure spaces were typical of a fifteenth-century craft or trade fraternity hall. Several years after acquiring a property on Maiden Lane in 1458, for example, the Haberdashers' guild employed master carpenter Robert Wheatley 'for making the porch the skreene the hall dores, the Armorie, the Entrie from the kitchen to the Parlour, the seeling over head of the Parlour and the staires to the Raven Chamber and dresser boards and other things in the kitchen'.[35] Boundaries between institutional spaces and neighbouring commercial and domestic architectures were often relatively fluid. Suggestively, in his late sixteenth-century survey, John Stow wrote of goldsmith Drugo Barentine, lord mayor in 1398, who 'gave fayre landes to the Goldsmithes: hee dwelled right against the Goldsmithes Hall. Between the which hall and his dwelling house, hee builded a Galory thwarting the streete, whereby he might go from the one to the other'.[36] The majority of medieval guild buildings in London were timber-framed, though there were some exceptions. The most affluent fifteenth-century mercantile companies used stone for general construction (as at Grocers' Hall) or particular features (Merchant Taylors' and Fishmongers' Halls); the late medieval Drapers' and Clothworkers' Companies used brick for certain rooms.[37]

Through their visual and material cultures, a range of symbolic meanings and identities existed in juxtaposition throughout these built fabrics, including imagery relating to Crown, City, and guild. There was often a strong emphasis too on the armorial bearings or craft symbols relating to particular families, and artisanal or mercantile dynasties. The imagery of saints also featured heavily in late medieval guild halls. In addition to devotional value within the community, saintly imagery could emphasise the antiquity of the mechanical arts and the unity of the craft guild. Across late medieval London, and urban England and Europe more broadly, craft fraternities and guilds adopted patron saints with a direct connection to the expertise of working members, through the saint's occupation in life or method of martyrdom.[38] And so the London Goldsmiths enjoyed the protection of St. Dunstan, said to be a tenth-century Glastonbury metalworker, while the Clothworkers' Company adopted St. Katherine of Alexandria, whose martyrdom included torture on the wheel (an object employed in production by guild members).[39] The direct working association of the saint with the guild must have endowed the labour of its artisans with significance and dignity.

The hall chamber

Akin to most hall chambers in substantial medieval London houses, the internal hall of the Pewterers' Company was probably located on the ground or first floor, towards the back of the site.[40] The great hall was the principal space for hosting the communal activities of the craft guild or fraternity such as the annual election feast, which established bonds of brotherhood, and simultaneously reinforced notions of institutional hierarchy.[41] Hall chambers contained the requisite furniture for hosting feasts and articulating social hierarchies. The craft fraternity of London blacksmiths had a great hall furnished with a table at the high dais of thirteen feet. and a table on the west and east sides of the hall, sixteen and thirteen feet, respectively.[42] Social and political distinctions were physically expressed and reinforced through the architectural design of the hall. The high or dais end was customarily the site for the feasting and conspicuous display of the most privileged members of the household or corporation (though by the late fifteenth century, in all but the very grandest and largest of England's houses, and except at very special occasions, the gentle or aristocratic family had retreated to first-floor rooms).[43] In domestic and institutional contexts the high and low ends of the hall were distinguished through material and structural features.[44] A bay window might be located behind the dais, as at Cutlers' Hall from the late 1480s.[45] A two-storied wooden screen was the traditional means from the fourteenth century of providing a formal entrance to the hall, enhancing the spectacle of the space from the perspective of the high table, and separating and concealing food preparation areas from the main body of the hall.[46]

The hall chamber served as a multifunctional space. The fifteenth- and early sixteenth-century court records of the Pewterers', Drapers', Blacksmiths', Cutlers', Brewers', Grocers', Carpenters', and Merchant Taylors' Companies all make references to the performance of 'plays' or 'players' within their halls, particularly as entertainments during election feasts.[47] These terms were heterogeneous, 'covering a full range of entertainment activity from dicing games to theatrical performances, and including satirical sketches, juggling acrobatics, sports, and the like'.[48] In the 1400s, pageants were held in Pewterers' Hall following the annual election feast, and a 'sword-player' provided additional entertainment.[49] The Carpenters paid for singers to perform during feast-time masses, and for ballads to be sung in the hall throughout dinner.[50] Hall chambers were also locations for the performance of the authority of guild elites in other, more punitive ways: for instance, apprentices were openly whipped there as punishment for misdemeanours.[51] And, in addition, this was the space in which the whole guild would gather on quarter days, the dates in the civic calendar when quarterage dues were collected, to listen to the recitation of guild ordinances and other speeches concerning governance and order.

In her work on the built fabric of the religious fraternities and craft guilds of late medieval York, Kate Giles has demonstrated how timber framing 'created complex hierarchical spaces with close parallels to the open halls of domestic buildings and the aisled nave and chancel of the medieval parish church'.[52] Documentary evidence indicates that these structural features were also employed in London's craft halls. In 1460 the Carpenters' Company employed its own members for 'werkmanship of the Celyng at the Highdeys of the Hall'. A decade later they 'paid for the bordyng of the high Dese'.[53] On account of their expertise in working with timber, these guildsmen would have been especially well-placed to interpret a 'grammar of carpentry', including 'rules about the conversion and use of timber' such as 'the placing of the fair face of timber towards the high-status end of the hall'.[54]

When Pewterers' Hall was rebuilt in the late 1490s, its artisanal fraternity also took great care over the choice of design for the new timber roof of the hall chamber. The principal craftsman employed for this building project was the carpenter Simon Birlyngham. Guild accounts show that in addition to the ordinary payments for construction, which amounted to £40, not including the materials which were purchased by the guild, the company also paid Birlyngham extra sums to 'vewe' with them Haberdashers' Hall, Carpenters' Hall, 'pappey' (the hall of the fraternity of St. Charity and St. John the Evangelist in the ward of Aldgate) and 'the Deans roof' at Hackney, probably the residence of the Dean of St. Paul's. In the design and rebuilding of their new institutional home the Pewterers were thus clearly taking inspiration from a range of existing roof structures within their surrounding built environment, particularly halls which belonged to fellow companies. In 1497–98 the Pewterers additionally paid for 'colours to peynt the [new] halle Roof' and 'the principal posts in the halle'.[55] It is not clear which type of roof structure the Pewterers finally decided upon – whether 'crown-post', 'up-right', or 'hammerbeam roof' – but they were engaging one of the foremost carpenters of London for the task, who had carried out a range of high status commissions.[56] Revealingly, at his death, master carpenter Simon Birlyngham was owed money for 'diverse stuff boughte for the King', in addition to significant outstanding sums from the Master of Lincoln's Inn, the Vintners' and Leathersellers' Companies, and numerous London churches, including All Hallows the Great and St. Mary-le-Bow.[57]

In London's late medieval craft buildings, the raised dais end of the hall chamber was ornamented with judiciously chosen furnishings. Citizens lavished funds, or undertook demonstrations of expert craftsmanship, for this site in particular. In 1428, for instance, the year in which Armourers' Hall was established, master armourers gave 'hallyngs to the high deysse [dais]' and 'the crest of the high deysse with three Angells'.[58] The crest feature was likely a wooden or plaster structure which framed the high table below. The 'hallyngs' were painted textiles, analogous to a cloth of state in a high status domestic context, which combined a visual representation of the company's patron saint, St. George, with celebratory textual verses by the poet John Lydgate.[59] In 1514 the new master William Clarke 'gave unto the said Hall two new formes [benches] to the hye deysse'.[60] The late fifteenth-century hall chamber of the 'Fraternity of St. Eligius of craft of blacksmiths of London' was decorated with four cloths: one for the high dais, 'the Westside', 'the Eastside', and 'the halle ende south'. The textiles were seven yards in length, three in width.[61] By 1542 the Pewterers' hall chamber was also decorated with 'iv hangyns', probably depicting the Virgin Mary, and in the reign of Mary I the guild acquired 'a pece of hanging of the xii apostles' for the hall.[62] Few hall chambers were as impressively furnished as at Merchant Taylors' Hall. This was among the largest and wealthiest companies in London, with members who 'had time out of minde beene great marchants, and had frequented all sortes of marchandises into most partes of the worlde'.[63] The Merchant Taylor's late fifteenth- and early sixteenth-century internal hall was hung with nine 'clothes of arrays [Arras]', worth £123, representing the life of their patron saint, St. John, as well as a 'cloth of Saint John ...

sette upon blewe velvet … browdered with floure de luces of venyce gold'.[64] When not on display the Arras were stored in '9 severall bagges of canvas'.[65]

In 1530 the Goldsmiths' Company commissioned a series of three tapestries from Flanders (the European centre of tapestry production) for the decoration of their high dais. This was the epitome of luxurious material import. The guildsmen specified a design for their 'ryche hangyngs of Arras', which represented scenes from the life of St. Dunstan. This textile, measuring 195 Flemish ells, cost a staggering £280 to produce. It took four artists sixteen days to make a black-and-white design. In addition to the costs for materials, workmanship, transportation, and customs fees, the guild paid 'for the translatynge of the [saint's] storye oute of Englyshe into Dutche'. Once the textiles had arrived at Goldsmiths' Hall the guild ensured the safekeeping of this new material investment by having a locked chest made especially for their secure storage.[66] These lavish and highly valuable textiles required close material maintenance. In March 1587 the 'decaied collors' of the Merchant Taylor's tapestries were refreshed by Thomas Bonde and James Burton, two 'workers in Arras'. These 'arras refreshers' proved their expertise for the job by presenting the citizens at Merchant Taylors' Hall with an old piece of arras, one side of which they had 'restored to his firste bewtie'. The restored half of the textile was, of course, 'very freshe and the collors livelie', while the untouched side was 'very duskie and so decaied in color that it seemed a thing unpossible to bringe it to the color and brightnes of the other part which was made cleane'.[67]

The Pewterers' inventory book shows how, in 1497–98, seventeen individual guildsmen and company widows paid for the glazing of window panels in the hall, including the bay window and 'the high window over the high dais' using 'flemysshe' and 'normandy' glass.[68] Company hierarchies were clearly established or confirmed through such material sponsorship, as the Master Lawrence Aslyn funded the most prestigious 'high' window, and the wardens and other senior or ambitious guildsmen funded additional panes (or 'half' panels) throughout Pewterers' Hall.[69] There was almost certainly an element of intra-guild competition articulated through this form of material patronage, a rivalry made rather more explicit in the case of coloured glass bearing benefactors' arms, as in the Merchant Taylors' and Carpenters' Companies' fifteenth-century halls.[70] Heraldic ornament featured prominently within company buildings, as within contemporary English palaces and opulent domestic interiors.[71] Liverymen who paid for the re-glazing of two windows on the north side of the Carpenters' hall chamber in 1586 had their names and timber marks engraved in the glass.[72] The armorial bearings of the monarch, company, and families of prominent artisans, merchants, and benefactors (living and dead) were displayed throughout guild halls in coloured glass, emblazoned upon textiles – including banners, streamers, and tablecloths – silver plate, wooden panels, chests, and even garden sculpture.[73]

The parlour and counting house

In 1498–99, a year after glass panes were affixed to window frames in the Pewterers' hall chamber, six artisans also gave money 'towards the makyng of the ii long formes [benches] in the said p[ar]lour' and Master Lawrence Aslyn likewise 'paide for the tymbre and werkemanship of the wyndowe atte the steire heed into the p[ar]lour And the crafte p[ai]d for the yren [iron] werke and glasse of the same wyndowe'.[74] During the late fourteenth and early fifteenth centuries, guilds with institutional homes began to add a parlour room to the building complex (the Goldsmiths in 1382; Drapers in 1425; Carpenters in 1442, and Cutlers in 1465). The parlour was usually located on the ground floor at right angles to the dais end of the hall chamber. The spatial proximity of the parlour to the high-status end of the hall and, using the language of space-syntax theory, its location 'deep' within the institutional building plan, is indicative of its prestige. Guild parlours might also overlook shared gardens.[75] The early sixteenth-century Bakers' Hall included a 'summer parlour' which ran the length of the garden, and a 'winter parlour' which was located on the opposite side of the courtyard.[76] As the etymology of the word suggests, the parlour was a room designed for relatively secluded conversation or conference, and the presence of benches and tables in this chamber further supports this likely function.[77] In the institutional context, the parlour was probably a room reserved for use by the most senior and authoritative artisans of the guild.

Though the parlour was to become richly decorated in the later 1500s, and a significant storage space for valuable documents, it was relatively bare in the fifteenth and early decades of the sixteenth centuries. In 1542 the Pewterers' parlour contained only basic furniture – including the aforementioned forms – and 'iv long ban[n]er staves'.[78] By contrast, the counting house (also known as the 'compting house'), which was the principal chamber for the keeping of accounts, was decorated in 1497–98 with 'xxxiiii yerds of peyntid clothes', and clearly functioned also as the principal storeroom for precious objects, including charters, seals, patents, and a significant collection of plate and textiles.[79] Royal charters were especially prized: 'they were not only practical devices, conferring sets of rights and privileges, but were also symbols of the particular relationship which the guilds had with the Crown, which characterized their development and influenced their evolving sense of their own histories'.[80] Multiple banners and streamers named in the inventory of 1490, and a fraternal 'blak cofyn with ii chaplet(s) of Red Saten with the ymage of our lady of assumpcion of sylver' were housed in relative security in the counting house and brought out into the communal hall and city streets during funerals, feast days, and civic processions, such as the Midsummer Watch.[81] The Cutlers' Company counting house window had bars for additional security.[82]

Gardens and recreational spaces

Pewterers' Hall had a garden with a 'vyne' and a bowling alley; these recreational spaces were also found to the rear of numerous other company halls within fifteenth- and early sixteenth-century London. The Carpenters' Company court accounts feature hundreds of entries relating to the careful maintenance of their box hedging (planted in the forecourt of the Hall in 1490), herbs, turf, privet hedging, and vines in an adjacent garden plot.[83] In the 1540s the Carpenters also constructed a bowling alley.[84] The Ironmongers on Fenchurch Street paid labourers for 'cutting the vines and hedges ... dressing the roses, and for the purchase of lavender to set the maze' in the early sixteenth century. They also paid a carpenter for 'ii dayes to repaire the gre[a]t frame of tymber that beryth up the vynes in the garden'.[85] The plan of Clothworkers' Hall on Mincing Lane, surveyed by Ralph Treswell in 1612, shows a well-established formal garden positioned at the rear of the site (see Plate 2). This garden was 'deep' with the Hall complex (relatively inaccessible with only one entrance); it was also overlooked by the ground-floor parlour. These were likely typical features of livery hall gardens.[86] Though we know little about their precise organisation and design, the relatively secluded setting of these City gardens, and the care lavished upon their upkeep, suggest that they were spaces associated with leisure and sociability for the most privileged guildsmen. In 1494 two wardens of the Pewterers' Company 'paide for the stuff and makyng of the bench of bri[c]k under the vyne in the south ends of the gardyne'. Liverymen across London sponsored material fixtures for their corporate gardens – such as sun-dials in the Ironmongers' Company garden – as they did for interiors.[87] We have seen that the Pewterers', Carpenters', and Ironmongers' Companies nurtured ornamental vines; so too did the Cutlers', Clothworkers', and Grocers' Companies.[88] The fifteenth-century Grocers enjoyed several bunches of grapes daily.[89]

Churches, chapels, and almshouses

The essential religious activities of the craft fraternity did not formally take place in Pewterers' Hall, but were hosted in the church of the Grey Friars and later the Church of All Hallows on Lombard Street. These included the provision of lights for the masses, obits, and dirges for the souls of deceased brothers, indicated in the Pewterers' inventories by multiple references to 'tapers of wax to set in [h]ono[ur] of our Blessid lady'.[90] Unlike the collegiate buildings of Oxford and Cambridge, a chapel was not an integral part of the livery hall complex. Chapels were only a feature of the most prestigious mercantile company halls, the Mercers (by 1391), the Merchant Taylors (by 1403–4) and the Grocers (1411).[91] Medieval London guilds typically had strong links with a neighbourhood church, upheld by regular corporate use of the building for worship, ceremony, and memorialisation. On the feast of their patron saint and on election day, guild members would attend services at their patronal church. Funerals of guildsmen might also be held there.[92] Guilds made contributions to the material fabric of their patronal church. Companies often sponsored an altar and funded one or more priests to pray for their guild members.[93]

On Maiden Lane, as well as Goldsmiths' Hall, lay the parish church of St. John Zachary, which many goldsmiths sponsored and would be memorialised within. Stow's *Survey* relates that it was a 'fayre church, with the monuments wel[l] preserved, of Thomas Lichfield, who founded a chauntrie there … Nicholas Twiford, Goldsmith, mayor 1388. And Dame Margery his wife: of whose goods the church was made & new builded, with a Tomb for them, and others of their race …', and so the list continues, naming nearly a dozen significant goldsmiths.[94] The goldsmith Henry Coote (d. 1513), left £70 to St. Dunstan's chapel in the church of St. Vedast, for the rebuilding of the chapel and a glass window 'to be made according to a pattern I have caused to be made containing the life of St. Dunstan and the figures of me and my two wives'.[95] In the parish church of St. Leonard, on Foster Lane, there was a monument to Robert Trappis, a goldsmith (d. 1526), with an epitaph that deliberately played with notions of remembrance: 'When the bel[l]s be merily roong, And the masse devoutly sung, And the meat merily eaten, Then shall Robert Traps his wives And children be forgotten'.[96]

Several guilds also built almshouses (charitable accommodation for the impoverished or elderly) adjacent to their halls or on nearby plots, from the early fifteenth century: the Merchant Taylors (1414), the Cutlers (1420–40), the Brewers (1423) and the Carpenters (1457–58).[97] Company almshouses that were developed from the mid-sixteenth century were 'on separate, often peripheral sites away from the city centre'.[98] Almshouses were also moved outside the City altogether (such as the Bowes almshouses at Woolwich, administered by the Goldsmiths, and the Wyatt almshouses for ten poor men at Godalming, managed by the Carpenters).[99]

By the 1530s, approximately forty company halls within the City of London had several key chambers, with a variety of functions and customary forms of furnishing and decoration. These buildings were organised according to a courtyard plan, with an internal hall to the rear of the site, perhaps with a small garden plot beyond. On the ground floor, at right angles to the hall, most guilds had a parlour room which was reserved for the deliberations of the company elite; a counting house sometimes adjoined this chamber. By the turn of the sixteenth century, some livery buildings also had basic food preparation and storage rooms.

Adaptations and rebuilding: change and continuity

A contemporary who approached an artisanal hall in the mid-sixteenth century with memories of the early 1500s would have noticed a number of significant changes to the built fabric. Company halls had been extended outwards and upwards. Exterior walls and gatehouses had been materially enhanced. Entry to the hall would reveal new chambers, rooms which contained greater quantities and varieties of material cultures. There were more locks on doors, and additional routes between rooms. Ceilings, windows, and doorways had been ornamented. Staircases had been inserted, expanded or embellished. If it were a quarter day, our imagined visitor to the hall would notice a greater number of journeymen in the immediate vicinity of the building and the courtyard. If it were a feast day, they would notice the culinary smells emanating from the kitchen, and the bustle created by porters and merchants delivering produce and extra furnishings to the hall. Significantly, the fundamental internal spatial organisation of chambers organised around a central courtyard remained the same as 'time out of mind'. Even when guilds entirely demolished the late medieval fabric and built anew, as with the Ironmongers' Company in the 1580s, and Goldsmiths' Company in the 1630s, the courtyard design was preserved. The spatial language of community, with its social and political distinctions, remained highly relevant and desirable.[100]

Across the sixteenth and early seventeenth centuries, guild buildings were customised according to the needs of particular artisanal communities. And thus, Founders' Hall uniquely incorporated a 'sizing house' for the assize of weights, and Goldsmiths' Hall an enlarged assay house for the testing of precious metals.[101] But there were several general trends which can be observed throughout the City. First, expansion: sites were enlarged, additional rooms built onto extant structures, chambers lengthened, storeys added, and routes between these spaces more clearly defined. Between the mid-sixteenth and mid-seventeenth centuries, additional parlours, assaying quarters, court and dining rooms, counting houses, kitchens, galleries, penthouses, domestic lodgings, and dedicated spaces for the storage and safeguarding of material possessions, including armouries, were added to artisanal company buildings. Second, rooms within remodelled artisanal halls became increasingly specialised in function; purposes and meanings were largely defined by material goods, which were used, displayed, and stored in growing quantities across this period. Third, interior decorative schemes, such as wainscoting and stone-work, were employed to articulate conceptions of artisanal skill, corporate hierarchy, and fraternity more explicitly than ever before, as well as notions of belonging and exclusion. Here we explore these adaptations and additions in more depth, and begin to consider the implications of these changes for the meanings and experiences of individual artisanal and collective identities.

Our previous discussion of the late medieval inheritance opened with the inventories of the Pewterers' guild. It is revealing that these late fifteenth- and early sixteenth-century lists of shared possessions are roughly organised according to materials. Things are listed in material groupings: objects made of velum and wax, fabric, precious metals, brick, glass, and timber. Particular chambers in Pewterers' Hall are only mentioned *en passant*. From 1540 there is a change. From this date the Pewterers' inventories are specifically ordered according to rooms in the hall, with goods listed as the inventory takers systematically moved throughout the building.[102] The guild officials began the process of recording their moveable goods on the ground floor, starting with the counting house, before moving into the hall chamber, and then passing through to the buttery, pantry, kitchen, and larder house. Having ascended a staircase to the first floor, the men composing the inventory itemised material goods in 'the parlour over the hall', and then the garret over the parlour, and finally, having descended two storeys back to the ground floor, objects located in 'the inner yard'. The inventory describes a courtyard house of several storeys. By 1559 the route of the appraisers began with the prestigious 'new parlour' (the original parlour chamber was now designated as the old parlour, or 'the olde greate parlor'). A gallery is mentioned in an inventory of 1604, and by the early 1620s goods in the armoury and court chamber were also itemised. The shift in organisational principle of these documents – from lists of material goods of a similar type, to objects ordered under separate room headings – is reflective of the larger and more complex built environment of Pewterers' Hall, and the acquisition of a greater number and variety of possessions. From the late 1550s objects in each chamber of the hall were even individually numbered. This new system of recording objects must have helped to keep track of growing volumes of things, and perhaps impose a sense of order on communal possessions. The guild appraisers were choosing to represent their company hall as a complex multifunctional space.[103]

Material cultures and guild spaces

Across the sixteenth and early seventeenth centuries, London's guilds accumulated a growing quantity and variety of material goods. Inventories reveal how halls were becoming more comfortable and richly furnished, and guilds were also better equipped to entertain on a grand scale. There is a notable increase in all categories of material cultures, including furniture, plate, textiles (including hangings, cushions, flags, and banners), and cooking equipment. Surfaces were also more richly ornamented with semi-permanent material fixtures like plasterwork and wainscot. Many of the material things utilised and displayed with artisanal architectures had been gifted or bequeathed to the guild by its particular members.

It is striking, too, how guild inventories became increasingly precise about where specific types of goods were stored in the hall. This is a reflection of the increased specialisation of particular rooms. It is a consequence also of the growing range of storage furnishings employed by London's guilds: caskets, settles, hampers, boxes, chests, presses, and cupboards were all named in institutional artisanal inventories. These various chests and boxes enabled the better organisation of large quantities of possessions.[104] Tara Hamling and Catherine Richardson have written of an 'organising and storing mentality' within the homes of England's early modern middling sort. The evidence discussed here supports their analysis for institutions also.[105] Storage containers in mercantile and artisanal halls marked out particular material cultures as being of high material, cultural, or political value, and provided additional security for these goods, beyond that afforded by a locked door. In the 1580s the Pewterers specifically itemised 'the napery in the great chest' (which was located in the counting house). In 1606–7 the Cordwainers Company paid a joiner 'for the new wainscot presse made … to lay in evidence and writinge of the howse'.[106] By the early 1630s the Ironmongers separately listed objects in 'the chest of linen', 'the press of pewter', and 'the great chest'. The latter contained textiles of especially high value: five pieces of tapestry hangings for the hall and a 'new piece of tapestry hanging for the upper end of the parlour of Sir Thomas Campbell's gift'.[107] The use of the new 'court cupboard of wainscot' in the Ironmongers' early seventeenth-century hall chamber additionally facilitated the display of silver plate at ceremonial occasions.[108]

Aside from boxes and chests, napery, armour, and books were the types of material things which were, relatively speaking, acquired in the largest quantities (as discussed in the next chapter, collections of pewter and silver plate fluctuated over time). The Pewterers listed thirty-one individual items of table linen in 1540. Their collection of napery had grown to 233 pieces by 1584, including table cloths, napkins, towels, and carving cloths. Most of these new pieces had been gifted to the company, and a number were also specifically itemised as high-quality damask. Less wealthy artisanal companies, including the Tallow Chandlers', Cutlers', Brown Bakers' and Carpenters' Companies did not record damask napery in the sixteenth century. Their tables would have been furnished with diaper and plain cloth.[109] At Ironmongers' Hall, the linen collection more than doubled in size from the mid-1550s to the late 1580s, from 61 to 140 individual pieces of linen. By the first decade of the seventeenth century, Ironmongers' Hall even had a dedicated 'linen chamber'.[110] Inventories itemise collections of linen and plate with associated lengths and weights in order to assess intrinsic monetary values. These lists also allowed company officials to monitor the movement (and disappearance) of valuable items. Almost all inventories are marked or annotated with the hands of later clerks. A typical note (of unknown date) on the Cutlers' inventory of July 1640 remarks that there is now 'one pye plate' and 'two trencher plat[e]s wanting'.[111] An amendment to the inventory of the yeomanry of the Tallow Chandlers' Company shows that the group rather disastrously 'lost at ye mayor's feast' of 1626 at Guildhall dozens of pewter items, including platters, saucers, and trenchers.[112] Furthermore, inventories enabled guilds to appraise the rate of deterioration of their goods, and thus reassess their re-sale value or decide whether repair or replacement was necessary. The Tallow Chandlers routinely described objects as 'good' or 'bad', depending upon the relative rate of wear and tear.[113] The Founders described objects as 'sore' or 'sere', meaning thin or worn.[114]

Due to high material values and associations with good-fellowship, napery was perceived as an especially appropriate gift from an artisan (or merchant) to his guild. A large napery collection enabled feasting on a grand scale. In 1566 the master and wardens of the Girdlers' Company each donated a dozen linen napkins during their year of service. Margaret West, wife of one of these company officials, also gave a table cloth.[115] Twenty years later, Master Thomas Sherman gave for 'the use of the Company one dozen of napkins wroughte with white worke and marked with the gredyron' (the Girdlers' Company's craft symbol, associated with the gruesome martyrdom of their patron saint St. Laurence).[116] An inventory taken 'of all such goods and ymplements as apperteyne unto the Company of Carpenters' in the early 1630s mentions dozens of 'drap napkins' 'brought by Mr Jerman', 'also he being then Master 1634'.[117]

From the 1580s, all guilds with property were obliged by the Crown to keep an armoury stocked with suits and weapons. This obligation explains the substantial growth in the acquisition of armour and weapons across London's late sixteenth-century company halls.[118] It is revealing, though, that the Armourers' Company was highly atypical in displaying its collection of suits and weaponry: first in the great hall, and later in a gallery set up over the hall chamber. London guilds stored their armour in garrets, largely out of sight from the guild body and visitors to the building. This concealment of arms and armour in low-status upper-floor storage rooms is in contrast to the common practice among mercantile elites of openly displaying collections of armour in the domestic 'symbolic hall'. This spectacle was a means of articulating 'the status of citizens in the urban militia and a sense of urban identity'.[119]

The growth in guild manuscript collections was undoubtedly a product of the burgeoning early modern record-keeping culture, of which civic institutions were a crucial part.[120] As Alexandra Walsham has written, 'record-keeping' was a polyvalent phrase, 'its meanings run the gamut from *making* and *creating* records to *watching*, *guarding*, *saving* and *preserving* them in proper order and form'.[121] Artisanal and mercantile guilds were very actively engaged in all such varied recording-keeping practices, particularly as their property portfolios and charitable bequest grew. The imperative to document guild business and preserve records actively shaped the organisation and use of the company hall. The volumes named in guild inventories were compiled and employed by company clerks for recording oaths, gifts, inventories, acts of parliament, accounts, ordinances, and statutes. Guild inventory-makers distinguished between dozens of different volumes according to their size, colours, materials, designs, aesthetic features, and subject matter. Descriptors included: books with clasps, books with velum covers, volumes embossed, 'great boarded books', 'newly binded' books, and 'an old paper book of building and diverse other matters'.[122] Such was the considerable increase in manuscript writings composed and preserved within company halls that the Tallow Chandlers' guild specifically numbered their charters, deeds, and 'wrytings' in inventories from 1576. The Ironmongers' Company adopted the same strategy for keeping track of their manuscript collection from 1584.[123]

The discovery that London's livery companies acquired greater quantities and varieties of material cultures will not come as a great surprise for scholars of consumption and material culture. London was the national centre – and a growing international hub – for the manufacture, trade, and consumption of luxury goods. Many city artisans and merchants were directly involved in luxury trades. Moreover, though we lack substantial archival evidence for London households before 1660, studies of surviving early modern English inventories indicate that middling, gentry, and mercantile households were acquiring greater volumes and types of material goods from *c.* 1550 (including furniture, kitchenware, linen and clothing).[124]

A sensitivity to social and spatial contexts is, however, vital in understanding the particular ways in which people experienced and valued material cultures.[125] In guild culture, objects did not belong to a specific individual (such as the head of the household), but were held in common. Material collections such as silver plate and linen, were actively utilised to construct and perpetuate a collective memorial, convivial, and specifically homosocial culture, at events like guild feasts and dinners. Material things were also used to manage social relations within guild communities which were undergoing particular experiences of growth and change, as when additional furniture was purchased to accommodate the growing yeomanry estate in the hall.[126] As we have seen, material cultures within artisanal company halls were also very often gifts from prominent and aspiring artisans. These objects were freighted with values, including masculine honour, authority, and workshop expertise that were especially meaningful within the artisanal hall as the centre of craft governance and regulation. The impact and significance of visual symbolism was also rooted in specific spatial contexts. Imagery of patron saints, for instance, was important precisely because these exemplars of (largely) masculine skilled sainthood were located within the communal built environment of a craft institution.[127] And so, growing quantities and varieties of material goods along with heightened specialisation of rooms were hardly phenomena unique to London's artisanal companies, but the ways in which they displayed, employed, and valued things were embedded in distinctive social, political, and cultural contexts.

Foundations enlarged

At the most fundamental level, the ground plan for the new Goldsmiths' Hall in the mid-1630s was on a substantially enlarged site. Ten houses and workshops that surrounded the building were demolished alongside (old) Goldsmiths' Hall in the very early stages of the rebuilding project. It was deemed to be 'a necessitie to alter the whole frame of the old buildinge into a more decent and comodious forme by some enlargement upon their owne grounde'.[128] The Goldsmiths' court minutes also show the often testy negotiations between company authorities and tenants as the hall expansion took place. Wardens were to 'send for such tenna[n]ts as dwell neere the hall whose houses or any parte thereof must of necessitie bee vsed in the new buildinge the hall and to treate w[i]th them for their seu[er]all termes and departures'.[129] Such neighbourhood strains over a major building project in a central urban site are a valuable reminder of just how deeply embedded were the craft company halls in the broader material fabric of the city.

The great hall

The dominant narrative of the hall chamber in domestic buildings in early modern England is of material decline, physical diminishment, and growing social and symbolic irrelevance. In the houses of the London mercantile elite, the space of the open hall, from the mid-fifteenth century, 'was no longer the centre of the house in the sense that it was the place for formal meals bringing together the urban household on a regular basis'.[130] The seventeenth-century London homes of the middling sort experienced 'the decline of the hall and rise of the dining room and parlour'.[131] In the grand country houses of the English gentry and aristocracy, and royal palaces, the familiar account is of a chamber with gradually declining social and architectural significance and prestige, from as early as the second half of the fourteenth century.[132] Though the hall had once been the 'supreme expression of power, ritual, wealth and hospitality', the importance of this communal space declined markedly as senior members of the household, and their large retinue, retreated to more specialised spaces of the house 'for reasons of privacy, comfort, or state'.[133] Grand halls were diminished to a single storey through their ceiling over, and the addition of high-status chambers above.[134] Simon Thurley has shown that with the retreat of the monarch to the Privy Chamber and the installation of grand, processional staircase in palatial residences, the hall chamber was neglected and bypassed.[135]

The position and status of great halls in craft company buildings by the mid-sixteenth century present a more complex picture. These were certainly not abandoned spaces or chambers that had been demoted to mere corridors, as in some grand domestic architectures. Halls remained functionally and symbolically important. The documentary evidence suggests that a large majority of hall chambers in artisanal and mercantile institutional buildings continued to have significant prestige and remained open to the roof. Crucially, the structural organisation and associated symbolism of 'high' and 'low' ends of the hall had enduring relevance and application in spatially, materially, and socially ordering complex artisanal communities. Ceremonially, the hall chamber remained the most significant semi-public space in the entire building complex (semi-public is taken to mean here the most frequently accessed chamber by the diverse guild body).

On election days the guild still 'repared unto the hall where were assembled the most part of the lyverye and yeomanrye unto whom was the ordynance re[a]d as of custome'.[136] The great hall was the chamber in which 'the longevity of the company, the liberality of its benefactors, and the importance of order and unity', were recited to the entire guild membership on quarter days.[137] The guild were summoned here for specific or extraordinary civic and royal announcements too, as in April 1593 when at the Pewterers' great hall 'ther was red unto the whole company' a precept sent by the lord mayor 'tuchyng that all howsholders shall governe ther servaunts and howsold'.[138] In March 1596, concerned that 'asmuche as the yeomanrye is greatly encreasyd so that there is nott in the hall sufficient roome for them to sit for want of place for them', the wardens of the Goldsmiths' Company ordered eight 'short formes [be] made for the better placyinge of them', and for more room the long tables to be lengthened – 'the longe tables are to be sett uppe on the benches, and the trestles carryed out for that instance'.[139] The yeomanry were to be accommodated, but through the use of furniture, and its spatial arrangement, as appropriate to their station. At the same time, with the expansion of artisanal building complexes, and the creation of more specialised spaces for governance, administration, and exclusive socialising, fewer social and political practices were focused upon the hall chamber, and elites retreated to first-floor high-status rooms on a more regular basis. Artisanal company halls were also not in such frequent use as in parallel institutional buildings, such as the Inns of Court and Oxford and Cambridge colleges, where members ate in hall chambers on an almost daily basis.[140]

Guild inventories show how the early modern hall chamber was richly furnished and decorated. The scale, materiality, and craftsmanship of halls was designed to impress the guild body, and a wider group of artisan, merchant, and gentleman visitors. The Tallow Chandlers' mid-sixteenth-century great hall contained a range of furniture and decorative items. In addition to 'a longe Tabill called the heighe Tabill' (for the seating of the guild elite) and two accompanying benches (for liverymen), which were permanent fixtures, the chamber was equipped with several other tables and benches, which were moved between hall and parlour. Spaces were adaptable, and furniture could be rearranged throughout Tallow Chandlers' Hall in order to host a range of events (such as dinners, feasts, and election ceremonies) with a variety of participants. The great hall was ornamented with a table of royal arms, a carpet of silk lined with linen, a gilded wooden lion, fourteen targets (shields) 'great and small', two cloths depicting the assumption of our lady and our lady and saint Elizabeth, and 'a gilt beame with v latyn candilsticks with the ymage of our Lady and a Turtle dove with iiii latyn cheynes longe or short'.[141] By 1576 the Tallow Chandlers also had two royal paintings on display in their hall: one of Henry VIII, and another of Edward VI.[142]

An early seventeenth-century inventory of Cutlers' Hall similarly reveals a richly decorated hall chamber with a variety of furniture. The room contained: three long tables, three dozen joint-stools, a carpet lined with canvas for the high table (seven yards long and a yard and a half broad), two other green carpets, several bankers (fabric coverings for benches, or walls) decorated with elephants and flowers, twelve cushions decorated with elephants, a great fire pan, five banner staves, a bible with a desk, eleven leaden weights, a table and a carving knife (gifted by a former cutler), nine shields with the Cutlers' arms, multiple streamers, banners, and flags, 'the storie of Noa in a table', and a table with the arms of the house. The decorative centrepiece of the hall was 'the angel with a beame hanging'.[143] This was likely an angel of the Annunciation, linked to the Cutlers' medieval fraternity dedicated to the Annunciation. In the early sixteenth century, there had been two angels: one suspended from a beam in the roof, and the other in the bay window.[144] Most unusually, by the mid-1580s the Cutlers' Company had a distinct 'yeomanry hall' chamber on the first floor. Presumably utilised for the yeomanry's quarter day feasts and funeral dinners, the room contained 'an old long table with a turned frame' and five benches (one with arms and a high back). Strikingly, the Cutler's yeomanry hall was 'hanged with stayned cloths of the storie of Shadrach, Meshach, and Abednego' (three young Jews from the Book of Daniel 3:16–28 who were sent to die in a blazing furnace because of their refusal to worship a golden idol of King Nebuchadnezzar II of Babylon; they were subsequently delivered from harm through divine intervention).[145]

This representation of young male heroes must have been particularly appropriate for a space dedicated to the relatively youthful yeomanry estate – men outside the livery who had not yet achieved 'full adult civic masculinity' – and the Old Testament figures' aversion to idol-worship a fitting biblical lesson in a post-Reformation context.[146]

The exceptionally long-running series of inventories of Ironmongers' Hall shows that its great hall was a chamber that became materially richer, and more impressive, over time. In the mid-1550s, it contained two tables, four trestles (which could be easily dismantled and removed), several forms, and half a dozen banner staves. By the late sixteenth century, among other additions, there were two cupboards with a desk to set plate upon, a carving table, and fifty scutcheons of wood hanging on both sides of the hall.[147] By the 1610s the inventory-makers separately itemised material goods in the hall, the chimney in the hall, and the hall window.[148] An inventory of 1640 lists seven pictures hanging in the hall chamber of (unidentified) benefactors.[149]

Documentary evidence also demonstrates how sixteenth- and early seventeenth-century hall chambers were enlarged and materially and architecturally embellished. In the mid-1570s and early 1580s, the Tallow Chandlers undertook substantial material aggrandizements to their hall chamber. First, they contracted a carpenter for his materials and workmanship for 'groundselling the Skrene in the hall'. Later, they employed painters, glaziers, carpenters, pavers, and plasterers for 'the Buylding of the hall windowes celyng and roofe of the hall', at a total cost of over £135.[150] The bills of account show that brown, white, blue, black, and red pigments were sourced for the decoration of the hall, including the 'paynting of the yomanrys [yeomen's'] wyndowe'. The walls of the hall were wainscoted and the floor was tiled.[151]

Amongst some craft companies, the funding of improvements to the hall chamber suggest that the symbolic meaning of this room, as the communal heart of guild life, continued to be relevant. In 1595, after a quarter of a century programme of improvements to their built environment, the Carpenters' Company carried out the substantial 'thenlarginge of the hall at the Eastend'. The total cost of the hall expansion was over £121.[152] This was a considerable sum for a guild that was decidedly artisanal in membership and character. As a basis of comparison, in the same year the income received from quarterage and search fines was just over £24. The income received for rents at London Wall, gardens at London Wall, and at Lime Street was £61. The guild paid £8 9s 10d for the feast at lord mayor's day.[153] Expenses for the rebuilding project included labour costs and materials for carpenters, bricklayers, plasterers, plumbers, and glaziers. The guild was also responsible for the transportation of bulky materials to artisanal workshops in the city, paying 4s, for example, for 'the cariage of a load of tymber from Charing Crosse to John Awnsells yard'.[154] It was presumably at this workman's site that the new timber frame was erected. Significantly, a large proportion of the costs for this project were met by a considerable group of liverymen and yeomen. For the reconstruction of the hall chamber, 120 carpenters personally contributed various quantities of timber or money, depending upon their place within the guild hierarchy. Master carpenter Elias Jerman gave 30s – this was among the six most generous donations.[155] This number of contributors represented just over a third of all members of the guild. Such donations would also have been 'extraordinary expenses', that is, in addition to the regular quarterage fee, which was a fundamental requirement of guild membership.

Likely there were considerable social pressures within the Carpenters' Company to make such a monetary or material subscription to the guild, but nevertheless the sense of communal responsibility for the extension of this particular chamber is suggestive.[156] The rebuilding of the original parlour and the construction of the new parlour chamber fifteen years earlier, in 1579, had been financed through 'the onlie costes and charges of suche money incident in the blak box to this misterie', that is to say, capital reserves stored in the guild's black box (which was itself kept in a 'cheste wy a loke and key').[157] The expenses for building the parlours were thus met through an incidental financial surplus; there was no special fund or subscription set up to ensure the completion of the work. The great hall was the chamber that best symbolised the communal ethos of a craft fraternity. It was traditionally the space within which the whole guild might gather, socialise, drink, and feast together. It was thus highly appropriate that over a third of the freemen of the company, from across the guild hierarchy, materially contributed to the expansion of this communal space, especially since this extension took place at 'the east ende' – the opposite side to the exclusive dais section.

Adjustments to hall chambers were both structural, as in the case of the Carpenters' extension, and involved investments in material fixtures. During the rebuilding of Goldsmiths' Hall in the 1630s, considerable expertise and materials were dedicated to the construction of a new screen for the great hall chamber, which, as previously noted, provided the customary means of formal entrance to the hall.[158] In January 1636/7 the 'manner of the skreene and wainscottinge of the hall according to the draught' were discussed at a committee meeting of the Goldsmiths' rebuilding project.[159] Master joiner Jeremy Kellett was commissioned to set up the screen and wainscot in the hall chamber, and the wooden panelling in the great chamber and new gallery. Thus, the interior decoration was conceptualised here as a coherent scheme running throughout high-status chambers. This marked a change from the usual accretion of interior adornments over time. The ornamentation of the new hall screen was carried out by Mr Taylor the carver. Taylor decorated the structure with five 'effigures [figures] of ffayth hope charitie St Peter and St Dunstane … sett up on the 5 pedastalls over the screene'.[160] In the early seventeenth century, pictures of SS. Peter and Dunstan had been set up on either side of the great window of the hall chamber (situated behind the high table) during the wardens' feast.[161] A sculptural scheme which incorporated saintly representations (fraternal origins) and godly values (such as charity) was particularly apposite at a time when London livery companies were expending unprecedented corporate funds upon charitable endeavours, for the benefit of their own members, and the wider population of the city (see Plate 5).[162] Before the injunctions of 1547 regarding superstitious practices, the guild's most prized communal possession had been a gilt statue set up on the hall screen, 'An image of Seint Dunston sett w[i]t[h] perle and stone'.[163] London's goldsmiths donated gold and precious jewels, 'towards the garnyshing' of the image.[164]

The 1692 ground plan of Goldsmiths' Hall shows a tripartite hall chamber paved with a black-and-white Purbeck marble floor, organised in a chequered pattern (see Plate 4). Purbeck marble was a highly valuable material in medieval and early modern England, sourced only from Corfe on the Isle of Purbeck. Additionally, as an especially dense limestone, it required particularly skilled hands to work it effectively.[165] The open courtyard floor of the Royal Exchange (built between 1566 and 1569) and the arcade floor of the New Exchange (built in 1609) were both also paved with black-and-white marble.[166] The use of this floor design, colour scheme, and high-status material for the Goldsmiths' great hall might thus have been an attempt to associate this institutional space with broader overtones of mercantile sociability, exchange, and commercial accomplishment. In June 1646, surgeon Lawrence Loe gifted to the Barber Surgeons' Company 'for the beautifying of the [upper end] of the Hall soe many stones of black and white Marble as shalbe sufficient for the Pavement thereof'.[167] These were certainly also material improvements to flooring; a century before, in 1540, the floor of the Ironmongers' Hall was simply covered with rushes and sand on prominent feast days.[168]

New and additional chambers: domestic institutional spaces

Homes were constructed within the sixteenth-century hall complex for the accommodation of company clerk, and sometimes beadle, and their respective families. Beadles were responsible for the general maintenance and management of the company hall and estates, for summoning guildsmen to court meetings and funerals, collecting quarterage, and administering punishments to errant apprentices. Clerks were employed to create, manage and preserve guild records and administrative papers; additionally they might provide legal advice.[169] As Matthew Davies writes, the clerks 'also had a public role, coordinating much of the communication with the City government, Parliament and the Crown'.[170] As the halls, estates, and charities of London's guilds expanded in the sixteenth century, so too did the responsibilities and workload of their salaried officials. Having these workers on site at the company hall must have become increasingly important. In November 1592, the assistants of the Pewterers' Company agreed that their clerk William Milles might dwell in 'the ii upper chambers and the ii lyttell garrettes over the sayed chambers' upon condition of payment of £3 per annum and 'his quyet behavyor in the house'.[171] By the mid-sixteenth century, Goldsmiths' Hall had separate 'dwelling houses' on site for company clerk, beadle, and master assayer.[172] The Carpenters' Company clerk's house was renovated in 1604, 'including the addition of a study – no doubt an indication of the growing burden of work carried by this official'.[173] The wife of the company beadle was often remunerated for washing linen after feast days. At Carpenters' Hall, the beadle's wife was paid for a range of essential work tasks, including the 'kepyng of the gardyn', scouring vessels and pots, and washing the textiles of the Hall.[174] These types of labour have been neglected in guild historiography, 'in part thanks to a long-standing bias that separates the productive and public work of making and regulation from the self-effacing 'domestic' or 'private' work of cleaning, maintenance and repair.'[175]

Kitchens, butteries, pantries, and larders

Between 1501 and 1505 a new kitchen, buttery, cellar, larder, and pastry house were added to the Guildhall. These important additions meant that the mayor's inaugural feast could be hosted in this centre of City government, rather than in the Merchant Taylors' and Grocers' Halls, as had been the former custom.[176] These annual banquets at Guildhall 'soon became part of a great seasonal cycle of feasts which joined together the civic, legal and court communities'.[177] The building works were the result of a fundraising initiative by John Shaa, a working goldsmith and master-worker of the Tower mint, mayor in 1501–2. Fifty-nine companies and two wealthy widows contributed a total of over £300 for the completion of the works (the sums donated reflected their position in the civic hierarchy).[178]

At early modern company buildings, kitchens and service rooms – butteries, pantries, and larders – were expanded, rebuilt, or newly added. These additions facilitated dining and feasting on a grander scale. The buttery was 'the principal service room', usually 'found between the hall and the main kitchen'. It was customarily a storeroom for alcoholic drinks.[179] The pantry was traditionally the room where bread and other provisions were kept; the larder was a chamber for storing meat.[180] In 1562 the Girdlers' Company recorded 'the benevolence of the livery towarde the biyldyng of the kytchyn and parlour' (totalling over £35).[181] In 1585 the Carpenters' Company built a new kitchen and ovens (costing over £27), and a year later they constructed a new pantry (costing £13).[182] At Fishmongers Hall 'there was considerable new building with ovens and chimneys in 1605, and that is probably when the great new kitchen was erected as an extension of the service wing'.[183] At Goldsmiths' Hall in 1621 a new cistern was built in the great kitchen to directly receive Thames water.[184]

Kitchens were located on the ground floor of these courtyard properties, and 'the medieval sequence of hall-screens-service rooms-kitchen' was typical.[185] As the Girdlers' Company example suggests, the establishment of food processing, preparation, and storage rooms was a further opportunity for material patronage. In 1522 armourer William Sympson donated to Armourers' Hall for 'the foundation of the chymney in the kitchin two loads of stone'.[186] The close connection of chimney to hearth and its fire, and the hearth's associations with 'the structural and psychological centre of the household' perhaps made this a symbolically significant (as well as functional) gift.[187] Other armourers gave dressing knives and iron pans.[188] At Girdlers' Hall the wardens and liverymen donated 'kytchyng stuff' in 1540. Donations included 'a chaffer' (a vessel for heating water), and 'a brasse pot'. The generous John Thompson gave 'a fryeng pan, a pottell pot, and a drinking pott'.[189]

The well-preserved inventories of the Pewterers' Company offer a valuable impression of the furnished livery hall kitchen, equipped for boiling, frying, roasting, and baking. In 1550 the Pewterers' kitchen contained a great brass pot, a 'lesse' brass pot, a lytle pan of brass, a great pan of brass, a 'spytte square and rounde', a great gridiron, a dripping pan, a pair of iron racks, a stone pestle and mortar, an iron cover 'for the ouyns [oven's] mouth', a dressing board with trestle, a cistern of lead for water, a latten colander, and a latten skimmer and ladle.[190] By 1589 'ii longe tables a kytchyn bourd ii dressyng bour[ds]' and a new great kneading board had been added.[191] The mid-sixteenth-century buttery and cellars contained a little bread chest with a cover, and storage vessels for beer. The pantry housed 'a great cheste bounde w[it]h Iron & a cord', and the larder had 'a boulyng pype to boult [sift or seperate] meale in'.[192]

The parlour

From the mid-sixteenth century there was a definite trend for the rebuilding and embellishment of parlours, and the addition of new parlour chambers. These were typically first or second floor rooms.[193] In 1562, for instance, the Girdlers' guild undertook to build a new parlour and kitchen. The Girdlers' gift book records the names of thirty-five liverymen who gave a grand total of £35 13s 4d towards the effort.[194] The Tallow Chandlers' Company likewise began an extensive parlour re-building scheme in 1569, which involved the relocation of this chamber to a higher storey. It was decided by the company court 'that the parlour and buylding next over shalbe taken downe from the west syde of the hall … And that the same shalbe raysed higher and buylded of new ageyne'. This building project was carried out under the guidance of the master, wardens, and four other tallow chandlers, and it was hoped that design inspiration would come 'by some patterne or example by them to be espied out'. Presumably this process involved close observation of building design throughout the city, including artisanal and mercantile architectures; we saw previously that the Pewterers engaged in a similar scrutiny of neighbouring buildings in the 1490s. The Tallow Chandlers' account book for this period records all the bills associated with 'the beautifyeing of the said house'.[195] Carpenter Thomas Watts was paid £60 'for the new frame Joyninge to our hawle', and £4 'for wetherbording of the owt syde of the greate frame'. Plasterer Barfield was paid over £16 for 'seling' [sealing] the parlour and a new court house, and two joiners presented a bill of £73 for wainscoting the two new rooms.[196] Later in the year a glazier was employed 'for iiii paynes with arms standing in the parlor windowe'.[197]

In 1579, a decade after the Tallow Chandlers' beautification project, the Carpenters' Company also remodelled their existing parlour, and built a new parlour chamber on a higher level: that 'thold parlor to be new mad[e] and one other parlor over that with the half ... storie shall forthwithe be made'.[198] The new parlour was subsequently 'celed with wainskote'; it was 'a major addition and might have almost doubled the size of the Hall'.[199] In an inventory of 1604 the Bakers' Company referenced 'the newe p[ar]llor'. Less than a decade later they had also constructed a 'new p[ar]llor over the courte parlor [chamber]'. Both were upper-storey rooms with fireplaces. The latest 'new' parlour was evidently the more comfortable and prestigious chamber as it contained three long tables, eighteen 'joyned' stools, and a 'faire new picture of King James'. By comparison, the older parlour room was sparsely furnished, containing a single long table with a frame.[200] A new 'great parlour' and gallery were added to Barber Surgeons' Hall in 1637, at a cost of over £263 (largely financed by forty-one members of the company, whose names were recorded in a building funds book). A tablet of stone was set in the front of the new parlour chamber inscribed with the date of establishment, and the names of master and wardens.[201]

The inventories of the Pewterers' Company are suggestive of the growing status of the parlour chamber across the sixteenth century. The early sixteenth-century parlour was relatively bare, containing basic furniture – long table, trestles, and joined forms – banner staves, and targets (or shields) of the gift of Robert Taylor, 'one of our lady assumption and one with the kyngs Armes'.[202] By comparison, the counting house at this date contained a wide range of precious belongings, including silver and pewter plate, moulds (for pewter plates, dishes, and saucers), election garlands, banners, napery, patents, and writings. The relative significance of these rooms had plainly shifted by the time 'the new parlour' is listed in 1559. The counting house has a more singular administrative function, as the room in which accounts are kept, whereas the parlour is the more socially and politically significant chamber – the centre of guild administration, regulation, and governance.

This alteration in status is evidenced by the changing situation of objects of great material and symbolic value. The new parlour room contained silver spoons, election garlands, multiple chests, boxes, cases, and caskets holding the common seal of the guild, significant artisanal wills, patents, and even 'the evydence of our hall and our lands in Lymestreate'. The parlour also housed 'grete Borded bokes of the acompts of the wardens', the guild's licence to search (artisanal workshops and retail sites), a wooden 'table with the names of the Clothing [livery] written', and a pewter table marked with 'the marcks of all the whole crafte'. By contrast, the Pewterers' counting house now accommodated much fewer, less precious, and rather more dated communal possessions, including basic wooden furniture, bags of books of complaints and old ordinances, and old ceremonial textiles, such as 'Banners of the olde armes of the Crafte' and 'olde Streamers of Saynt Mighell'.[203] The counting house of the Cutlers' Company was equipped with furniture appropriate for financial administration and organisation, including 'a folding table with a chest in it and a trestle for it', a great chest 'barred with iron', and 'a new press with boxes in it'.[204] No decoration or ornamentation is recorded for the Ironmongers' late sixteenth-century counting chamber.[205] The counting house was understood to be a necessary administrative adjunct to the parlour, as demonstrated by the construction of a counting house at Carpenters' Hall in 1592 from 2,000 bricks and tiles, 'made oute of the well yard to serve for the parler next adjoyninge unto the hall'.[206] At contemporary London properties surveyed by Ralph Treswell, the counting house 'could be found at the back of a warehouse or at the back of a shop', and alongside a gallery.[207]

At the mercantile Ironmongers' Hall the growing status of the parlour was even more clearly marked with material fixtures. By the first decade of the seventeenth century, wainscot partitions had been inserted into the chamber to create a distinct 'upper end of the parlour'. This space was further distinguished through being furnished with what was effectively a high table, and 'a settle [long bench] of wainscot with turned pillars round about'. Evidently here the traditional 'high' and 'low' spatial organisation and syntax of the hall chamber had been transplanted to the parlour. By the same date the parlour chamber even had its own dedicated buttery, separate from the buttery which serviced the main hall. This storeroom contained additional furniture which could be 'set in the parlour if needs require'.[208]

Although the parlour room had always had associations of relative privilege and exclusivity, there is considerable evidence from *c.* 1560, across the London companies, that guild governance, regulation, and elections were becoming progressively concentrated within this space. The relative privacy of the parlour, and the ability of assistants to withdraw from the commonality to discuss matters of policy and finance, was central to a system of governance in which access to words, policies, and documents of authority were closely monitored. Secrecy, Paul Griffiths contends, 'protected existing structures of authority'.[209] And 'exclusion from knowledge' more generally 'tracks the topography of power'.[210] Across guild, civic, and parochial government in London, elites 'preferred to meet behind closed doors, and the exclusive nature of proceedings helped to institutionalize inequality by restricting access'.[211] Notably at Guildhall, the heart of civic governance, it was decided in 1611 that a new council chamber was to be constructed (initially the plan was for the new chamber to be built of 'the best free stone', but it was later decided to use brick 'w[i]th much less charge ... and the windowes onely of freestone').[212] A gallery and a 'bookehouse' were added in the same decade, and the treasury 'for keeping the Cittyes othes and records' was enlarged. These architectural additions were evidently intended to facilitate political withdrawal and privacy for the mayor, 'his bretheren the Aldermen, and the learned Councell and officers of this Cittye'.[213] It was decided in October 1619 'that the place intended for a bookehouse at the end of the gallery enteringe into the Councell Chamber shalbe a retiringe place for the Lord Maior and Aldermen'.[214] To heighten the 'delight' of these civic elites and provide 'a place of recreac[i]on', 'the carpenters yarde and the yard next beyond that beinge in sight of the Councell Chamber' were 'converted into a garden' in 1620.[215]

At craft company halls, the structural and material embellishments of parlours and their physical relocation to first and second floors, which has just been evidenced, were hugely important to this political choreography of withdrawal. In the early 1570s this trend towards spatial exclusivity in Goldsmiths' Hall was keenly noticed by those who lacked the social and professional privileges to partake in the processes of governance. Complaints were received from the yeomanry that guild matters were being determined in the parlour in a 'hugger mugger' (secretive) fashion.[216] Lena Cowen Orlin has written of 'the development, by the mid-sixteenth century, of the corporate parlor as an exclusionary space'.[217] Robert Tittler has remarked upon an analogous tendency within the town halls of provincial government during this era.[218] In middling and elite domestic residences, too, parlours 'responded to a desire for greater comfort and privacy, while advertising wealth and status through the display of impressive material goods'. Moreover, Tara Hamling and Catherine Richardson have found that in the homes of the middling sort there was a meaningful 'relationship between urban office-holding, authority and the developing space of the parlour'.[219] In company halls the development of the parlour room and the increasingly secretive nature of social and political practices among London's most authoritative artisans were mutually reinforcing processes. For instance, it is highly revealing that the Pewterers' court of assistants – consisting of all guildsmen who had formerly served as master and wardens – was formally established in 1560, a year or two after the new parlour had been built and furnished.[220] At Pewterers' Hall the new parlour space enabled more exclusive political activities to take place.

The treasury

A dedicated treasury – a chamber specifically designated for storage of precious or valuable items – was a relatively rarity within institutional artisanal or mercantile architectures in London. Typically it was the wealthiest livery companies who had what the Merchant Taylors (alternatively) referred to in an inventory of 1512 as a 'Jowell House'.[221] At Goldsmiths' Hall the treasury housed plate, and from the later sixteenth century it also accommodated significant books and papers drawn up by the company clerk.[222] We can thus see this treasury chamber operating as a type of guild archive, access to which was very closely controlled. The treasury door was permanently locked and the keys to the chamber were kept solely in the custody of the upper warden.[223] On 'give up' day in May (the scripted handover of official responsibilities following the election) the keys were exchanged – between former and current upper wardens – along with an inventory of the treasury's contents.[224] Certainly, 'the possession of keys unlocked secrets', as well as access to material treasures, and custody of keys 'was also a mark of status, a function of responsible office and seniority'.[225]

Discussions at the Goldsmiths' Company court in March 1635/6 reveal the practical and symbolic significance of the position of the treasury within the newly rebuilt Goldsmiths' Hall. It was decided by a large majority at the ballot box that the treasury was to be placed 'betweene the hall and parlor and the dore to open into the parlor' (namely, the more exclusive and inaccessible of the two chambers).[226] The ground plan of Goldsmiths' Hall shows that only those with substantial political capital – citizens who might be seated or circulate at the high end of the hall – thus had access to the route which led directly into the treasury and parlour. The image of the interior of the communal hall, painted from the perspective of the dais end looking out towards the screen shows the doorway to the treasury and parlour, complete with elaborate cornice, on the right-hand side of the high table (see Plate 5). On account of its precious contents, the treasury was, in the language of space syntax, a 'terminal space', connected to the rest of Goldsmiths' Hall by a single entrance.[227] The physical proximity of treasures to the governing body of the guild must have been a necessity – for reasons of security and ease of access for service at the high table in the hall chamber – but such closeness might also be construed as a symbolic statement of value and familiarity. The governing body of

1 John Ward, *Goldsmiths' Hall: bird's-eye view*, watercolour, 1692. This is effectively a representation of the building from the late 1630s.

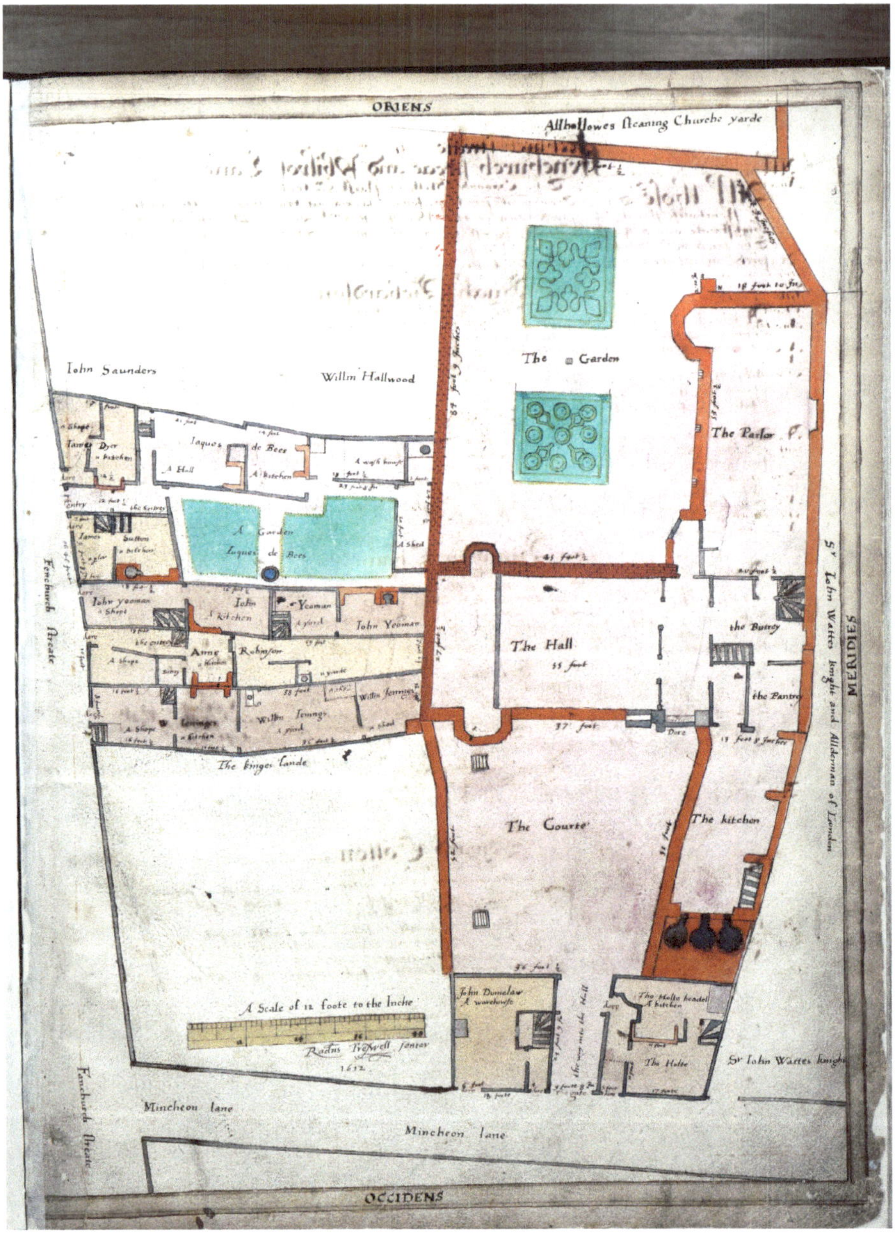

2 *Clothworkers' Hall, Mincing Lane, and 47–8 Fenchurch Street*, 1612. The Clothworkers' Company, Treswell Plan Book, CL/G/7/1, fo. 12r.

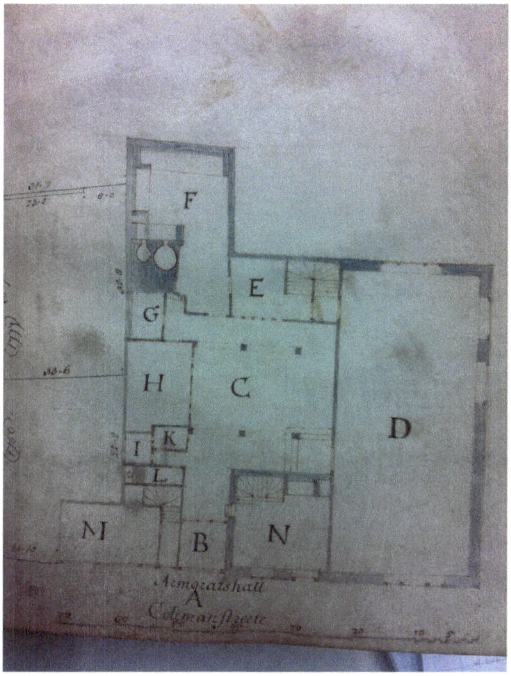

3 Joseph Titcombe, *Armourers' Hall, Coleman Street*, 1679. GL, MS 12104. Eighteenth-century building extensions added to the left-hand side of the building plan.

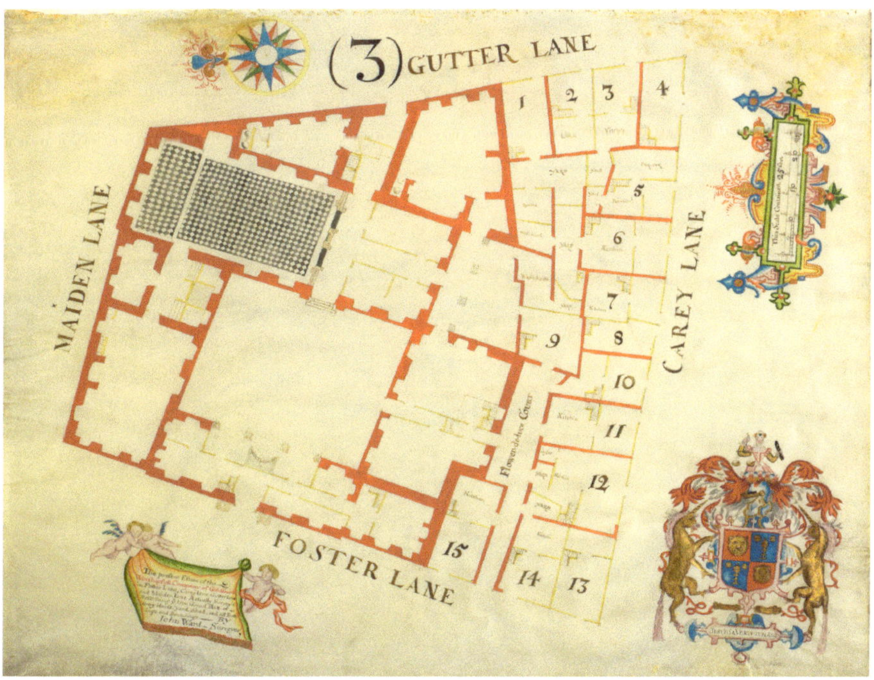

4 John Ward, *Goldsmiths' Hall: ground-storey plan*, watercolour, 1692.

5 John Ward, *Goldsmiths' Hall: interior of the hall chamber* (from the perspective of the dais end), watercolour, 1692.

6 John Ward, *Goldsmiths' Hall: elevation of Foster Lane front*, watercolour, 1692.

7 *Noah and the construction of the ark*, engraving by F. W. Fairholt of the original sixteenth-century wall painting at Carpenters' Hall (now lost), 1848.

8 *King Josiah ordering the repair of the temple*, wall painting on lime plaster, Carpenters' Hall, *c*. 1570.

9 *A youthful Christ in St. Joseph's workshop*, wall painting on lime plaster, Carpenters' Hall, *c.* 1570.

10 *Christ teaching in the synagogue*, wall painting on lime plaster, Carpenters' Hall, *c.* 1570.

11 *William Portington, Master Carpenter*, oil on panel, *c.* 1637, attributed to Emmanuel De Critz. This painting is based upon a (lost) portrait undertaken in *c.* 1626. The textual inscription reads: 'Will[ia]m Portington Esq. M[aste]r Carpenter in ye office of his Ma[jest]es buildings: who served in ye place 40. yeeres and departed this life ye 28 of march 1628 being aged 84 yeeres, who was a well wisher to this societie this being ye gift of Mathew Bankes who served him 14 yeeres and is at this present M[aste]r of the said co[m]panie. Aug. 19 1637.'

12 William Vynyard, *St. George and the Dragon*, oak, iron, leather, and horse hair, h. (excluding sword) 84.5 cm, *c.* 1528. Gifted by Vynyard to the Armourers' and Brasiers' Company.

13 *Roger Tyndall, Master Armourer*, 1585. Tyndall was a major benefactor of the Armourers' and Brasiers' Company. He served as master of the guild three times between 1559 and 1577.

14 Sixteenth-century ceremonial crowns, Carpenters' Company.

the Goldsmiths' Company and their plate and treasures effectively shared one wing of the new hall, and their proximity mutually reinforced their significance.

The treasury at Barber Surgeons' Hall on Monkwell Street comes into very clear archival focus on the occasion of a dramatic break-in on the night of 7 November 1615. After 'the Robbinge of o[u]r Hall', the guild 'plate was carried to Westm[inster] and our monie was devided amongst the theves'. Following orders from the master, the company clerk 'went to Westm[inster] and upon search there made found our plate locked up in a trunke in the howse of … a shoemaker'. Four men were apprehended, sentenced, and executed for the crime. The clerk, beadle, and porter were each given a financial reward for 'their paynes taken in apprehending the theves and obteyninge our plate'. Tellingly, in response to the treasury breach, it was immediately decided at the Barber Surgeons' court that 'a present course be taken for the spedie repaieringe' of the treasury, 'and that the same shalbe forthwith stronglie borded and made up'.[228]

In the absence of a dedicated treasury, artisanal guilds stored valuable and precious things in counting houses, parlours, butteries, and garrets. In 'the Roome behind the old Parlor' the Armourers' Company stored 'two presses with lockes and keyes, one for the Company leases and other writings, the other for the Company Gownes Banners and Streamers'.[229] The Founders' guild kept significant papers and books and their plate collection in a chamber described as 'the inner buttery'. This small chamber operated as their corporate archive. The security of this room was closely managed with a series of locks and keys, and the keys were in the custody of authoritative guildsmen. The wardens accounts of 1614–15 relate that a particular valuable 'bonnd is lockte with the housse plate within the inner buttry … in a cheste with three lockes and the keys remayne in the handes of the Master, Upper Warden and Senior Assistant and the dore key with the Younger Warden'. By the mid-1640s the Founders 'inner-buttery' collection had grown considerably: 'In the iner buttery in the great trunke this plate following: 13 peeces of plate waying 128 ounces and 37 spoones, sume white, sume gilte … Mr. Rowding's leaces of 2 howses standing in Lothburie, which comes into the Companies handes uppon Michaelmus next, 1647, and the Merchantes bond of 300 li with the Companis Corporation, with many other ould wrightinges belonging unto the said Company.'[230]

For City guilds that lacked a hall of their own, a single wooden chest might come to represent, house, and preserve the entire guild archive.[231] The seventeenth-century Clockmakers' Company (incorporated in 1631) had such a chest, which moved between various private, commercial, and institutional city locations. This trunk contained all the guild's 'writings and papers' and plate.[232] Company business required the master and wardens 'to open the company chest'.[233] In the early 1650s the company's chest was stored at Painter Stainers' Hall (for which privilege the guild paid £3 per annum), but by March 1657/8 it was 'kept in Dunstanes Vestery house' (the vestry house of St. Dunstan-in the-West in Fleet Street).[234] By the end of the decade the chest had been moved to the guild master's house, with the guild charter 'locked into the Chest', and an inventory taken 'of all thinges locked therein'.[235] From that point onwards the chest was stored in the guild master's house and would be moved annually to its new home at the inauguration of the latest official.[236] For example, in October 1672 when clockmaker Samuel Home was 'sworne and tooke his place ... Mr Nicholas Coxeter the late Master delivered up to him' the guild chest.[237] The Clockmaker's court minutes outline very clear 'directions to unlock and lock the companyes chest'. These guidelines established that opening and locking the chest required three separate keys for three locks, with keys in the custody of the guild master, upper warden, and renter warden.[238]

Staircases and galleries

In late sixteenth- and seventeenth-century guild halls the installation of new staircases worked to create novel and exclusive routes through institutional buildings. Stairways were typically established on the ground floor and led directly to high-status chambers on the first floor. At Barber Surgeons' Hall it was decided in September 1605 to 'proceed w[i]th worcke now in hand for the erectinge of a steyre and steyrecase to be made to passe through the p[ar]lor into the ... garden plott'.[239] At the Tyler and Bricklayers' Company Hall there was 'new building of stairs into [the] parlour' in the 1630s.[240] The rebuilding of Goldsmiths' Hall allowed for a substantial expansion and reconfiguration of staircases. In November 1637 it was decided to demolish the old 'paire of staires leadinge up into the dyneing roome over the Butteries ... there shalbee aanew paire of staires erected in their sted w[hi]ch shallbee more large and convenient for the companyes use'. At the same court meeting it was also decided to go ahead with 'the makeinge of the great pairre of staires leading up into the great chamber [from the courtyard] upon view of the ground designed for the same'. Both new staircases were designed by mason Nicholas Stone.[241] The prestige of this new route was materially reinforced through 'the carveinge of turned pillers and railes of the great staires leadinge vp into the great chamber'. Taylor, the carver, had also been employed for his work on the '5 effigures of ffayth hope and charitie St Peter and St Dunstane ... sett vp on the 5 pedastalls ouer the [hall] screene'.[242] This was an era in which the staircase emerged as an elaborate showcase for the artisanal skills of joiners and carvers. As on their screen in the communal hall, it is probable that the newels, turned balusters, and finials of the Goldsmiths' Company's staircases were ornamented with heraldic symbolism and sculpted figures.[243]

Evidently at Goldsmiths' Hall there was a coherent plan to create more grandiose and direct access routes from the ground floor to the first floor of the new building. The creation of lavishly decorated direct routes to chambers of governance and authority allowed for the circumvention of any ground-floor rooms associated with food preparation, domestic, or administrative labour. Use of the new staircases would likely have been a privilege associated with livery status; it also reinforced this honoured position. Unless specifically brought before the assistants to answer for a particular offence, or to present an apprentice, the yeomanry of the guild would have been restricted to the courtyard, hall chamber, and assay office. The installation of new staircases was probably also motivated by the desire for clear processional routes to privileged first-floor spaces of governance, conviviality, and recreation. This was particularly apposite in the early seventeenth century, when civic ceremony, specifically the lord mayor's show, was becoming an increasingly extravagant and competitive event.[244]

Together with staircases, galleries were another notable structural addition that reorganised the flow of guildsmen and visitors around the building. Through restricted use they could also work to emphasise internal guild hierarchies. The Armourers' Company had a 'harniss' gallery from the 1580s, specifically for displaying armour. But by the mid-seventeenth century Armourers' Hall also had an 'Outer Gallery' and a 'Gallery over the hall'.[245] The 'Outer Gallery' was likely the building feature which encircled the courtyard and is visible on their property plan of 1679 (see Plate 3). In 1572–73 the Carpenters' Company itemised in their accounts charges towards the setting up of a wainscoted gallery, and in 1614 the 'chardges layd out about makinge the Gallerye in the Court before the Hall, the Staire Case and Staires leadinge to it'.[246] An inventory taken by the Carpenters' Company in the 1630s lists a 'long gallery', a 'crosse gallery' and an 'upper gallery'.[247] By 1609 the Ironmongers' Company was including a gallery in its hall inventories (it contained twelve staves and twenty-two scutcheons of wood 'for men to beare').[248] A gallery was added to Barber Surgeons' Hall in March 1636/7 immediately following the construction of an anatomy theatre (it appears to have led directly from parlour to theatre).[249]

Galleries served a variety of purposes. They could operate as corridors linking high-status rooms (as at Barber Surgeons' Hall), or else as viewing platforms above the hall chamber or courtyard (as at the Armourers' and Carpenters' institutional buildings). Galleries acted as relatively secluded spaces for display, conversation, and indoor exercise, as was likely the case with the prestigious 'long galleries' located in the Clothworkers' and Goldsmiths' Company Halls (both furnished with fireplaces).[250] During the early seventeenth-century rebuilding of Goldsmiths' Hall it was resolved by vote amongst the company elite '14. against. 1. That both a Gallery and Tarras shall be made'.[251] A 'tarras' or 'terrace' was an elevated place for walking, often open on one or both sides.[252] The Goldsmiths' new gallery was situated on the first floor, most likely along the 'front' of the new building, facing out onto Foster Lane. Since galleries in large late medieval and early modern houses customarily lay deep within buildings, often alongside gardens, we might speculate that the new placement of the Goldsmiths' gallery along the street-front was intended to suggest, by contrast, a novel dialogue with the broader built environment.[253] The 'outward looking' gallery at Goldsmiths' Hall (which also allowed for a symmetrical face for the new building) existed in tension with the 'inward looking' courtyard formation within the walls. Internally, the company assistants closely regulated social access to the new gallery.[254]

Interior decorative schemes

From the mid-sixteenth century, interior surface decoration, such as plasterwork and wainscot, was widely applied throughout remodelled and new high-status chambers within institutional artisanal buildings, including halls, parlours, great chambers, and galleries. Tellingly, the Ironmongers' Company referred to their parlour as 'The parlar joyned rownd a bowght' (no other chamber had such a material descriptor).[255] These ornamental features undoubtedly contributed to the general beautification of architectures, but their application also enabled the material articulation of routes of status and authority through buildings. In 1561 the Armourers' Company decided to 'wayneskott the neither ende of their hall and to make iii dores half wayneskott … that is to saye the hall dore the buttre dore and the officers parlor doore'.[256] Routes of prestige through the building were thus highlighted through wooden panelling.[257] Similarly, at Goldsmiths' Hall, stonework traced paths of status throughout the building. The use of Portland stone and marble for significant features of the hall chamber, great chamber (including for 'the dorecase at the great staires head leadinge into the greate chamber'), and gallery articulated clear visual cues for how guildsmen or visitors should proceed within these spaces (with suitable decorum), or indeed which individuals might pass through at all.[258]

At Carpenters' Hall the materiality of wainscot might also have been central to its value and significance. The first major early modern adaptation to Carpenters' Hall was the setting up of a wainscoted gallery and the wainscoting of their hall chamber in 1572–73 (probably only at the dais end). Through the wainscoting of their walls, the sixteenth-century Carpenters' Company encased the guild body within a material demonstration of wood-working craft skills. Wainscoting was generally the preserve of joiners, though the assembly and installation of wainscot panels could require the combined artisanal endeavours of both joiners and carpenters.[259] Whilst there is evidence that other guilds painted their wainscot panels – green was the preferred colour – the Carpenters' Company left their boards unadorned.[260] Bare wainscot would have drawn attention to the basic materiality of the craft. Significantly, the panels installed in the gallery, hall, and later the 'new' parlour, were considered to be of substantial

Figure 4.1 Carved wooden panels from Carpenters' Hall, 1579. The panels feature the arms of the guild and tools of the craft, the trade mark of master Thomas Harper, and the names of the wardens. The panels commemorate the rebuilding of the company parlour and building of a new parlour chamber.

cultural value to the Carpenters' Company for many generations beyond their initial installation. When the sixteenth-century building was entirely demolished in the nineteenth century (1876–1880) selected panels were preserved (along with Jacobean oak chimney pieces) and installed in the new Carpenters' Hall. Three of these original sixteenth-century carved panels survive and are displayed in the latest company hall (opened in 1960) (see figure 4.1). Marked with the arms of the guild, tools of the craft, the date of their installation, and the names and trade or craft marks of the master and wardens, these panels are clear exemplars of the physical incorporation of civic and craft identities into beautified built fabrics. Across London livery halls, interior decorative schemes provided opportunities for particular craftsmen or artisanal dynasties to make their mark on the communal built fabric. In the next chapter we will see how artisans competed through material donations to have their initials, craft symbols, and armorial bearings embedded within the hall through the media of wood, stone, plaster, and glass.

Notably, the structural and material changes undertaken at Carpenters Hall in the early 1570s were accompanied by a striking addition to the hall chamber. Around the same time as wainscot was installed, several senior members of the Carpenters' Company commissioned a series of four wall paintings depicting the illustrious biblical history of the craft of carpentry for the decoration of the dais end of their communal hall (see Plates 7–10).[261] These images, approximately three feet high and twenty-three feet in length, were organised as a coloured narrative frieze, with each image framed and separated from the others by a classically inspired architectonic border.[262] Three of the wall paintings are still extant, displayed in the current Carpenters' Hall. In the sixteenth century the images were directly applied upon a surface of brown earth and clay, spread with a thin layer of lime plaster.[263] A sketch made of the original location of the paintings at the west end of the hall – upon their rediscovery under painted canvas in the mid-1840s – gives a clear sense of their centrality and visibility at the high end of the chamber (see figure 4.2). The paintings depict the crucial role of carpentry throughout Old and New Testament biblical history: Noah receiving the command of God for the construction of the ark, and his three sons at work (Genesis 6.9–22); King Josiah ordering the rebuilding of the Temple at Jerusalem (2 Kings 22.1–7); a youthful Jesus (and Mary) obediently aiding Joseph in his carpentry workshop (Luke 2.41–52); and Jesus, 'the carpenter's son', teaching in the synagogue (Matthew 13.53–58).[264] Each image is accompanied by the associated biblical verse in a black letter inscription. The clear emphasis on the 'process of a story' was perhaps a self-conscious attempt to avoid allegations of idolatry.[265]

Conspicuously, in three of the frames, full-bearded mature male figures are featured wearing contemporary livery dress of the 1560s/1570s, with distinctive black caps and fur-trimmed gowns, alongside those dressed in 'traditional' biblical costume.[266] As a material signifier of civic prestige and privilege, gowns or 'liveries' were highly valued possessions. To wear the full livery (gown and hood) was to be a liveryman, and thus part of the City's artisanal and mercantile elite (see figure 4.3). As Barbara Hanawalt has written, 'outward appearances measured a man's and a gild's status, setting them apart in the streets [and in the company hall] and showing where they stood on the social ladder in a very hierarchical society'.[267] Liveries were frequently named in mercantile and artisanal testamentary bequests as distinguished movables, bestowed on particularly favoured family members, kin or members of the workshop.[268]

It is probable that the liverymen within the Carpenters' Company tableau were likenesses of the commissioners of the paintings, and thus the guildsmen in question were immortalised in these historic narratives alongside senior biblical figures. In the Josiah and the carpenters scene, a single figure, dressed in sixteenth-century livery, gazes directly at the viewer; in the Joseph carpentry workshop painting, a liveryman directly intervenes in the visual narrative, directing our attention to the large horizontal plane of wood that Joseph works. This personal inclusion in the mural might

Figure 4.2 *Wall paintings at Carpenters' Hall.* This engraving was undertaken in 1846, following the re-discovery of the sixteenth-century paintings.

Figure 4.3 *Civic costume*, engraving, *c.* 1600.

have been an enterprising means of establishing individual authority and memorialisation within a broader visual statement about communal craft identity and antiquity.[269] Such a personal rendering within a wider pictorial narrative would also have alluded to the fraternal tradition, throughout late medieval Europe, of patronal representation within ecclesiastical fixtures such as stained glass and altarpieces – for instance, the representation of 'the life of St Dunstan and the figures of me and my two wives' designed and commissioned for a window of St. Dunstan's chapel in the church of St. Vedast by the goldsmith Henry Coote in 1513.[270]

We can imagine how these paintings projected an apposite statement of civic authority, particularly when the hall was set up for feasts and dinners, with guildsmen hierarchically organised throughout the chamber and the most authoritative liverymen dining directly below their visual counterparts. Situated in the most 'public' space of Carpenters' Hall and positioned at the dais end of the internal hall, thus visible to all freemen looking towards the privileged west end of the room, the Carpenters' wall paintings might have been interpreted as a didactic statement about the ideal nature of social and political relations within a guild community. In each image of the Carpenters' frieze, a senior, respected male figure of authority is depicted in the act of instruction: God commanding Noah; Josiah ordering the rebuilding of the Temple; the figure of the liveryman directing Joseph's labour; Christ preaching in the synagogue.[271] The hierarchies embedded within the masculine institution of the guild – political relations that intensified as the century progressed – were shown to have scriptural or historical precedents. By the late 1630s, another representation of mature artisanal masculinity, 'Mr Portingtons picture', was displayed in the hall chamber alongside the murals.[272] This posthumous portrait of the carpenter William Portington, former master of the Carpenters' Company, and the king's Master Carpenter for half a century from 1579 to 1629, presented this hugely accomplished artisan in sombre civic dress with the tools of his craft, dividers and rule, in his hands (see Plate 11).[273] Based upon an original portrait of *c.* 1626 (now lost), the corporate version of Portington's likeness was undertaken in 1637, and, according to a textual inscription at the base of the portrait, gifted and presented for display in Carpenters' Hall by Matthew Bankes, 'who served him 14 years'. The representation of this great guildsman with his workshop tools, 'in the action of conducting measurement', was a clear visual memorial of Portington's artisanal skills and civic identity.[274] It signified also a continued connection to the living artisanal community, including carpenter Bankes, who had trained within Portington's workshop and was master of the guild himself in 1637.

The wall paintings at Carpenters' Hall were perhaps also a commentary on current rebuilding practices and the centrality of the guild to these exercises. The murals marked a significant event in the communal life of the guild: they were undertaken at the start of the rebuilding of Carpenters' Hall, and were likely commissioned at the same time as the dais end of the internal hall was wainscoted (the early 1570s), and a wood panelled gallery was also established. Within the next twenty years a new parlour had been built, a counting house was constructed, and the internal hall was substantially enlarged 'at the east ende'.[275] The paintings were thus not simply an isolated visual statement about the genealogy of the craft but were themselves an integral element of the new built environment. Visual representations of reconstruction or rebuilding were highly apposite at a time of structural remodelling, drawing attention to the surrounding materiality of the new Carpenters' Hall – in particular, the oak panelling. In a cultural context within which painting was not understood 'as an autonomous art object', and boundaries between 'wall' and 'painting' were yet to be precisely defined, a narrative history of the craft of carpentry was embedded in the built fabric of Carpenters' Hall and memorialisation of eminent guildsmen inseparable from collective physical structures.[276]

Conclusion: why adapt or rebuild?

Rebuilding(s), and adaptations to domestic, commercial, and civic structures, were widespread across early modern England, in both rural and urban contexts. A wide variety of social groups, including yeomen farmers, middling urban sorts, merchants, gentry, and the aristocracy, were engaged in rebuilding practices, particularly from the mid-sixteenth century.[277] But there is no single comprehensive explanation to account for this re-investment in the built environment. Pioneering work by archaeologists and historians has repeatedly stressed the socially, politically, and culturally specific meanings and uses of buildings, and adaptations to them. Moreover, the idea that a growth in affluence necessarily and straightforwardly resulted in rebuilding initiatives has been shown to be largely unsatisfactory in explaining changes to civic and domestic buildings.[278] In the case of guildhalls in provincial towns, decisions to restructure or adapt came not from 'any particular desire for ostentation' during a time of prosperity, or a change in styles or techniques of vernacular construction, but rather a political need: 'to symbolize the attainment of civic authority from seigneurial hands and the exercise of that authority over the community'.[279] Hamling and Richardson found that the mutable nature of middling status was precisely what fuelled 'investment in buildings, decoration and furnishings'. Improvements to the domestic built fabric 'became so notable and significant a priority for those engaged in consolidating and exhibiting their social position'.[280]

In accounting for the very considerable expense, time, materials, and craftsmanship invested in company buildings, as well as the substantial changes to building layout, circulation patterns, furnishings, and in some instances external design, there is no specific, straightforward rationale. In their archives, early modern artisanal and mercantile guilds provide no explicit motivation, beyond vague statements of material improvement and, perhaps, enhanced comfort. In the mid-1580s the Ironmongers simply stressed 'that the hall belongeinge to the Comp[a]nie beinge ruinous and in greate decaye shalbe furth[er]with newe builded'.[281] Fairly typical was the declaration in 1622 by the assistants of the Plumbers' Company, that 'the hall and house which is our usuall place of resort … to be repayred and made decent and comely'.[282] But in this discussion of continuity and change in the artisanal built fabric, we have encountered several explanatory themes, none of which is exclusive. These include the social and political organisation of the guild body, the management of growing collections of material possessions, and the mutually reinforcing relationship between material sponsorship of the built environment and the promotion of individual and collective statuses.

Livery hall rebuilding was associated with the attempted ordering of social and political relations. The expansion of halls and modifications to chambers and access routes were clearly important in structuring growing artisanal communities. The new interior configurations of halls, particularly the installation of staircases and galleries, and the relocation of high-status rooms to upper storeys, inscribed hierarchy into the built fabric and social organisation of space. As Helen Hills contends, 'architecture does not simply frame a pre-existing practice; it serves to produce specific social practices and social relations. It is both the locus and the agent of change.'[283] The experiences of living, working within, and visiting these artisanal buildings shaped what it meant to be an authoritative artisan and a member of a craft company in late sixteenth- and early seventeenth-century London. Key features of institutional artisanal lives, including feasting and the testing of products and materials, were both fashioned by the changing material fabric of the guild and helped shape it. The forms, uses, and perceptions of company halls worked to define relationships and hierarchies within the guild, and framed its external civic and political relations.

Changes to company halls were also closely related to the proliferation of material goods within the guild 'house'. Growing quantities and varieties of material cultures needed to be displayed, stored, and managed in secure and culturally meaningful ways. Many of these objects and interior decorative features were gifted. Hence, we have begun to observe the mutually constitutive relationship between institutional built environments and artisanal and civic social behaviours and cultural identities. London's leading artisans reinforced and perpetuated status and reputation through contributions to the design, built fabric, and furnishings of craft company buildings. Individual identities could be defined or enhanced through close material association with the artisanal hall. The collective splendour and status of the guild – especially in relation to other artisanal companies – were reciprocally enhanced in the process. Architectural changes and material enhancements must have been perpetuated and extended by an internal competitive dynamic within guilds, and a keen awareness of the improvements taking place at neighbouring company halls. The competitive intra-guild dimension of sponsorship of the urban material fabric was likely extended also to the parish churches with which guilds were closely associated. From the 1590s, 'and gaining considerable momentum during the reign of James I', London's parish churches underwent considerable programmes of repair and ornamentation.[284] City guilds, keen to 'have their ties to the parish, as well as their contributions, publicly recognized', might for instance sponsor the new glazing of a church window, such as the Salters' Company arms in a stained-glass window at All Hallows Bread Street.[285] Others invested in the repair of the steeple, as concerned the Goldsmiths' Company at the church of St. John Zachary in 1628, and the Pewterers' Company at the church of St. George in Southwark in 1629–30.[286] It is to the themes of competitive material gifting, expertise, and identity formation within the spatial context of the livery hall to which we now turn.

Notes

1 GL, MS 5817, fos 1–2. Andrew Hunt also 'willed that the two chambers standyng by the voyde grounde which are those Chambers that stande in the South part by the ground of our entering into our hall that two of the Livery of our Companye Decayed to have free dwelling in the same for Ever'.
2 GL, MS 5817, fo. 3. A 'solar' referred to a chamber on an upper floor. 'Maud Moundevyle' was Matilda, wife of Thomas Maundevill. See W. Dumville Smythe, *An Historical Account of the Worshipful Company of Girdlers* (London: Chiswick Press, 1905), p. 206.
3 Schofield, *Medieval London Houses*, p. 44.
4 *Ibid.*, pp. 199–200; Edward Basil Jupp, *An Historical Account of the Worshipful Company of Carpenters of the City of London: Chiefly Compiled from Records in their Possession* (London: W. Pickering, 1848), p. 217.
5 Stow, *A Survey of London*, I, p. 176.
6 Vanessa Harding, 'Space, property, and propriety in urban England', *Journal of Interdisciplinary History*, 32:4 (2002), 549–69, at p. 557; Reddaway and Walker, *The Early History of the Goldsmiths' Company*, pp. 71–2.
7 Caroline Barron, *London in the Later Middle Ages: Government and People, 1200–1500* (Oxford: Oxford University Press, 2004), p. 225.
8 Welch, *History of the Worshipful Company of Pewterers*, I, p. 59.
9 Barron, *London in the Later Middle Ages*, p. 216.
10 BL, Harley MS 541, fos 225v–226v; Barron, *London in the Later Middle Ages*, p. 216.
11 John Schofield, 'City of London gardens, 1500–c.1620', *Garden History*, 27:1 (1999), 73–88, at p. 77.
12 Schofield, *Medieval London Houses*, p. 44; Katherine Giles, *An Archaeology of Social Identity: Guildhalls in York, c.1350–1630* (Oxford: J. and E. Hedges, 2000), pp. 114–15.
13 Justin Colson, 'Commerce, clusters, and community: a re-evaluation of the occupational geography of London, c.1400–c.1550', *Economic History Review*, 69:1 (2016), 104–30, at pp. 107, 115, 120.
14 Sylvia L. Thrupp, *The Merchant Class of Medieval London, 1300–1500* (Chicago, IL: University of Chicago Press, 1948), p. 144.
15 Barron, *London in the Later Middle Ages*, p. 199.
16 Epstein, 'Craft guilds, apprenticeship, and technological change', pp. 701–2.
17 Welch, *History of the Worshipful Company of Pewterers*, I, p. 154.
18 *Ibid.*, I, p. 87.
19 Lancashire, *London Civic Theatre*, p. 86.
20 Likewise, Fabrizio Nevola has suggested in relation to early modern streets: 'individual and collective actions and behaviors inscribe spaces with meaning that accumulates over time'. See 'Street life in early modern Europe', p. 1334.
21 GL, MS 3115, fo. 51v. The Cooks' Company counted their blessings at a meeting of the court of assistants in mid-September 1666 for 'the goodness of god in sparing this hall being surrounded with those dreadfull flames'.
22 Chris King, 'The interpretation of urban buildings: power, memory and appropriation in Norwich merchants' houses, c. 1400–1660', *World Archaeology*, 41:3 (2009), 471–88, at p. 473.
23 Margaret Spufford, 'The limitations of the probate inventory', in Joan Chartres and David Hey (eds), *English Rural Society, 1500–1800: Essays in Honour of Joan Thirsk* (Cambridge: Cambridge University press, 1990), pp. 139–74.
24 Giorgio Riello, 'Things seen and unseen: the material culture of early modern inventories and their representation of domestic interiors', in Paula Findlen (ed.), *Early Modern Things: Objects and their Histories, 1500–1800* (Basingstoke: Routledge, 2013), pp. 125–50, at p. 129.

25 GL, MS 12071/2, fos 474v–475r.
26 GL, MS 14357.
27 GL, MS 6152/1, fos 154v, 156r.
28 GL, MS 6152/1, fos 109v, 154v, 162v.
29 MS 6152/1, fos 233r–v.
30 Before the late sixteenth century, any drawn survey of urban or rural property was very unusual. See Gerhold, *London Plotted*, pp. 1–3.
31 *The London Surveys of Ralph Treswell*, ed. by John Schofield, figures 25 and 33.
32 *Ibid.*, p. 15; Schofield, *Medieval London Houses*, p. 34, 'This courtyard type has been called Type 4 in a London typology of house-plans shown in the Treswell surveys of 1607–14.'
33 Matthew H. Johnson, 'Meanings of polite architecture in sixteenth-century England', *Historical Archaeology*, 26:3 (1992), 45–56, at pp. 48–9.
34 GL, MS 7110, fos 1r–4v.
35 GL, MS 15874, fo. 26.
36 Stow, *A Survey of London*, I, p. 305.
37 John Schofield, 'The construction of medieval and Tudor houses in London', *Construction History*, 7 (1991), 3–28, at pp. 3, 8, 21.
38 Robert Bartlett, *Why Can the Dead Do Such Great Things? Saints and Worshippers from the Martyrs to the Reformation* (Princeton, NJ; Oxford: Princeton University Press, 2013), p. 277.
39 David Hugh Farmer, *The Oxford Dictionary of Saints*, 5th rev. edn (Oxford: Oxford University Press, 2011), pp. 128–30, 80–1.
40 Schofield, *Medieval London Houses*, p. 65.
41 Kate Giles, 'The "familiar" fraternity: the appropriation and consumption of medieval guildhalls in early modern York', in Sarah Tarlow and Susie West (eds), *The Familiar Past? Archaeologies of Later Historical Britain* (London; New York, Routledge, 1999), pp. 87–102, at p. 90.
42 GL, MS 2883/1, fo. 6.
43 Mark Girouard, *Elizabethan Architecture: Its Rise and Fall, 1540–1640* (New Haven, CT: Yale University Press, 2009), p. 62.
44 Matthew Johnson, *Housing Culture: Traditional Architecture in an English Landscape* (London: UCL Press, 1993), p. 59, 'At the level of spatial text, it signified several different things: it asserted communality and community, but it also denoted inequality and segregation at the same time'.
45 Welch, *History of the Cutlers' Company*, I, p. 316.
46 Giles, *An Archaeology of Social Identity*, p. 127; Nicholas Cooper, *Houses of the Gentry: 1480–1680* (New Haven, CT; London: Yale University Press, 1999), p. 275.
47 Lancashire, *London Civic Theatre*, pp. 73–117.
48 *Ibid.*, p. 71.
49 Welch, *History of the Worshipful Company of Pewterers*, I, viii.
50 Lancashire, *London Civic Theatre*, p. 90.
51 Prideaux, *Memorials of the Goldsmiths' Company*, I, pp. 78–9.
52 Giles, 'The "familiar" fraternity', p. 90.
53 Jupp, *An Historical Account*, p. 220.
54 Giles, 'The "familiar" fraternity' [referencing R. Harris, 'The grammar of carpentry', *Vernacular Architecture*, 20 (1989), 1–8].
55 Welch, *History of the Worshipful Company of Pewterers*, I, pp. 82–3, 85–6.
56 Schofield, *Medieval London Houses*, pp. 95–6.
57 John Harvey, *English Medieval Architects: A Biographical Dictionary Down to 1550: Including Master Masons, Carpenters, Carvers, Building Contractors and others Responsible for Design* (Gloucester: Sutton, 1984), p. 26.
58 GL, MS 12105, fo. 2.
59 Mark Girouard, *Life in the English Country House: A Social and Architectural History* (New Haven, CT: Yale University Press), p. 34; Jennifer Floyd, 'St. George and the

"steyned halle": Lydgate's verse for the London Armourers', in Lisa H. Cooper and Andrea Denny-Brown (eds), *Lydgate Matters: Poetry and Material Culture in the Fifteenth Century* (New York; Basingstoke: Palgrave Macmillan, 2008), pp. 139–64.

60 GL, MS 12105, fo. 9.

61 GL, MS 2883/1, fos 5–6.

62 GL, MS 7110, fos 14v, 26v.

63 Stow, *A Survey of London*, I, p. 182.

64 *Memorials of the Guild of Merchant Taylors of the Fraternity of St. John the Baptist, in the City of London; and of its Associated Charities and Institutions*, compiled and selected by Charles M. Clode (London: Harrison & Sons, 1875), pp. 84–5.

65 Schofield, *Medieval London Houses*, p. 129.

66 GHA, WA/CM, D, fos 418–19.

67 Rebecca Olson, *Arras Hanging: The Textile that Determined Early Modern Literature and Drama* (Newark: University of Delaware Press, 2013), p. 149.

68 GL, MS 7110, fo. 3v; Richard Marks, 'Window glass', in John Blair and Nigel Ramsey (eds), *English Medieval Industries: Craftsmen, Techniques, Products* (London: Hambledon Press, 1991), pp. 265–94, at p. 267, 'Normandy glass was generally considered to be superior both to Rhenish and English glass and this is reflected in the price.'

69 GL, MS 7110, fo. 3v.

70 Schofield, *Medieval London Houses*, p. 106. The fifteenth-century windows might have been glazed, or 'filled with oiled paper, linen or silk'. See Fredrick Morris Fry and Walter Lloyd Thomas, *The Windows of Merchant Taylors' Hall* (London: Burrup, Mathieson and Company, 1934), pp. 10–11.

71 Maurice Howard and Tessa Murdoch, '"Armes and Bestes": Tudor and Stuart Heraldry', in Olga Dmitrieva and Tessa Murdoch (eds), *Treasures of The Royal Courts: Tudors, Stuarts and the Russian Tsars* (London: V&A Publishing, 2013), pp. 56–67.

72 Alford and Barker, *A History of the Carpenters' Company*, p. 63.

73 Prideaux, *Memorials of the Goldsmiths' Company*, I, p. 65. In 1565, 'Robert, the lute player ... set in a fair book of parchment all the Arms now painted in the common garden of the Hall, he is to have 2 s. for every of the said Arms so to be set forth'.

74 GL, MS 7110, fo. 5r.

75 Michael J. Dawes and Michael J. Ostwald, 'Space syntax: mathematics and the social logic of architecture', in B. Sriraman (ed.), *Handbook of the Mathematics of the Arts and Sciences* (Cham: Springer International Publishing, 2019), pp. 1–12, at p. 6; Schofield, *Medieval London Houses*, pp. 66–7.

76 Sylvia L. Thrupp, *A Short History of the Worshipful Company of Bakers of London* (Croydon: Galleon Press, 1933), p. 164.

77 'parlour | parlor, n. and adj.' *OED Online*. Oxford University Press, June 2020 [accessed 19 July 2020]. GL, MSS 7164, 6r; 16988/2, 83r.

78 GL, MS 7110, fo. 15r.

79 Welch, *History of the Worshipful Company of Pewterers*, I, pp. 86–7. 'counting-house, n.' *OED Online*. Oxford University Press, June 2020 [accessed 19 July 2020].

80 Matthew Davies, 'Crown, city and guild in late medieval London', in Matthew Davies and James A. Galloway (eds), *London and Beyond: Essays in Honour of Derek Keene* (London: Institute of Historical Research, 2012), pp. 247–68, at pp. 258–9.

81 GL, MS 7110, fos 1r–2r; Lancashire, *London Civic Theatre*, pp. 50–2, 153–70.

82 Welch, *History of the Cutlers' Company*, I, p. 319.

83 Jupp, *An Historical Account*, p. 222.

84 Schofield, *Medieval London Houses*, p. 91.

85 GL, MS 17155, fo. 6.

86 Schofield, 'City of London gardens', p. 81.
87 GL, MSS 7110, fo. 3r; 17155, fo. 6.
88 Schofield, *Medieval London Houses*, p. 89; Schofield, 'City of London gardens', p. 79.
89 Barron, *London in the Later Middle Ages*, p. 224.
90 GL, MS 7110, fo. 2r; Welch, *History of the Worshipful Company of Pewterers*, I, iv; Vanessa Harding, *The Dead and Living in Paris and London, 1500–1670* (Cambridge: Cambridge University Press, 2002), pp. 194–5.
91 Schofield, *Medieval London Houses*, p. 69.
92 Laura Branch, *Faith and Fraternity: London Livery Companies and the Reformation, 1510–1603* (Leiden; Boston, MA: Brill, 2017), pp. 28, 32–3.
93 Barron, *London in the Later Middle Ages*, p. 217.
94 Stow, *A Survey of London*, I, p. 305.
95 Reddaway and Walker, *The Early History of the Goldsmiths' Company*, p. 293.
96 Stow, *A Survey of London*, I, pp. 306–7.
97 Schofield, *Medieval London Houses* p. 56. The two houses at Carpenters' Hall were not almshouses for long; they were soon let for commercial rents. See Alford and Barker, *A History of the Carpenters' Company*, p. 50.
98 Schofield, 'The topography and buildings of London', p. 314.
99 Alford and Barker, *A History of the Carpenters' Company*, pp. 102–3. C. E. Challis, 'Bowes, Sir Martin (1496/7–1566), goldsmith and mayor of London.' *Oxford Dictionary of National Biography*. 3 January 2008. Oxford University Press [accessed 22 July 2020].
100 The basic courtyard design was preserved too after a huge wave of livery hall rebuilding following the Great Fire. Notably the 'compact plan' was becoming more desirable for contemporary high-status homes. See Colin Platt, *The Great Rebuildings of Tudor and Stuart England* (London: UCL Press, 1994), ch. 6; Nicholas Cooper, 'Rank, manners and display: the gentlemanly house, 1500–1750', *Transactions of the Royal Historical Society*, 12 (2002), 291–310, at pp. 300–1.
101 *Wardens' Accounts of the Worshipful Company of Founders of the City of London, 1497–1681*, transcribed, calendared, and edited by Guy Parsloe (London: Athlone Press, 1964), pp. 239, 252, 256, 263; Prideaux, *Memorials of the Goldsmiths' Company*, I, p. 100.
102 This was a precocious shift on the part of London's guilds. On a national level 'it was common to organize details of household possessions in inventories by room location' by the early seventeenth century, although there was regional variation in adopting this change. See Donald Spaeth, '"Orderly made": re-appraising household inventories in seventeenth-century England', *Social History*, 41:4 (2016), 417–35, at p. 423.
103 Seen from the perspective of the appraisers, inventories 'should be viewed as representations, created through a process of conscious reflection'. See Spaeth, '"Orderly made": re-appraising household inventories', 421.
104 For the importance of boxes, chests and trunks in managing a paper archive see Heather Wolfe and Peter Stallybrass, 'The material culture of record-keeping in early modern England', in Liesbeth Corens, Kate Peters, and Alexandra Walsham (eds), *Archives and Information in the Early Modern World* (Oxford: Oxford University Press, 2018), pp. 179–208, at pp. 199–201.
105 Tara Hamling and Catherine Richardson, *A Day at Home in Early Modern England: Material Culture and Domestic Life, 1500–1700* (New Haven, CT: Yale University Press, 2017), p. 154.
106 GL, MS 7351/1.
107 GL, MS 16988/4, fos 212v–213r.
108 GL, MS 16988/3, fo. 263r; Mark Overton, Jane Whittle, Darron Dean, and Andrew Hann, *Production and Consumption in English Households, 1600–1750* (London: Routledge, 2004), p. 92.

109 David Mitchell, 'Fine table linen in England, 1450–1750: the supply, ownership and use of a luxury commodity' (PhD dissertation, University College London, 1999), p. 209.

110 GL, MS 16988/3, fo. 262r. There was a trend across England from the late sixteenth century for the 'acquisition of great quantities of linen, and better quality linen'. Overton et al., *Production and Consumption*, p. 109.

111 GL, MS 7164, fo. 75.

112 GL, MS 6155/2.

113 For example 'ii ould curtaynes hanging in the [parlour] window' [MS 6152/1, fo. 115v].

114 *Wardens' Accounts of the Worshipful Company of Founders*, p. 414.

115 GL, MS 5817, fo. 16.

116 GL, MS 5817, fo. 34. St. Laurence (d. 258) was said to have been roasted on the gridiron. See Farmer, *The Oxford Dictionary of Saints*, p. 263.

117 GL, MS 4329A.

118 Herbert, *The History of the Twelve Great Livery Companies*, I, p. 89.

119 Roger H. Leech, 'The symbolic hall: historical context and merchant culture in the early modern city', *Vernacular Architecture*, 31:1 (2000), 1–10, at p. 8. Arms and armour were also commonly displayed in halls in Kent. See Hamling and Richardson, *A Day at Home*, p. 123.

120 Markus Friedrich, *The Birth of the Archive: A History of Knowledge in the Early Modern World*, trans. by John Noël Dillon (Ann Arbor: University of Michigan Press, 2018), pp. 37–8.

121 Alexandra Walsham, 'The social history of the archive: record-keeping in early modern Europe', in Corens, Peters, and Walsham (eds), *The Social History of the Archive*, pp. 9–48, at p. 17.

122 GL, MS 7710, fos 13v, 58r.

123 MSS 6152/1, fos 189r–v; 16988/2, fos 325v–326v.

124 Joan Thirsk, *Economic Policy and Projects: The Development of a Consumer Society in Early Modern England* (Oxford: Clarendon Press, 1978); Lorna Weatherill, *Consumer Behaviour and Material Culture in Britain 1660–1760* (Cambridge: Cambridge University Press, 1988); Carole Shammas, *The Pre-Industrial Consumer in England and America* (Oxford: Clarendon Press, 1990); Overton et al., *Production and Consumption*.

125 Grassby, 'Material culture and cultural history', pp. 595–6.

126 Prideaux, *Memorials of the Goldsmiths' Company*, I, p. 89.

127 Similarly, 'one of the main goals of confraternity art … was to assert the group's corporate identity… and educate new members about its mission and history'. See Alyssa Abraham, 'Iconography, spectacle, and notions of corporate identity: the form and function of art in early modern confraternities', in Konrad Eisenbichler (ed.), *A Companion to Medieval and Early Modern Confraternities* (Leiden; Boston, MA: Brill, 2019), pp. 406–32, at p. 406.

128 GHA, WA/CM, S1, fo. 12r. Emphasis added.

129 GHA, WA/CM, S1, fo. 118r.

130 Leech, 'The symbolic hall', p. 6. See also Frank E. Brown, 'Continuity and change in the urban house: developments in domestic space organisation in seventeenth-century London', *Comparative Studies in Society and History*, 28:3 (1986), 558–90, at pp. 580–2.

131 Eleanor John, 'At home with the London middling sort – the inventory evidence for furnishings and room use, 1570–1720', *Regional Furniture*, 22 (2008), 27–51, at p. 40.

132 Cooper, *Houses of the Gentry*, pp. 275–89; Girouard, *Life in the English Country House*, pp. 30–8; Simon Thurley, 'Henry VIII and the building of Hampton Court: a reconstruction of the Tudor palace', *Architectural History*, 31 (1988), 1–57, at p. 11.

133 Girouard, *Life in the English Country House*, p. 30.
134 Cooper, 'Rank, manners and display', p. 297.
135 Simon Thurley, *The Royal Palaces of Tudor England: Architecture and Court Life, 1460–1547* (New Haven, CT: Yale University Press for the Paul Mellon Centre for Studies in British Art, 1993), pp. 113–20.
136 GHA, WA/CM, N, fo. 19.
137 Ian W. Archer, 'Discourses of history in Elizabethan and early Stuart London', *Huntingdon Library Quarterly*, 68 (2005), 202–26, at p. 205.
138 Welch, *History of the Worshipful Company of Pewterers*, II, p. 11.
139 GHA, WA/CM, N, fo. 83.
140 Mark Girouard, 'The halls of the Elizabethan and early Stuart Inns of Court', in Jayne Archer, Elizabeth Goldring, and Sarah Knight (eds), *The Intellectual and Cultural World of the Early Modern Inns of Court* (Manchester; New York: Manchester University Press, 2011), pp. 138–56, at pp. 143–4; Louise Durning, 'The Oxford college as household, 1580–1640', in Sandra Cavallo and Silvia Evangelisti (eds), *Domestic Institutional Interiors in Early Modern Europe* (Farnham: Ashgate, 2009), pp. 83–101, at p. 88.
141 MS 6152/1, fo. 69v.
142 MS 6152/1, fo. 188v.
143 MS 7164, fos 20r–v.
144 Welsh, *History of the Cutlers' Company*, I, pp. 15–16, 164.
145 GL, MS 7164, fo. 8r.
146 I have taken the phrase 'full adult civic masculinity' from Ruth Mazo Karras, *From Boys to Men: Formations of Masculinity in Late Medieval Europe* (Philadelphia, PA: University of Pennsylvania Press, 2003), p. 110.
147 GL, MS 16988/2, fo. 398v. Hamling and Richardson, *A Day at Home*, p. 125, 'the traditional trestle table, which had two or more moveable supports or trestles on which a table board rested, so that it could be easily turned up and put aside when the space was needed for other purposes'.
148 GL, MS 16988/3, fos 262v–263r.
149 GL, MS 16988/5, fo. 93r.
150 GL, MS 6152/1, fos 195r, 233r–v.
151 GL, MS 6152/1, fos 233r–v.
152 GL, MS 4326/5, fo. 16r. The total charges for the enlarging of the east end of Carpenters' Hall came to £121 12s.
153 *Records of the Worshipful Company of Carpenters*, VII, pp. 37–8, 51.
154 GL, MS 4326/5, fo. 16r.
155 GL, MS 4326/5, fos 13v–14r. 27 members of the livery; 93 members of the yeomanry.
156 Notably, at the end of the wardens' accounts for 1595 is a list of ten men in arrears for their promised contribution towards the enlarging of the hall. See GL, MS 4326/5, fo. 17v.
157 *Records of the Worshipful Company of Carpenters*, VI, p. 104; Alford and Barker, *A History of the Carpenters' Company*, p. 46.
158 Giles, *An Archaeology of Social Identity*, p. 127; Cooper, *Houses of the Gentry*, p. 275.
159 GHA, WA/CM, S2, fo. 236v.
160 GHA, WA/CM, T, fo. 96v.
161 Prideaux, *Memorials of the Goldsmiths' Company*, I, p. 137. St. Peter was the patron saint of the Fishmongers' Company, with whom the Goldsmiths had a long-standing amity.
162 Archer, 'The livery companies and charity', pp. 15–28.
163 BL, Add. 34307, fo. 1r.
164 GHA, WA/CM, C, fo. 119.
165 John Blair, 'Purbeck marble', in Blair and Ramsey (eds), *English Medieval Industries*, pp. 41–56.

166 Donatella Calabi and Derek Keene, 'Exchanges and cultural transfer in European cities, c.1500–1700', in Donatella Calabi and Stephen Turk Christensen (eds), *Cultural Exchange in Early Modern Europe. Vol. 2, Cities and Cultural Exchange in Europe, 1400-1700* (Cambridge: Cambridge University Press, 2006), pp. 286–314, at p. 302; Claire Walsh, 'Social meaning and social space in the shopping galleries of early modern London', in John Benson and Laura Ugolini (eds), *A Nation of Shopkeepers: Five Centuries of British Retailing* (London; New York: I. B. Tauris, 2003), pp. 52–79, at p. 58.
167 *The Annals of the Barber-Surgeons of London*, compiled from their records and other sources, by Sidney Young (London: Blades, East & Blades, 1890), p. 218.
168 GL, MS 17155, fo. 8.
169 Barron, *London in the Later Middle Ages*, p. 224.
170 Matthew Davies, '"Monuments of honour": clerks, histories and heroes in the London livery companies', in Hannes Kleineke (ed.), *The Fifteenth Century X Parliament, Personalities and Power. Papers Presented to Linda S. Clark* (Cambridge: Cambridge University Press, 2013), pp. 143–63, at p. 147.
171 GL, MS 7090/3, fo. 42r. In September 1601 Milles and his wife moved into 'the beadles house', described as 'the chamber with the chymney' [fo. 122v].
172 Prideaux, *Memorials of the Goldsmiths' Company*, I, pp. 56, 62.
173 Alford and Barker, *A History of the Carpenters' Company*, p. 96.
174 *Records of the Worshipful Company of Carpenters*, IV, p. 33 [1548–49]. 7s for garden work, 12d for scrubbing vessels, and 4s for washing the clothes.
175 Helen Smith, 'Gender and material culture in the early modern London guilds', in Hannah Greig, Jane Hamlett, and Leonie Hannan (eds), *Gender and Material Culture in Britain since 1600* (Basingstoke: Palgrave Macmillan, 2015), pp. 16–31, at p. 26.
176 Stow, *A Survey of London*, I, pp. 272–3.
177 Berlin, 'Civic ceremony', p. 18.
178 Caroline Barron, *The Medieval Guildhall of London* (London: Corporation of London, 1974), p. 32; E. B. Buxton, 'Shaw [Shaa], Sir John (c. 1455–1503), goldsmith and mayor of London.' *Oxford Dictionary of National Biography*. 13 September 2019. Oxford University Press [accessed 22 July 2020].
179 Schofield, *Medieval London Houses*, p. 71; 'buttery, n. 1.' *OED Online*. Oxford University Press, June 2020. Web 19 July 2020.
180 'pantry, n.' *OED Online*. Oxford University Press, June 2020. Web 19 July 2020; 'larder, n.1.' *OED Online*. Oxford University Press, June 2020. Web 19 July 2020.
181 GL, MS 5817, fo. 14.
182 Alford and Barker, *A History of the Carpenters' Company*, p. 64.
183 Priscilla Metcalf, *The Halls of the Fishmongers' Company: An Architectural History of a Riverside Site* (London: Phillimore, 1977), p. 31.
184 Prideaux, *Memorials of the Goldsmiths' Company*, I, p. 133.
185 *The London Surveys of Ralph Treswell*, p. 19.
186 GL, MS 12105, fo. 10.
187 Sara Pennell, '"Pots and pans history": the material culture of the kitchen in early modern England', *Journal of Design History*, 11:3 (1998), 201–16, at p. 202.
188 GL, MS 12105, fo. 10.
189 GL, MS 5817, fo. 9.
190 Welsh, *History of the Worshipful Company of Pewterers*, I, pp. 167–8.
191 *Ibid.*, II, p. 4.
192 *Ibid.*, I, pp. 167–8.
193 In middling and elite seventeenth-century homes 'the parlour developed into a comfortable room (nearly all parlours had a fireplace), with increasingly specialised functions: sitting, entertaining and dining'. See Overton et al., *Production and Consumption*, p. 132.

194 GL, MS 5817, fos 14–15. Most girdlers gave 20s each, though amounts varied.
195 GL, MS 6152/1, fos 156r–157v.
196 GL, MS 6152/1, fos 162v–163r.
197 GL, MS 6152/1, fo. 163r.
198 *Records of the Worshipful Company of Carpenters*, VII, p. 104.
199 Alford and Barker, *A History of the Carpenters' Company*, p. 64.
200 GL, MS 5201, fos 1r, 2r.
201 Young, *The Annals of the Barber-Surgeons*, pp. 132–4, 213–15.
202 GL, MS 7110, fo. 15r.
203 GL, MS 7110, fos 30r–32r. In domestic spaces too, an 'unwillingness to dispose of still serviceable and presentable goods is evident in their relocation around households.' See Sara Pennell, 'Material culture in seventeenth-century "Britain": the matter of domestic consumption', in Frank Trentmann (ed.), *The Oxford Handbook of the History of Consumption* (Oxford: Oxford University Press, 2012), pp. 64–83, at p. 81.
204 GL, MS 7164, fo. 7r.
205 GL, MS 6988/2, fos 396r–397r.
206 *Records of the Worshipful Company of Carpenters*, VI, p. 305.
207 *The London Surveys of Ralph Treswell*, p. 22.
208 GL, MS 16988/3, fo. 263r.
209 Griffiths, 'Secrecy and authority', p. 927.
210 Lenore Manderson, Mark Davis, Chip Colwell, and Tanja Ahlin, 'On secrecy, disclosure, the public, and the private in anthropology', *Current Anthropology*, 56:12 (2015), 183–90, at p. 184.
211 Griffiths, 'Secrecy and authority', p. 928.
212 LMA, COL/CA/01/01/033, fos 273v, 279v.
213 LMA, COL/CA/01/01/030, fo. 96r.
214 LMA, COL/CA/01/01/038, fo. 226v.
215 LMA, COL/CA/01/01/039, fos 71v, 220v.
216 Prideaux, *Memorials of the Goldsmiths' Company*, I, p. 75; 'hugger-mugger, n., adj., and adv.' *OED Online*. Oxford University Press, June 2020 [accessed 19 July 2020].
217 Orlin, *Locating Privacy in Tudor London*, pp. 114, 146–51.
218 Tittler, *Architecture and Power*, p. 36, 'it is easy to understand how the demand for such a room would grow with the increasing authority of the mayor and the other senior officials in the sixteenth and seventeenth centuries … Such additions not only meant an increase in dimensions, but also an upgrading of style and even of comfort.'
219 Hamling and Richardson, *A Day at Home*, pp. 185, 189.
220 Welch, *History of the Worshipful Company of Pewterers*, I, p. 213.
221 *Memorials of the Guild of Merchant Taylors*, I, 84–92.
222 Bishop, 'The clerk's tale', p. 17 (footnote 11), from the later sixteenth century 'the Goldsmiths' Company decreed that only those papers and books in current use should be kept in the clerk's paper office, with other documents moved to the company treasury for safer keeping'.
223 GHA, WA/CM, R1, fo. 25r.
224 GHA, WA/CM, S1, fo. 91r.
225 Griffiths, 'Secrecy and authority', p. 935. On the development of specific muniment rooms in provincial guildhalls, see Robert Tittler, '"… and no loose people to trouble the hall": oligarchy and the division of space in the English civic hall to 1640', *History Compass*, 10:9 (2012), 622–32, at pp. 626–7.
226 GHA, WA/CM, S2, fo. 182r.
227 Julienne Hanson, *Decoding Homes and Houses* (Cambridge: Cambridge University Press, 1998), p. 173.
228 Young, *The Annals of the Barber-Surgeons*, p. 208.

229 GL, MS 12107, fo. 11v.
230 *Wardens' Accounts of the Worshipful Company of Founders*, pp. 262, 329.
231 Markus Friedrich has suggested that individual cabinets 'could be directly called and labelled an "archive"'. See *The Birth of the Archive*, p. 134.
232 GL, MSS 2710/1, fo. 65; 2710/2, fo. 67r.
233 GL, MS 2710/1, fo. 219.
234 GL, MS 2710/1, fos 65, 94.
235 GL, MS 2710/1, fos 99, 104.
236 GL, MS 2710/1, fo. 148.
237 GL, MS 2710/1, fo. 257.
238 GL, MS 2710/1, fo. 333.
239 Young, *The Annals of the Barber-Surgeons*, p. 199.
240 GL, MS 3043/1, fos 79–80.
241 GHA, WA/CM, T, fo. 31r.
242 GHA, WA/CM, T, fo. 95v.
243 Walter Hindes Godfrey, *The English Staircase, an Historical Account … to the End of the XVIIIth Century* (London: B. T. Batsford, 1911), pp. 22–35.
244 David M. Bergeron, *English Civic Pageantry, 1558–1642* (London: Edward Arnold, 1971), pp. 126–7, 139; Berlin, 'Civic ceremony'.
245 GL, MSS 12071/2, fo. 475r; 12107, fos 5v–6r.
246 *Records of the Carpenters' Company*, VII, p. 493.
247 GL, MS 4329A. Few furnishings are listed: this is entirely typical for the gallery space.
248 GL, MS 16988/3, fo. 262r.
249 Young, *The Annals of the Barber-Surgeons*, p. 213.
250 Schofield, *Medieval London Houses*, pp. 84–6; Rosalys Coope, 'The "long gallery": its origins, development, use and decoration', *Architectural History*, 29 (1986), 43–71, at pp. 51, 60–2.
251 GHA, WA/CM, S2, fo. 182r.
252 'terrace, n.' *OED Online*. Oxford University Press, June 2020 [accessed 19 July 2020].
253 On the typical location of galleries see Schofield, 'City of London gardens', p. 81; Orlin, *Locating Privacy*, pp. 234–8.
254 Discussed in greater depth in Chapter 7.
255 GL, MS 16988/2, fo. 83r.
256 GL, MS 12071/2, fo. 33.
257 Giles, *An Archaeology of Social Identity*, p. 126.
258 GHA, WA/CM, T, fos 112v–113r. See also Graham Fairclough, 'Meaningful constructions – spatial and functional analysis of medieval buildings', *Antiquity*, 66 (1992), 348–66, at p. 354, 'decoration on doors between the hall, state stair and the private chambers on the principal floors (i.e. ground and first) form a progression of successively more private rooms creating increasing "depth" as more private areas are reached'.
259 Welch, *History of the Worshipful Company of Pewterers*, I, p. 274.
260 Schofield, *Medieval London Houses*, p. 123.
261 The date of their commissioning and completion is hard to ascertain precisely. See Jupp, *An Historical Account*, pp. 239–41.
262 Francis W. Reader, 'Tudor Domestic Wall-Paintings', *The Archaeological Journal*, 92 (1935), 243–86, at p. 248, 'pictorial panels were often enclosed in an architectural framework of painted columns, arches, etc.'
263 Jupp, *An Historical Account*, p. 236.
264 All references from *The Bible* (Geneva, 1560).
265 Tessa Watt, *Cheap Print and Popular Piety, 1550–1640* (Cambridge: Cambridge University Press, 1991), p. 209.
266 Reader, 'Tudor domestic wall-paintings', p. 275.

267 Barbara A. Hanawalt, *Ceremony and Civility: Civic Culture in Late Medieval London* (New York: Oxford University Press, 2017), p. 116.
268 *Calendar of Wills Proved and Enrolled in the Court of Husting, London, A.D. 1258–A.D. 1688*, ed. by Reginald R. Sharpe, 2 vols (London: John C. Francis, 1889–90), II, 668–82. A 'girdler' Laurence Robiout (d. 1558), distributed his gowns to brothers, kin, and a trusted apprentice.
269 Tittler has suggested that 'civic portraits' were distinct from 'personal portraiture': the former were often directly commissioned by a civic institution; 'civic' paintings were displayed within institutional interiors; the figures demonstrated civic rather than personal virtues. See Robert Tittler, *The Face of the City: Civic Portraiture and Civic Identity in Early Modern England* (Manchester: Manchester University Press, 2007), pp. 4–6.
270 Eamon Duffy, *The Stripping of the Altars: Traditional Religion in England c.1400–c.1580* (New Haven, CT: Yale University Press, 1992), p. 163; Reddaway and Walker, *The Early History of the Goldsmiths' Company*, p. 293.
271 It is notable that the 'micro-architecture' of authority – Josiah's throne and Christ's pulpit – were evidently crafted from wood.
272 GL, MS 4329A, fo. A.
273 Gerbino and Johnston, *Compass and Rule*, p. 63.
274 Tarnya Cooper, *Citizen Portrait: Portrait Painting and the Urban Elites of Tudor and Jacobean England and Wales* (New Haven, CT; London: Yale University Press, 2012), p. 197.
275 GL, MS 4326/6, fo. 42r.
276 Lucy Gent, '"The rash gazer": economies of vision in Britain, 1550–1660', in Lucy Gent (ed.), *Albion's Classicism: The Visual Arts in Britain, 1550–1660* (New Haven, CT; London: Yale University Press, 1995), pp. 377–93, at p. 282; Juliet Fleming, *Graffiti and the Writing Arts of Early Modern England* (London: Reaktion Books, 2001), p. 32, 'Where paintings are more readily painted on than hung on walls ... questions as to what is meant by a "surface" – admit no easy answer.'
277 W. G. Hoskins, 'The rebuilding of rural England, 1570–1640', *Past and Present*, 4 (1953), 44–59; R. Machin, 'The great rebuilding: a reassessment', *Past and Present*, 77 (1977), 33–56; Johnson, *Housing Culture*; Tittler, *Architecture and Power*; Platt, *The Great Rebuildings*; Giles, *An Archaeology of Social Identity.*
278 Giles, *An Archaeology of Social Identity*; Johnson, *Housing Culture*; Chris King, 'Domestic buildings: understanding houses and society', in Catherine Richardson, Tara Hamling, and David Gaimster (eds), *The Routledge Handbook of Material Culture in Early Modern Europe*, pp. 115–29, at p. 117.
279 Tittler, *Architecture and Power*, p. 93.
280 Hamling and Richardson, *A Day at Home*, p. 9.
281 GL, MS 16967/1, fo. 165v.
282 GL, MS 2208/1, fo. 4r.
283 Helen Hills, 'Theorizing the relationship between architecture and gender in early modern Europe', in H. Hills (ed.), *Architecture and the Politics of Gender in Early Modern Europe* (Aldershot: Ashgate, 2003), pp. 3–22, at p. 4.
284 J. F. Merritt, 'Puritans, Laudians, and the phenomenon of church-building in Jacobean London', *The Historical Journal*, 41:4 (1998), 935–60, at p. 942.
285 *Ibid.*, p. 945–6.
286 Prideaux, *Memorials of the Goldsmiths' Company*, I, p. 146; Welsh, *History of the Worshipful Company of Pewterers*, II, p. 87.

5

Material gifting: artisanal virtuosity and material memorialisation

In 1528 master armourer and active citizen William Vynyard presented a spectacular gift to his guild, originating from his own workshop. He gave to the Armourers' Company a polychromed oak sculpture of St. George and the Dragon, with the saintly hero clad in an exceptionally intricate miniature steel armour (see Plate 12). Vynyard's material gift went on to play a significant role in the ceremonial life of the guild, as when the company travelled by boat to Greenwich in 1540 to celebrate the marriage of Henry VIII to Anne of Cleves, 'with our baners, targattes and our George standyng ouer ye Raylles [rails]'.[1] Vynyard's sculpture also inspired the further donation, by other sixteenth- and seventeenth-century artisans, of sculptural armoured masterpieces. This object is still in the possession of the guild, and the moment of its donation is recorded in the company's extensive gift book.[2]

This chapter uncovers the fundamental importance of material cultures to the articulation and establishment of individual artisanal reputations and collective craft culture. Having already traced the changing spatial boundaries of artisanal communities through practices of rebuilding and architectural reorganisation, our focus here is firmly upon the material dimensions of identity and experience. Objects were not just representative of desirable characteristics and values such as expertise, honour, and generosity, but were also active agents of cultural and social change.[3] Material cultures can thus be read in terms of their symbolism and designs, the materials and techniques employed in their construction, and the 'trajectory' of the life of the 'thing', within networks of artefacts, spaces, and people.[4] This chapter employs these methodologies in order to flesh out the relationships between artisanal identities and diverse material cultures.

Institutional artisanal records, such as company court minutes and inventories, and more personal accounts such as citizens' wills, are saturated with references to material cultures, primarily in the form of gifts. Gift-giving is thus a uniquely rich avenue through which to encounter and trace the impact of artisanal material cultures. Take, for example, a typical inventory of a late sixteenth-century artisanal company, listing the 'goodes and other moveables remaininge and beinge within the Common Hall of the Company of Cutlers'. It is striking that a considerable proportion of the objects listed by the appraisers were specifically recorded as 'gifts', donated by company members and friends of the guild. Material donations included a carpet of broad cloth, 'stayned' cloths, napery, silver, pewter and stone pots, a large collection of silver spoons and a considerable quantity of weaponry and knives that had been made by the donor's own 'hand'. Other citizens gave a bible with a desk, a portrait picture, 'the storie of Noe [Noah] in a table', 'a table of the armes of the misterie' and 'a table of the companys of London'. The Cutlers' diverse range of gifts for display, ritual use, and storage in the various rooms of their institutional building, including hall, parlour, 'drinking howse', buttery, yeomanry hall, and armoury, was not unusual.[5]

The established literature on gifting and London's livery companies is exclusively focused upon the gift as an act of civic philanthropy by the city's most successful mercantile elites.[6] By contrast here we explore a significant but overlooked culture of material gifts within London craft companies, and consider a series of questions. Which people gave gifts? What, when, and how did they give? And, perhaps most important, why did they give? What did donors hope for and expect in return? The argument here is that returns were in terms of honour, status, and memorialisation. That makes this culture rather different from that of medieval religious gifting, with its very specific spiritual returns, or the secular culture of gifts designed to secure favours or patronage from courtiers and office holders. Moreover, within the craft guild – an urban institution composed of highly discerning producers and consumers of material cultures, including apprentices, journeymen, master craftsmen, retailers, and regulators of the crafts and trades – the gift could have particular and unusual significance. Artisans were especially well placed to assess the symbolic, design, and material qualities of judiciously commissioned or personally crafted offerings. Citizens were closely attuned to the importance of suitable temporal and spatial contexts for both the initial gift presentation and subsequent 'social life' of their offering. The chapter further demonstrates that across the sixteenth century gifting was embedded into the ritual calendar of elections and commemoration, and into the built fabric of the City's livery halls.

The rationale for this investigation into traces of tangible, physical gifts derives from both the abundance and variety of archival evidence of gifting practices within guild societies, and from the methodological understanding that a material approach offers a new and enriching perspective on company cultures. Examining a range of primary sources, including company court minutes and accounts, books of gifts, benefactors, and inventories, in addition to rare material survivals within guild collections, we can see that a complex material gift 'economy' existed alongside the philanthropic culture of charitable endowments that has been so comprehensively elucidated in the historiography.[7] Material gifts were a means through which early modern guildsmen expressed competing claims to civic status and professional artisanal accomplishment. The donation of goods for display or use in one's livery hall were tools through which citizens established and sustained their status and memorials within complex guild hierarchies. This chapter considers: first, the distinctive nature of gifts within guilds; second, the ways in which gifts were managed, recorded, and remembered by the recipient company; third, the range of gifts and multiplicity of motivations for gifting (the anticipated 'returns' of the gift bearer); fourth, the ideal spatial, gestural, and temporal contexts for the presentation of gifts; and finally, patterns of continuity and change across the sixteenth and early seventeenth centuries.

This examination of material gift-giving draws on evidence from the archives of a dozen craft guilds with especially rich cultures of object-exchange, including the Armourers', Carpenters', Cutlers', Founders', Girdlers', and Tallow Chandlers' Companies. Case-studies are also included from the records of the Goldsmiths', Ironmongers', and Merchant Taylors' Companies. It cannot be said definitively why certain artisanal companies showed a greater propensity to gift than others. However, we can speculate on a combination of possible factors, including the relative prosperity of members, the opportunities for gift presentation and display created by livery hall rebuilding projects, and the suitability of the particular artisanal craft as a material gift. Metalworkers, including armourers, cutlers, goldsmiths, and pewterers, were especially well-positioned to present customary hand-wrought gifts, such as knives and plate, from their own workshops.

The gift and the guild

Building upon sociological and anthropological theory, a growing body of recent historical scholarship has demonstrated the significance of gifting cultures throughout early modern English society.[8] Gift relations, from the (apparently) altruistic to the market-like exchange, from the 'symmetrical' to the 'asymmetric', have been shown to be a fundamental, dynamic element of social, economic, and political relations. In middling and aristocratic households the exchange of presents such as clothing, plate, and food gifts, at significant stages of the life-cycle and on holidays and festivals, particularly New Year, was a means of demonstrating affection and loyalty.[9] At the universities and the Inns of Court, gift exchanges were an essential form of social interaction and political negotiation, which materialised 'obligations and expectations between giver and receiver'.[10] At court the asymmetrical relationship between monarch and subject, or patron and client, and associated notions of deference and honour, were structured through the presentation and receipt of gifts judged appropriate.[11]

First theorised by Marcel Mauss, the idea that a gift is never without expectation on the part of the donor but an act that inherently entails an exchange (or imposes a 'burden' on the recipient), now features prominently in all studies of gift exchange.[12] In early modern England no donor presented a gift without some hope of appropriate 'return'. In guild culture, since the monetary or material donation was presented to the institution, a citizen 'gave unto this house' rather than to an individual. In consequence, the nature of the return could be somewhat intangible; it lay with the corporate body as a whole.[13] Gifting within late medieval craft guilds and fraternities was embedded within Catholic religious culture, principally the performance of the Mass, which bound living and dead guildsmen together in perpetual cycles of material and spiritual exchange. Purgatory was undermined and fraternities were abolished in the 1540s, but the significance of material, social, and (reformed) spiritual reciprocity remained paramount to the sustained vitality of London's craft and mercantile guilds.[14]

The existing research on London's post-Reformation livery companies has conceptualised the act of gifting in terms of large-scale charitable donations of money, land or property, by exceptionally affluent merchants to their companies. Gifting was a strategy through which 'godly' civic reputations and cultures were founded and perpetuated.[15] Robert Tittler's pioneering work on the 'civic portrait', a genre of late sixteenth- and seventeenth-century panel portrait painting, has demonstrated how ideals of philanthropic gifting were linked to the material collections of London companies. Gifted or bequeathed by major donors and their families and displayed within livery halls, these portraits 'reiterated in visual terms the virtues of fraternal obligation and pious benefaction'.[16] Urban institutional identities, 'attributes, virtues and achievements', were self-fashioned through visual culture.[17] A fairly typical example of the 'civic portrait' is that of armourer Roger Tyndall (or Tindall), completed in 1585, when he was aged seventy-five (see Plate 13). Tyndall, who had served three times as master of the Armourers' Company, was also a major charitable benefactor to the guild and bequeathed his 'Counterfet [portrait] to be had to the [Armourers'] Hall and there for ever to remain and by my Brethren to be maintained in some decent place for my memorial'.[18] Company inventories show that in 1585 the portrait was displayed in the hall, and by the mid-seventeenth century the gift had been moved to the gallery.[19] The painting shows Tyndall dressed in livery robes, resting his left hand upon a skull, a typical *memento mori* symbol.[20] Textual inscriptions emphasise his generosity and the importance of crafting one's post-mortem reputation and legacy; written on the table ledge is 'Whatsoever thou dost, mark thy end', and a witty mnemonic to the right of Tyndall's head reads 'Tyme glydes away One God obey. Let truth bear sway So Tindal still did say'. Conspicuously, under his livery robes a sword is depicted – a visual reference both to his role as gentleman at arms, and his professional identity as a working armourer. Portraits of contemporary office-holders or historic benefactors for display in company premises were, however, exceptional gifts, representing a very small fraction of the objects donated by guildsmen. Outside the largest and wealthiest mercantile companies these were very rare gifts indeed.[21]

This chapter adopts a more wide-ranging perspective on types of gifts and incentives for giving, beyond grand philanthropic gestures and the civic portraits to which these donations were closely associated. It is concerned with material gifts of all kinds, and with the craft guild itself as the designated recipient.[22] Donations to London companies ranged from the technically innovative and intrinsically valuable artefact for use in exclusive company rituals, such as silver gilt and rock crystal election cups, to everyday objects made from quotidian materials, like wooden trenchers for feasting, which were viewed and touched by a range of estates and stored in the less prestigious rooms of the hall (the kitchen, pantry, or larder). Gifts included: textiles and soft furnishings such as carpets, cushions, banners, tapestries, painted cloths, and hearse cloths; furniture such as tables, chairs, forms and stools, cupboards, chests, and presses. Silver and pewter plate, cooking apparatus, weaponry and armour, books and manuscripts were also considered suitable gifts. Against the backdrop of major rebuilding projects and structural adaptations to guild architectures across the City, the gifting repertoire also included decorative material features such as wainscot, painted glass panels, and plasterwork. Even the physical supplies required for building projects, such as timber, stone, and mortar, could be conceptualised as gifts and recorded as such. Thus, the armourer William Gurr 'gave the carriage of certaine timber from Trigglane to the [Armourers'] Hall for the chymneys'.[23] The donation of building supplies could take the form of semi-obligatory donations, offerings which were still framed as 'gifts' in the court minutes and accounts. As, for example, when the Carpenters' Company undertook a major extension of their hall chamber in 1594 – 'thenlarginge of the Hall at the east ende' – and 120 members of the livery and yeomanry gifted timber from their workshops, or money, depending upon their status within the guild.[24] Similarly, perishable goods, such as food stuffs and alcoholic beverages for collective consumption at guild feasts and dinners, constituted another strand of guild gifting culture.[25] Gifts of consumables could also express loyalty, foster 'fellowship', or mark social distinctions.[26] The symbolic richness of the food (and drink) gift within artisanal companies merits separate discussion, and is explored further in Chapter 6.

The status of the gift within guild culture is most clearly demonstrated through the careful recording of material donations within company inventories and books of gifts or benefactors. The many objects and material fixtures specifically labelled as 'gifts' reveal that citizens valued the opportunity to make their mark on the interior decoration or physical structure of their company hall. From the institutional perspective, these narratives of gifting, typically compiled over centuries and across generations of office-holders, show that recording material donations, including what was given, when, and by whom, was of considerable social and cultural value. Symbolically, inventories and gift books acted as coherent and permanent records of institutional reciprocity. They worked to construct a material corporate community with lists of 'gifyts of such goodmen that be alyve and they that be paste oute of this worlde'. From the 1540s the Pewterers' Company clerk even self-consciously noted down in the guild inventory 'this present book of Inventories (in which the gifts of good people are written) which is the gift of Walter Walshe, whose name is written in it'.[27] Long after things had been mislaid, stolen, exchanged, or simply worn out, the entry in the inventory or gift book could also stand in for the original gifted object and memory of the donor. In November 1637, for instance, the hard-pressed Goldsmiths' Company recorded 'the particuler waight and Armes and other remarkable expressions of the donors' with regard to their corporate silver, just as the collection was about to be sold, so 'that when the Companye shalbee of abilitie then they may supplye and restore the said guifts of the Donors'. Gifted objects were indeed re-made at a later date (see figure 5.1).[28] Similarly, when selling off their silver plate collection in October 1642, the Barber Surgeons ensured that for 'every parcell of that plate which shalbe sold a patterne or fashion of it shalbe drawne in paper and the perticuler Letters Writeings or Graveings shall likewise be written on that paper'.[29]

After inventories, books of gifts and benefactors are the richest manuscript sources for gifting within craft guilds. Though these books were typically compiled in the later seventeenth and eighteenth centuries, they provide vital evidence of gifting practices in the sixteenth and early seventeenth centuries. The Girdlers' Company's Benefactions Book lists gifts of land, property, material culture, and money, from 1431 to 1638. A great number of sixteenth-century 'Gyfts to Thall' are noted within this volume, including silver and pewter plate, textiles, painted tables, books, and 'newe glasse wyndoes' engraved with the donors' names.[30] Similarly the Coopers' Company's Benefactors' List, running from the late fifteenth to the late eighteenth century, and first compiled by the clerk in 1718, includes both charitable endowments and material legacies.[31] Unlike inventories, which were, in part, working documents enabling company officials to keep track of their moveable property, record the value of plate and napery, and assess rates of deterioration, books of gifts and benefactions, compiled retrospectively, served a more explicitly self-aggrandising purpose. The Book of Benefactors compiled by the Armourers' Company from the early 1660s,

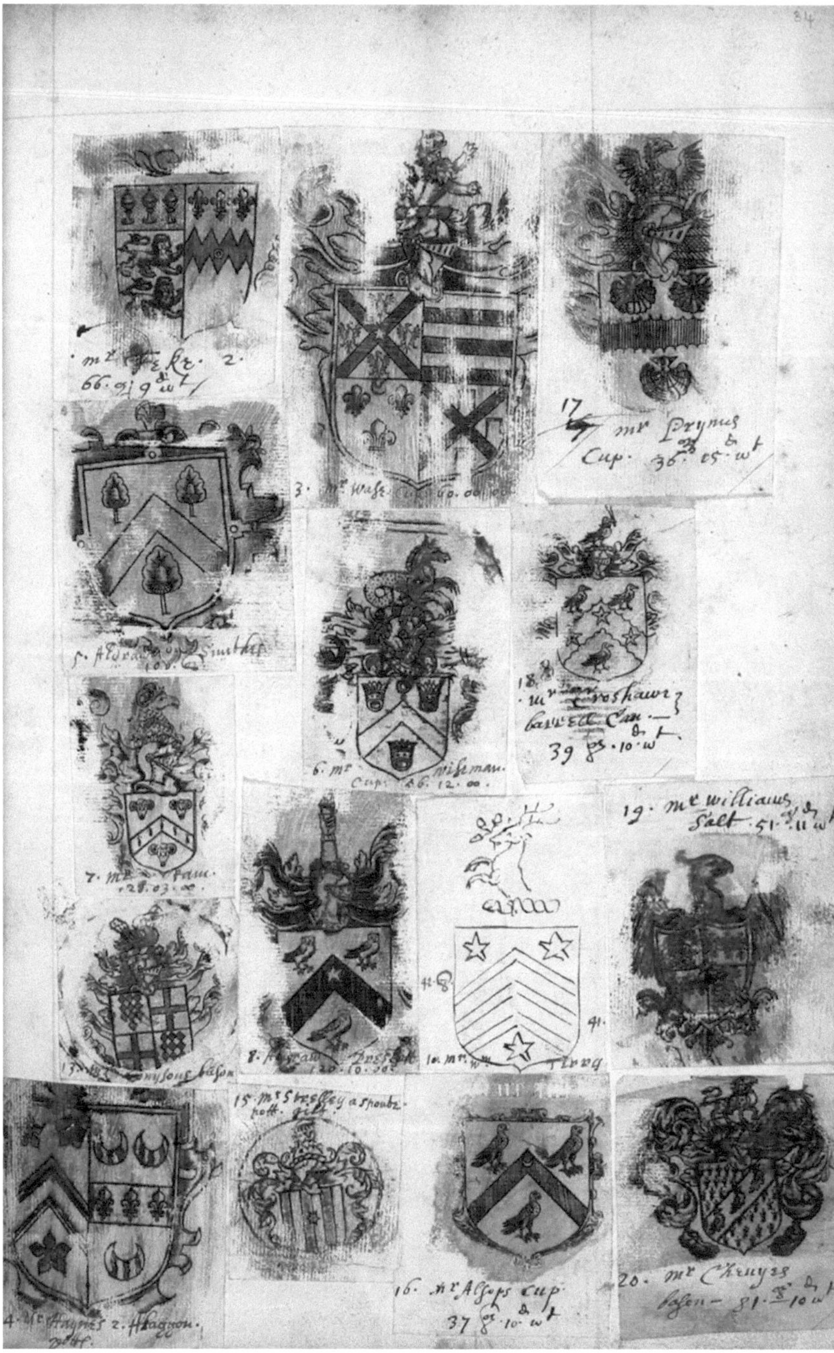

Figure 5.1 Etchings and drawings of 'the particuler waight and Armes and other remarkable expressions of the donors' of plate to the Goldsmiths' Company. November 1637, WA/CM, T, fo. 34r. The 'waight' refers to the weight of the individual pieces gifted.

for instance, lists 'plate, goods and money' donated to the guild from the acquisition of their hall in 1428, and was evidently intended to be a permanent record of the generosity and virtuosity of guild patrons and worthies.[32] This careful commemoration of civic philanthropy was no doubt also intended to spur additional donations and bequests.[33]

For the historian, the limitation of gift and benefaction books lies in their inevitable selectivity. Often writing generations after the initial donation, company clerks recorded benefactions that the liverymen themselves deemed to be significant and which required a 'return', in the form of ceremonial memorialisation in company archives, on commemorative boards in the hall, and in quarter day speeches.[34] The objects recorded in gift books (and inventories) were things which the assistants had decided were 'gifts' and were thus labelled as such. It is entirely feasible that there were a host of other objects, whose presence is now forever lost, which were not thought worth recording because of the social status of the donor, or because they were rejected or considered unsuitable. As a consequence this chapter is inevitably focused on the gifting patterns of the company elites, the liverymen, and especially those who formed the core of this group, the court of assistants, though there is also some evidence of material presentations from within the yeomanry. The account book of the yeomanry 'governor' and wardens of the Tallow Chandlers' Company, a group who had their own dedicated chamber within the company hall, features an inventory of the yeomanry's possessions for nearly every year of the accounts, from 1519 to 1627.[35] There are also occasional, tantalising hints in the archival record that the gifting process could sometimes be disrupted, and that the donation might even generate controversy. For example, when the goldsmith George Smithes bequeathed a cup to the Goldsmiths' Company, the assistants expressed their 'dislike of some of the verses graven on the cup, which they desire to be altered'.[36] Moreover, changing political and religious circumstances meant that objects which were once deemed 'good' gifts and were entered into official records might subsequently come to be viewed as unsuitable, even subversive, and so be deleted from the archive, removed from the hall, and destroyed or hidden.

Motivations for material gifts

Why give? What motivated the presentation of material gifts by artisans to their companies? Donors never stated their motives explicitly, but the nature of the gift, its timing, and physical placing can yield clues. Broadly there were four principal anticipated returns on the guild gift, none of which were mutually exclusive: the establishment of civic status and memorial cultures, the construction of craft identity, the material production of 'company', and the reinforcement of civic authority.

If the guild gifting 'repertoire' ranged from the 'freely given' to the 'obligatory', the presentation of silver stands at the latter end of this spectrum.[37] However, through inscriptions of crests, names, personal mottos, and craft symbols, there was considerable scope for an individualised and competitive dimension. Silver plate and cutlery, including covered cups, bowls, spoons, and knives, were the most ubiquitous type of gift recorded; they were also often compulsory offerings within most City companies. Gifts of plate, especially silver gilt drinking vessels with lids, and silver spoons of a certain weight, were the customary donations made by an individual upon admission to a guild, acceptance into the livery, as a fine for unacceptable behaviour such as trade offence, or compensation for declining office.[38] Typical was the order of the court of the Pewterers' Company, recorded at the end of an early sixteenth-century inventory that any man entering the livery 'shall bring in and hand over to the Master and Wardens a silver spoon weighing an ounce or more. And this rule is to continue till the Hall has a stock of spoons for as many people as may be seated in the Hall and Parlour.'[39]

The particular significance of the gift of silver plate lay in its intrinsic material value and potential for mutability and exchange. Collections of silver formed essential reserves of ready bullion and at times of political and financial pressure, or extraordinary expenditure, guilds sold or melted down their collections of plate, accumulated through generations of individual donations. 'Gre[a]tly impoverished by reason of the dayly charges and taxes' levied by both City and Crown, the Founders' Company had sold off all their admission spoons by 1635, each marked with the donor's initials or name, all except Humphrey Bowen's spoon, gifted in 1624–25, and inscribed on both sides of the handle: 'If You Love Me, Keep Me Ever. That's My Desire and Your Endeavour.'[40] In this instance the inscription evidently proved instructive and the single object stood in for the entire dispersed collection. Following an expensive building project – the construction of an anatomy theatre at their hall – the Barber Surgeons' Company sold off the yeomanry's entire collection of plate in 1636, except a single gifted beer bowl.[41] The aspiration to keep up with changing fashions in plate design and the shifting prestige of object types also resulted in the dispersal and remodelling of existing plate collections. In 1579 the assistants of the Armourers' Company paid a goldsmith for the 'changing of vi owld platters and ii pottell potts into ii great chargers and ii newe pottell potts'. In 1602 they decided to 'change awaye so manie of [the] silver spoones belonging to this Companie as should amount unto the value of three salts ... which were set up in the counting house amongst the other plate'.[42]

The (often) obligatory nature of these gifts and the intrinsic value of company silver, which made it both a gift and a commodity, did not, however, negate the potential for plate to act as a conveyor of status and memory. Through designs, markings, and inscriptions these objects acted as tangible bearers of identity. Gifts of plate marked an individual's term of civic office or transition from non-citizen to citizen, or from yeomanry estate to that of the livery.[43] These objects also played an active role in the ritual and social life of the company, observed on the buffet or table in the hall or parlour and touched and utilised by company elites at feasts and dinners. Records of the inscriptions on silver and pewter plate speak of the significance of sociability and affective bonds between citizens, and how these objects facilitated convivial interactions. This language of fellowship was particularly appropriate at the feasting table, which epitomised – in theory, if not always in practice – the reciprocal culture of guild gifting, mutual obligation, and 'brotherly love'.[44] The silver spoon presented by cutler and 'younger warden' William Cave to his company, 'marked on the handle thereof be ye all of one mynd love as brethren' was a typical offering.[45] Bequests of silver cups with engraved armorials and inscriptions, objects which were customarily used for the first time at the remembrance dinner of the donor in the company hall, after the citizen's burial and funeral sermon, played strongly on the connections between institutional fellowship and personal memorialisation. Gifts presented to the early seventeenth-century Goldsmiths' Company included silver gilt cups inscribed with the arms of the donor and the following mnemonics: 'This guifte I leave amongst my friends, Of that which God did give, That when I dye this guifte of myne Amongst my friends may live'.[46] And, 'When at your Hall doth shine with plate, And all your dishes served in state, When mirth abound, and wine is free, Then (freely drinking) think on me'.[47] Through interactions with such objects at guild feasts and dinners, 'amongst my friends', the symbolic community of guildsmen extended beyond the present company.[48] Gifts of plate were undoubtedly investments, forming essential reserves of institutional silver, but they also perpetuated the 'social memory' of previous generations of artisans in the minds of the living civic community.

Words or the armorial bearings of a donor or the company were not the only symbols upon gifts of silver and pewter plate. Craft marks of master artisans and mercantile dynasties were also inscribed, providing a strong link between the identity of the donor as a skilled workshop practitioner, and the gift for ritual use within the guild community. In 1519 carpenter Thomas Smart did 'give and bequeath … A Cupp of silver and cleane Guilt with my name and my timber mark in it weighing 27 oz' so 'that I the said Thomas may be the better rememb[e]red and prayed for in the said fellowship of Carpenters while our world shall endure'. In 1559 girdler John Cooke 'gave unto this house A Cupp with a Cover graven and gylt and with his mark'.[49] Though religious and memorial cultures had changed considerably since Smart's day, the craft mark continued to operate within the guild as a meaningful mnemonic device. Upon serving a successful apprenticeship, receiving the freedom, and thus becoming a citizen and active artisan, a maker's mark (which often incorporated the letters of his name or the tools or products of the trade) had to be formally approved and registered at the appropriate company hall. Inventories show that pewter or lead tables 'with the marks of all the whole craft' were prominently displayed within company parlours, the key site of civic governance and craft regulation.[50] Bert De Munck has argued that every hallmarked object represented collective material quality and was in a sense a gift offering that anchored 'the spirit of the giver to the product'. Here it is suggested that, in London, the individual maker's marks were especially potent, signifying the particular expertise and identity of the donor.[51]

The association between gifted object, mark, and donor must surely have had a further charge, within an institution of producers and retailers, when the artefact was created from the materials with which the giver had artisanal expertise. Thus a 'stope pot … vi lb markid with his owne marke' was presented by pewterer Robert Turner to his company in 1594.[52] Members of the Pewterers' Company frequently gave pewter plate to their guild, including 'pottell potts', spoons and dishes. Goldsmiths gave plate from their own workshops; armourers working in the City or at Greenwich gave suits and tools for display at Armourers' Hall on Coleman Street.[53] These were artefacts which demonstrated the donor's personal labour and expertise in the craft of the company, a feature of civic identity and status overlooked in existing interpretations of urban cultures.[54] The 'spirit' of the maker (and donor) was inextricably and uniquely linked to these gifts. The early sixteenth-century French craftsman Marion Garret, for example, Henry VIII's personal bladesmith, presented 'a table knyf and a carvynge knyf of [his] guift' to the Cutlers' Company, possibly a donation associated with his naturalisation and admission to the English guild.[55] This presentation was perhaps intended both to foster goodwill between himself and the London Cutlers, and also showcase his personal expertise in the craft. This strategy seems to have worked. By the late sixteenth century these knives were displayed in the same hall chamber as Garret's portrait, demonstrating that working identities were closely in dialogue with what have conventionally been perceived as 'civic' virtues.[56] The status that such a hand-wrought gift might hold within the guild in the years following its presentation is indicated by 'a knyf of the guifte of Mr Richard Mathewe' being placed first on the list of objects in the parlour, the most exclusive room in the late sixteenth-century Cutlers' Hall.[57] Mathew also presented knives for use at the lord mayor's feasting table in Guildhall and a sword of state, 'well and workmenly wrought and gylded' to the City Corporation, 'desiring onely ye reasonable favour of this Court in suche his honest sutes'. Mathew was an active citizen and working cutler with an unrivalled expertise in the manufacture of knives.[58] He was even praised in John Stow's *Survey of London* for his innovative workshop practices: 'the first Englishman that attained to the Skill of making fine Knives and Knife-hafts'.[59]

Gifts to guilds worked not only to demonstrate the personal expertise of the associated donor, but also to make the ideal of institutional 'companie' material.[60] The link between gifting and the physical construction of corporate community is most explicit in the case of the sponsorship of the material apparatus of the guild feast. In the 1550s, for example, a member of the Girdlers' Company 'dyd gyve to this howse one playne table cloth ii dozen playne napkyns and the frame for the high table', a parcel of gifts which ensured that he had single-handedly sponsored the entire top feasting table.[61] An early seventeenth-century armourer even gave 'three dozen of Brasse hookes … for to hang hats upon as the Co[mpany] sitteth at dinner'.[62] Gifts from the yeomanry to their guild were typically items for use in the yeomanry's quarterly feasts, including mazers, horns, wine and beer pots, trenchers, long spits, and 'dripping pannes'.[63] The significance of provisioning these events, to which all yeomanry members were invited, suggests the strong institutional and social identity these meals fostered. Amongst the livery, the donation of napery, especially table napkins and cloths, by a master or a warden in the year of his service – and marked with his initials and/or craft mark – was a custom across the craft guilds. The gift of the master pewterer Sir Thomas Curtis, on 1 January 1549/50, of 'a playne table clothe for the hye table [and] a dd [dozen] of playne napkyns markyd with his marke', demonstrates that a citizen's mercantile or craft mark might act as a powerful status symbol on textiles as well as plate.[64] As each individual seated at the high table would be provided with a napkin 'markyd with hys marke', Curtis was explicitly demonstrating ownership over the social and material worth of the gift itself and the legitimacy of his place at this privileged site of fellowship.[65] In this particular instance, the longevity and representational authority of Curtis's craft mark upon the table napkins was further enhanced through being reproduced by the company clerk in the margin of the archival record on which the gift was recorded (see figure 5.2).[66]

The gift of painted wooden surfaces in the form of framed 'tables', hung and displayed in the court room, parlour, gallery, but most frequently in the communal hall, did not have intrinsic material value, but were nevertheless a highly visible means through which a donor might assert a personal association with the good government, biblical history, or antiquity of his company. Depictions of biblical scenes or the patron saints of companies – such as the 'storie of Noyes [Noah's] flude' on a table in Cutlers' Hall or 'a table of joyners worke with the picture of St George upon it in vellom' in Armourers' Hall – were popular choices.[67] As we saw in Chapter 4, a group of liverymen of the Carpenters' Company sponsored a mural at the high end of their late sixteenth-century hall representing the fundamental role of carpenters and the craft throughout Old and New Testament history (see figure 4.2).[68] Within the guild context, such representations of biblical ancestry no doubt served to bolster both

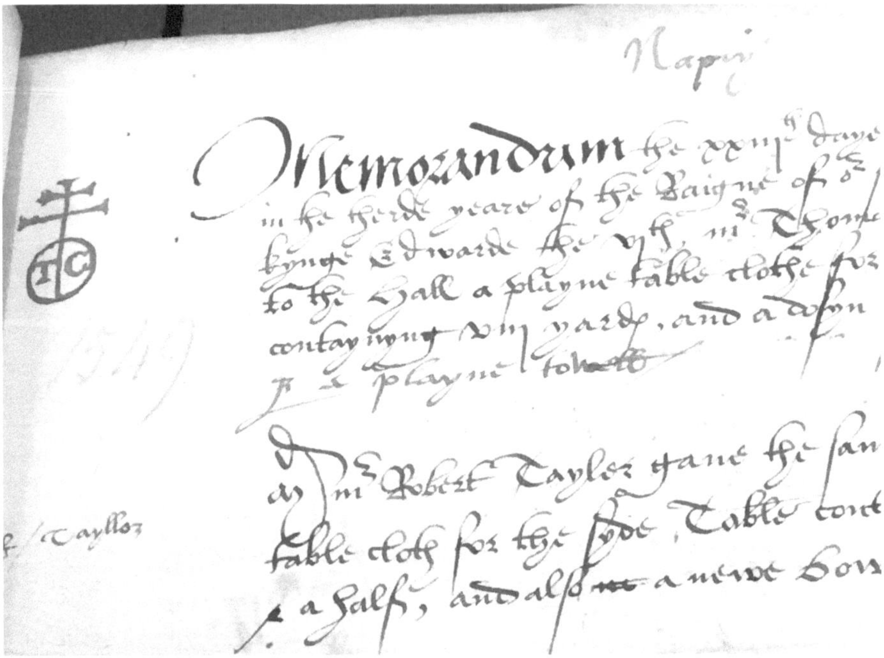

Figure 5.2 The craft mark of Thomas Curtis (or Curtyes) in the margin of the Pewterers' Company inventory book, GL, MS 7110, fo. 11r.

the occupational identity of the craft practitioners and the legitimacy of the company elites who had sponsored the image.[69] The Old Testament scenes chosen for the Carpenters' wall paintings were those that demonstrated the intimate connection between the skills and materials of carpentry and the survival and salvation of mankind: Noah constructing the ark and thus ensuring the existence of God's creation; the central role of 'the artificers and carpenters and masons' in the rebuilding of Josiah's Temple, artisans who were said to 'deal' and 'work' 'faithfully'.[70] The New Testament depictions of Christ and the Holy Family make Jesus's ancestral relationship to the craft of carpentry absolutely explicit. In the third painting we see him observing and aiding his earthly father within Joseph's carpentry workshop; in the final image we witness the disbelief of the crowds in the synagogue, 'Is not this the Carpenter's Son?'[71] The trees depicted in the first and third paintings of the frieze – those of Noah and the Holy Family – were perhaps also an allusion to the Tree of Jesse, the ubiquitous late medieval symbol for the genealogy of Christ (the carpenter). Clearly the absent image of ultimate salvation is that of Christ on the wooden cross. A visual representation of the Passion would have been wholly unsuitable in the post-Reformation context, though it is possible that the horizontal plane of wood, which dominates our field of vision in the depiction of Joseph's workshop, was intended to act as a figurative reference to the Crucifixion (see Plate 9).

In depicting the labours of the carpenters, and in giving the material of their trade such visual prominence, the frieze must have also drawn attention to the extensive contemporary re-building work at Carpenters' Hall, undertaken by prominent members of the guild. A mural which celebrated the skills and historic importance of carpenters was thus embedded in a broader timber showpiece of the carpenters' collective ingenuity. The visual emphasis on historic antiquity was perhaps all the more significant for the City's craft companies, which lacked the extensive endowments, philanthropic cultures, and 'merchant heroes' of the City's wealthiest and most prestigious mercantile companies.

Ubiquitous in guild buildings were tables displaying text related to the ordinances of the company, regulations of the craft, and the founders and benefactors of the guild – gifts which unambiguously represented civic authority, particularly in relation to the yeomanry, the predominantly artisanal; and occasionally unruly element of the guild body.[72] In the Pewterers' hall chamber from the late 1580s hung a board with a 'wrytten acomendation of love and justyce'.[73] The display of these tables in the common hall specifically ensured that they were viewed by the largest number of guild members and visitors. By contrast, there was a parallel trend of displaying 'civic portraits' in the more exclusive and generally inaccessible rooms of parlour and great chamber.[74] In the 1550s the Girdlers' Company was presented with five tables from John Nicholls, including 'a joyned table to hang in t[he] hall wherein he hath wrytten with his owne hand the Actes and ordinances of t[he] howse to be reade ev[e]ry quarter daye'. The other tables related to the taking and enrolling of apprentices, the making of 'lawfull' wares, and 'of all the evidence and wrytinge that be in t[he] hows of this daye'. The association between Nicholls and these gifts was reinforced by each being 'of his owne hand wryting'.[75] Likewise a donor to the Armourers' Company 'did make and give … a table faire written in meeter of the Antiquity of this Co[mpany]'.[76] The Cutlers' guild had in their 'great hall' a framed table of 'the orders of the Companye fayrelye written and lymmed' in addition to a table listing the names of 'divers of first beginners of this company in the tyme of Edward third', with two doors 'to shut together'.[77] It is tempting to see an allusion to the closed panels of a triptych in this design, with folding doors which were perhaps only opened to reveal the names of 'the ancient beginners of the societie of cutlers' on quarter days and the election feast (which coincided with the patronal feast day).[78]

The presentation of wooden chests, boxes, and presses, which proliferated within company buildings from the mid-sixteenth century, for the storage of charters, manuscripts, books, seals, jewels, and plate, and the carrying out of elections, symbolically linked the donor to significant administrative and governmental processes and the company's most precious material collections. The armourer John Pasfield – master of the associated company six times between 1583 and 1597 – gave 'a wainscot box made to serve for the choice or like of ... fines leases tenants rents or any other thing that shall be put to election' in the 1590s. He also gave a 'fair large chest bound with iron. A lock in the midst and fower hanging locks to it the chest' for the storage of documents, with keys for each of the three wardens, and one for himself.[79] This was not an unusual gift for a man of his civic position and responsibilities, particularly during an era in which ownership and access to guild archives and treasures was becoming increasingly restricted and contentious.[80]

Conspicuous so far by their absence from this discussion of gifts and returns have been female donors. Women could not hold office or attend court meetings, and female donors were almost always the wives (or more usually the widows) of the guild elite. Textiles were the gifts most commonly given, an unsurprising discovery in view of the cultural value of textiles within female gifting networks.[81] Since needlework was perceived as a female accomplishment, it is probable that these textile gifts were personally produced or modified by their female donors, thus combining a symbol of identity and status with a demonstration of skill and devotion.[82] Mary Bishop left to the Stationers' Company in her will of 1613 'ten pounds foure arras wrought cushens a cubberd cloth and two long flaxen table-clothes of her owne spinning'.[83] These hand-wrought gifts often incorporated the initials of the married couple. The 'six lowe stooles for women' presented in 1606 by widow Agnes Sherman to the Girdlers Company were covered with green fabric 'and marked on the toppe in the middle with letters embrodered of black velvet T. S. A: for the name of her .... And Mr Thomas Sherman her said husband'.[84] These seats were used by Agnes and her fellow city wives and widows on the relatively rare occasions that women were admitted into the hall for dinners and festivities.[85] In 1570 another widow, Mystres Wyet, had given to the Girdlers a 'cupboard clothe wrought with blacke silke and a blacke and white fringe for the windowe in the hall to set plate vpon'. An armourer's wife likewise gave 'to the high cuboard in the [Armourers'] Hall a fine cuboard cloath'.[86] The cupboard cloth was a highly strategic gift choice since it was placed under the most prestigious window in the hall (usually a bay window), and provided an opulent backdrop for the silver buffet during occasions of civic significance, including election dinners, and funeral feasts.[87]

Spatial contexts of the material gift

The political culture of guild gifting was firmly embedded within the particular spatial and architectural contexts of the livery hall. On walls, ceilings, staircases, gates, and within window frames, and through the mediums of wood, stone, plaster, and glass, guildsmen competed to have their initials, marks, words, or armorial bearings displayed in the most prestigious spaces and chambers within company buildings (see figure 4.1).[88] As shown in Chapter 4, the comprehensive inventory of the Pewterers' Company includes a list from 1497–98 of guildsmen and company widows who had gifted glazed window panels for the hall, parlour, and counting house, including a bay window, 'the high wyndowe over the high dais', and 'the wyndowe next to the gardyne dore', using 'flemysshe' and 'normandy' glass. Company hierarchies were both affirmed and negotiated through this process of material sponsorship. Master Lawrence Aslyn funded the most prestigious 'high' window in the internal hall, and the wardens and former office-holders were responsible for additional panes (or 'half' or 'third' panels) throughout the chamber. Whereas the hall windows were sponsored by current and former masters and wardens, the parlour windows were exclusively funded by men with no official title but with evident ambition to enhance their social and civic status. Company accounts show that Thomas Chamberleyn, Robert Langtot, John Magson, William Pecke, and Richard Taylor all supplied 'glasid' panes for the parlour in 1497–98 and subsequently went on to hold company office over the next two decades.[89] More than half a century later, as the Pewterers were again engaged in a project of building improvement and expansion, civic hierarchies were made material through the institutional built fabric. Between 1551 and 1553 members of the Pewterers' Company competed over the precise locations of their contributions towards the 'seallyng [wainscoting] of the hall'. Heraldic symbols were also set up in the form of carved and painted wooden devices, displaying the company insignia and familial arms of benefactors. These were not always by the same individuals who had paid for the general panelling, thus creating a complex material surface of patronage and status.[90] Material sponsorship of the livery hall was a defining feature of civic ambition, and institutional architectures were themselves conceived of as gifts.

London's early modern citizens also demonstrated an acute awareness of the ceremonial value of the very act of gifting, 'the politics of representation'.[91] Though benefaction books and inventories are generally thin on contextual detail concerning the precise circumstances in which a moveable gift was bestowed, occasional entries in court minutes relating to especially grand donations demonstrate that artisans timed their performances of generosity with care. For example, following a meeting of the court of assistants in 1562, and just before their dinner at Armourers' Hall began, armourer John Bell 'in the presence of all … afore sayd gave unto this hawll one dosande of playn nappkyns markyd with a J and a B and he gave at the same tyme a tabull knife to take uppe ye tabull'.[92] Ideally a large number of citizens, particularly those belonging to the political elite, would witness the act of gifting, and preferably the donor's peers might be assembled within the livery hall on a day of customary importance in the ritual calendar, thus amplifying the status of the giver and gift. At guild feasts, held on days of craft, religious, or political significance, the upper echelons of the company were present and the hall was hung with banners, streamers and tapestries (see Plate 5). Further, the feast was customarily a convivial event associated with civic reciprocity and generosity, including the distribution of alms and pensions.[93] In 1567 the accomplished armourer John Kelte was at the peak of his professional career, as a liveryman of the Armourers' Company and Master Workman at the royal armour workshops at Greenwich. He presented his gift to the company, a model pattern harness in the latest Greenwich style, at the master's election feast that year. Kelte placed his gift on a platter and theatrically processed it, before the multiple serving dishes of food, to the high table.[94] The court minutes describe this suit as a 'mannakyne' and it was kept in a specially made cupboard and dressed in satin and blue silk on feast days.[95] The highly ritualised giving of this hand-wrought gift, in imitation of civic ceremony, evidently mirrored its future use within the corporate community.

Objects specifically associated with company election rites, such as election garlands, hats or crowns, or election cups, were especially charged gifts, which might only be presented by those who had served as guild master. Election artefacts had an unusual type of agency within guild culture, for it was through drinking from the election cup, and/or having been crowned with the election wreath that one formally became a new master or warden. Rather like a crown at the royal coronation, these garlands did not merely represent authority, but through their use, brought about a new status.[96] The Goldsmiths' Company's court of assistants stressed that a warden was only invested with civic authority 'at the feast daye by the garlands then sett upon their heads'.[97] Through their theatrical presentation at the election feast and subsequent use at all such future election rituals these artefacts materially linked the memory of the donor with the election ceremony and civic office, long after his lifetime. For the guild community, the use of ritualised objects also provided a sense of continuity and stability across the generations.[98] The connections between personal reputation, craft identity, and durable political legitimacy are nicely illustrated by a gifting example from August 1575, when Master Cuthbert Beeston

> of his owne free will gave unto the use of the Master of the said [Girdlers'] Companye yerely to be elected and chosen forever, one crowne Garlande of blacke velvet imbrodered with the letters of his name … and a gridyron of golde, and the girdle with the buckles of brodered gold lace compassinge the crowne.[99]

As Beeston's gift choice suggests, the objects presented for use at election ceremonies were highly valuable, both in their use of precious natural and manufactured materials, such as gold, silver, rock crystal, pearl, and velvet, and through exquisite craftsmanship. Election garlands, crowns or cups were very often the most intrinsically valuable object in a company's entire collection of plate and linen; the quality of the materials and workmanship heightening the visual and material splendour of the rite. At the Goldsmiths' election feast of 1560, Master Sir Martin Bowes presented for use at all future election ceremonies four 'fair garlands of crimson velvet, garnished with silver and gold, and set with pearls and stones' and 'a fair gilt Standying Cuppe, weighing 80 ounces ... with a manikin on the cover holding a skutchyn whereon his arms be graved in an annealed plate of gold' (see figure 5.3).[100] The iconography of objects for use at election typically incorporated craft symbols and patron saints, presumably valued because of their antiquity. The 'iiii garlandes of crimson velvet' acquired by the Tallow Chandlers' Company in 1564 were ornamented with 'vii Turtle doves of silver and iiii St Johns hedes of silver and gilte'. The Pewterers' four election garlands were decorated with silver pendants of 'the image of our lady'. The yeomanry wardens of the Haberdashers' Company were crowned at their election feast with garlands of crimson velvet with silver pendants depicting SS. George and Katherine.[101]

Figure 5.3 *The Bowes Cup*, silver-gilt, enamel, rock crystal, h. 49.3 cm, d. 19.3 cm, 1554. Gifted in 1560 to the Goldsmiths' Company by Martin Bowes. The enamelled shield on the lid finial features the arms of Bowes.

Across the City companies, a discernible chronological pattern emerges in relation to the gifting of election artefacts. From *c*. 1560 the spaces within the livery hall where election ceremonies took place were expanded, materially improved and embellished, and the ritual election objects presented underwent a similar transformation. Despite repeated assertions in company archives that all things were observed and performed as 'of ancient tyme it hath bene accustomed', election rites were also being newly codified and adapted.[102] During the 1560s it was decided by the governors of the Armourers' Company that 'where as afore tyme there was no place apoynted for the old wardens', now former wardens would sit with the current authorities at the 'feast dener', and might all 'ryse jointly together and goe with their garlands'. In 1595, by a command of the court of the Ironmongers' Company, the precise seating arrangements and order of service at the annual election feast for the 'Highe Table', the 'Seconde Table', and the 'Thirde Table' were codified for the first time.[103] The splendour of election ceremonies reflected upon the status of the guild and officers were keenly aware of parallel ritual practices in each other's halls. It is telling that in 1560 the court of the Goldsmiths' Company decided that 'the ceremony of choosing the wardens with garlands on our feast day (as the use is in other Companies) shall be used in this Company'.[104]

Continuity and change: gifting practices and material collections

We turn finally to the issue of continuity and change to gifting practices and material collections across the sixteenth and early seventeenth centuries. The evidence of objects for use at election ceremonies shows that there were some innovations in gifting practices in the types of things given and methods of presentation from the second half of the sixteenth century. This was a trend linked, in all likelihood, to the enlargement of company halls and the broader elaboration of civic ceremony.[105] The opportunities for very senior freemen to perpetuate their reputations through ritualised material gifts were enhanced. The embellishment of rites of gift-giving, events focused upon reciprocity between citizen and company, also look to be further evidence for the rise of associational 'bourgeois' culture in this period.[106] Furthermore, the synchronisation of gifting and feasting rituals within guild communities from the mid-sixteenth century, rites which were both intended to reinforce bonds between citizens, is suggestive of the increasing prevalence of civic sociability or 'company' in early modern urban England.[107]

We might anticipate that the Reformation had a profound impact upon guild gifting cultures. The 'intensely iconoclastic opening phase of the English Reformation' is often said to have dealt a weighty blow to provincial urban culture.[108] Adding an important religious dimension to the pessimistic social and economic analysis of sixteenth-century urban England, Robert Tittler suggests that the comprehensive process of 'refashioning … a useful collective memory' by England's citizens from *c*. 1540, resulted in a truly distinctive post-Reformation culture. Religious iconography and mythology were replaced with new forms of civic regalia, civic portraiture, and historical writing.[109] The evidence of London's craft companies presents a rather more nuanced picture of continuity and change.[110] Practices of material gifting and memorialisation survived the Reformation upheavals with relatively few significant changes. Some prominent objects were removed from company halls as no longer acceptable. But many other gifts survived. The guild archives provide no explanation for this pattern, but we can speculate on possible factors, including: the variable balance of reformed or conservative sympathies among the livery and assistants of each guild; corporate pride in guild traditions; and the close association of patron saints with the particular craft of guild members. It is probable that the symbolic meanings of gifts also underwent modification in new spatial and material contexts.

From the surviving evidence it is clear that following the Edwardian injunctions of 1547 certain iconographies and materialities, those undeniably devotional, were no longer acceptable within London company collections.[111] Among the gifts initially accepted but later removed from guild inventories, gift books, and halls were: the gilded statue of St. Dunstan in Goldsmiths' Hall, set with precious stones; 'the crest of the high deyesse [dais] with three Angells' in Armourers' Hall; and a table for an altar with 'an ymage of Seint Clement', belonging to the Founders' Company.[112] The gift of a gilt image of St. John the Baptist, 'standyng in a Tabernacle' in Merchant Taylor's Hall in the early sixteenth century, is conspicuous by its absence in the next surviving company inventory, taken in the first decade of the seventeenth century.[113] In a reformed religious context in which the intercessory role of saints was denied, three dimensional, gilded images of these figures were unsuitable. But livery halls were not stripped of all religious material culture. The craft guilds of London showed a sustained enthusiasm for visual imagery of their late medieval patron saints well into the Elizabethan Reformation, as evidenced by representations of saints on gifts of silver plate, banners and flags, wall paintings and hangings, wooden shields, and election garlands. In 1562 the Tallow Chandlers still had hanging from the high end of their company hall 'a gilt beame with v lattyn candilsticks with the ymage of our ladie and a turtill dove'. And covering the walls they still had 'ii clothes the one of the ymage of the Assumpcion of our ladie and the other of our ladie and seynt Elizabeth'.[114] The most prized possession of the yeomanry of the Tallow Chandlers, from its donation in 1536, remained a mazer with 'the image of saint Katheryn in the bottome of the gift of Mr Choppin'.[115] Though in a reformed religious context patron saints could no longer be invoked, the direct working relationship to the craft, combined with the historic antiquity of the saints, evidently endowed these figures with sustained cultural value, across the Reformation divide.[116] Perhaps, as in the case of the Carpenters' wall paintings, saintly lives continued to provide a worthy example of artisanal skill acquisition, specifically the collective 'mystery' of the craft guild.[117] Nor is this picture of iconographic continuity wholly surprising. Research on the decoration of English domestic interiors, and cathedrals and parish churches, shows a similar pattern of religious material culture removals and survivals across the 'long Reformation' period.[118]

Once they were part of a company collection the meanings of a gift could also change over time, and explicitly devotional associations might be detoxified. Take, for example, the polychromed oak sculpture of St. George and the Dragon, presented to the Armourers' Company in 1528 by William Vynyard, premier citizen and artisan at the peak of his civic ascendancy, which we encountered at the beginning of the chapter (see Plate 12). This exceptional gift, encased in miniature steel armour of the latest Italian fashion, had been made in Vynyard's own workshop and started life as a devotional object – as evidenced by its donation with 'a Lattin Candlestick that is before it' – located before the high table in Armourer's Hall (another sculpture of St. George was displayed in the Armourers' chantry at St. Pauls).[119] By the late sixteenth century, long after the death of its donor and in a different religious climate, Vynyard's sculpture of St. George (patron saint of the company) was the inspiration not for religious piety but stood rather as an exemplar of the armourers' technical skills. A number of other working guild members crafted and presented miniature armoured St. Georges (or 'mannakynes') and 'Twelve Compleats foot Armors' (full-sized suits), which were conspicuously displayed as a group, with Vynyard's original gift, in the new 'Gallery over the Hall'.[120]

As with the iconography of gifts, the mnemonic function of material cultures in London's sixteenth- and early seventeenth-century guilds suggests more continuity than change. The Reformation brought a certain fundamental alteration to the memorial cultures of the City's artisanal guilds, namely that with the rejection of the doctrine of good works and the suppression of fraternities and chantries, gifts could no longer directly invite prayers from the living on behalf of the soul of the deceased. But memorialisation within the guild involved a broad understanding of the reciprocal relationship between living and dead company members. Commemoration meant more than intercessory prayers.[121] The evidence of material gifts, and their continued ritualised uses during feasts, funerals, elections, and civic ceremonies, shows that the social obligation to remember the honour and generosity of former generations of civic office-holders was deeply woven into the fabric of guild culture.

Inventories and books of gifts and benefactors show that the practice of giving material things was a thread of institutional cultural continuity within late medieval and early modern City companies – a means by which identity, legitimacy, and memorialisation were negotiated within London's craft guilds. The culture of guild gifting was so deep-rooted and significant that it could survive the disruptions of the Reformation with relatively few changes. A focus upon the nature and meaning of objects of exchange within craft companies has shown that when fashioning contemporary and post-mortem reputations, notions of skill and workshop technique were highly valued by London's citizens, alongside philanthropic ideals.

Notes

1 GL, MS 12071/1, fo. 14.
2 GL, MS 12105, fo. 10. William Vynyard also sponsored the built fabric of Armourers' Hall, including 'the lattice [work] that be about the galleryes into the [hall] chamber and making the white seates in the parlor and the laying of them'.
3 Alfred Gell, *Art and Agency: Towards an Anthropological Theory* (Oxford: Clarendon Press, 1998).
4 Appadurai, 'Introduction: commodities and the politics of value', pp. 3–63; Igor Kopytoff, 'The cultural biography of things: commoditization as process', in Appadurai (ed.), *The Social Life of Things*, pp. 64–91; Bruno Latour, *Reassembling the Social: An Introduction to Actor-Network-Theory* (Oxford: Oxford University Press, 2005), pp. 70–82.
5 GL, MS 7164, fos 5r–13r.
6 Robert Tittler, 'Sir Thomas White of London: civic philanthropy and the making of the merchant-hero', in Tittler, *Townspeople and Nation: English Urban Experiences, 1540–1640* (Stanford, CA: Stanford University Press, 2001), pp. 100–20; Archer, 'The livery companies and charity'; Ward, *Culture, Faith and Philanthropy*.
7 Material survivals are limited as a consequence of the Reformation, the Great Fire of 1666, and the aerial bombardment of the City of London in the early 1940s.
8 Felicity Heal, *Hospitality in Early Modern England* (Oxford: Clarendon Press, 1990); Felicity Heal, *The Power of Gifts: Gift-Exchange in Early Modern England* (Oxford: Oxford University Press, 2014); Ben-Amos, *The Culture of Giving*.
9 Heal, *The Power of Gifts*, pp. 63–82.
10 Durning, 'The Oxford college as household, 1580–1640', p. 90.
11 Linda Levy Peck, *Court Patronage and Corruption in Early Stuart England* (London: Unwin Hyman, 1990), pp. 18–20; Heal, *The Power of Gifts*, pp. 31–59; *The Elizabethan New Year's Gift Exchanges, 1559–1603*, ed. by Jane A. Lawson (Oxford: Oxford University Press for the British Academy, 2013).
12 Marcel Mauss, *The Gift: The Form and Reason for Exchange in Archaic Societies*, trans. by W. D. Halls (London: Routledge, 1990), p. 3.
13 GL, MS 5817, fos 7–8.
14 Brigden, 'Religion and social obligation', pp. 94–102.
15 Joseph Ward, 'Godliness, commemoration, and community'; Ward, *Culture, Faith and Philanthropy*; Ben-Amos, *The Culture of Giving*, pp. 242–55.
16 Robert Tittler, 'Portraiture, precedence and politics amongst the London liveries, c. 1540–1640', *Urban History*, 35:3 (2008), 349–62, at p. 355.
17 The distinguishing features are mapped out in Tittler, *The Face of the City*, pp. 3–7.
18 GL, MS 12106, fo. 53.
19 GL, MSS 12071/2, fo. 474v; 12107, fo. 6r.
20 Cooper, *Citizen Portrait*, pp. 200–3.

21 Tittler lists only nine 'civic portraits' acquired by companies outside the 'great twelve', all but one in the early seventeenth century [*The Face of the City*, pp. 174–5].
22 Compared to the 'great twelve', most guilds had much more modest charitable endowments, and in some cases none at all. See Ben-Amos, *The Culture of Giving*, pp. 102–4.
23 GL, MS 12105, fo. 11.
24 GL, MS 4326/6, fo. 39r.
25 Gervase Rosser, 'Going to the fraternity feast: commensality and social relations in late medieval England', *Journal of British Studies*, 33:4 (1994), 430–46.
26 Felicity Heal, 'Food gifts, the household and the politics of exchange in early modern England', *Past and Present*, 199:1 (2008), 41–70.
27 GL, MS 7110, fos 1v, 13v.
28 GHA, WA/CM, T, fos 29r–30v.
29 Young, *The Annals of the Barber-Surgeons*, p. 496.
30 GL, MS 5817, fos 7–37.
31 GL, MSS 5618/1–2.
32 GL, MS 12105.
33 Ian Archer, 'The arts and acts of memorialization in early modern London', in Julia Merritt (ed.), *Imagining Early Modern London*, pp. 89–113, at pp. 90, 97–8.
34 *Ibid.*, p. 99.
35 GL, MSS 6155/1–2; *Records of the Worshipful Company of Tallow Chandlers*, ed. by M. F. Monier-Williams, 2 vols (London, 1897–98), II, p. 255.
36 Prideaux, *Memorials of the Goldsmiths' Company*, I, 125.
37 Natalie Zemon Davis, *The Gift in Sixteenth-Century France* (Oxford: Oxford University Press, 2000), pp. 14–15.
38 Philippa Glanville, *Silver in England* (New York; London, 1987), pp. 308–9.
39 GL, MS 7110, fo. 6r.
40 William N. Hibbert, *History of the Worshipful Company of Founders of the City of London* (London: privately printed, 1925), p. 274; Guy Hadley, *Citizens and Founders: A History of the Worshipful Company of Founders, London, 1365–1975* (London: Phillimore, 1976), pp. 72–3.
41 Young, *The Annals of the Barber-Surgeons*, p. 495.
42 GL, MSS 12065/2, fo. 14v; 12071/2, fo. 663.
43 A parallel argument has been made in relation to the 'symbolic or representational meaning' of gifts of silver plate within the Oxford colleges. See Durning, 'The Oxford college as household', p. 90.
44 The assistants of the Armourers' Company lamented in 1610 that as a result of the 'neglect' of quarterly dinners, 'discords have arisen and brotherly love decreased' [GL, MS 12071/2].
45 GL, MS 7164 fo. 61r.
46 Prideaux, *Memorials of the Goldsmiths' Company*, I, p. 150.
47 *Ibid.*, pp. 156–7.
48 Shelia Sweetinburgh, 'Remembering the dead at dinner-time', in Tara Hamling and Catherine Richardson (eds), *Everyday Objects: Medieval and Early Modern Material Culture and its Meanings* (Farnham: Ashgate, 2010), pp. 257–66, at pp. 264–5.
49 GL, MSS 4332, fo. 2; 5817, fo. 13.
50 GL, MSS 7164, fo. 6r [Cutlers' Company]; 12107, fo. 3r [Armourers' Company]; 7110, fo. 31v [Pewterers' Company].
51 Bert De Munck, 'Artisans, products and gifts: rethinking the history of material culture in early modern Europe', *Past and Present*, 224:1 (2014), 39–74, at p. 64. For Mauss's original formulation of the 'spirit' of the gift, see *The Gift*, pp. 14–16.
52 GL, MS 7110.
53 GL, MSS 7110, fo. 32v–33r; 7164, fo. 6v.

54 There is a parallel here with the intellectual 'labour' associated with the gift of a manuscript or poem presented to a court patron. See Heal, *The Power of Gifts*, pp. 46–9.
55 Welch, *History of the Cutlers' Company*, I, p. 208; GL, MS 7164, fo. 5v.
56 Welch, *History of the Cutlers' Company*, II, p. 116.
57 GL, MS 7164, fo. 6r.
58 Welch, *History of the Cutlers' Company*, I, pp. 222–4. Richard Mathew was Master of the Cutlers' Company three times during the 1580s.
59 Cited in *ibid.*, p. 224.
60 Withington, 'Company and sociability', p. 300.
61 GL, MS 5817, fo. 11.
62 GL, MS 12105, fo. 14.
63 GL, MS 6155/2, fos 42v–43r.
64 GL, MS 7110, fo. 11r. Curtis was the first member of the Pewterers' Company to serve as lord mayor in 1557–58.
65 For 'paraliturgical' features of the late medieval guild feast, see Rosser, 'Going to the fraternity feast', pp. 433–7.
66 GL, MS 7110, fo. 11r.
67 GL, MSS 7164, fo. 7r; 12105, fo. 9.
68 Alford and Barker, *A History of the Carpenters' Company*, pp. 62, 150, 225–7.
69 Keith Thomas, *The Perception of the Past in Early Modern Europe: Creighton Trust Lecture* (London, 1983), p. 2; Archer, 'Discourses of history', p. 206.
70 Genesis 6.14–15; 2 Kings 22.7.
71 Elizabeth A. Lehfeldt, 'Ideal men: masculinity and decline in seventeenth-century Spain', *Renaissance Quarterly*, 61:2 (2008), 463–94, at p. 474, 'Joseph was the ideal male artisan, offering his productive labor as evidence of his virtue and devotion.'
72 Systemic tensions between the yeomanry and the livery should not be exaggerated. See Rappaport, *Worlds within Worlds*, pp. 219–32; Archer, *The Pursuit of Stability*, pp. 106–11.
73 Welch, *History of the Worshipful Company of Pewterers*, II, p. 4.
74 Robert Tittler, 'Faces and spaces: displaying the civic portrait in early modern England', in Hamling and Richardson (eds), *Everyday Objects*, pp. 179–87.
75 GL, MS 5817, fos 11–12.
76 GL, MS 12105, fo. 13.
77 GL, MS 7164, fo. 69r.
78 GL, MS 7164, fo. 69v. For spectacular surviving examples of early modern Netherlandish guild altarpieces, which combine craft imagery and patron saints, see Ria Fabri and Nico Van Hout, *From Quinten Metsijs to Peter Paul Rubens: Masterpieces from the Royal Museum Reunited in the Cathedral* (Antwerp: De Kathedraal VZM & BAI Publishers, 2009), pp. 13–43.
79 GL, MS 12105, fo. 13.
80 Griffiths, 'Secrecy and authority', pp. 934–5.
81 Sara Mendelson and Patricia Crawford, *Women in Early Modern England, 1550–1720* (Oxford: Clarendon Press, 1998), pp. 223; Lorna Weatherill, 'A possession of one's own: women and consumer behaviour in England, 1660–1740', *Journal of British Studies*, 25:2 (1986), 131–56, at p. 143.
82 Lisa M. Klein, 'Your humble handmaid: Elizabethan gifts of needlework', *Renaissance Quarterly*, 50:2 (1997), 459–93, at pp. 471–6.
83 W. A. Jackson (ed.), *Records of the Court of the Stationers' Company, 1602–1640* (London: Bibliographical Society, 1957), p. 62.
84 GL, MS 5817, fo. 37.
85 Female testamentary bequests were also targeted at women. See Claire Schen, *Charity and Lay Piety in Reformation London, 1500–1620* (Aldershot: Ashgate, 2002), p. 244.

86 GL, MSS 5817, fo. 18; 12105, fo. 11.
87 Schofield, *Medieval London Houses*, p. 131.
88 The display of portraits upon 'tables' in company halls could also be immensely competitive. See Tittler, 'Faces and spaces', pp. 184–5.
89 GL, MS 7110, fos 3v–4r.
90 Welch, *History of the Worshipful Company of Pewterers*, I, p. 274.
91 Gadi Algazi, 'Introduction: doing things with gifts', in Gadi Algazi, Valentin Groebner, and Bernhard Jussen (eds), *Negotiating the Gift: Pre-Modern Figurations of Exchange* (Göttingen: Vandenhoeck & Ruprecht, 2003), pp. 9–27, at p. 18; Archer, 'The arts and acts of memorialisation', p. 105.
92 GL, MS 12071/2, fo. 87.
93 Rosser, 'Going to the fraternity feast', pp. 436–7; Ben-Amos, *The Culture of Giving*, pp. 173–4.
94 Elizabeth Glover, *Men of Metal: History of the Armourers and Brasiers of the City of London* (Huddersfield: Jeremy Mills for The Worshipful Company of Armourers and Brasiers, 2008), p. 65.
95 GL, MS 12071/2, fo. 474v.
96 Edward Muir, *Ritual in Early Modern Europe*, 2nd edn (Cambridge: Cambridge University Press, 2005), p. 272.
97 GHA, WA/CM, K I, fo. 220.
98 For civic regalia in the post-Reformation urban provincial context see Tittler, *The Reformation and the Towns*, pp. 272–3.
99 GL, MS 5817, fo. 20. The gridiron related to the martyrdom of St. Laurence (d. 258).
100 Prideaux, *Memorials of the Goldsmiths' Company*, I, p. 63. The Bowes Cup is still within the Goldsmiths' Company's plate collection.
101 GL, MSS 6152/1, fo. 31r; 7110, fo. 12r; 15868, fo. 8r.
102 GHA, WA/CM, P1, fo. 28r.
103 GL, MSS 12071/2, fo. 33; 16960, fo. 64v.
104 Prideaux, *Memorials of the Goldsmiths' Company*, I, p. 63.
105 Berlin, 'Civic ceremony', pp. 18–19.
106 Barry, 'Bourgeois collectivism?'
107 Withington, *The Politics of Commonwealth*, pp. 129–37; 'Company and sociability', pp. 297–300; *Society in Early Modern England*, pp. 102–33.
108 Robert Tittler, 'Reformation, civic culture and collective memory in English provincial towns', *Urban History*, 24:3 (1997), 283–300, at p. 286.
109 Tittler, *The Reformation and the Towns*, ch. 13. Tittler was chiefly responding to the established narrative of the decline of sixteenth-century urban society and economy. See Peter Clark and Paul Slack, 'Introduction', in Clark and Slack (eds), *Crisis and Order in English Towns, 1500–1700* (London: Routledge, 1972), pp. 1–56.
110 Laura Branch has suggested that London's mercantile elite (specifically members of the Drapers' and Grocers' Companies) had diverse responses to religious change in the sixteenth century. See *Faith and Fraternity.*
111 Margaret Aston, *England's Iconoclasts, vol. 1, Laws against images* (Oxford: Clarendon Press, 1988), pp. 254–57.
112 GHA, WA/CM, I, fos 7, 16, 22; MS 12105, fo. 2; *Wardens' Accounts of the Worshipful Company of Founders*, p. 413.
113 *Memorials of the Guild of Merchant Taylors,* pp. 84, 92–6.
114 GL, MS 6152/1, fo. 97v.
115 GL, MS 6155/1.
116 Rosser, 'Going to the fraternity feast', p. 444.
117 Carol Piper Heming, *Protestants and the Cult of the Saints in German-Speaking Europe* (Kirksville, MO: Truman State University Press, 2003), p. 106; Bartlett, *Why Can the Dead Do Such Great Things*, p. 90.

118 Tara Hamling, *Decorating the 'Godly' Household: Religious Art in Post-Reformation Britain* (New Haven, CT; London: Yale University Press, 2010); Julie Spraggon, *Puritan Iconoclasm During the English Civil War* (Woodbridge: Boydell Press, 2003), ch. 1.

119 GL, MS 12105, fo. 10; Glover, *Men of Metal*, p. 26.

120 GL, MS 12107, fos 2r, 6r, 9r. On the subject of the spatial re-location of objects and the neutralisation of devotional significance, see Maurice Howard, 'Art re-formed: spiritual revolution, spatial re-location', in Tara Hamling and Richard Williams (eds), *Art Re-formed: Re-assessing the Impact of the Reformation on the Visual Arts* (Newcastle-Upon-Tyne: Cambridge Scholars, 2007), pp. 267–71.

121 Peter Sherlock, 'The reformation of memory in early modern Europe', in Susannah Radstone and Bill Schwarz (eds), *Memory: Histories, Theories, Debates* (New York: Fordham University Press, 2010), pp. 30–40, at p. 31; Archer, 'The arts and acts of memorialization', pp. 91, 113.

6

Shaping artisanal and civic identities

In 1610–11 the governors of the Carpenters' Company 'Paid the smyth for ii locks for the Drawers in the Parlour'. They also 'Paid for ii Keys one for the outward parlor door and an other for the Larder'.[1] The Founders' Company paid over 4s in 1617–18 'for mending two lockes & for two new kees & iron boulte for the gate'.[2] Several years earlier they had employed a locksmith for 'mendinge a locke in the settell in parlour'.[3] In 1609 the governing elite of the Goldsmiths' Company made a series of pronouncements concerning doors, locks, bolts, and the possession of keys. These might appear to be mundane details about building fixtures and fittings, but in fact they are highly revealing of broader attitudes to access and exclusion within company properties. These orders also give a flavour of how conceptions and experiences of institutional spaces in London varied according to social order and civic privilege. At Goldsmiths' Hall the company court

> agreed that the back door going into the Clerk's hall shall be shut up by the Clerk. That the Beadle's door going into the great chamber, as also the door at the foot of the stairs, shall have locks and bolts set upon them by the Wardens, who shall keep the keys, and open the same doors when needful. That the Beadle only shall have a key of the outer great gate, and that if any shall apply for entrance after 10 o'clock at night he shall pay the Beadle 4d. to be let in.[4]

This chapter explores the ways in which adapted built spaces in sixteenth- and early seventeenth-century London shaped the experiences, identities, and behaviours of artisans and broader groups of urban inhabitants. It also considers how the performance of particular artisanal and civic activities impacted upon the meanings and significance of certain spaces. The previous discussion of artisanal company buildings established patterns of adaptation, growth, and material enhancement. Further, we observed how material sponsorship of artisanal built environments could heighten and reinforce civic status and notions of artisanal skill and honour. Building on this, we turn now to the multiple ways in which artisanal communities were in turn fashioned by interactions with their built environments. Writing about early modern domestic environments and their inhabitants, cultural archaeologist Matthew Johnson has observed that 'the house and social life acted recursively, back-and-forth on one another'.[5] More recently, Tara Hamling and Catherine Richardson have explored 'the connections between spaces, objects and human activity: the mutually constitutive relationship between people and their houses'.[6] Here, the focus is institutional artisanal built spaces and the social and cultural practices of the guilds, and, as we will see, these were similarly mutually constitutive. Notions of belonging, status, and hierarchy were articulated and experienced through institutional architectures. Further, conceptions of relative 'secrecy' and 'openness' were enacted and reinforced through the use and appropriation of company halls. The emphasis in this chapter is upon the internal organisation and structuring of guild communities. The next chapter considers how exterior designs signified order and uniformity in the wider urban environment of the City of London.

This examination of the manifold ways in which built environments shaped guild communities, and how the users of company halls appropriated company halls, considers specific spaces such as galleries, parlours, kitchens, halls, assay houses, and domestic sites, as well as particular activities and cultural practices, like material testing and feasting. These highly ritualised activities derived significance from their performance in certain spaces, and in turn shaped the meanings and import of the rooms in which they were enacted. As Janette Dillon contends: 'space is not really a fixed material feature, but is constructed by the way it is occupied. Our mental maps of physical structures stem from our understanding not only of the material elements of those spaces but of how their occupants functioned within them.'[7] The spectrum of activities undertaken by guild members and employees in these buildings and their environs was considerable, ranging from food preparation to deliberations on legal matters, from gardening to testing the quality of material products of city producers and sellers. Company halls were hives of human activity and social and commercial exchange. The variety and intensity of such endeavours depended upon the season, and the particular point in the ritual calendar of civic governance and celebration. Some were everyday activities (like maintaining the basic cleanliness of the hall), others highly ceremonial and meticulously choreographed (such as election ceremonies and feasts).

One's experience of artisanal or mercantile and civic spaces was not uniform, but varied according to social status, gender, and political authority. Unless read with a suitably critical gaze, institutionally produced sources can, however, obscure the multiplicity of contemporaries' understandings and interpretations of space. A map of Armourers' Hall on Coleman Street, dating from a property survey of 1679, is a rare visual representation of an early modern livery hall, and illustrates this point nicely (see Plate 3).[8] Though outside the primary chronological parameters of this book, it is an important survival, for Armourers' Hall was largely unscathed by the Great Fire of 1666 and thus this plan shows its early modern configuration. The Armourers' survey signifies each interior ground-floor chamber with a letter, which corresponds to an adjoining textual key.[9] So, for instance, the letter 'C' designates the space of the courtyard, and 'K' represents the Beadle's study. A recommended route through the building is inferred from these lettered spaces/chambers. A visitor should start at 'A' – 'the front of Armorars-hall and the Beadles house And a Tenement situate in Coleman street' – and then proceed through to 'B' – 'the passage into the Court yard' – and so on, through the remaining letters of the alphabet and associated rooms and storeys of Armourers' Hall. A sense of the materiality of the space is also provided: 'the passage, the Court yard, the Kitchin, and Pantry, and beer Cellar, are all paved with Purbeck Stone'; whereas the great hall is 'ffloored with boards, and Wain=Scotted round'.[10] But what is being presented here is in actuality a highly privileged experience of this building. This is an (official) route through Armourers' Hall which would only have been possible for a man with full civic authority and relatively exclusive access rights to all sites of governance, administration, production, and display. The itinerary proposed by the Armourers' survey (taking in the gallery and court room, for example) would not have been how most urban inhabitants (including non-citizens and women) conceptualised this space, or physically negotiated that particular environment.

This chapter reads institutional records – primarily company court minutes and accounts – against the grain to reveal evidential traces for the mutually reflexive relationship between artisanal architectures and identities. The first part of the chapter uncovers the ways in which ideals of exclusion and belonging, secrecy and openness, were structured and perceived through lived experiences and negotiations of the built fabric. As companies acquired novel or adapted and newly furnished rooms of high status and specific function, such as galleries, court chambers, and parlours, issues of access were more carefully managed, often through new doors, locks, and other fixtures. Guild elites also exhibited heightened sensitivity to the management of access routes within guild buildings. In so doing, professional and social distinctions were materially articulated and reinforced. Our discussion begins with issues of access and restriction to high status chambers from the perspective of the labours and movement of clerks and beadles within company halls. We then consider the notion of secrecy in relation to the management of workshops within guild buildings, specifically the assay office within Goldsmiths' Hall.

The second part of the chapter explores the spatial arrangement and choreography of a particular practice: guild dining and feasting. Close analysis of this highly significant civic activity, which took place principally in halls, parlours, and great chambers, shows how guild, generational, and gender hierarchies were repeatedly enacted and negotiated through the spatial and material choreography of collective consumption and display. Further, from the latter decades of the sixteenth century there was a heightened sensitivity on the part of feast planners and participants to the spatial arrangements and movements of people and things at the feast. Notably, such concerns were concurrent with major projects of civic adaptation and rebuilding.

'A convenient house': the domestic within the institutional interior

Beadles and clerks were essential for the day-to-day operation of the guild and smooth running of the company hall and its estates. Their employment was often long-standing. A considerable number of guild officers were involved in the administration of a company's affairs for decades.[11] As observed in an earlier discussion, the beadle was the principal caretaker of the physical fabric of the guild hall. He ensured that rooms were clean and ordered in advance of court meetings, dinners, and feasts. The beadle was also responsible for regulating movement in and out of the hall gate ('the Beadle only shall have a key of the outer great gate'), rather like a porter in a Cambridge or Oxford University college.[12] This institutional employee also had a significant communication role within the craft company and wider environs of the city: in advance of court meetings and special assemblies of the guild he summoned company men to the hall.[13] The beadle of the Barber Surgeons' Company additionally had the unique and entirely unenviable task of 'bringing home dead bodies from Tyburn' to facilitate surgical demonstrations at Barber Surgeons' Hall.[14] By contrast, the clerk's primary function was record-keeping, management, and preservation. He kept minutes during meetings of the court and extraordinary assemblies of the company. The clerk compiled inventories of guild property. Clerks also dealt with legal matters, such as the drawing up of contracts and leases. As Joseph Ward writes, 'the clerk was the only person who had not risen through the company's ranks who had access to its records'.[15] The sensitive nature of guild accounts, and their significance in constructing a sense of institutional continuity and memory, meant that discretion was a highly prized attribute in a clerk. On taking up the role, his oath included a vow of secrecy.[16] In general he was 'to behave and demean himself to the Company with all due respect'.[17]

The lived experiences of these institutional employees exemplify the ways in which professional and social distinctions were marked out and reinforced through the built environment of the company hall. Sixteenth-century artisanal and mercantile institutional architectures began to incorporate domestic spaces for the accommodation of guild officials (and their families), including clerks, beadles (and assayers, in the case of the Goldsmiths' Company).[18] As semi-permanent residents within guild buildings, the experiences of the beadle and clerk give us unique perspectives on the social, political, and material ordering of guild spaces. At Goldsmiths' Hall the clerk and the assayer shared a house, which was roughly divided into two separate living areas.[19] Across the City companies it was quite typical for the beadle to inhabit rooms within, or adjacent to, the gatehouse of the hall. At Drapers' Hall the clerk lived next to the principal gate and courtyard: his rather substantial accommodation included 'the office by the gate, two third parts of the cellar under the same, the low chamber next to the said office, the scullery house for his kitchen, a dark chamber or coal house. Three chambers over the Ladies Chamber and over the pantry with the garrets over the same.'[20] While guild archives give few indications as to the interior furnishings of these chambers, court minutes provide valuable insights into the perceived challenges of managing a domestic space embedded within an institutional built environment.[21] Moreover, it becomes evident that small adaptations were made to company buildings, such as the addition of doors and locks, in order to manage different degrees of access to privileged spaces such as galleries and court chambers, and to regulate movement within artisanal halls. In so doing, the wardens of craft companies made manifest, and reinforced, varied degrees of social and political privilege between company officials and guild members, and between different institutional employees.

In November 1619 the court of the Tallow Chandlers' Company decided 'that our Clark Roger Pryne his wife and family shall inhabit and dwell w[i]thin our hall called Tallowchandlers Hall'. To accommodate these new residents, 'this Court have viewed the sev[er]all Romes in the same and do find that … A convenient house maye be made on the Maisters side (w[hi]ch o[u]r Clark is willinge to do w[i]thall convenient speede).' It was further decided that 'bycause the way into the hall lyeth open for all passengers out of the gate w[hi]ch is very inconvenient yt is thought fit that o[u]r said Clark shall at his owne use make two double shuttinge dores for the same and in leu thereof shall have a peece of old [timber] w[hi]ch is for one p[ar]t thereof'.[22] At Tallow Chandlers' Hall, then, the clerk was responsible for making contributions towards the construction of his own house. Moreover, the new addition of 'two double shuttinge dores' which regulated movement through the gate was presumably of mutual advantage to Roger Pryne and the court of the Tallow Chandlers. Both Pryne, as a resident, and the guild authorities, would have benefitted from enhanced security and greater control of human traffic in and out of the building. Three months later, when the necessary adaptations to Tallow Chandlers'

Hall had been completed, the spatial privileges of the clerk within the building were further refined:

> That o[u]r said clark shall hold and enioy the same Romes and dwellinge and egresse and regresse into and from the same for his owne life onely: he the said Roger Pryne not at anie tyme hind[e]ring the Master or wardens of the said company of the use of the larder or anie other Romes of the said hall but onely of his privat lodgeings and chambers.[23]

Evidently the clerk was being encouraged here to remain relatively isolated within his 'privat lodgeings and Chambers', apart from the elite ruling company, and certainly not to have free circulation of the hall building. The specific mention of the larder hints at the significance of storing, preparing, and provisioning food within the company – a theme explored in depth below.

During the rebuilding of Goldsmiths' Hall from the mid-1630s, the concerns of the company assistants regarding access rights of company clerk and beadle to high status spaces within the new building were more numerous, and, to their mind, required a more drastic solution of debarring passageways. In July 1637 the Goldsmiths' clerk, William Haselfoote, petitioned the company assistants 'for a dore way or passage into the Gallerye at Gouldsmiths Hall out of the dwelling House which is appoynted for him there'.[24] The clerk did not give a reason for this particular appeal, though we might conjecture that an entranceway or direct route from his domestic quarters into the gallery for personal recreation and use of his guests, when not occupied by goldsmiths, would have enhanced his social status. Over at Grocers' Hall the clerk 'controlled access to the garden and tower by the company hall, a perquisite that might gain him favour from members'.[25] Haselfoote's request was refused. The court minutes state in opaque fashion that 'for some reasons to the contrary shewed it is not now thought fit to graunte his requeste'.[26] However, five years later, in May 1642, the clerk made his appeal to the guild governors once again, this time with a positive outcome. On this occasion, the broader spatial and political concerns of the guild governors about relatively free movement within the building were also made rather more explicit. The wardens had initially been concerned that if the clerk had access to this exclusive gallery chamber within Goldsmiths' Hall, damage might be sustained and responsibility would be hard to ascertain: 'that if the Companye should beautifie the Gallery by painteinge itt or adorne[ing] itt with pictures that if itt were any waye spoyled or defaced the Company could not tell whome to charge therewith if hee had a dore into itt'.[27] In the early 1640s a passageway between the clerk's domestic quarters and the gallery was only established on the specific condition that 'the Companye will sett a lock and bolte upon the passage dore from his house into the Gallerye on the inside to debar him the entrance thereinto when they please'.[28] The 'lock and bolte

... on the inside' ensured that the company assistants controlled access on their own terms.

For contemporaries, the long gallery was closely associated with the ability to conduct private conversations.[29] At Goldsmiths' Hall the essential exclusivity and 'privacy' of the gallery space were to be strictly maintained and confidential recreations of artisanal and mercantile elites were not to be disrupted by the clerk. While the clerk was trusted in general with guild business and archives, this plainly did not give him *carte blanche* to engage in all company discussions. In all likelihood, the concern of the assistants of the Goldsmiths' Company was not centred wholly on the possibility that unregulated access might lead to spoliation of collections and decorative interiors. Rather, the exclusive nature of the site of the gallery also made free and unsupervised entrance a controversial social proposition. Tellingly, the company beadle was entirely 'exclude[d] ... whereby the Clerke onely may stand blamable if the gallery or any thinge theren shalbee att any time injured wronged or defaced by him'.[30] The beadle did, however, have a passage made 'out of his house ... into the great chamber for keeping of them cleane and ready upon all occasions for the Companyes service'. By setting up a hierarchy of spatial privilege between clerk and beadle, the wardens of the guild were reinforcing a sense of social distance between these officials; the former was chiefly engaged in literate, paper work, the latter tied up with the more physically labour-intensive work of building and estate maintenance. Notably, the beadle's access to the Goldsmiths' Company's great chamber was specifically for the purpose of making the room 'cleane and ready'.

Through this close recording of the gradual process of working out patterns of spatial privilege throughout the new Goldsmiths' Hall, passageways, doors, locks, and bolts emerge as articulations of social distinction, even between members of the same institutional household. The artisanal built environment might be adapted in order to reflect and crucially reinforce social difference and political hierarchies. The focus of the next case-study is the practice of material testing and regulation, specifically the supervision of the working and living space of the company assayer within Goldsmiths' Hall. The assay office is an intriguing example for it complicates a conception of spaces within company halls as either essentially 'open' (e.g. courtyard) or 'restrictive' (e.g. parlour or long gallery) in character. The nature of the assayer's work, and the official role of the guild in overseeing the legitimacy of his labour, meant that access to his workshop required a careful negotiation of the principles of secrecy and openness.

The assay office at Goldsmiths' Hall: regulating secrets

From December 1478 an assay house and a salaried assayer were located in Goldsmiths' Hall. The Goldsmiths' Company's assayer was variously known as the common assayer, assay master, and deputy assayer, and these terms are used interchangeably in the company's archival records. The centralised system of daily testing and marking (or 'touching') the wrought plate of London's goldsmiths replaced the custom by which company wardens periodically assayed plate in the premises of individual goldsmiths. Christopher Elyot, a liveryman of the guild, was appointed as the first common assayer.[31] As discussed earlier, the common assayer was also allocated a domestic residence within Goldsmiths' Hall. This highly skilled practitioner tested the raw materials – silver and gold ingots – used by London's goldsmiths, and their wrought silver articles, to ensure that all were of the correct standard. The assay master also checked the weights used by precious-metalworkers. The company oath of the common assayer emphasised the significance of his personal integrity:

> You shall swear to ... truly assay all such gold and silver as shall be brought to you to assay. And also you shall melt all pieces of gold and silver delivered to you truly and impartially, without any deceit, to the least waste and damage possible ... And every article of gold and silver that you receive you shall keep safely, recording it all in writing and returning it honestly when you are asked to do so, making a true account of it uninfluenced by favour or affection, hatred or ill-will.[32]

A printed representation from the 1670s of the interior of the assayer's workshop at Goldsmiths' Hall reduced the complex workshop processes, and social relationships, to a series of numbered illustrations (see figure 2.4). Notably we see at '14' the 'Assay-Master making Assays' (his hand resting on the balance for accurate weighing), and at '16' the company warden 'marking the Plate on the Anvil'. Once marked the plate might legitimately be displayed and purchased at '19', 'A Goldsmiths Shop'.[33]

The lived reality of the common assayer's working practices at Goldsmiths' Hall proved to be much more complicated than this oath and visual depiction suggested, not least because the testing process was inherently subjective and volatile. As we saw in earlier discussions of *The Gouldesmythes' Storehowse*, a metallurgical treatise authored by London goldsmiths, assay by fire involved an experiential understanding of many workshop variables, including furnace temperatures and the malleability of metals. Materials and elements might behave in unexpected ways. A fourteenth-century manuscript note from the Royal Mint recommended that in every instance of testing 'at least three impeccable assays should be made, lest through overheating or otherwise the silver should have spurted out from one of the assays and lest from draughts or a failure of the fire, the assay should have cooled, or by the fall of coals or in any other way the assay or silver should have been diminished'.[34] The assayers at Goldsmiths' Hall and the Tower mint (sometimes, controversially, the same man) were also enmeshed in a complex series of institutional and patronage relationships; hence, acting 'truly and impartially'[35] in the eyes of guild and Mint governors, merchants, and working goldsmiths was often a challenge. But for our purposes, fortunately, it was precisely when relations between the goldsmiths and their assayer broke down that accounts of expected standards, customs, and values are most clearly articulated in the company archive. Moreover, it is evident that the working practices and reputation of the company assayer and built space of the assay office at Goldsmiths' Hall were seen to be mutually constitutive on quite a profound level. Notably, across Renaissance Europe the architecture of mints and sites of metallurgical testing were intended to express notions of respectability, integrity, and stability.[36]

The famed metallurgist Georgius Agricola recommended that the assayer 'should close the doors of the room in which the assay furnace stands, lest anyone coming in at an inopportune moment might disturb his thoughts when they are intent on the work'.[37] This was a nice ideal, but managing the physical space of the assay house at Goldsmiths' Hall was a perennial and unique challenge for the guild. In part this was a consequence of its location; the workshop was embedded within a multifunctional institutional space. The deputy assayer in early modern London did not work in splendid isolation. A survey of Goldsmiths' Hall dating from the 1690s shows the extent to which the assayer's working and living space was embedded in the company building and the wider urban environment (the numbered spaces are domestic, working, and commercial spaces owned by the guild; house number '9' on the plan is the common assayer's house) (see Plate 4). At any one time within Goldsmiths' Hall numerous political, social, domestic, and commercial spatial practices were undertaken by men and women of varying status. As we will see, unsolicited eyes observed workshop activities, and ears overheard company secrets.

Significantly, the wardens' concerns about interferences with the assayer's labour were typically more pointed than mere distraction. There was also a distinct corporate cultural ambiguity about the extent to which the common assayer's working practices ought to be made visible to interested parties. The deep-rooted ideal of secrecy in relation to the craft mystery (the valuable collective embodied skills and techniques of the guild) meant that the assayer's workshop ought to be shielded from prying eyes and inquisitive ears from outside of the goldsmiths' guild.[38] The Goldsmiths' ordinances stressed secrecy.[39] More specifically, the trials undertaken by institutional assayers were meant to be discreet and private in order to uphold the allegedly impartial nature of the process, and they were thus ideally concealed from all but the workshop employees and institutional authorities. And yet this very secrecy, and apparent lack of transparency concerning the deputy assayer's workshop activities, repeatedly led to complaints and controversies from among the city's artisans and merchants. In the hands and judgements of London's assayers lay the purity of specie and the livelihoods of craftsmen and merchants. The honesty and quality of their work also reflected upon institutional reputations. Thus a balance was continually renegotiated between 'secrecy' and 'openness' in relation to the working space of the Goldsmiths' Company's assay master. Unlike, for example, the company parlour – a site of civic governance that became progressively more exclusive over the course of the sixteenth and early seventeenth centuries – regulating access to, and views of, the assay house was an altogether trickier endeavour.[40]

The Goldsmiths' Company archive sheds light on the challenges faced in restricting observation and entry to institutional assay workshops. First, craft secrets were a marketable commodity, and thus might be communicated and performed outside of the workshop and sold.[41] Engaged in the separation and transformation of matter, assayers and the affairs of their workshops were a growing curiosity for gentlemen interested in the secrets of nature.[42] Furthermore, against the backdrop of the Elizabethan 'gold rush' the assayer's knowledge and techniques became an especially valuable commodity.[43] In 1560 the Goldsmiths' assistants chastised their assay worker John Kirk for bargaining with certain gentlemen of the Court 'to teach them the feate of assayes making'. The wardens told him that it was unlawful, and contrary to his oath, 'to open that or any other secret of his mystery to any man that is not free thereof'. Kirk said that 'he had taught others', and 'would do it again for money', and 'stood stoutly on his defence'.[44] In the early seventeenth century workmen employed by the deputy assayer were gossiping about the 'secrets of the assay house' to stranger goldsmiths on a street adjacent to Goldsmiths' Hall.[45] The physical boundaries of the assayer's workshop, especially doors and windows, also had to be closely monitored when trials were taking place. In August 1601, for instance, the company governors ruled that no man should walk on the terrace while the assayer and touch wardens were at work 'and doe sitt and debate about the affaires of this societie'; from the vantage point of the elevated terrace one could covertly observe the activities taking place in the assayer's chamber.[46]

The built space of the assay house at Goldsmiths' Hall was also understood by contemporary artisans to be intimately associated with the skill and integrity of its office-holder. *In extremis* the physical state of the built environment, and the (dis)honourable reputation of the assay master, were even seen to be mutually reinforcing.[47] This perceived association is amply demonstrated by two especially contentious and long-running disputes between the assay master and the wider body of London's goldsmiths. In the 1560s common assayer Richard Rogers was in repeated conflict with the assistants of the company.[48] Tensions were generated in part because he held a prominent position at the Mint, in addition to his company role.[49] As the assayer at Goldsmiths' Hall was called upon to be a check on the assayer at the Tower, through highly ritualistic testing of the coinage at the trial of the pyx, Rogers was said to be in effect 'his owne judge, not without great suspicion of partiality'.[50] To borrow a description from Lauren

Jacobi, and to apply it to the London context, the assay workshops at Goldsmiths' Hall and the Tower mint were central to 'the spatio-architectural network of places of monetary production and exchange'.[51] Suspicions about Richard Rogers were also focused upon his keeping an open shop on Cheapside 'where he also dwelleth'. The ordinances of the guild stated that the common assayer should reside in Goldsmiths' Hall: 'that he should not have his dwellynge in any other place but onely in the tenement belonging and annexed unto the said office'. And yet, Rogers would not 'give over his occupueyncye and dwellynge in Chepe [a premises named the Goat], and come dwell in his house ... w[i]thin goldsmiths hall'.[52] The assistants lamented in December 1564 that the tenement which rightly belonged to the office 'now standeth and of long tyme hathe stande voyde and emptie to the great harme and decay of the same'. The governors of the guild here equated the increasingly decrepit edifice of the assayer's institutional residence with the diminishing integrity of the office-holder. Three years later, the assistants were still complaining of Rogers's 'frivolous delays' in removing himself from Cheapside to the 'house belongyng to his office of assayes makynge as other his pr[e]decessors ... tyme out of mynde have done'. When Rogers was finally dismissed from the company post in 1567, he pointedly kept in his possession the physical contents of the Assay Office, including the weights and tools for trials, belonging to the guild, until the matter was resolved to his satisfaction.[53] The holding back of instruments from the workshop – company property, and necessary apparatus for undertaking assay – was evidently a form of protest at his treatment by the wardens of the guild. Early in the seventeenth century a disgruntled clerk stripped from his institutional house 'doores, locks, wainscott and suche like' as a form of remonstration. The wardens claimed he had maliciously 'spoiled and defaced the howse in everie place'.[54]

The exceptionally protracted early seventeenth-century disagreement between deputy assayer John Reynolds and a group of working goldsmiths also speaks directly to matters of skill and integrity, and legitimate oversight of the space of the assay house.[55] In May 1629, a group of thirteen working goldsmiths presented a petition thoroughly besmirching Reynolds's personal honour and professional integrity. Clearly their grievances had been mounting for some time. The document detailed eight reasons why 'wee the workemen ... conceave that neither hee the said assayer nor his servants are fit to judge or refuse our plate'. The root of their objection was that, far from acting with the integrity that his office required, Reynolds, having 'sett aside all fear of God hath violated his annual oath by favour, affection, hate and evil will to diverse ... men of this mistery'. Reynolds was said to be 'partial in his office, allowing plate of the fineness of the standard to be touched for them that he favoureth and causing the wardens to break some far better of such workemen disaffected by him'. In a revealing insight regarding the anticipated personality traits of a master assayer,

Reynolds was said, contrariwise, to have a lack of control of his passions or senses; he had rather an irrepressible 'fury or rather madness … in his rage hath misused many… [braking plate, which was later proved by other assayers to be up to standard] without all pity or humanity'. The petitioners especially resented the idea that Reynolds presumed himself to have royal protection, on account of his dual role at Goldsmiths' Hall and the Tower, 'affirming himself to be his majesties servant daring any man whome he hath wronged once to touch him, commanding the wardens in the kings name to do as he would have them'.[56]

Reynold's counterpetition to these accusations of partiality, maliciousness, and mismanagement addresses the matters of skill, honesty, and regulation of the space of the assay office with which we are concerned. Reynolds assured the wardens that the oath of his office was 'a bond of Integrity laid upon his conscience his sufficiency of skill and knowledge required for that place, being not inferior to any his predecessors'. Further, the master assayer proposed that the primary cause for the workmen's discontent was the new spatial context within which the assayer's judgements were enacted. Reynolds suggested that the 'innovation' of destroying 'men's stuffe' in the assay house rather than the parlour, and 'without due ceremonie and solemynitie' was encouraging 'turbulent spirits'.[57]

Reynolds was dismissed from his role as common assayer at Goldsmiths' Hall, but his comments regarding the witnessing of work and judgements in particular civic spaces were acknowledged and acted upon. The company court decreed that all deceitfully made plate should be broken in the parlour before two wardens, not in the assay house, or elsewhere, and that the clerk should certify the deceit, and the workman's name, to the next court.[58] This was a clear reaffirmation of the parlour as a site of civic authority. Moreover, it was also necessary to open up the assay house to wider scrutiny. Select groups of working goldsmiths were encouraged to come to the assay house at Goldsmiths' Hall personally to observe the assayer's trial.[59] Making the workshop activities of the company assayer visible to the wider body of goldsmiths was significant at this moment to repair the trust and accountability of the assay house.

In a representational sense, publicly displaying the imagined space of the assayer's workshop could be significant in terms of broadcasting the honour and legitimacy of the goldsmiths' guild. The connection between the skill and integrity of the assayer at Goldsmiths' Hall and the regulatory oversight of the Goldsmiths' Company was brought vividly to life during the inaugural procession of goldsmith Sir James Pemberton as lord mayor of London on 29 October 1611, a device presented in a printed version as *Chruso-Thriambos: The Triumphs of Gold*. Authored by Anthony Munday (who also provided the costumes), Pemberton's civic spectacle was one of the magnificent investitures which marked 'the zenith of the mayoral Shows in the early seventeenth century'.[60] The Goldsmiths' Company contributed

200 marks towards the festivities: 'a more liberall benevolence than hath bene formerlie granted to any Lord Maior of this Companie'.[61] Pemberton's procession snaked across the River Thames to his swearing-in at Westminster, back across the Thames to Baynard's Castle, on foot to the south gate of St. Paul's Churchyard, onward to Lawrence Lane, and thence to St. Paul's Cathedral; the civic pageant ended at the lord mayor's new residence, Camden House on Maiden Lane, a mansion which almost neighboured Goldsmiths' Hall.[62] This elaborate water and land route was typical of the mayoral Shows; linking royal and civic authority, this extended journey also 'provided the occasion for a show of pageant devices'.[63] A central feature of Pemberton's procession was a magnificent pageant (or 'orferie') shaped like a golden mountain, 'On a Quadrangle frame, of apt constructure, and answerable strength, we erect a Rocke or Mount of Golde, in such true proportion, as Art can best present it'. Upon the 'Mount' in ascending order were characters representing the labours and crafts essential to the goldsmiths art: 'the Pioners, Miners, and Deluers, doe first vse their endeuour and labour, to come by the Oare of gold and Siluer hidden in the Rock ... the industrious Finer [..] the Mint-Maister, Coyners, Gold Smithes, Iewller, Lapidarie, Pearle-Driller, Plate-Seller, and such like. All liuely acting their sundry professions.' Towards the very summit of this rock of gold (positioned just below the figure of *Justice*), 'to distinguish those precious Mettals of Gold and Siluer, from base adulterating or corruption, wee show there also an ingenious Say-Maister'. This artisan was displayed with 'his Furnaces, Glasses of parting each Mettall from other, his Table, Balance, and Weightes, euen to the very smallest quantitie of true valuation, in Ingots, Iewells, Plate or Monies, for the more honour of the Prince and Country, when his Coynes are kept from imbasing and abusing'.[64] Dramatically and, we might assume, very conspicuously from the perspective of the crowd, the sole fireworks of the event emerged from the assayer's furnace. By transforming the representational space of the assayer's workshop into a public spectacle, and performing the sourcing, refining, testing, and manufacture of precious metal on a 'Mount of Gold', London's early seventeenth-century Goldsmiths' Company advertised on the City streets the fundamental significance and authority of the guild in regulating and upholding material integrity.[65] Intriguingly, the material props and sets from the pageant which signified these themes had conspicuous afterlives; they were displayed in Goldsmiths' Hall (possibly in a gallery space) until 1622.[66]

On a day-to-day level, managing the spaces, activities, and skilled practitioners involved in material quality regulation was an ongoing challenge for London's goldsmiths. When trials were underway the assayer's workshop was ideally a restricted site to all but its employees and the governors of the guild. And yet the significance of the testing process also meant that it required legitimation and, at times of social and political tension, it required witnessing by a wider artisanal and mercantile audience. The final section of this chapter turns to consider a very different sort of cultural and social activity undertaken in all company buildings across London's crafts and trades, performed according to a very prescribed spatial and material choreography: guild feasts and dinners.

Feasting

At the turn of the seventeenth century John Stow reported how:

> *Bartholomew Read*, Goldsmith, Mayor in the yeare 1502. kept such a feast in this [Goldsmiths'] hall as some haue fabuled, is far incredible, & altogether vnpossible, considering the smalnes of the hal & number of the guests, which as they say, were more then an hundreth persons of great estate. For the messes and dishes of meates to them serued, the paled [enclosed] Parke in the same hall, furnished with frutefull trees, beastes of venery [game], and other circumstances of that pretended feast well weighed, Westminster hall would hardly haue suffised, and therefore I will ouerpasse it, and note somewhat of principall Goldsmithes.[67]

Stow might have doubted some of the extraordinary details about this early sixteenth-century banquet at Goldsmiths' Hall, but the prominence of guild feasts in the civic imaginary is telling. Feasting rites were an essential and deep-rooted part of guild culture, and highlights of London's festive calendar. From their foundation in the late medieval period, guilds and craft fraternities invariably celebrated the patronal feast day. This annual rite of commensality embodied the fraternal and charitable aspects of guild culture. As Gervase Rosser has written, 'by its participants, the fraternity banquet was commonly described as being intended "for the promotion of love and charity among the members"'.[68] Indeed, around the same time that Stow was writing, the wardens of the Armourers' Company worried that as a consequence of the recent 'neglect' of quarterly dinners at Armourers' Hall, 'discords have arisen and brotherly love decreased'.[69] Their concerns reflected the widespread understanding in civic culture that sharing a meal was a celebration of all participants 'as members of one societie'.[70] As discussed in previous chapters, one of the new features of company halls in the sixteenth and early seventeenth centuries was the extension or new building of kitchens, butteries, and pantries. The improvement of facilities for food preparation and storage was no doubt motivated by the desire to feast on a grand scale, and vastly improve the ability to do so.

Feasting hierarchies

Hierarchy was integral to civic feasting culture, and thus at Guildhall no two livery companies had quite the same experience of dining. At the lord mayor's feast of 1532, the ranking of City guilds was materialised – and reinforced – by numbers of invitees and the quantity of dishes provisioned, served, and consumed. The Goldsmiths' Company, ranked fifth in the civic hierarchy, brought the wardens and ten other liverymen to Guildhall; this group were served three messes (a course, or dish). By contrast, the Wax Chandlers' guild, placed seventeenth in the City, was allowed the wardens and six other men, and they received two courses at the feasting table. The Joiners' Company, ranked forty-fourth, was permitted three feast-makers; this small group consumed a single course.[71] As Lars Kjaer and A. J. Watson have argued, 'the feast remained a useful tool for speaking about, enacting and conceptualising status and solidarity'.[72]

For London's leading merchants and artisans, contributions and attendance at guild dinners and feasts were understood to be a fundamental element of guild membership. Communal eating and drinking on significant dates of the ritual calendar helped to construct a distinctive sense of community. This was a model of community which was intensely hierarchical, as well as fraternal. Full participation was typically restricted to men (and sometimes women) of particular status. Moreover, not all diners ate from the same table, or even in the same room; nor did they necessarily enjoy the same food and alcohol.[73] Certainly, only a select few men had access to the company treasures which furnished the meal and played an increasingly significant role in its successful choreography. This section of the chapter explores the spatial and social dynamics of guild feasting. Differentiation between participants at the feast had always been a significant aspect of the ritual, but guild members were especially preoccupied with the spatial and material dynamics of communal consumption from the second half of the sixteenth century. And thus, at the same time that adaptations and material improvements were being made to the built fabric of artisanal companies, their most significant collective rites were also under close scrutiny. The built spaces and material cultures of the guild fundamentally shaped individual and collective identities during rites of commensality; at the same time the highly performative practice of feasting also endowed particular civic spaces with especial significance.

At guild meals hosted in company halls, consumption of food and drink was similarly stratified according to rank. The variety, type, and quality of foodstuffs and alcohol offered to participants depended upon an individual's place in the guild or civic hierarchy.[74] At Drapers' Hall in 1564 'there was no quails' at the 'second table', 'but pigeons only there instead'.[75] On quarter days at Goldsmiths' Hall ale and spiced bread were consumed by all guild members, but a 1620 'order for the distributing of ye cheise' recommended that the wardens take home a third of a cheese each, and the remainder of the livery a sixth. We can only assume that the yeomanry departed empty handed.[76] The spatial organisation and choreography of service at guild feasts also reflected and reaffirmed the social and political status of participants. The feasting tables laid out in the great hall and parlour, and occasionally gallery and great chamber, were organised hierarchically. The master, wardens and most senior liverymen and guests would be seated at the high table, located at the dais end of the hall chamber. The remaining participants at the feast were seated at tables according to their relative social rank (often in a horseshoe shape spatial organisation) (see Plate 5). Civic seating in urban England more broadly was customised to physically and symbolically 'elevate the rulers of the post-Reformation town above their fellow citizens'.[77] At livery halls the high table was lavishly furnished, with tablecloths, cushions, and carpets, whereas the lesser tables were left unadorned, or else equipped with less valuable material cultures.[78] In Pewterers' Hall the distinction between the 'table clothis of damaske' and those described as 'playne' reflected and reinforced the varied statuses of those sitting at different tables within the hall chamber.[79] We have seen how authoritative guildsmen might sponsor the material apparatus of this feasting culture, particularly the top table, including tables, linen, and plate. Moreover, senior guildsmen were customarily served by youthful men with considerably less political authority (routinely described in court records as 'comely you[n]ge men of this companie').[80] This choreography of service reinforced the relatively submissive position of the yeomanry at the same time as it bolstered the seniority of the liverymen at the feasting table. The provision of table service reinforced the ideals of subordination and humility within the guild's masculine hierarchy of relationships. At the feast table the yeomanry could be quite literally at the service of older, more established men, in possession of full patriarchal manhood.[81]

The choreography of table service was adjusted if a member of the guild held mayoral office. It was decided in December 1611, the year that goldsmith James Pemberton held office, that whereas 'of ancient tyme it hath bene accustomed that a certain nomber of the Yeomanrie should wayte in their gownes at the Renters feast' now 'there shall be 20 of the riche batchelers appointed to carry the service unto the highe Table and the other tables in the hall in their gownes ... and satten hoodes ... there shalbe none of the Yeomanrie employed in that service'.[82] 'The bachelors' were a distinct livery of the yeomanry, created when a member of one of the great companies was elected mayor. Notably the 'riche batchelers' wore the full livery, both 'gownes ... and [crimson] satten hoodes', thus distinguishing themselves sartorially from other yeomen, at considerable personal expense.[83] Crucially, the material and spatial dynamics of feasting were not merely reflective of relationships – and tensions – within the guild (and not infrequently, the city at large); they were also reflexive, giving shape and substance to an artisan's reputation and manhood within a highly complex and competitive civic environment.[84]

The feasting calendar

Guild feasts and dinners were held on numerous occasions throughout the year. At Carpenters' Hall in the 1540s members made provisions for dinners or feasts on the day the mayor went to Westminster (the mayoral inauguration in October), on quarter days (when quarterage was collected from all members), on St. Lawrence's day, on the feast or 'denner' day (which marked the election of guild officials), and at the 'Reconyng Day' (when the accounts for the year were settled).[85] This festive calendar was typical across the City guilds. The wealthier companies additionally organised meals following 'view days', which entailed the collective inspection of corporate property.[86] And, as discussed previously, funeral dinners were also hosted in company halls, funded by the deceased and organised by their executors. Funeral dinners or dinners of commemoration 'became increasingly popular after the abolition of obits and were funded by bequests of a few pounds for a dinner or a series of dinners in their memory'.[87] The aforementioned armourer and benefactor Roger Tyndall (d. 1587) left funds for a sermon and feast in his honour on the day of his funeral (see Plate 13).[88] He also established a perpetual trust for an annual sermon to be delivered 'by a godly learned preacher' at the parish church of St. Dionis Backchurch, and a feast at Armourers' Hall on St. George's Day. Tyndall specifically requested that 'such as the same yeomanry as goeth to church' and attend the sermon 'should dine and make merry together with the same [liverymen]'.[89]

The feast day, which celebrated the transfer of authority from one small group of guild officials to another, was universally the most extravagant event in the ritual calendar. The main feast was customarily preceded by a mass. Guild officials would proceed from the company hall to a neighbouring church in their full livery. After the service the guildsmen would return in procession to the company hall for the splendid repast.[90] Following the religious changes of the reformation, this custom was not shattered but adapted; masses were replaced with appropriate religious observances. The Goldsmiths' Company recorded in 1550 that instead of mass, there was a sermon and communion.[91] The officials of the Carpenters' Company handed out money 'to the poore at comminge from Churche'.[92] Such visible acts of corporate charity were mirrored across the City on feast days.

The precise choreography of the election ceremony is largely opaque, particularly for guilds outside of the great twelve, though occasional items in court minutes are suggestive of increasingly elaborate and codified rites from *c.* 1550. As established in the previous discussion of gifted artefacts, materially elaborate election garlands or crowns were becoming an increasingly significant element of the ritual investiture throughout London (see Plate 14); important too were the election cups from which departing and new guild officials would have drunk. In the early 1590s, for instance, there was presented in Pewterers' Hall 'a standyng cuppe duble guylt waying 32 ounces of the guyft of mr Rychard hustwayght deseased geven to the wardens of the yomandry and to ther successors to be vsed at all there dynnars and at all ther choyse of wardens, for A remembra[nce] for ever of his good will'.[93] A scantily recorded act 'for the election of the ii wardeyns at the tabull at dener' at Armourers' Hall included the directive: 'to drinke to hym whome he doth chose at the tabull and let the olde wardeyn geve hym his garlande ... to the other warden who is chosen before by the hoil bodye of the company'.[94] The Drapers' Company minute books provide an unusually vivid insight into the material and spatial dimensions of the order of election:

> at the middle of the second course ... our Master, arising from the outside of the high table went into the parlour, and after a little pause made came out again into the hall along the high table with the minstrels, a Bachelor bearing a cup of hippocras afore him. He did ... set the garland on Mr Sadler's head and drank to him to be Master the year following. And immediately after the old Master Wardens went into the parlour ... came out again after the ancient Warden with the minstrels and before every Warden a Bachelor bearing a cup of hippocras. They went compass wise to the middle of the hall and chose the new Master Wardens according to the former nomination ... And those two being here at dinner were chosen in the hall, the Second Warden at the north table and the Third at the south table.[95]

As historian Lena Cowen Orlin has observed of this ritual, in particular the movement in and out of the hall and parlour, 'each officer made a show of retiring to the place in which the leadership had privately appointed their initiates, pausing in this select space before bringing their secrets back with him to the hall and the rest of the fellowship'.[96] Suggestively, at the order of the election in 1575, the choreography included a humorous gesture towards those (women and men) who were precisely excluded from civic authority. The Drapers' minutes relate that:

> after the last course was served the four Master Wardens in their lined gowns saluted those that sat at the high table and the rest of the tables, which thing done, they required Mr Alderman Pullison, our Master, to rise to the election of the new Master, who tendered his garland first to the ladies and gentlewomen and other strangers, and in the end drank to Mr John Quarles as Master of this Company for the year next ensuing.[97]

The main feast day was not an isolated event but was followed by a meal the next day, usually for a smaller group of guild officials. At Armourers' Hall there was an 'election breakfast' on the morning after the feast dinner.[98] Preparations for the feast day(s) also involved improvements to the company hall. In 1611 the Carpenters' Company paid 4s for 'trymminge the Garden against thelleccion'. They also paid 'Mr Stanleye the plasterer for worke done about the hall'.[99]

It is important to stress that the actual decision-making process and voting for the new wardens took place in advance of the election feast, among a much smaller group of liverymen (usually only assistants), as compared to the number of citizens and guests as were present on the feast day.[100] Significantly, by the later sixteenth century the election process would have also taken place in a more tightly controlled and private space, namely the company parlour. At Goldsmiths' Hall, for example, the wardens were elected in April, and took up office on 19 May, the feast day of St. Dunstan. The Goldsmiths' Company detailed in their court records of April 1563 how for 'the elec[t]ion of the newe wardens' the master, four wardens and four 'others' (assistants), 'departed together out of ye halle into ye parlor. W[here]fore they did secretly among themselfs elect and chose wardens for ye yeare ensueynge.' In May 1563 it was decreed that the names of the newly elected wardens must absolutely be 'kept secret'. It was forbidden (upon payment of a substantial fine) for the men who had witnessed the event in the parlour the month before to 'utt[er] and disclose ye names ... of ye newe wardens ... before they shalbe knowne at ye feast day by ye garlands then sett upon their heads'. If the company clerk were to demonstrate such a lack of discretion he would 'lose his office for so doynge'.[101]

Provisioning dinners and feasts

Conspicuous consumption was central to festivities. At the feast day a wide range of meat, poultry, and fish was prepared for a single meal of multiple courses. Largesse was intended to impress participants and observers, and thus promote the status and worshipful nature of the guild. At Goldsmiths' Hall in 1530 'for the drinking and dinner on St. Dunstan's day and eve' the wardens sought provisions from a baker, a brewer, a fishmonger, a chandler, a grocer, and even a 'waferer'.[102] At the Carpenters' Company feast day in 1546 participants consumed sirloin of beef, leg of mutton, swan, goose, capon, chicken, and rabbit, all prepared with spices including cloves and saffron. Pike and 'salt fyshce' were also on the menu. Dates, prunes, raisins, and pears were consumed afterwards. These delicacies were washed down with copious quantities of ale, beer, gascon and muscadel (sweet dessert) wine.[103]

As we might expect, the wealthiest mercantile guilds had the most spectacular feasts. They also hosted the most illustrious guests from civic and court contexts. In April 1638 the Barber Surgeons invited to dine in the company parlour 'the Lords of ye privye Counsell & other Lords & p[er] sons of state at the dedicac[i]on of the Theatre & first anatomicall publiqe opa[ra]c[i]ons'. For this event the guild hired 'Venice glasses' and splendid silver plate, and even paid 'John Bludder of the Kings Wardrobe for bringinge and hanginge the great Parlour w[i]th Tapestry'.[104] At their annual 'Feast Dynner' in 1566, the Drapers' Company spent over £112 on a menu which included swan, venison and 'red deer' pasties, quail, 'jelly dishes' and 'marzepaynes'. The Drapers' extraordinary 'Dinner Book'– a detailed account kept of feast expenses and organisation from 1564 to 1602 – reveals that a painter was even hired specifically to gild the desserts with gold leaf.[105]

Unsurprisingly, the Drapers also consumed a wide variety of alcohol. 'Wynne of all sorts' is listed in the Drapers' Dinner Book, including 'gaskon', 'ffrenche', and Rhenish, which was sourced from several different vintners. The geographical range of vineyards was no doubt intended to signify their mercantile networks and overseas connections. Quantities were also designed to impress. At the 'Feast Dynner' in 1566 four gallons of wine was ordered simply for infusion into the 'Jelly'. We should bear in mind that not all who witnessed the feast were full participants in the event. The Bachelors of the Drapers' Company who served the guild elite their dinner at Drapers' Hall were provided afterwards with the relatively humble menu of boiled capon, roast goose, and custard.[106]

At the feasts of the distinguished mercantile guilds and some artisanal companies, the principal food stuff was deer. Venison, sourced from the deer parks of the aristocracy and greater gentry, was the ultimate luxury food-gift.[107] In the words of Felicity Heal, 'venison was marked by its prestige and its ability to confer a measure of honour on the recipient'.[108] At Drapers' Hall the mercantile elite, particularly outgoing wardens, had a tradition of gifting bucks to the hall. This gifting could be competitive. In 1567 John Isham mercer 'agaynst the tyme of the feast [he did] gather togeither 33 fatt and Large buckes, Which he showed to divers of his company, Lyinge alltogeither in a gallery ... yt was thought, that not one man before his time nor sens had the Lyke by a great many'.[109] Several years later the Drapers' Company's court of assistants were informed that 'the nobility and gentlemen about the Court are much offended at the great number of bucks being consumed in the halls of Companies within London at their feast dinners'.[110] Unsurprisingly, venison was consumed by the chief guests at company halls; but deer carcasses were also transformed into baked pasties that could be 'geven awaye by the M[aste]r Wardens to their ffrendes, to officers of thoswe and others' (including the cook and the porters at the feast day).[111] Based on the evidence of the Drapers' Dinner Book, Sarah H. Milne has calculated that 'the number of leftover pasties ranged from 184 in 1567 to fifty-eight in 1570'.[112] The distribution of such a high-status food gift to the worthy poor, officers of the guild, and influential 'ffrendes' of the wardens was evidently a means of garnering loyalty, and of publicly advertising the worshipful status of the feast-makers.[113]

Contributions of food and drink were also made by some tenants of the London livery companies. An obligatory consumable gift could be stipulated as part of the rental contract. And thus, an apothecary and a vintner renting property from the Pewterers' Company in the early seventeenth century each contributed a 'fat buck yearly' to the guild's feast day. Most appropriately Thomas Colle a 'confectionarie' (confectioner) who leased a house from the guild in March 1640/1, was requited to give a marchpane at the annual election feast.[114] The Goldsmiths' Company rented out *The Horn* tavern on Fleet Street in 1624 on the condition that the leaseholder provided 'one good fat buck of the season and one tierce of wine, to be delivered at the Hall the day before the Wardens shall take their oaths and places'.[115]

Food and alcohol were not the only highlights; musical and theatrical entertainment were also a central part of the festivities. A published seventeenth-century description of the Printers' election feast plausibly claimed that guildsmen were served 'beer, Ale, and Wine, of all sorts, to accommodate each Guest according to his desire. And to make their Cheer go cheerfuller down, are entertained with Musick and Songs all Dinner time.'[116] Rather more majestically, at the Goldsmiths' Company's election feast in 1560 'all ye dynner tyme ye syngynge chyldren of paules [the choirboys of St. Paul's Cathedral] played upon their vialles and songe verye pleasaunt songes to ye great delectacion and rejoysynge of ye whole companie'. Eight years later the Queen's trumpeters played while the food was being served.[117]

Participants at the feast

The evidence suggests that by the middle of the sixteenth century, across nearly all crafts and trades, only liverymen participated in the annual feast day.[118] This was an event largely funded by the company wardens. Quarter day festivities were more inclusive events, and in the smaller crafts these meals probably included all guild members. At Armourers' Hall the whole company were served spice cakes, cheese, ale, and beer.[119] A Pewterers' Company quarter day dinner of 1615-16 was composed of seven messes, including carp and roast capons. In addition to food and alcohol, expenses included 'laborer dishe washers', a 'porter of the gate' and a 'water bearer'.[120] Dinner was funded from a mixture of sources: in addition to the quarterage paid by each guildsman, 'the house' allowed £3; there were contributions from two wardens, and extra funds were also 'gathered at the table of the liverie'.[121] In some guilds the yeomanry also hosted their own feast day celebrations. For the annual yeomanry feast in Armourers' Hall every man and his wife were charged 16d, single men 12d, and single women 4d for attendance. The charge was the same for 'forrens, strangers and denysons'.[122]

Lists of attendees at guild meals were not typically recorded, and yet, fortunately, sixteenth-century clerks of the Armourers' Company did keep records of attendance for the annual feast dinner. The Armourers' records show that at the inaugural dinner of Master George Brades in 1546, forty persons (men and women) were in attendance. A little over half that number, twenty-four (men and women) attended a more exclusive breakfast on the subsequent morning.[123] In 1562 forty-six, and thirty-seven persons were at the election dinner and breakfast, respectively, for Master John Smyth.[124] Men are listed here in order of seniority. Moreover, on some recorded feast days, the grouping of names together in separate columns likely correlated to table seating plans. For example, an attendance list for a dinner and supper at Armourers' Hall in October 1556, in celebration of the inauguration of Sir Thomas Offley as lord mayor, features men and women in separate columns of names (almost certainly representing gender segregated tables in the hall).[125]

By the early seventeenth century the Carpenters' Company makes reference in their accounts to highly exclusive events in Carpenters' Hall and at local taverns, specifically for the assistants of the guild. This was in addition to customary quarterly suppers and the election day dinner. In 1603, for instance, there were at least four 'court of assistants dinners' held at Carpenters' Hall. In 1611 there were additionally collations in the parlour when the assistants worked late. Exclusive dinners were also being held after court of assistant meetings at Pewterers' Hall from the 1630s, if not before – the culinary highlight was roast beef.[126] Notably these meals were hosted in the parlour not the main hall. A list of 'reasonable' annual projected expenses for dinners, compiled by the Goldsmiths' Company in 1609 – at a moment when the court of assistants desired to reform excessive expenditure on dinners – included relatively informal meals hosted in inns and taverns after guild business, such as the search of workshops, had been undertaken.[127] The Carpenters' Company recorded seven such search dinners in a single typical year of the early seventeenth century.[128] As well as refreshing participants and presumably providing opportunities for further discussion of guild (and other) matters, these meals no doubt served to bolster the visible authoritative presence of guild authorities and 'attract a substantial body of witnesses to the assertion of urban rights' within the wider metropolitan environment.[129]

Wardens sometimes complained about the exorbitant costs of provisioning feasts, or even refused to contribute altogether.[130] Refusal to participate could be perceived as a serious violation of civic responsibility. In March 1629/30 renter wardens Gabriel Newman and Robert Jenner of the Goldsmiths' Company refused to pay for the wardens' election dinner on St. Nicholas's day, despite being 'men of habilitie and worthe'. This neglect was interpreted by the company assistants as a 'breache of the laudable customes of the said company', which 'doe muche leade to the violac[i]on and breach of good order and governement within this Cittie'. In reprimanding the unwilling feast-makers, the court of assistants stressed that the planned meal was intended as an occasion for company governors to meet 'in a loveing and brotherly manner as members of one societie'. They also laid on heavily the weighty rhetoric of custom: it was 'well warrented by anntient custome, and had bin auntiently kept and duly and constantly observed by all the precedent Rentors of that Company beyond the memory of man'. Newman quickly agreed to pay his half after a strong verbal warning, but Jenner was confined to Newgate gaol, 'to remayne untill hee shall conforme' (he repented pretty rapidly).[131] Against the backdrop of inflation and growing financial demands from the Crown the responsibility for laying on these lavish meals felt especially burdensome in the late sixteenth and early seventeenth centuries. But we should be wary of seeing avoidance of feast-making simply as an early modern phenomenon. As early as the 1360s a controversy erupted in the Goldsmiths' Company because many members absented themselves from the city on the feast of St. Dunstan.[132]

As the Armourers' Company's seating arrangements suggest, women were in attendance at some guild dinners and feasts, but they were frequently seated on separate tables from male participants.[133] In elite mercantile spaces wives and widows of eminent guildsmen might even be seated and served in a separate room altogether. At Drapers' Hall women were seated on separate hall tables in the first half of the sixteenth century; from the mid-1560s, 'they were seated separately at a special table positioned either within the parlour or a gallery'.[134] Moreover, any invitation to engage in civic sociability of this kind was, of course, predicated upon a woman's status as a wife or widow, and the relative seniority of her husband within the guild and wider civic hierarchy. And thus at funeral dinners hosted in Carpenters' Hall in the early seventeenth century the spouses of the company assistants were invited, but the liverymen dined unaccompanied.[135] When aldermen were invited to dine at Goldsmiths' Hall their wives were typically invited too; but the wives of liverymen of the guild were not permitted, unless their husbands had served as company renters.[136] At times of particular financial hardship, women were excluded from guild meals entirely in order to make the rite more economical.[137] Moreover, lacking formal civic authority, women would never participate in the meals which followed the exclusively male meetings of the court of assistants.

All this being said, women did play a role in provisioning and preparing dinners and feasts, and in arranging and cleaning the hall. At Drapers' Hall citizen wives and widows even had a role in scenting the feasting chambers with perfumes stored in pans specifically for that purpose.[138] Women at the lower end of the social spectrum were employed 'for labour in the kitchen', 'for scraping of trenchers', and 'washing the dishes'.[139] One Goodwife Parkinson was paid 18d 'for three days washing the [Drapers'] house before the dinner and after and also washing dishes in the kitchen the day of the Great Dinner'. On other years she was paid for 'dressing up the house'. The daughters of the Drapers' Company clerk were rewarded in 1580 for 'helping to dress up the house and Ladies' Chambers'.[140] At Carpenters' Hall a woman turned the spit at the court of assistants' dinners.[141] Following the death of her husband Robert Gray, cook to the Barber Surgeons' Company, Margaret Grey even took over the role of cook in 1601, with the same 'fee and salary therefore as at any tyme heretofore hath beene graunted' (and despite there being 'divers [male] Cookes' as suitors for the place).[142]

Women might also be engaged in maintaining the material cultures of feasting rites. At Goldsmiths' Hall in 1609 it was ordered that 'the napery belonging to the Company shall be delivered up by inventory to the Renters' wives, who shall have custody thereof, and shall deliver and receive the same by tale from time to time to and from the Beadle's wife, when the same shall be foul, and thereby to be by her washed again'.[143] Thus, we see how citizen wives might be given responsibility for safeguarding and cleaning the napery, a very valuable collective guild possession. Moreover, the respective roles of the women mirrored their husbands' work for the guild, thus reinforcing gendered social hierarchies. Whereas the renters' wives had overall responsibility and 'custody' of the textiles, the beadle's wife was responsible for washing the napery. The former role was akin to the significant task of safeguarding archives and treasures, for which their husbands were collectively responsible as wardens; the latter task of cleaning was parallel to the manual tasks undertaken by the company beadle.

Contentions at the feasting table

Marking out the relative spatial location of participants at feasting tables was evidently significant in terms of codifying a hierarchical order. But neat plans could not fix a messier human reality in which social relations were in flux. Sensitivity to spatial arrangements and hierarchies is evidenced by quarrels at the dinner table. Political and social tensions between fellow citizens were repeatedly expressed and shaped through disputes over material contributions to feasts, spatial hierarchies at the table, and privileged access to the company plate and treasures. As guild dinners were intended to be living enactments of the hierarchical community, refusal to partake in feasts or take one's allocated seat, or subversion of the rituals of communal consumption were an effective means of expressing competing claims to status, or articulating disapproval of some aspect of internal governance.

Tension or protest could take the form of uncivil speech acts or gestures at the feast table. Company court minutes recount verbal outbursts, such as the 'brabbling that he [armour Robert Jones] made sitting at the table'. The assistants claimed that such behaviour 'dyd disquiet all that dyd sytte here at the tabull' (but 'when the mr and wardeyn[s] dyd rebuke hy[m] for his faulte he mayd but a fyllyp [fillip; a gesture with the hand] at them').[144] At Barber Surgeons' Hall there were 'unseemely and unfitting words' uttered by one John Newman as he was 'sitting at dinner with the rest of the assistants'.[145] There was an expected standard of civil discourse within guilds, with verbal disputes mediated, and language directly regulated by company courts. 'Uncivil' words threatened to rupture the harmony of the corporate community and undermine the honourable reputations of the artisans involved.[146] Company employees might also create verbal disturbances, as when one Sebright was 'dismissed from his place of beinge Cook to this howse [Barbour Surgeons' Hall] as well for that he did dresse their last dynner very badlie as for his ill usage in speeches towards the maisters wyves'.[147]

Disruption at the feast table might also take the form of interference with the customary choreography of table service. In August 1600 an order was made for the reformation of abuses at Barber Surgeons' Hall. It was claimed that 'the bodye of this Company hath susteyned much disparagement by reason that some of the livery and others ... have not onely by themselves but alsoe by their servants and apprentices disfurnished the tables att ffeastes whereat they have sitten to pleasure their private frendes contrary to all modestie and good government'.[148] To 'disfurnish' was 'to deprive or divest of that wherewith it is furnished'.[149] In the late 1630s 'upon the complaint of the losse of a silver spoone the last dinner in the Hall and diver other times napkins and pewter dishes' the Barber Surgeons court ordered 'that when dinner goes in, the outer Wickett doore shalbe alwayes locked and the key thereof brought in and layed by o[u]r M[aste]r for the time being till dinner be ended'.[150] At the mid-seventeenth-century Tylers' and Bricklayers' Hall feasting tables were also unacceptably 'disfurnished'. The assistants attempted to curb such unruly behaviour. The court minutes relate that:

> Whereas great abuse hath bin formerly comitted by many and seuerall p[er] sons of this Company in sending forth of meate and other provisions abroad unto strangers and others by reason whereof the Company is much disgraced and abused and their tables disfurnished, and much lynnen thereby hath bin lost and gon.[151]

Here we see how the unauthorised stripping of tables could relate to both food stuffs and the material cultures of feasting. The practice of 'sending forth of meate abroad or out of doores from the Tables' at Tylers' and Bricklayers' Hall perhaps hinted at a deeper tension within the company concerning the relationship between citizens and strangers. In 1638 the company court had ordered that 'noe strangers shall be invited by any man of the livery unto such feast or feasts unles the master and wardens please'.[152]

For guildsmen of significant rank, abstention from the feast could also be a disruptive strategy. Absence created conspicuous gaps at the feasting table, which visibly undermined the ideal of a united fellowship. Non-attendance could also involve the withholding of essential material apparatus for the successful performance of the meal. At Goldsmiths' Hall in 1574 there were absentees from the dinner as a consequence of internal strife within the guild. Gardiner and Brandon, in possession of the keys of the company chest, were specifically sent for so that the guild might safely store their plate – but these goldsmiths would not attend the dinner. Their absenteeism was likely connected to a certain dissatisfaction concerning the mode of guild government.[153] Non-attendance at the feast was thus here an explicit vehicle for expressing discontent. In 1596 there was no silver plate to serve at dinner in Goldsmiths' Hall as a consequence of the pointed absence of goldsmith Brode who had the custody whereof.[154]

More dramatically, guildsmen might leave the table mid-feast. Among artisans and merchants of substantial authority, this theatrical departure from the table was a means of rejecting the pre-arranged hierarchy at the dinner table. Disputes over table precedence in guild halls took place between near social equals.[155] And thus in October 1612 at Goldsmiths' Hall the table plan proved to be unpalatable to certain participants. Following a meeting of the court of assistants, the company were about to 'repaire into the hall for dynner' when a contention arose between Sir William Herrick (goldsmith, teller of the exchequer, and large-scale lender to the Crown) and Alderman George Smithes (goldsmith and prime warden 1610–11) about their respective precedence at the table. After the matter had been 'well argued' between the two men, the City Remembrancer, William Dyos, was specifically summoned to Goldsmiths' Hall to resolve the dispute. It was decided by Dyos that 'Aldermen of the City should in all places within the City have precedence before the Knights Commoners. Thereupon Sir William departed, and would not be entreated to stay dinner, leaving Mr. Sheriff Prescott and his other guests in the Hall'.[156] Conversely, at a feast in 1617 a renter warden refused to leave the table at Goldsmiths' Hall when the renters were told to depart, because he was also a company assistant.[157] Here we see how tensions within and between guild, civic, and court hierarchies manifested themselves, and were worked through, as precedent disputes at the feast table.[158]

Managing the expectations pertaining to these discrete and yet overlapping hierarchies of social order was especially challenging when a guildsman held senior civic office. Mayoral office, for example, entailed the hosting of civic drinking rituals and feasts in the citizen's particular company hall. Predictably, these events were carried out according to a highly prescribed spatial and material chorography of order and hierarchy (which attempted to take into account guild and civic sensibilities). In 1611–12, the year that goldsmith James Pemberton was lord mayor, his livery company was required by 'anncient custome' to make choice in Goldsmiths' Hall of the king's sheriff. The decision would be confirmed by a 'drinke to him in a great cup of yppocras … w[i]th one of the flaggon potts of the Citie of the second sort filled w[i]th yppocras and a boxe of waffers'. The Goldsmiths' Company's wardens' accounts laid out in minute detail the seating arrangement of the (all male) company for this significant civic event, 'at the upper table in the hall':

> the Lo[rd] Maior sitting on the bench syde in the myddest of the table accompanied w[i]th two anncient Knights and Aldermen ... sitting on the right hand and [... two men] of this Companie on the left hand, and on the out syde right over against them Mr Sheriffe Smithes being mr warden of this Companie on the upper hand and Mr Sheriffe Barkham on the left hand the Lo[rd] Maiors Carver standing in the myddest and onely the Wardens and Assistants in theire several degrees sate at table w[i]th them ... at the syde table next the parlour doore ... the Clarke, Assayer and Beadle of this Companie w[i]th 2 other guests.

Despite the careful planning a tension arose as to whether 'the mr warden or the renter should rise and present the Lo[rd] Maior w[i]th the cup of wyne to welcome him'.[159] Here the relative status and associated privilege of wardens and renters was articulated through competing claims of access to precious civic plate and service during the ritual performance of welcome to Goldsmiths' Hall. Authority was seen to be invested in access to the flagon pot and privileged ritual movement through the great hall.

Managing the movement of people, food, and precious things on feast days also extended to men and women in receipt of corporate charity. Customarily, the poor were meant to have a presence at the guild feast and receive leftovers from the table; they sometimes acted also as servers at the meal.[160] In some early modern guilds the almsmen and/or women were provided with their own distinct meal. Sponsorship of these events could be a valuable avenue for philanthropic impulses. At Carpenters' Hall from 1611 twelve 'poore of the Companye' were invited to an annual supper of 'joyntes of meate bread and drink' (grace was said before and after the meat was served). They also received alms at the meal. This repast was sponsored by carpenter Richard Wyatt, though his particular identity as a benefactor was initially a secret, and only revealed after the yearly meal had been instituted. Wyatt even paid for a special table and bench to be made for the 'twelve poore to sit at'.[161] This special piece of furniture might have elevated the respectable (yet admittedly materially poor) status of the feast participants; though on the other hand, perhaps the joint use of the same benches for livery and receivers of alms was perceived as somewhat distasteful. Carpenter Richard Wyatt, who made his fortune in the early seventeenth century as a city wharf owner and dealer in timber, was a major property benefactor too. In his will of 1620, he bequeathed to the Carpenters' Company land at Henley-upon-Thames (thirteen poor women were to be supported by the rents from this land), and a gift of £500 to be used to construct ten almshouses for poor men at Godalming.[162]

The involvement of the poor in feasting activities, whether at their own designated meal, or as part of the main company festivities, was based upon certain behavioural and social criteria. However, their actions within company halls and broader urban sites of corporate sociability could be perceived as disruptive of the planned ceremonial order of proceedings. In 1622 the assistants of the Goldsmiths' Company expressed concern that:

> The waiting of the almsmen [at dinner] is thought unseemly, and unlike what is done at other Companies. Six waiters are therefore chosen instead of the almsmen. Ordered also that *no relief be given to the almsmen at the table in the Hall*, as heretofore, but that what food is left *shall be distributed amongst them at their own places*, and that none of the almsmen come to the tavern at such times as any of the Wardens or Assistants dine or sup there.[163]

This was clearly not the end of the matter. In December 1636 the company wardens 'reproved the Almesman for their forward sollicitac[i]ons of the new Rentors for their benevolens in giveinge them Beefe according to custome'. The almsmen were reminded that the food was a gift of 'charity unto them and not as of right belongeinge unto them'. Overall the wardens were 'the more Angry' at the presumption of due benefit because the almsmen had been approaching feasting tables before the 'wardens had concluded ... the makeinge of their accustomed dynners and other busines incident to their places'.[164] Moreover, contemporaneously to the disagreeable matter of 'forward solicitations' at the feast table, the governors of the Goldsmiths' Company were also concerned about the sartorial standards of their almsmen. It was agreed by the court that 'Mr Wardeins shall buy the clothe for the Almes mens gownes: and the goodness of the cloth ... may bee for the creditt of the Company' and 'the Badges of the Leopards heads shalbee sett upon each gowne'. It was stressed that if the almsmen should 'bisbehave themselves then their gownes and penc[i]ons to bee taken from them and conferred upon others'.[165] Plainly it was not just men of high civic station who might upset the delicate choreography of guild feasting.

Conclusion

Architecture 'organizes all aspects of life spatially through the body', it is 'adept at organizing, separating and ranking bodies'.[166] Artisanal company halls, through their spatial organisation and ritualised uses, ordered bodies relationally according to social, gender, and generational differences. Attendance at feast days in the company of their high-ranking husbands must have reinforced the standing of certain city women, but their subordinate gendered status was simultaneously reinforced through their seating at separate tables, or even discrete rooms. For worthy male artisans, the coveted identity of full patriarchal manhood was signified and reinforced through placement on a particular table, or participation in a ritual of civic significance.[167] But this delicate status might be slighted or threatened by a perceived verbal insult at the table, or one's position at the table relative to other men of honourable standing. The inclusion of younger guildsmen in rites of commensality was premised on them being excluded from the full delicacies of the meal, from seating of status, or from ritualised movement through the hall, as when the most senior goldsmiths 'departed together out of ye hall into ye parlour' to discuss secret matters.[168] Younger men witnessed or served their male seniors, but they were not full participants in guild rites. The bodies of the worthy urban poor were welcome in halls only if they complied with particular sartorial standards and presented themselves with suitable deference and humility.

As artisanal company halls were expanded and beautified from the mid-sixteenth century, their users and visitors became increasingly conscious of how access, movement, and placement within these institutional spaces reflected upon personal and collective identities. Privileged access to particular chambers, and witnessing of protected or 'secret' guild practices (such as material testing or election rites), signified and produced artisanal status.[169] Additionally, proximity and contact with the treasured material apparatus of feasting rites worked to bolster status and hierarchies within the artisanal or mercantile guild. More elaborate ceremonials matched the enhanced and expanded material fabric of halls, parlours, galleries, and staircases, though codified spatial arrangements and movements did not always go according to plan. Though in principle tightly choreographed, disputes over contributions, service, seating arrangements, attendance, and material standards of presentation at feasts show that rites did not go uncontested by feast-makers, or those largely excluded from festivities. Fundamentally, the materially augmented built environment of London's artisanal companies both shaped and was shaped by the guild community.

Notes

1 *Records of the Carpenters' Company*, VII, p. 399.
2 *Wardens' Accounts of the Founders' Company*, p. 268.
3 *Ibid.*, p. 244.
4 Prideaux, *Memorials of the Goldsmiths' Company*, I, p. 112.
5 Matthew Johnson, *English Houses 1300–1800: Vernacular Architecture, Social Life* (Harlow: Longman, 2010), p. 16.
6 Hamling and Richardson, *A Day at Home*, p. 6.
7 Janette Dillon, *The Language of Space in Court Performance, 1400–1625* (Cambridge: Cambridge University Press, 2010), p. 6.
8 GL, MS 12104. This professional survey included Armourers' Hall on Coleman Street and the broader company estate holdings on Thames Street and Bishopsgate Street. It was 'Measured and Drawne … by Joseph Titcombe member of the same Comp[any] and one of the ffoure sworne Viewers of this City and approved of to be well done by the three other Viewers of the said City'.
9 The Armourers' plot represents only the ground floor of the building (as was typical of seventeenth-century plans) but the accompanying textual key describes a multifunctional building of at least three storeys.
10 GL, MS 12104.

11 Ward, *Metropolitan Communities*, p. 91.
12 Prideaux, *Memorials of the Goldsmiths' Company*, I, p. 112.
13 Ward, *Metropolitan Communities*, p. 86.
14 Young, *The Annals of the Barber-Surgeons*, pp. 299, 301.
15 Ward, *Metropolitan Communities*, p. 86.
16 Griffiths, 'Secrecy and authority', p. 932.
17 Prideaux, *Memorials of the Goldsmiths' Company*, I, p. 367.
18 Across early modern society more broadly, an increasing number of people lived within institutions. See 'Introduction', in Cavallo and Evangelisti (eds), *Domestic Institutional Interiors*, pp. 1–23.
19 GHA, WA/CM, R1, fo. 11v; S2, fo. 242v; T, fo. 118r.
20 Sarah Milne, 'Merchants of the City: situating the London estate of the Drapers' Company, c.1540–1640' (PhD dissertation, University of Westminster, 2016), p. 204.
21 Interestingly – in terms of perceived hierarchies of what was worth recording – domestic residences of clerk and beadle (and, in the Goldsmiths' Company's case, assayer) are not listed on any surviving company inventories.
22 GL, MS 6153/1, fo. 47.
23 GL, MS 6153/1, fo. 49.
24 GHA, WA/CM, V, fos 191v–192r.
25 Ward, *Metropolitan Communities*, pp. 88–9.
26 GHA, WA/CM, T, fo. 7r.
27 GHA, WA/CM, V, fos 191v–192r.
28 GHA, WA/CM, V, fo. 192r.
29 Lena Orlin has argued that the long gallery was an essential space for conducting private conversations in aristocratic houses and royal palaces: *Locating Privacy*, ch. 6.
30 GHA, WA/CM, V, fo. 192r.
31 Reddaway and Walker, *The Early History of the Goldsmiths' Company*, pp. 164–5.
32 GHA, MS 2524, fo. 13v.
33 William Badcock, *A Touchstone for Gold and Silver Wares* (London, 1677), frontispiece.
34 *The De Moneta of Nicolas Oresme and English Mint Documents*, trans. by C. Johnson (London; New York: Nelson 1956), p. 81.
35 GHA, MS 2524, fo. 13v.
36 Lauren Jacobi, *The Architecture of Banking in Renaissance Italy: Constructing the Spaces of Money* (Cambridge: Cambridge University Press, 2019), ch. 2.
37 Georgius Agricola, *De Re Metallica*, trans. by Herbert Hoover and Lou Hoover (New York, 1950), p. 223.
38 For craft guilds and secrecy, see Long, *Openness, Secrecy, Authorship*, pp. 3–4, 6–7, 13–14, 72–101; Davids, 'Craft secrecy in Europe in the early modern period'.
39 GHA, MS 2524, fo. 55v.
40 For a discussion of 'secrecy as a dynamic social relation' see Koen Vermeir and Daniel Margocsy, 'States of secrecy: an introduction', *The British Journal for History of Science*, 45:2 (2012), 153–64.
41 For secrets as a commodity see Daniel Jütte, *The Age of Secrecy: Jews, Christians, and the Economy of Secrets, 1400–1800*, trans. by Jeremiah Riemer (New Haven, CT: Yale University Press, 2015), esp. ch. 4.
42 Jasmine Kilburn-Toppin, '"A place of great trust to be supplied by men of skill and integrity": assayers and knowledge cultures in late sixteenth- and seventeenth-century London', *The British Journal for the History of Science*, 52:2 (2019), 197–223.
43 Donald D. Hogarth, 'Mining and metallurgy of the Frobisher ores', in William W. Fitzhugh and Jacqueline S. Olin (eds), *Archaeology of the Frobisher Voyages* (Washington, DC; London: Smithsonian Institution Press, 1993), pp. 137–45; Harkness, *The Jewel House*, ch. 4.
44 Prideaux, *Memorials of the Goldsmiths' Company*, I, p. 62.

45 Forbes, *Hallmark*, p. 99.
46 GHA, WA/CM, O2, fo. 194.
47 For a broader discussion of 'the profound interrelations between house and individual', see Daniel Jütte, 'Living stones: the house as actor in early modern Europe', *Journal of Urban History*, 42:4 (2016), 659–87.
48 Richard Rogers was employed as company assay master from 1559 to 1567.
49 In 1566 Rogers was appointed assay master at the Tower mint.
50 GHA, WA/CM, K1, fo. 316.
51 Jacobi, *The Architecture of Banking*, p. 77.
52 GHA, WA/CM, K1, fos 271, 321.
53 GHA, WA/CM, K1, fos 271, 361, 382.
54 GHA, WA/CM, P1, fo. 37v. As a consequence, the Goldsmiths' Company's workmen 'were required to view the howse and put downe in writing the particular spoiles thereof under their hands'.
55 John Reynolds was in post as company common assayer for a decade, from 1619 to 1629.
56 GHA, WA/CM, Q1, fos 112r–v.
57 GHA, WA/CM, Q1, fo. 113r.
58 Prideaux, *Memorials of the Goldsmiths' Company*, I, p. 152.
59 GHA, WA/CM, Q1, fo. 122v.
60 Hill, *Pageantry and Power*, p. 16.
61 Quoted in *ibid.*, p. 58.
62 Anthony Munday, *Chruso-Thriambos: The Triumphes of Golde* (London, 1611); Martin Wiggins and Catherine Richardson, *British Drama, 1533–1642: A Catalogue. Volume VI: 1609–16* (Oxford: Oxford University Press, 2015), p. 196.
63 Curtis Perry, *The Making of Jacobean Culture: James I and the Renegotiation of Elizabethan Literary Practices* (Cambridge: Cambridge University Press, 1997), p. 199.
64 Munday, *Chruso-Thriambos*, sigs. A4r–A4v.
65 In a similar vein, in fifteenth- and sixteenth-century Chester and York innovative dramatic civic cycles included representations of craftwork and were employed by artisans to construct a distinctive cultural identity and social status based upon 'particularized claims to honor, profit and charity'. See Nicole R. Rice and Margaret A. Pappano, *The Civic Cycles: Artisan Drama and Identity in Premodern England* (Notre Dame, IN: University of Notre Dame Press, 2015), p. 18.
66 Wiggins and Richardson, *British Drama, 1533–1642*, VI, p. 199.
67 Stow, *A Survey of London*, I, pp. 305–6.
68 Rosser, 'Going to the fraternity feast', p. 431.
69 GL, MS 12071/2.
70 GHA, WA/CM, Q2, fo. 167r. For broader British examples of urban feasts 'as a means to reduce social conflict and enhance solidarity internally', see Heal, *Hospitality in Early Modern England*, p. 303.
71 Stow, *A Survey of London*, II, pp. 190–1.
72 Lars Kjaer and A. J. Watson, 'Feasts and gifts: sharing food in the middle ages', *Journal of Medieval History*, 37:1 (2011), 1–5, at pp. 2–3.
73 In domestic contexts, 'a complex interrelation of gender, age and place determined where a person sat to eat their dinner'. See Amanda Flather, *Gender and Space in Early Modern England* (Woodbridge: Boydell, 2007), p. 63. For the great households of the gentry and aristocracy, and their carefully graded hierarchy of seating and eating, see Heal, *Hospitality in Early Modern England*, pp. 30–2.
74 More generally in this society, 'the food and drink that people ingested provided resonant markers in the expression of worth and the articulation of status.' See Adam Fox, 'Food, drink and social distinction in early modern England', in Steve Hindle, Alexandra Shepard, and John Walter (eds), *Remaking English Society: Social Relations and Social Change in Early Modern England* (Woodbridge: Boydell, 2013),

pp. 165–87, at p. 165. Ken Albala has argued that in the sixteenth century 'dietary prejudices based on class intensified'. See *Eating Right in the Renaissance* (Berkeley, CA; University of California Press, 2002), p. 187.

75 Drapers Company Archive [hereafter DCA], DB1, fo. 14v.

76 GHA, WA/CM, P2, fos 225v–226v.

77 Robert Tittler, 'Seats of honor, seats of power: the symbolism of public seating in the English urban community, c. 1560–1620', *Albion*, 24:2 (1992), 205–23, at p. 214.

78 *The Dinner Book of the London Drapers' Company, 1564–1602*, ed. by Sarah Milne (Woodbridge: The Boydell Press, 2019), xxiii.

79 GL, MS 7110, fo. 32v.

80 GHA, WA/CM, K1, fos 125, 140.

81 Shepard, *Meanings of Manhood*, pp. 35–6.

82 GHA, WA/CM, P1, fo. 28r.

83 Rappaport, *Worlds within Worlds*, p. 226.

84 Notably, following their service at the lord mayor's show, twenty (out of eighty) of the bachelors were chosen to be in the livery, paying £10 each. Prideaux, *Memorials of the Goldsmiths' Company*, I, p. 120.

85 *Records of the Carpenters' Company*, IV, pp. 13–16.

86 GHA, WA/CM, K1, fo. 202; Branch, *Faith and Fraternity*, p. 34.

87 *Ibid.*, p. 52.

88 GL, MS 12106, fos 37, 48.

89 *Ibid.*, fos 39, 43.

90 Rosser, *The Art of Solidarity*, p. 125.

91 Prideaux, *Memorials of the Goldsmiths' Company*, I, p. 55. Likewise, from 1543, before the election dinner, the Drapers' Company 'would attend church where "Divine Service and sermon be done and Holy Communion ministered"'. See Branch, *Faith and Fraternity*, p. 47.

92 *Records of the Carpenters' Company*, VII, p. 402.

93 Welch, *History of the Worshipful Company of Pewterers*, II, p. 12.

94 GL, MS 12071/2, fo. 33.

95 DCA, MB1B, fo. 696.

96 Orlin, *Locating Privacy*, p. 150.

97 DCA, MB9, fo. 19v.

98 GL, MS 12071/1, fo. 219.

99 *Records of the Carpenters' Company*, VII, p. 402.

100 For restricted participation in election ceremonies, and variation in such regulations among companies, see Rappaport, *Worlds within Worlds*, pp. 245, 252–3; Archer, *The Pursuit of Stability*, pp. 103–4.

101 GHA, WA/CM, K1, fo. 220.

102 Prideaux, *Memorials of the Goldsmiths' Company*, I, pp. 45–7; Hanawalt, *Ceremony and Civility*, p. 108.

103 *Records of the Carpenters' Company*, IV, pp. 15–16.

104 Young, *The Annals of the Barber-Surgeons*, pp. 452–4.

105 DCA, DB1, fos 41r–49v.

106 DCA, DB1, fos 45v, 43r. At feasts held in the Inns of Court social distinctions were also signified by the food served at different tables. See Wilfrid R. Prest, 'Readers' dinners and the culture of the early modern Inns of Court', in Archer, Goldring and Knight (eds), *The Intellectual and Cultural World of the Early Modern Inns of Court*, pp. 107–123, at p. 115.

107 The Drapers' Dinner Book meticulously records the aristocratic, courtly, and mercantile networks through which the wardens obtained bucks.

108 Heal, *The Power of Gifts*, p. 40.

109 Quoted in Archer, *The Pursuit of Stability*, p. 117.

110 Quoted in Orlin, *Locating Privacy*, p. 139.

111 DCA, DB1, fo. 85r.
112 *The Dinner Book of the London Drapers' Company*, xxxv.
113 Heal, *The Power of Gifts*, p. 41.
114 Welch, *History of the Worshipful Company of Pewterers*, II, pp. 94, 105, 107.
115 Prideaux, *Memorials of the Goldsmiths' Company*, I, p. 140.
116 Moxon, *The Mechanick Exercises*, pp. 364–5.
117 GHA, WA/CM, K1, fo. 125; Prideaux, *Memorials of the Goldsmiths' Company*, I, p. 69.
118 There were some exceptions to this – the whole guild were invited to the election feast of the Brewers' and Weavers' Companies until the late 1550s and late 1570s respectively. See Archer, *The Pursuit of Stability*, p. 118. The trend towards exclusivity in guild feasting was experienced throughout Europe. See, for example, H. Deceulaer and F. Verleysen, 'Excessive eating or political display? Guild meals in the Southern Netherlands, late 16th–late 18th centuries', *Food and History*, 4:2 (2006), 165–85.
119 GL, MS 12071/1, fo. 486.
120 The total dinner bill was £8 6s 1d. The dish washers, porter, and water bearer were paid 2s 11d in total.
121 GL, MS 22181 [not paginated].
122 GL, MS 12073, fo. 29r.
123 GL, MS 12071/1, fo. 219.
124 GL, MS 12071/2, fo. 80.
125 GL, MS 12071/1, fos 464–5.
126 See GL, MS 22191 [not paginated].
127 Prideaux, *Memorials of the Goldsmiths' Company*, I, p. 113.
128 *Records of the Carpenters' Company*, VII, pp. 397–408.
129 Heal, *Hospitality in Early Modern England*, p. 328.
130 The burdens of being feast-maker could be felt in urban centres across England, particularly during the 1590s. See Heal, *Hospitality in Early Modern England*, p. 339; Ben R. McRee, 'Honesty and dissent: resisting the Company of St George in Tudor Norwich', *Urban History*, 47:1 (2020), 23–40.
131 GHA, WA/CM, Q2, fos 167r–v.
132 Prideaux, *Memorials of the Goldsmiths' Company*, I, p. 5.
133 In parish churches women frequently sat in separate blocks from men too (and they might be seated according to their particular status as wives or mothers). See Christopher Marsh, 'Order and place in England, 1580–1640: the view from the pew', *Journal of British Studies*, 44:1 (2005), 3–26, at pp. 10–11. For a broader discussion of wives as participants in elite urban commensality (sometimes at separate events to their husbands), see Heal, *Hospitality in Early Modern England*, pp. 336–7.
134 *The Dinner Book of the London Drapers' Company*, xxiii–xxiv.
135 *Records of the Carpenters' Company*, VII, p. 403
136 Prideaux, *Memorials of the Goldsmiths' Company*, I, p. 87.
137 *Ibid.*, p. 60.
138 DCA, DB1, fos 28r, 48r, 107r, 126r, 132r.
139 DCA, DB1, fos 27v, 98r.
140 DCA, DB1, fos 123v, 129r, 132r.
141 *Records of the Carpenters' Company*, VII, pp. 180–1.
142 Young, *Annals of the Barber-Surgeons*, p. 448.
143 Prideaux, *Memorials of the Goldsmiths' Company*, I, p. 112–13.
144 GL, MS 12073, fo. 35v.
145 Quoted in Celeste Chamberland, 'Honor, brotherhood, and the corporate ethos of London's Barber-Surgeons' Company, 1570–1640', *Journal of the History of Medicine and Allied Sciences*, 64:3 (2009), 300–32, at p. 321.

146 Withington, *The Politics of Commonwealth*, pp. 137–49, 176–7; Jennifer Bishop, 'Speech and sociability: the regulation of language in the livery companies of early modern London', in Justin Colson and Arie van Steensel (eds), *Cities and Solidarities: Urban Communities in Pre-Modern Europe* (London: Routledge, 2017), pp. 208–24.

147 Young, *The Annals of the Barber-Surgeons*, p. 450.

148 *Ibid.*, pp. 447–8.

149 'disfurnish, v.' *OED Online*. Oxford University Press, June 2020 [accessed 19 July 2020].

150 Young, *The Annals of the Barber-Surgeons*, p. 454.

151 GL, MS 3043/1, fo. 135.

152 GL, MS 3043/1, fo. 75.

153 Prideaux, *Memorials of the Goldsmiths' Company*, I, pp. 79–80.

154 *Ibid.*, p. 89.

155 Similarly, in parish churches, 'most quarrels occurred among the relatively powerful as they competed for places at the front of the church'. See Marsh, 'Order and place in England', p. 26.

156 Prideaux, *Memorials of the Goldsmiths' Company*, I, p. 120; GHA, WA/CM, P1, fo. 49r.

157 Prideaux, *Memorials of the Goldsmiths' Company*, I, p. 129.

158 At Drapers' Hall there were also social frictions relating to seating and associated internal and external hierarchies. See *The Dinner Book of the London Drapers' Company*, xxiii, 'Tensions ran especially high when Company officers or Assistants rejected City offices, as they frequently did, but were still entitled to a seat closer to the centre of the high dais simply on account of their nomination.'

159 GHA, WA/CM, P1, fo. 41r.

160 Heal, *Hospitality in Early Modern England*, pp. 320, 332–3; Rosser, 'Going to the fraternity feast', pp. 436–7.

161 GL, MS 4326/5, fos 106r, 163r.

162 Alford and Barker, *A History of the Carpenters' Company*, pp. 88, 102–3.

163 Prideaux, *Memorials of the Goldsmiths' Company*, I, p. 135. Emphasis added.

164 GHA, WA/CM, S2, fo. 229r.

165 GHA, WA/CM, R1, fo. 8v.

166 Hills, 'Theorizing the relationships between architecture and gender', p. 6.

167 Amanda Bailey and Roze Hentschell, 'Introduction: gendered geographies of vice', in Bailey and Hentschell (eds), *Masculinity and the Metropolis of Vice, 1550–1650* (Basingstoke: Palgrave Macmillan, 2010), p. 12, 'perceptions and experiences of masculinities in early modern England were predicated on one's access to and mobility across particular spaces'.

168 GHA, WA/CM, K1, fo. 220.

169 Martha C. Howell, 'The spaces of late medieval urbanity', in Marc Boone and Peter Stabel (eds), *Shaping Urban Identity in Late Medieval Europe* (Leuven: Garant, 2000), pp. 3–23, at pp. 9–10.

7

'Outward walls' and 'publique workes'

In 1579 the Armourers' Company paid 'for paving the streatt befor[e] the hall gate and a lode of sand and a lode of stone'.[1] In the early 1600s, the Ironmongers' Company organised for the 'outside of the Hall to the streete (to) be mended, plaistered, oyled, and collered'.[2] City guilds were very much aware of how the exterior façade of their institutional buildings – or 'outward walls' as the Goldsmiths phrased it – might reflect upon the status and honour of the corporation. Livery halls were highly conspicuous civic buildings, in 'dialogue' with multiple political, social, and aesthetic audiences, including their own guildsmen but also artisans of diverse crafts, merchants, foreign dignitaries, and members of the royal court. 'Private' buildings were also in constant dialogue with 'public' spaces, such as the street and marketplace, and thus the state of structures like guild halls impacted upon the prestige of public throughways, and vice versa. As Vanessa Harding has suggested, 'public space derived some of its character – architectural and social – from the private units around it', but 'the converse was also true ... Public uses and private values complemented and reinforced one another.'[3] The primary focus in this work has been upon the internal structure and organisation of institutional artisanal buildings and their guild communities. The view here, however, is extended outward, to consider what exterior walls, designs, and materials signified in the wider urban environment of the City of London.

This chapter explores external walls and political relationships. At the same time that modifications and improvements were being made to interior designs and material cultures across artisanal company halls in London, their outer walls were also subject to enhancements and remodelling. Exterior walls had, of course, always been of importance – in providing security, and a sense of a physically bounded corporate community – but the early seventeenth century was a moment at which exterior façades came under particular scrutiny. 'Improvements' to company halls were part of a broader cultural and political movement for the material enhancement and design regulation of the built fabric of the City and its environs. From a royal perspective, uniform architectural design signified a stable, ordered political community. Accordingly, royal building proclamations repeatedly stressed the significance of uniform building and design. Significantly, under James I and Charles I 'regulation became notably prescriptive', and particularly during the personal rule (1629–40) 'their language lent itself to interpretation as that of a would-be proprietor at best, a tyrant at worst'.[4]

This discussion of exterior walls and the negotiation of political and social relations attends to three central case-studies. First, the enhancement of guild and City gatehouses; second, dialogues over the exterior designs of Goldsmiths' Hall; and third, the long-running debate over the contested location of London's goldsmiths' shops and work sites – many of which had spread outside the City walls by the early seventeenth century. Linking these case-studies is a deep-rooted concern on the part of both civic and royal authorities to regulate space and enhance the material fabric of London. Thematically central too is the question of what exactly constitutes 'public' space. The Goldsmiths' Company described their rebuilding project of the mid-1630s in somewhat contradictory terms, as 'a publique worke for a never dyeing body', referring to the guild's incorporated status and concomitant privilege to own private property.[5] Indeed, extensive discussions over the positioning and design of Goldsmiths' Hall reveal an inherent tension between the complex interior spatial organisation of company buildings (the prerogative of the guildsmen) and their façades (adapted in accordance with the royal concern for 'uniformity'). To resolve tensions over the extent to which company architectures were 'public' buildings, guild office-holders made a distinction between 'inward' works, over which they exerted close control, and 'outward' walls, where responsibility was largely delegated to those with architectural expertise and close royal connections. Congruently, the well-documented campaign to return all 'remote' goldsmiths (located in western suburbs) to Cheapside (their customary City location) – initially orchestrated by City and Crown, but by the 1630s imperiously pushed as an issue by the royal council – shows that contested interpretations of 'private' or 'public' space, in workshops and city streets as within company halls, came to define an artisan's or trader's place within the body of the guild or, indeed, his exclusion from it.

Previous chapters showed how early modern urban spaces, including buildings and streets, were not absolutely public or entirely private. As Riitta Laitinen and Thomas Cohen have eloquently phrased it: 'multiple aspects and tones of publicity and privacy figure in our early modern streetscapes'.[6] The case-studies under focus here illuminate the different ways in which rebuilding projects sharpened awareness and negotiations as to the comparatively public or private nature of artisanal and mercantile spaces (and indeed surfaces, such as exterior walls). Improvements to exterior walls and gateways enabled a firmer material and symbolic boundary between the 'public' street and the 'private' institutional interior. Lengthy civic debates over the placing and design of Goldsmiths' Hall, in particular, resulted in a deepened understanding and articulation of how interior surfaces and 'Outward walls' might map onto institutional understandings of the respective demands of relatively private corporate interests and public concerns. The increasingly heated discussions and petitioning related to the location of goldsmiths' workshops within and outside the City walls was centred on contested interpretations as to what was legitimate public space. The chapter shows how this dialogue was taking place between citizens and within artisanal and mercantile communities, but it was also an increasingly fraught negotiation between City and Crown.

Gates and access to halls

On approaching a craft company hall in early modern London, one's first material encounter would have been a wall, or walls, and most likely a gate. Gates and gatehouses, prominent entrance points to institutional buildings, and their immediate environs, underwent substantial enhancement and material improvement from the last quarter of the sixteenth century.[7] At Founders' Hall there were a series of investments for 'mendyng of the gate' (1571–72), 'panting [painting] of the hall gate' (1620–21), and 'for mending of the hamar at the gatt' (1627–28).[8] The latter payment perhaps referred to the visual representation of a tool on a trade sign positioned above the gateway.[9] In 1607 the Carpenters' Company undertook improvements to their gatehouse, a considerable structure which had its own roof and a 'tenemente scituate [situate] within' (this probably housed the beadle).[10] The Carpenters paid for 'plancks for the twoe seats at the Gate; for twoe men to hang the gates and make the seats … For a man to cutt the Inner gate and amend it and sett on bolts'. Several years later, they paid 'Wiltsheine the smyth by bill for an Iron barr, a lock and a key to the Gate next the street', and another artisan for 'paintinge the Gate next the streete'.[11] The complete rebuilding of Goldsmiths' Hall in the 1630s included the construction of a materially and architecturally elaborate gateway. In the case of both the Carpenters' and Goldsmiths' remodelled gates we see a firmer material demarcation of the relatively private interior space (within the gates) from the exterior public space (the street). Gates signified, and created, 'insiders' and 'outsiders'.

In early modern urban culture, gates were freighted with symbolical meaning. As Daniel Jütte writes, in antiquity and the middle ages 'a gate stood as *pars pro toto* [a part [taken] for the whole] for its city, as illustrated on coins, coats of arms, and seals'.[12] Across Europe, city gates signalled civic authority and antiquity. From AD 200 London was a walled city with gates, and by the seventeenth century the City possessed seven major gates in the old wall.[13] Temple Bar on Fleet Street, west of Ludgate, was effectively an extra honorary (eighth) gate, its importance rooted in being 'the main point of transition between the Cities of London and Westminster'.[14] London's gates were the ceremonial entrance (and departure) points for receiving royal and civic dignitaries and processions, and thus their ornament, inscriptions, and sculptures balanced civic interests and royal honour.[15] On a practical level gates also formed a moveable material barrier that could act as a type of 'social filter'.[16] Movement through the City gates was monitored, and each evening they were shut. At moments of political turmoil, the gates had an even more pointed defensive purpose. During the Civil War 'the old wall, bulwarks and gates provided a second line of defence to the larger fortifications that were constructed in 1642–43'.[17] Some of the City gates also served further functional purposes, such as prison buildings (Newgate and Ludgate) and domestic residences for the lord mayor's household officers.[18] As controller of the customs of the port of London, Geoffrey Chaucer had lived above Aldgate from the mid-1370s for twelve years.[19]

At the beginning of his renowned *Survey*, the origins, antiquity, and vicissitudes of the City gates are carefully accounted by John Stow, and presented as one of the principal features of the urban built fabric – alongside the City wall, bridges, towers and castles. For instance, Stow writes of how: 'In the West is the next, and sixt principal gate, and is called Ludgate, as first builded (saith Geffrey Moumouth) by king Lud a Briton, about the yeare before Christs natiuitie 66 ... This gate I suppose to be one of the most auncient.'[20] He goes on to develop Ludgate's turbulent history:

> In the year 1260 this Ludgate was repayred and beautified with Images of Lud, and other Kinges ... These Images of Kings in the raigne of Edward the sixt had their heads smitten off ... and in the raigne of Queene Marie were repayred ... The 28 of Queene Elizabeth [when] the same gate being sore decayed, was cleane taken downe ... and the same yere the whole gate was newly and beautifully builded, with the Images of Lud, and others, as afore, on the East side, and the picture of her Maiestie, Queen Elizabeth on the West side. All which was done at the common charges of citizens, amounting to 1500 poundes or more.[21]

This rich description of the trials and tribulations of Ludgate is significant for what it reveals about the symbolism of the City gates. Royal imagery was common on these edifices, but we should not read this as a simplistic statement of civic loyalty to the Crown. As Christine Stevenson has argued, 'the very prestige and prominence of this (royal) ornament paradoxically underlined civic autonomy, for the gates' royal arms and statues allegorized a partnership of interests, which was also enacted when distinguished visitors entered'.[22] Stow's exploration of Ludgate's history is also highly revealing of practices of civic rebuilding. Ludgate (a prison gate) was rebuilt in 1585–86, and Aldgate and Aldersgate in the early seventeenth century. Between 1620 and the disastrous conflagration of 1666 citizens were especially active in the 'repair and making good' of the City gates. As Emily Mann contends, 'the City authorities were highly conscious of how their care of the gates – "by ancient custom" – connected themselves with London's prestigious founders and past'.[23] The substantial material improvements to the gates of company halls, and the enlargement of gatehouses, were thus clearly taking place at the same time (or slightly preceding) the wider civic project of enhancing City entrances.

At company halls a gatehouse enabled guilds to closely regulate the movement of people and goods in and out of their institutional homes. Particular, or personal, instances of the experience of gate use are beyond our reach, but we do have references to general prescriptions suggestive of typical patterns of use, such as the early seventeenth-century directive from the Goldsmiths' Company, 'that the Beadle only shall have a key of the outer great gate, and that if any shall apply for entrance after 10 o'clock at night he shall pay the Beadle 4d. to be let in'.[24] The guild thus had an inner and outer gate, controlled by the beadle (the Carpenters' Company also referred to 'a man to cutt the Inner gate').[25] Moreover, it is evident that the gates of company halls were locked at night – an echo of the wider civic curfew enacted through the closing of the City gates in the walls each evening. The seventeenth-century survey of Goldsmiths' Hall, which reveals the interior spatial organisation of the ground floor of the gatehouse, integrated within the range (as it was from the late 1630s), provides further evidence of the social regulatory function of guild gatehouses (see figure 7.1). The Goldsmiths' gatehouse was evidently substantial; the interior staircase symbols show that this was a multi-storey structure. An exterior gate – with gateposts and hinges – and an interior gate, complete with keyhole, are represented on the survey. This double gate system would have facilitated scrutiny of all those who entered the gatehouse before they passed through to the courtyard. The chamber to the immediate right of the gatehouse (from the perspective of a visitor approaching Goldsmiths' Hall from Foster Lane) was almost certainly the beadle's residence. Internally, this dwelling was connected to the symmetrical gatehouse. Thus, even at times of day when the exterior gates were open, the company beadle was in a prime position to monitor comings and goings from the hall.[26] Similarly, Ralph Treswell's survey of Clothworkers' Hall on Mincing Lane shows how the gatehouse incorporated the beadle's house (see Plate 2). During significant civic events, such as feast days, men would be specifically positioned at the gate for the purposes of enhanced security (at Carpenters' Hall a man was paid 'for keepinge the gate', and another for 'keepinge the porch').[27]

Grand guild gatehouses and gateways must also have enhanced the ceremonial experience of feasts, processions, and celebrations. Guests

Figure 7.1 Close view of the gatehouse at Goldsmiths' Hall; detail from *Goldsmiths' Hall: ground-storey plan*, 1692.

would have passed through the gatehouse into the courtyard and hall for feasts and dinners. On these occasions the entryway might have advertised the status and prestige of the guild, and simultaneously its bounteous hospitality (gates customarily had such generous associations at country houses; notably, the Drapers' Company gave out pasties to the poor and other food gifts from their gatehouse).[28] In advance of civic processions and pageants, guildsmen gathered and were arranged into an appropriate hierarchy in the courtyard, before parading through the gate and onto the City streets. For instance, on the occasion of the inauguration of Sir John Wollaston as lord mayor on 28 October 1643 (on the feast day of St. Simon and St. Jude), the wardens and assistants of the Goldsmiths' Company met at 8am at the hall and proceeded 'to the Lord electe's house in their gownes and hoodes to wayte upon him to the Guildhall to take his oath of Maioraltye'. And thus, having gathered in the parlour, and proceeded down the grand staircase to the courtyard, the guild officials would have passed through the magnificent new gateway onto Foster Lane, 'beeinge ushered from Goldsmithes Hall to his [Wollaston's] house by 4 almesmen, in their gownes, and white staves in their handes, leading the waye, and the Assistantes in their degrees, the Clerk and Beadle goeinge last'. After cakes and wine at his home, the goldsmiths repaired to Guildhall for the swearing-in ceremony. The corporate gatehouse here literally framed the opening ceremony, and notably ritual proceedings ended at the domestic gates of the old and new civic officials. Accordingly, 'when the Fishmongers came to the now Lord's gate [Wollaston], they made a stand of the other side of the way, and the Assistants of this [Goldsmiths'] Companye went in to the now Lord Maior's house, and dyned with him, and the old Lord takeinge his leave of the new att his gate, the Fishmongers attended the old Lord home to his house, and dined with him according to custome'.[29]

More architecturally elaborate gatehouses allowed for closer scrutiny and regulation of ingress and egress from company halls. These increasingly elaborate structures also symbolically marked a threshold between exterior public streets and interior civic spaces. Entrance through the outer and inner gates into the courtyard did not, however, equate to free movement across the building. The gatehouse was but the first barrier or point of social filtering. As seen in previous chapters, an individual's gender, age, and civic or social seniority largely determined the extent to which they might have legitimate passage throughout the livery hall. Experience of the space was highly subjective.

'Outward lines' and 'inward worke'

Previously we encountered the circumstances through which Nicholas Stone, master mason to the Crown, became involved in the Goldsmiths' Hall rebuilding project. During the winter months of 1634, at the same time as Nicholas Stone was establishing his role as surveyor for the Goldsmiths' Hall (re)building project, debates amongst the committee for building centred on the issue of 'outwarde Walls'. The question was this: 'w[hi]ch plott [design] the Company would begin their new building for the out lines in respect that one of the plotts had the hall gate leadinge out Mayden Lane and the other leading out of Foster Lane' (we might notice the firm emphasis here placed upon the gate as the centre point or 'face' of the building). Put to the vote 'it was resolued by 10. Against 7. That the Company should proceed accordinge to the plot leadinge out of Foster Lane for the settinge out of the outward walls'. This preferred design had been authored by Stone.[30] Two months later, the surveyor's 'seuerall draughts' for the new Goldsmiths' Hall were presented to the building committee. These plans showed 'the ffronte and sides to the streetside and the patterne of the greate gate to ffoster lane ward as alsoe the ffronte of the hall parlor and dyneinge chamber towards the greate courte'. Nicholas Stone made known to the court, 'that in the doeinge thereof Mr Jones his Ma[jes]tyes Surveyor tooke especiall care and did advise and direct before the p[er]fectinge and finishinge of each piece accordinge to the seurerall draughts now shewed'.[31] Subsequently the Goldsmiths gifted Jones a gold

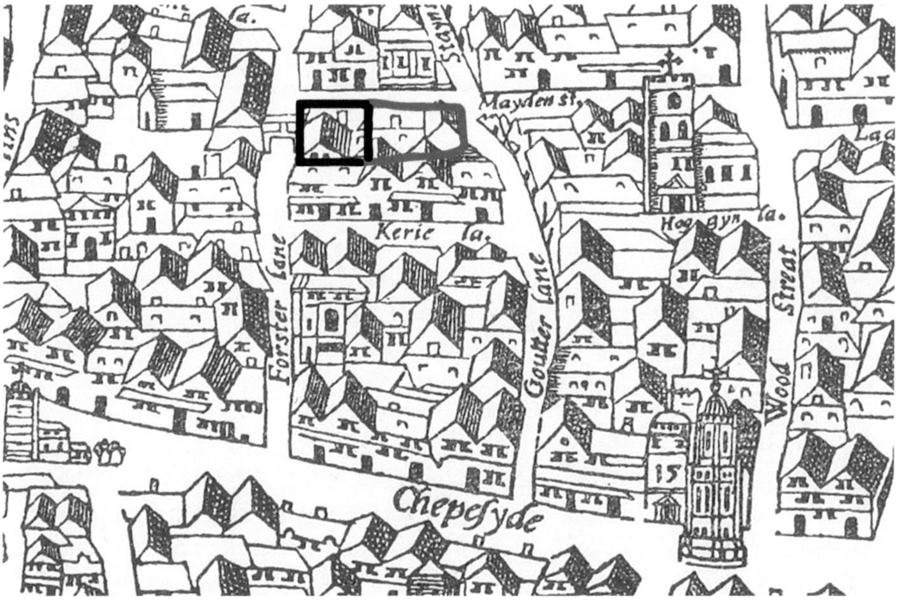

Figure 7.2 Close view of City location of Goldsmiths' Hall. Original site indicated by bold rectangle on the left; approximate outlines of extended hall site from mid-1630s indicated on the right. Detail from the *'Agas' Map of London* c. 1561, this edition published c. 1633, sheet 7.

plate and a Spanish gold chain, 'as a token of this Company's love', for the trouble he had taken over the rebuilding of Goldsmiths' Hall.[32] Such a choice concerning the positioning of the new building represented a clear statement of civic magnificence. If the great gate had been on Maiden Lane, the building would have faced towards the walls and away from the City centre. By contrast, an entrance facing onto Foster Lane ensured that Goldsmiths' Hall was seen to be connected directly to Cheapside, the main artery of ceremony, luxury trade and commerce through the heart of the City (see figure 7.2).[33] The east end of Cheapside was additionally an area in which goldsmiths, individually and as a corporation, were major property owners.

These deliberations about the position of the new guild hall demonstrate how the Goldsmiths' Company and their surveyor were highly conscious of the external, material 'face' which they might present to the rest of the City. Moreover, the remarks show that when the committee for building conceptualised and negotiated the rebuilding of their dilapidated late medieval hall into an impressive new structure that befitted their civic status, firm distinctions were repeatedly made between 'outward' and 'inward' works, between plans for the external walls and 'the settinge out of any inward worke either for hall parlor or greate Chamber and for the … seuerall offices and habitacons for the seuerall officers of the hall'.[34]

The designs for the 'outward lines' – those facing 'the streeteside' – were left largely to the discretion of the external project manager, an individual highly familiar with classical architectural language. But crucial decisions about the internal spatial organisation of the new Goldsmiths' Hall were understood to be principally at the discretion of the guildsmen themselves. Whilst the internal material and spatial organisation of the guild community was becoming increasingly complex – in part a reflection of the expanding and diversifying body of guildsmen, and their growing collections of material possessions – the exterior walls and façades of guild halls ideally demonstrated order and harmonious proportion (see Plates 1 and 4).

Throughout early negotiations conducted between senior members of the Goldsmiths' Company and their surveyor, Nicholas Stone, distinctions were repeatedly made by the guild between responsibility for the design and construction of the exterior walls, and authority over the internal spatial organisation of the new Goldsmiths' Hall. The sources give the overall impression that the assistants of the guild were prepared to give Stone a relatively free rein in terms of the architectural design of the façade – presumably they recognised his relative expertise in this matter – but they were keen to collaborate very closely when it came to the spatial layout of the interior complex. In December 1634, having agreed upon Nicholas Stone as surveyor for the project, it was stated very plainly that 'This Plott is agreed vpon by the Company of Gouldsmithes for the outward lines provided that the inward workes may be altered as wilbe most convenient for the Company *within their owne grounde*.'[35] Over a year later, in March 1635/6, as building proceeded apace, it was decided that the committee for rebuilding should 'consider of the offices and buildinges now to bee erected for the better ordereinge contriveinge and fittinge thereof and of all or any of the officers houses and roomes thereto belongeinge and for the p[ro]videinge of materialls for the same'.[36] Nicholas Stone was very closely involved in this process, and expected to provide thorough 'advice', but the emphasis for the spatial reorganisation of the building was on the 'best conveniency of the Company and Officers as to them shall seeme best'.[37]

The building project of the mid-1630s was explicitly presented by the Goldsmiths' Company as a 'publique' work. Having approved Nicholas Stone's plots for rebuilding, a petition was prepared to send to the king 'for licence to build accordinglye and for a warrant to send for one hundred tun of Portland Stone out of his Maj's Quarry It beeinge for a *publique worke* for a neuer dyeinge body'.[38] 'Public' had a multiplicity of meanings in the early seventeenth century, but we might presume in this context that it referred to the livery hall being open to general observation or, in other words, being conspicuous, a prominent visual landmark in the centre of the City. The use of 'public' in their communication with the Crown was likely also rooted in the notion that the building, in further beautifying the City, was of significance to the wider urban community, or even commonwealth as a whole.[39] This reading is bolstered by the language used by the Goldsmiths in a petition to the Crown in February 1634/5: 'And for the better effectinge of soe *publique a worke* in continueinge the beauty therof to posteritie for the service of the state and kingdome.'[40]

This language of 'publique' can be mapped on to the Goldsmiths' Company's firm distinction between 'outward lines' and 'inward works', discussed above. Indeed, as we have seen, the company emphasised 'their owne ground' within the walls of the hall as a rather more private matter, principally of corporate concern. This laboured emphasis on the building works being undertaken on their own soil was a strong assertion of independent corporate identity. As demonstrated in earlier chapters, there was a close association between incorporation and the ability to hold real property.[41] In their dialogue with the royal court over the construction of their new company hall, the governors of the guild were thus reaffirming their incorporated status and privileges. Contemporaneously, certain individual goldsmiths residing and working apart from Cheapside were asserting their rights to hold private property in 'public' places outside the City walls.

The original design sketches of Goldsmiths' Hall, the 'severall draughts' produced by Nicholas Stone and presented to the Goldsmiths in spring 1634/5 for 'the frronte and sides to the streetside and the patterne of the great gate towards Ffoster lane ward', have not survived.[42] It is likely that Stone never intended for these drawings to be preserved for posterity's sake. These plots were not finalised blueprints, but designs in progress, sketches to be discussed with company men and building craftsmen on site. Though lacking the original 'draughts', we do have the extant plan of the ground storey, elevation of the Foster Lane front, and bird's-eye view perspective of Goldsmiths' Hall, produced by John Ward, the company's surveyor between 1691 and 1693. It is striking that despite the irregular shape of the internal building, the external façade of Goldsmiths' Hall, specifically the Foster Lane face of the structure, was symmetrical and proportioned (see Plate 6). This façade was composed of a stone frontage of eleven bays, 110ft long. A central projection of five bays reflected the width of the courtyard within (60ft). The central point was emphasised with a great gateway crafted from West Country marble, with an escutcheon of the Goldsmiths' arms carved over the doorway, and Corinthian pilasters at either side. When first conceptualising the external 'dress' of Goldsmiths' Hall, Nicolas Stone was clearly confronted with a design problem – namely, a desire to create a seemingly well-proportioned classically inspired building, in which 'the street front formed the main architectural expression externally', and yet he was working with a structure that was based upon a medieval plan, with domestic quarters and only the 'ends' of significant rooms fronting Foster Lane. Architectural historian John Newman has persuasively argued that the design inspiration for Stone's ingenious plot was the seventh book of sixteenth-century Italian architectural writer and theorist Sebastiano Serlio, particularly chapters which advised 'planning a building on an irregular site'.[43]

By comparison to the internal spatial organisation of Goldsmiths' Hall, which was structured according to the medieval courtyard plan, an architectural language of 'inward looking' community and spatial (and social) distinction, external aesthetics were clearly expected to communicate a rather more contemporary visual message, to a broader urban audience.[44] The external uniform stone façade of the new Goldsmiths' Hall might enhance the glory of the City and the Crown, and enter into a complimentary aesthetic and design dialogue with recent architectural developments in the surrounding urban environment.[45] These public projects included the construction of the Banqueting House at Whitehall Palace (1619–22), the remodelling of St. Paul's Cathedral (1631–42) two hundred yards south-west of Goldsmiths' Hall, and the development of Covent Garden by the Earl of Bedford (1630s).[46] Inigo Jones was the 'architect' behind all three projects, and Nicholas Stone the master mason for the Banqueting House. Fundamental to all these building schemes was the projection of a uniform and self-conscious 'monumental classicism', the 'deliberate use as models of the structures of the ancient Romans', which Jones recognised from books and had seen in person. This was an architectural embodiment of royal imperialist ambition.[47]

The choice of language by the Goldsmiths' Company in their petition to the king, particularly references to 'publique' works and 'service of the state and kingdome', was clearly intended to chime positively with royal concern regarding the quality (and density) of housing within the City of London, an urban space which Charles I pointedly regarded as 'being the Kings Chamber, the Seat Imperiall of this Kingdom, and renowned over all parts of the Christian world'.[48] Concern for the state of the built environment was not new. From the beginning of his reign – and like Elizabeth I before him – James I had attempted to control the energetic pace of new building in the City and suburbs and improve the outward appearance of extant structures 'looking towards the Streets', with forefronts of brick and stone and of 'uniforme order and forme'.[49] The royal desire was for structures that 'shall both adorne and beautifie this said City', rather than a ramshackle collection of wooden structures that posed a serious fire and infection risk, as well as being aesthetically unappealing.[50] In a royal proclamation of 16 July 1615, the king infamously declared, 'that as it was said by the first Emperour of Rome, that he had found the City of Bricke, and left it of Marble, So that Wee … mought be able to say in some proportion, That Wee had found Our Citie and Suburbs of London of stickes, and left them of Bricke'.[51] In the same proclamation James I heartily praised 'all Edifices, Structures, and workes which tend to *publique use and ornament* ... as the paving of Smithfield, the planting of Moorefields ... the reedifying of Algate, Hicks Hall, and the like workes'.[52] Charles I echoed all his father's proclamations concerning new building and the essential 'uniformitie' of those that currently stood; adding that no persons should attempt to 'support or strengthen any Buildings so ruinous and olde, as are unfit to be continued'.[53]

The direct royal interest in the uniform development of the capital city demonstrates very clearly that in their rebuilding projects guilds were operating within a particular political and aesthetic climate, one which encouraged institutions to outwardly display civic magnificence in a self-consciously classical style. With Nicholas Stone, royal master mason, as surveyor for their project – almost certainly at the suggestion of Inigo Jones – the Goldsmiths were clearly under pressure to construct a new institutional home which fulfilled the royal desire for external order, uniformity, and beauty. Royal expectation is unquestionably hard to disentangle from the motivations of the Goldsmiths themselves, who also wished to present an impressive front to the rest of the City. The court minutes show that even before the approach of Inigo Jones, the Goldsmiths had accepted the possibility that a total rebuilding of their institutional home might be necessary – for 'repayringe and amending the same from time to time or to newe build as occasion shall require'.[54] The Goldsmiths might also have been driven by a competitive civic impetus. The Mercers' Company, first in order of precedence of all livery companies, improved the external façade to their guild hall in 1632–33, just before the Goldsmiths' project commenced.[55] The Mercers inhabited a structure, rebuilt in the 1530s, whose impressive battlemented stone façade of five bays, over ninety-eight feet long, fronted on to the east end of Cheapside.[56] This was 'a most curious peece of worke' in the opinion of John Stow, though sadly no visual representations exist of the building before the late 1660s (it was rebuilt again 1668–82).[57] Mercers' Hall was located in an area of the City densely populated by mercers' shops and residences, standing as monument to their growing corporate affluence and civic authority.[58] The existence of a stone altarpiece within Mercers' Hall chapel, commissioned from a sculptor based in Antwerp, has led to some speculation that the entire external shell of Mercers' Hall might have been Flemish in design.[59] It is probable that improvements to this institutional façade in the early 1630s were also linked to a royal political imperative for the material enhancement and uniformity of Cheapside.

When the Goldsmiths' rebuilding project was finally completed in the early 1640s, their new institutional home attracted interest and comment among contemporary observers. Significantly, the new Goldsmiths' Hall was no longer set back from the street but, like the Mercers' Hall on Cheapside, bordered the lane. Discerning viewers recognised the 'antique' language articulated through the external walls of the new building, identifying the order and rule inherent in the spatial relationships between gateway and windows, and their relative degrees of ornamentation.[60] The French traveller and diarist Balthasar de Monconys (1611–65) noted in his *Journal des Voyages* that 'the house of the Goldsmiths ... is not only the most beautiful in London for its architectural lines, but is second to none in Italy'. Further, he went on to reflect upon its materiality: 'its fenestrations, portals and cornices, which divided the two storeys, all of cut stone of a beautiful and bold architectural style that is the same in the gates, windows and porticos'.[61] Even those bystanders with little textual or architectural basis for comparison would have noticed – in a city predominately constructed of wood – that the impressive new outer shell of the Goldsmiths' Hall, like the great new portico, of ten forty-foot high Corinthian columns, before the west front of St. Paul's, was crafted from stone (see figure 7.3). From the perspective of the external observer, the outer, ordered 'dress' of the new building suggested a singularity of purpose. According to Leon Battista Alberti, the renowned fifteenth-century Italian architect, in the ideal city particular structures would have specific functions, which

Figure 7.3 Daniel King, *View of St Paul's Cathedral's west end*, etching, c. 1634.

were indicated by their architectural form and ornamentation.[62] The classical allusions embedded in the symmetrical stone-clad shell of the new Goldsmiths' Hall screened the multifunctional reality of the structure and projected a visual message of order, authority, and control to a 'publique' audience.

Goldsmiths' Row: remote goldsmiths and the nature of 'publique and open' space

> ye petic[i]oners doe justly find themselues agreeved at … many others (Goldsmithes) who have dispersed themselves into sundry places aswell without as within this Cittye farre remote from Cheapside Lombardstreete and other places thereunto adiacent, the anntient and most proper inletts for o[u]r trade.[63]

In the opening days of 1635, a warden of the Goldsmiths' Company was verbally abused by a fellow goldsmith in the street. Mr Warden Mannynge complained to the company's court of assistants of 'some ill speeches in some passages of a conferrence had between them in the rowe in Cheapside'. Mannynge asserted that 'every member of this Company according to the rule of good government ought to give that due respect to the p[er]son of a Warden which the place requireth'.[64] Notably, this ugly confrontation took place on a street that had deep-rooted associations with the products and labour of goldsmiths, but by the mid-1630s was at the centre of a major contention concerning spatial, architectural, and political uniformity. The Goldsmiths' Company's principal route of search was the street front of luxury shops and workspaces known as Goldsmiths' Row, situated at the west end of Cheapside, the chief ceremonial and commercial street in the City of London.

Cheapside was by far the widest and most prestigious thoroughfare within the walls.[65] It was the site of a large permanent market of perishable goods, and a location for the enacting of exemplary punishment, particularly of those who deceitfully contravened the ethics of the 'public' market.[66] The street was framed by high-status retail spaces and domestic residences on both sides, and it was, accordingly, the location for the most significant public ceremonies of City and Crown. From the early seventeenth century the most remarkable of these public spectacles was the lord mayor's show, 'the high point of the civic calendar'. As we saw with James Pemberton's spectacular event, this was an annual pageant that included a procession and a dramatic performance which marked the inauguration of the new mayor.[67] As shown in the illustration of Edward VI's coronation procession of 1547, during ceremonial rituals the built environment of Cheapside was itself a stage of civic magnificence, as well as a viewing platform for members of the urban elite (see figure 7.4).[68] The domestic residences and shop fronts of Cheapside were a veritable showcase of crafts and trades; gold

Figure 7.4 *Coronation procession of Edward VI passing the Cheapside Cross*, from a painting of 1547, engraving executed in 1809.

and silver wares, painted textiles, highly skilled plasterwork, joinery, and carpentry.

One section of Cheapside attracted particular acclaim. Sixteenth-century residents and foreign visitors alike were united in their praise for the magnificence and splendour of Goldsmiths' Row. John Stow wrote of:

> the most beautiful frame of fayre houses and shoppes, that bee within the Walles of London, or else where in England … It contayneth in number tenne fayre dwelling houses, and foureteene shoppes, all in one frame, uniformly builded foure stories high, bewtified towardes the streete with the Goldsmithes armes and the likenes[s] of woodmen in memory of his name [Thomas Wood, goldsmith and fifteenth-century founder], riding on monstrous beasts, all which is cast in lead, richly painted over and gilt, these he gave to the Goldsmithes with stockes of money to be lent to yong men, having those shops, &c.[69]

The Goldsmiths' Company was the freeholder of the great majority of properties along the Row and the west end of Cheapside – sixty-three tenancies in total – and their ordinances stated that tenants had to be both members of the company and practising goldsmiths. Plainly the objective was to keep this quarter of the City as a site specifically for working goldsmiths. Some of these tenancies consisted of shops or stalls on the ground floor, with domestic residences located above; others were simply retail spaces.[70] Artisanal labour undoubtedly took place on site as there are repeated references in company court minutes to gilding or melting houses and furnaces on Cheapside. An analysis of three lists of occupiers of houses and shops on the Row, compiled between 1558 and 1569 by the Goldsmiths' clerk, shows that there was a very close connection between seniority within the company and occupancy on the Row, 'the great majority of those who gained firm footing there also attained the carefully limited haven of the livery'. Richard Rogers, assayer at Goldsmiths' Hall and at the Tower mint, also ran two businesses in the Row in the late sixteenth century. Sir Richard Martin, liveryman, master of the Mint from 1582, and four-time prime warden of the Goldsmiths' Company, resided in a house on the Row during his mayoralty in 1593–94. Having a presence on the Row was highly desirable in the sixteenth century, such that the Goldsmiths' Company kept a 'waiting list' of applicants should any space on this prestigious street fall vacant.[71] If Goldsmiths' Hall on Foster Lane was the social and ceremonial heart of the body of the guild, and the centre of craft regulation, then the workshops and residences upon Cheapside and Lombard Street were its gilded veins.

The wardens of the Goldsmiths' Company were endowed with the right and responsibility to search the workshops of all silversmiths, goldsmiths, and retailers of gold and silver goods, powers of search that were principally established and upheld through royal charter. Their focus was Cheapside, Lombard Street, and Foster Lane.[72] The regulation of goldsmiths, in particular, had always been a priority of the Crown because of the material interrelationship between plate and coinage.[73] Search was a guild activity undertaken in the suburbs and liberties, not just within the City walls.[74] However, the Goldsmiths' Company were unusual in having the right to inspect wares not simply two miles beyond the City walls, but also (admittedly much less frequently) in many towns across the country.[75] In August 1635, for example, the wardens searched premises in Newcastle upon Tyne, York, Lincoln, Lyme Regis, Norwich, Ipswich, Colchester, and Chelmsford.[76]

On search days the company hall was the site from which the perambulation of guild officials, in groups of three or four and dressed in their liveries, would begin and end. As Patrick Wallis and Catherine Wright have written, on the search the 'backdrop to most regulatory encounters was the interplay of their personal experience, technical ability, and perceptual authority in judging the qualities of things'. This 'roving panel of experts' was composed of searchers whose status was a composite of 'age, experience, success, and corporate office-holding'.[77] The search took in workshops, retail sites, and fairs, with guild officials checking for substandard wares (in the case of precious metals, suspicious commodities would be confiscated and assayed at Goldsmiths' Hall). Since search records rarely note the location of the offender's workshop, it is frustratingly hard to plot the routes of the company searchers.[78] The Goldsmiths' Company's court minutes are replete with instances of 'bad workeinge' and 'deceitful' practices, goldsmiths who 'cloggingeľd] their worke with unnecessary sauder', or put 'new ffeete to the bodyes of old boules'.[79] Defective wares (those below the standard) would be broken up by company wardens, and wrongdoers fined. Persistent (fourth time) offenders would face humiliating public-facing punishments in Goldsmiths' Hall, including stocks 'in the open eye of the whole Com[mon]altie for example to others to avoide the like deceite in workmanshipp'.[80]

The ritual of 'searching' workshops and retail spaces at regular intervals was thus one of the principal means through which the geography or spatial bounds of guild authority were repeatedly and publicly reasserted within the urban environment. As with the rites of 'beating the bounds' of the parish on Rogation Days by parish authorities (men often involved too in guild governance), the routes of the company searchers symbolically bound the wider community of guildsmen to a fraternal whole. The premises of every freeman were linked, through the circuits of company officials, to his livery hall.[81] This is not to say that the authority of the guild elite, and their legal rights to enter private premises, always went unchallenged. For the Goldsmiths' Company, cases in which company searchers were denied access to workshops and retailing spaces increased from *c.* 1630.[82] Court minutes from across the companies reveal that on searches guild representatives might be subject to verbal, even physical, abuse by freemen who refused to recognise the authority of guild officials. In 1636 a silversmith named Thomas Duffield caused quite a scene following the breaking up of two great kettles and the nozzles of three great candlesticks by Jackson, the company assayer. Jackson claimed that 'hee was in fear of his life and because hee [Duffield] thrust him out of the [assay] office hee broke a greate parte of the glass windows'. Duffield had also threatened the company assayer that 'hee would let his guts out about his heeles'.[83] Some guildsmen even threatened – or attempted – to take legal action against searchers who appeared to lack legitimacy, had violated their sense of good government, or who seemed incapable of making accurate or honest judgements about the quality of their craft products.[84]

John Stow's effusive praise for the Row as 'the most beautiful frame of fayre houses and shoppes' was written in the last years of the sixteenth century, when the street fronts had been recently refurbished – under the direction of goldsmith Sir Richard Martin – and were still the subject of much admiration. But in the following decades this language of praise turned into an alarmist commentary of ruin and decay.[85] From the 1610s

City authorities, the king, and foreign visitors began to remark upon the poor material appearance of the Row, and the distasteful mixing of trades. The once uniform display of goldsmiths' wares had been disrupted by the arrival of 'mean' trades, including mercers, haberdashers, and perfumers. Critics of the disorderly appearance of Cheapside were quick to link the declining material and commercial value of Goldsmiths' Row to the movement of prominent goldsmiths to workspaces and shops west of the City walls.

By the 1630s approximately seventy-five goldsmiths were 'remote' from the City; most had set up businesses in Holborn or on Fleet Street and the Strand, the flourishing extra-mural areas which were attracting some of the wealthiest residents and clientele in the growing metropolis, as well as the most luxurious trades.[86] At the same time that Goldsmiths' Hall was being remodelled, its members were also engaged in a fierce negotiation concerning spatial conformity within and outside the walls. These two issues – rebuilding and the Row – dominated discussions at the Goldsmiths' court of assistants for the entirety of the 1630s. From the perspective of many liverymen the rebuilding project on Foster Lane and the reform of the Row were unmistakably part of the same drive to improve the reputation and built fabric of the company, and reclaim authority over contested spaces.

The wardens of the Goldsmiths' Company had initiated the drive for the improvement of the Row and the spatial unity of the trade in a petition to the Crown in 1619. This led to a City and Crown campaign to force 'remote' goldsmiths to return to their customary City centre location – an operation with little success, that had petered out by 1625.[87] The campaign for the return of 'remote' goldsmiths, which gained momentum from the mid-1630s, was spearheaded by the royal council. A series of directives addressed to the City government, and the Goldsmiths' Company specifically, articulated an increasingly frustrated royal authority, for 'the rotting Row was very visible'.[88] At Star Chamber in November 1634, the Privy Council complained to the summoned wardens of the Goldsmiths' Company that:

> in the Goldsmithes Rowe in Cheapside and Lumbardstreete, divers shopps are held and occupyed by persons of other trades, whereby that uniforme shew and seemelynes w[hi]ch was before an ornament to those places, and a luster to the Cittye, when all the shopps were used w[i]th Goldsmiths w[i]thout the mixture of any other, is now greatly blemished; Of w[hi]ch incongruous change his Ma[jes]ty takeinge notice, is therew[i]th much offended.[89]

The disorderly appearance of the Row was an affront to the aesthetic sensibilities of Charles I. This was no trivial matter, when we consider the close association between political authority and 'uniform' architecture, and the allied royal drive to create a truly imperial capital city.[90] Moreover, the 'blemished' face of Cheapside demonstrated the blatant absence of goldsmiths, who 'not regardinge those places w[hi]ch are most proper for them, have seated themselves scateredly in sondrye streets, and some of them in obscure places'.[91] The 'absenteeism' of these goldsmiths and their continued refusal to return to Cheapside was interpreted as flagrant insubordination by citizens who should ultimately defer to the authority of the king. The Crown insisted the goldsmiths obey 'vpon the penalty of beeinge put out of the places of Assistants and of the Liverye'. And yet, a small group refused to be moved, in the words of the royal council: 'preferringe their owne humors and ends before the respect and obedience w[hi]ch they owe to order and Gouverment and to the authoritye of the Boarde'.[92]

Through recorded petitions, the institutional archive gives us insights into the perspectives of early seventeenth-century goldsmiths within and outside the City walls. In a 'humble petic[i]on' to the Goldsmiths' Company's court of assistants in December 1634, 'the Goldsmithes Inhabitants in Cheapside' set out their case for the importance of the spatial clustering of the craft and trade in 'Cheapside Lombardstreete and other places thereunto adiacent, the anntient and most proper inletts for o[u]r trade', and outlined the dangers of the existing situation. Primarily, the dispersal of workshops 'farre remote' from the Row was said to have resulted in a growth of unregulated activity, undertaken both by goldsmiths and 'divers that are not bred up in the Misterye of Gouldsmithes' having not 'served seaven yeares as Apprentises thereunto'. Of chief concern was the allegation that the spatial splintering of the craft had resulted in a situation whereby 'much stollen goods are consealed to the prejudice of the owners, w[hi] ch would bee discovered if it were brought into the open m[ar]ket'.[93] The 'open' character of Cheapside, here equated with the legitimacy and public nature of commercial activity, is contrasted with the 'remote' places, outside the walls, where illegitimate goods and activities are 'consealed'.[94] Guild governors had a long-established concern about goldsmiths living and working in 'secret' spaces. This anxiety related to 'both aliens and Englishmen' who were said to 'often keep chambers in secret places and shops in dark lanes within London, and in such places often purchase [dishonest] plate and other goods', and also 'make sub-standard gold and silver ware contrary to the constitutions and ordinances of the craft'. The Goldsmiths' Company's fifteenth-century ordinances prescribed that 'no man may work in lanes or chambers or secret places, but only in the high street in shops publicly that men may see that their work is truly done and that the wardens may exercise their right of search'. [95]

Moreover, according to the Cheapside goldsmiths, the movement away from the Row, a set of premises with leases collectively controlled by goldsmiths, had resulted in unchecked ambition. The petitioners reported that 'certaine others of the same trade in this Cittye whoe by inlargeinge their shopps have ingrossed amongst them almost the whole trade ... to the great prejudice of the Major parte of o[u]r Company'. The goldsmiths of Cheapside suggested that these damaging trends might be reversed, 'the inlett wilbee still forestalled', if 'they bee all brought generally within the walles of the Citty'.[96] The wardens of the Goldsmiths' Company responded to this petition by undertaking a special search of various premises in the Royal Exchange, one of the areas identified by the petitioners as a hotbed of unregulated activity.[97]

When challenged by their fellow guildsmen and requested to take up premises upon the Row, the goldsmiths outside the walls re-framed their situation and outlined a number of their own objections. Notably they presented themselves as 'poore Goldsmithes inhabiteinge in Fleetstreet the Strand and other publique places in and neere the Cittye of London and Westminster'. The principal petitioners in June 1635 – including Michael Barkstead, William Wheeler, Francis Allen, and James Prince – were liverymen of the Goldsmiths' Company.[98] These goldsmiths alleged that a wholesale relocation to the Rows was simply not logistically possible. They argued that 'the number of shopps either emptye or ... to bee disposed of are not above xxxiiii and the Gouldsmithes who are enjoyned to conforme to the said orders are one hundred familyes and upwards'. Moreover, these premises on Cheapside were not affordable. Though the properties were meant to be leased and 'enjoyed by young men of the said mistery at easie and indifferent rents', as had been intended by 'charitable benefactors', in reality 'unreasonable ffines and excessive rents' were applied. Most significantly, the 'remote' goldsmiths stressed that though outside the City walls, their workshops and retail spaces were located upon 'Publique and open streets'. Their premises were not liminal spaces, thus, they should be permitted to 'still exercise their trades in the places where they now dwell ... and where the peticoners have expended the greatest p[ar]te of their estates to settle themselves for the Comodious exercising of the trades in which they have bin trayned up'.[99] The demand that they might remain apart from the customary district of Cheapside was thus allied to an assertion of their artisanal (guild-sponsored) training and the 'openness' of their workspaces and, by implication, their trading practices. These goldsmiths were explicitly refuting the charge of their peers that they were residing in 'obscure spaces'.[100] Under pressure from the Crown, in June 1635 seven liverymen (Giles Allen, John Perryn, John Parker, Michael Barkstead, William Maddox, John Prince, and George Courthop), were 'suspended from beeinge of the Assistants and Livery of the company ... untill they shall conforme'.[101] Their spatial non-conformity had led to their expulsion from the Goldsmiths' Company and deprivation of the freedom of the City. By the mid-1630s, then, the spatial location of a goldsmith's workshop and trading premises had come to (re)define his civic and social position within (or even outside) the guild.

Conclusion

The divisive issue of the disorderly Row and absent goldsmiths was never resolved. It proved impossible to force a return to an era in which the topography of the trade was tightly organised, with all 'uniform' goldsmiths' shops within the same City neighbourhood (and considering the fifteenth-century prescriptions concerning 'secret' places, we might question if this was ever more than a civic fantasy). The inability, and in certain cases unwillingness of the Goldsmiths' Company to collectively bring all workers of gold and silver within the City walls, was in part a result of ambiguity as to the very nature of 'publique' space. Individual goldsmiths had diverging conceptions as to the limits and ambitions of corporate, and certainly royal authority. Nonetheless it is striking how in their opposing petitions, both 'the Goldsmithes Inhabitants in Cheapside', and 'the Goldsmithes inhabiteinge in Fleetstreet the Strand and other publique places' explictly engaged with the notion of public space. The arguments for being 'brought … within the walles' were clearly linked to the notion that customary marketplaces and open streets ensured public scrutiny of artisanal and trade practices, and were primary sites for company searches and the enforcement of guild authority.[102] The principal 'remote' goldsmiths repeatedly asserted that developing sites of luxury trade, in extra-mural areas, should also be considered to be 'Publique and open streets'.[103] The development and expansion of the built environment of London generated heated discussion and dissension as to the nature and limits of urban public space. Simultaneously, the rebuilding of Goldsmiths' Hall, and the material embellishment of gates and outward walls at institutional artisanal and mercantile architectures, sharpened thinking and boundaries as to relatively public and private zones of influence and authority. It mattered to the Goldsmiths to assert the organisation of building works 'within their owne ground'.[104] When it came to streets, guild halls, workshops, and retail spaces in 1630s London, spatial clustering and architectural uniformity were becoming markers of political acquiescence (and its opposite, an explicit challenge).

Notes

1 GL, MS 12065/2, fo. 15v.
2 GL, MS 17155, fo. 7.
3 Harding, 'Space, property, and propriety', p. 562.
4 Stevenson, *The City and the King*, pp. 34–6.
5 GHA, WA/CM, S1, fo. 56v.
6 Laitinen and Cohen, *Cultural History of Early Modern Streets*, p. 196.

7 Following John Goodall, I too have taken the term 'gatehouse' 'to be broadly understood. It can refer to any entrance structure that amounts to more than simply an opening in a wall or a decorative archway.' See 'The English gatehouse', *Architectural History*, 55 (2012), pp. 1–23, at p. 1.
8 *Wardens' Accounts of the Founders' Company*, pp. 182, 275, 289.
9 For signboards see Andrew Gordon, '"If my sign could speak": the signboard and the visual culture of early modern London', *Early Theatre*, 8:1 (2005), 35–51.
10 *Records of the Worshipful Company of Carpenters*, VI, p. 33.
11 *Ibid.*, VII, pp. 300, 486.
12 Daniel Jütte, *The Strait Gate: Thresholds and Power in Western History* (New Haven, CT: Yale University Press, 2015), p. 221. For the intimate association between 'wall' and 'city' see also James D. Tracy, 'Introduction', in Tracy (ed.), *City Walls: The Urban Enceinte in Global Perspective* (Cambridge: Cambridge University Press, 2000), pp. 1–15, at p. 1.
13 Schofield, *The Building of London*, p. 67. In early modern London 'the lord mayor's jurisdiction covered an area that extended beyond the City's ancient wall'. See Ward, *Metropolitan Communities*, p. 9.
14 Emily Mann, 'In defence of the City: the gates of London and Temple Bar in the seventeenth century', *Architectural History*, 49 (2006), 75–99, at p. 75.
15 Stevenson, *The City and the King*, p. 70.
16 The phrase 'social filter' is from Jütte, *The Strait Gate*, p. 225.
17 Mann, 'In defence of the City', p. 80.
18 Stevenson, *The City and the King*, p. 72.
19 Oliver Creighton and Robert Higham, *Medieval Town Walls: An Archaeology and Social History of Urban Defence* (Stroud: Tempus, 2005), p. 168.
20 Stow, *A Survey of London*, I, p. 38.
21 *Ibid.*, pp. 38–9. Several of the Tudor (Elizabethan) statues which decorated Ludgate have survived, and are currently housed in the church of St. Dunstan in the West, Fleet Street. See John Schofield, *London 1100–1600: The Archaeology of a Capital City* (Sheffield; Oakville, CT: Equinox, 2011), p. 17.
22 Stevenson, *The City and the King*, p. 70.
23 Mann, 'In defence of the City', p. 78.
24 Prideaux, *Memorials of the Goldsmiths' Company*, I, p. 112.
25 *Records of the Worshipful Company of Carpenters*, VII, p. 300.
26 The gatehouse also had a monitoring function at Oxford colleges. See Geoffrey Tyacke, *Oxford: An Architectural Guide* (Oxford: Oxford University Press, 1998), p. 42, 'The room over the gateway [at New College, Oxford] was, and still is, part of the Warden's house or Lodgings (a term also used in contemporary aristocratic houses), and its strategic placing enabled him to keep an eye on visitors and on the activities of the Fellows.'
27 *Records of the Worshipful Company of Carpenters*, VII, p. 407.
28 Goodall, 'The English gatehouse', p. 3; Heal, *Hospitality in Early Modern England*, pp. 34–5; Milne, 'Merchants of the City', pp. 263–4.
29 Prideaux, *Memorials of the Goldsmiths' Company*, I, pp. 216–17.
30 GHA, WA/CM, S1, fo. 39r.
31 *Ibid.*, fos 56r–v.
32 *Ibid.*, fo. 77r; S2, fo. 166r. The gold plate was worth £10, the chain £30.
33 Harding, 'Cheapside: commerce and commemoration'.
34 GHA, WA/CM, S1, fo. 39v.
35 *Ibid.*, fo. 41v.
36 GHA, WA/CM, S2, fos 182r–v.
37 *Ibid.*, fo. 176r.
38 GHA, WA/CM, S1, fo. 56v. Emphasis added.
39 Erica Longfellow has suggested that 'we tend to agree – as did early modern people – that that which is public is that which has national or community relevance'.

See 'Public, private, and the household in early seventeenth-century England', *Journal of British Studies*, 45:2 (2006), 313–34, at p. 315.
40 GHA, WA/CM, S1, fo. 72r. Emphasis added.
41 Harding, 'Space, property, and propriety', p. 557.
42 GHA, WA/CM, S1, fos 56r–v.
43 Newman, 'Nicholas Stone's Goldsmiths' Hall', p. 35; Sebastian Serlio, *Tutte l'opere d'architettura* (Venice, 1575), VII, p. 143.
44 Johnson, 'Meanings of polite architecture', pp. 48–9.
45 Maurice Howard, 'Classicism and civic architecture in Renaissance England', in Gent (ed.), *Albion's Classicism*, pp. 29–49, at p. 33, 'Public buildings, unlike the country houses of this period which were increasingly isolated within great parks, enter into dialogue with the urban space around them.'
46 Derek Keene, Arthur Burns, and Andrew Saint (eds), *St Paul's: The Cathedral Church of London 604–2004* (New Haven, CT; London: Yale University Press, 2004), pp. 171–90; John Newman, 'Inigo Jones and the politics of architecture', in Kevin Sharpe and Peter Lake (eds), *Culture and Politics in Early Stuart England* (Stanford, CA: Stanford University Press, 1993), pp. 229–56, at p. 246; Smuts, 'The court and its neighbourhood', p. 120.
47 Newman, 'Inigo Jones and the politics of architecture', pp. 229–30; Anderson, *Inigo Jones and the Classical Tradition*, ch. 7.
48 *Stuart Royal Proclamations*, ed. by James F. Larkin and Paul L. Hughes, 2 vols (Oxford: Clarendon Press, 1973–), II, p. 21 [Proclamation no. 9].
49 *Ibid.*, I, p. 112 [Proclamation no. 51].
50 *Ibid.*, I, p. 172 [Proclamation no. 78].
51 *Ibid.*, I, p. 346 [Proclamation no. 152].
52 *Ibid.*, I, p. 346 [Proclamation no. 152]. Emphasis added.
53 *Ibid.*, II, pp. 24–5 [Proclamation no. 9]. See also James Robertson, 'Stuart London and the idea of a royal capital city', *Renaissance Studies*, 15:1 (2001), 37–58.
54 GHA, WA/CM, R2, fo. 216v.
55 Jean Imray, *The Mercers' Hall* (London: The London Topographical Society and The Mercers' Company, 1991), p. 19.
56 *Ibid.*, p. 16; Schofield, *Medieval London Houses*, p. 174.
57 Stevenson, *The City and the King*, p. 39.
58 Stow, *A Survey of London*, I, p. 269.
59 Imray, *The Mercers' Hall*, p. 15.
60 Howard, 'Classicism and civic architecture', p. 31, 'For a start they would not have understood the term 'classical' as such but might have used the words 'antique' or 'Roman' according to the different literary or historical resonances buildings were thought to convey.'
61 Balthasar de Monconys, *Journal des Voyages*, 2 vols (Lyon, 1665–66), I (1666), p. 75. Translation is my own.
62 Howard, 'Classicism and civic architecture', p. 42.
63 GHA, WA/CM, S1, fo. 34r. In the company court minutes fifty-five of the 'remote' goldsmiths are said to be living in the West End.
64 GHA, WA/CM, S1.
65 Harding, 'Cheapside: commerce and commemoration', p. 78, 'some four hundred yards long and fifty to sixty feet broad before the Great Fire of 1666. Some of the streets leading off it were only five or six feet wide at the junction.'
66 Harding, 'Cheapside: commerce and commemoration', pp. 86–90; James Masschaele, 'The public space of the marketplace in medieval England', *Speculum*, 77:2 (2002), 383–421, at p. 405, 'The crimes or misdemeanours that merited public punishment in a marketplace were typically committed in the marketplace: they were, in other words, acts usually committed *in* public.'
67 Berlin, 'Civic ceremony', p. 18.
68 Harding, 'Cheapside: commerce and commemoration', p. 85.

69 Stow, *A Survey of London*, I, pp. 345–6.
70 Thomas F. Reddaway, 'Elizabethan London – Goldsmiths' Row in Cheapside, 1558–1645', *Guildhall Miscellany*, 2 (1963), 181–206, at pp. 182–3.
71 *Ibid.*, pp. 184, 189.
72 Prideaux, *Memorials of the Goldsmiths' Company*, I, p. 93.
73 John Forbes, 'Search, immigration and the Goldsmiths' Company: a study in the decline of its powers', in Gadd and Wallis (eds), *Guilds, Society and Economy in London*, pp. 115–25, at pp. 115–16.
74 Ward, *Metropolitan Communities*, pp. 27–44; Rappaport, *Worlds within Worlds*, p. 113.
75 Ian Anders Gadd and Patrick Wallis, 'Reaching beyond the city wall: London guilds and national regulation, 1500–1700', in Epstein and Prak (eds), *Guilds, Innovation and the European Economy*, pp. 288–315.
76 GHA, WA/CM, S2, fos 125r–139r.
77 Wallis and Wright, 'Evidence, artisan experience, and authority', pp. 139–40, 143.
78 Ward, *Metropolitan Communities*, p. 28.
79 GHA, WA/CM, V, fos 53v–54r.
80 Quoted in Janelle Day Jenstad, 'Public glory, private gilt: the Goldsmiths' Company and the spectacle of punishment', in Anne Goldgar and Robert Frost (eds), *Institutional Culture in Early Modern Society* (Leiden; Boston, MA: Brill, 2004), pp. 191–217, at p. 210.
81 Michael Berlin, 'Reordering rituals: ceremony and the parish, 1520–1640', in Griffiths and Jenner (eds), *Londinopolis*, pp. 47–66, at pp. 55, 57.
82 Forbes, 'Search, immigration and the Goldsmiths' Company', p. 117; Mitchell, *Silversmiths in Elizabethan and Stuart London*, p. 178.
83 GHA, WA/CM, S1, fos 108–9.
84 Wallis, 'Controlling commodities: search and reconciliation', in Gadd and Wallis (eds), *Guilds, Society, Economy*, pp. 90–1.
85 Griffiths, 'Politics made visible', pp. 176–7.
86 *Ibid.*, p. 178; Smuts, 'The court and its neighbourhood'; Peck, *Consuming Splendor*, pp. 46–7.
87 Griffiths, 'Politics made visible', pp. 178–82.
88 *Ibid.*, p. 177. Notably the Privy Council also became involved in the rebuilding of the church of St. Michael le Querne, located on an island site at the west end of Cheapside. By the 1630s this church 'was evidently in a serious state of decay'. Inigo Jones's intervention in this architectural project was resented by a number of parishioners, even to the extent that 'some of his drawings were (so he alleged) deliberately mislaid'. See Howard Colvin, 'Inigo Jones and the Church of St Michael le Querne', *The London Journal*, 12:1 (1986), 36–9.
89 GHA, WA/CM, S1, fo. 29r.
90 Griffiths, 'Politics made visible', pp. 182–5; Newman, 'Inigo Jones and the politics of architecture'.
91 GHA, WA/CM, S1, fo. 29r.
92 *Ibid.*, fo. 29v.
93 *Ibid.*, fos 34r–v.
94 Dave Postles, 'The market place as space in early modern England', *Social History*, 29:1 (2004), 41–58, at p. 42, 'the market place was recognizably a public and open space, open in the sense that many (but certainly not all) social interactions were visible'.
95 GHA, MS 2524, fos 37r, 45v.
96 GHA, WA/CM, S1, fos 34r–v.
97 *Ibid.*, fo. 35v.
98 It is notable that a number of these 'remote' goldsmiths, including Francis Allen and Michael Barkstead, were later listed as exceptions in the Act of Indemnity and Oblivion of 1660.

99 GHA, WA/CM, S1, fos 98r–v.
100 *Ibid.*, fo. 29r.
101 *Ibid.*, fos 105v–106r. It was later reported in January 1635/6 that 'imediately then after the aforesaid [court of assistants] John Perryn seated himself in the Goldsmithes Rowe in Cheape who therevpon was restored into the livery againe' [GHA, WA/CM, S2, fo. 171r].
102 GHA, WA/CM, S1, fos 34r–v.
103 *Ibid.*, fos 98r–v.
104 *Ibid.*, fo. 41v.

8

Conclusion

On the evening of Friday 18 August 1632, following the 'ancient custome' of a search of 'Ffanchurch Streete Lumber Streete Cheapside and Foster Lane', the wardens of the Goldsmiths' Company 'repayred to the hall where there was prepared a small banquett of ffruite and plomes'. These practices of collective workshop inspection and consumption, centred on Goldsmiths' Hall and its immediate urban environs, were largely unremarkable. But on this evening, the wardens were presented with a most extraordinary gift: Simon Gibbon donated to his guild – 'as a free guifte of his love'– a silver-gilt and rock-crystal standing salt, 35cm high and weighing 57 oz (see figure 8.1).[1] Salts were prestigious objects which might combine novel designs, complex techniques, elaborate details, and precious materials. A key decorative centrepiece at the high table, salts showcased the creative and technical ingenuity of the goldsmith and were customarily placed at the right-hand side of the host, in front of the most eminent guest at the feast.[2] The presentation of silver plate to one's guild was hardly uncommon, but the architectural design of this 'fair gilt salte', with four iconic columns supporting a square upper canopy, was highly distinctive and unusual. Undoubtably its makers were inspired by contemporary architectural treatises that espoused the increasingly fashionable *all'antica* style. The Goldsmiths' court minutes describe this object as 'a faire gilt salte … with four pillors and a figure of a man in the midle of the salte inclosed with crisstall curiously cut'.[3] Around the underside of the base is inscribed: 'The guift of Simon Gibbon Goldsmith 1632', '57-oz'. The salt is also stamped with a craftsman's mark of three trefoils within a larger trefoil (an unidentified maker's mark), and a 1576 London hallmark.

Gibbon was a Cheapside goldsmith, with at least twelve apprentices indentured to his workshop from 1600 until his death in 1644.[4] He was also an assistant of the Goldsmiths' Company and would become actively

Figure 8.1 *The Gibbon Salt*, silver-gilt and rock-crystal, h. 30.4 cm, 1576. Gifted in 1632 to the Goldsmiths' Company by Simon Gibbon.

involved in the rebuilding of Goldsmiths' Hall from the mid-1630s. The timing of Simon Gibbon's splendid gift hints that it was, perhaps, related to a trade infraction discovered that summer day on the company search. Most significant, though, is its curious and atypical longevity within the Goldsmiths' Company's plate collection. Some 400 years after it entered the hall with its eponymous goldsmith, the 'Gibbon Salt' is still a centrepiece of the corporation's material treasures. Despite the necessary decimation of the company's plate collection in the 1630s, and again in the 1660s, the Gibbon Salt remained; evidently its cultural value outweighed its material worth. An object crafted from precious materials and styled upon the Vitruvian orders might have had cultural cachet in any early seventeenth-century domestic or institutional interior, but the Gibbon Salt's prominent sculptural display of classical design acts as a particular reminder of the goldsmith's engagement with architecture; it is a material 'site for a dialogue' between precious metalwork and architecture.[5] Displayed within the new Goldsmiths' Hall, a monumental building with an outward façade modelled on Serlian designs, the micro-architectural salt must have been a constant reminder both of the magnificence of the wider built environment and the collective virtuosity of London's goldsmiths. This final material article brings together some of the key themes with which this book has been centrally concerned: improvements to built space; meaningful furnishings and material gifts; artisanal skill as a valued attribute and a symbolic artefact; and the interrelationship between individual and collective identities.

Crafting Identities has shown how London witnessed a decided trend for livery hall rebuilding and adaptation from *c.* 1550 to 1640. Craft companies, from the relatively minor to the most affluent and politically influential, invested significant collective funds and corporate energy in the redesign and beautification of their built environments. This development can be framed as part of a broader resurgence of civic culture in this era, but it also points towards a more particular assertion of artisanal culture within the urban milieu.[6] In their design, furnishing, and ornamentation, company halls celebrated and memorialised a distinctive craft culture of expertise and regulation, and honourable masculine artisanal identity. Artisanal, workshop-based skills were a form of cultural capital in the civic environment, and hence the display of craft marks, hallmarks, tools, instruments, and working bodies. Repeatedly in these pages, whether exploring the building site with the City Viewers, the feasting table alongside artisanal and mercantile elites, or the guild-sponsored procession, we have encountered the significance of craft mastery as a civic accomplishment. Tellingly, at goldsmith James Pemberton's lord mayor's show in October 1611, at the apex of 'a Rocke or Mount of Golde' was the character of St. Dunstan, who 'had no little delight in the Arte of Gold-Smithery, and shewes himselfe now (as then) acting that profession'. In Anthony Munday's printed account of proceedings 'venerable' St. Dunstan was described as being 'very practique, and so well skild in Goldsmithery'.[7] The cultural and political significance of artisanal expertise – as related to the individual and the collective – alongside attributes such as respectability, authority, moderation, self-control, independence, honesty, and good fellowship, has been underestimated in previous accounts of London's civic culture.[8]

The evidence presented here of substantial building projects establishes the significance of guilds as patrons of the urban fabric. We have hitherto undervalued the extent to which craft guilds in sixteenth- and early seventeenth-century London shaped the aesthetics and materialities of urban space. This book has demonstrated how such an engagement with the built environment had social and cultural valence for particular craft companies and their memberships, but was also meaningful to wider urban audiences and political relationships. In their designs, materials, and furnishings, livery company halls were part of an ongoing communication (or means of ordering relations) between guild, City, and Crown. Certainly, as we saw in the discussion of goldsmiths, external walls, and workshop locations, this was a dialogue which was becoming increasingly challenging and fraught by 1640, the chronological endpoint of this study. Substantial investments in company halls had ceased by this date, no doubt in large measure a consequence of the mounting financial pressure applied by the Crown to a 'hard-pressed citizenry' in the form of forced loans.[9]

A new focus upon rebuilding projects at all stages of their development – from construction sites to furnished halls, negotiated by journeymen, masters, and civic elites – has also illuminated significant features of metropolitan artisanal knowledge cultures. Skilled craftsmen, including those engaged in architectural design at the highest political levels, did not perceive a fundamental division between theoretical and embodied knowledge. Expertise was communicated through the spoken word, text, drawing, object, or by manual demonstration, or through a combination of these different mediums. Preferences might depend upon the relative status or craft specialism of the interlocutors, or the location in which they made their assessments. Indeed, the social dimensions of artisanal knowledge cultures have also come to the fore in this study. We cannot speak of craft knowledge without acknowledging the web of social relations within and through which artisans operated. While the 'collaborative nature of artisanal production' in the workshop context is an acknowledged theme, this book has shown that the collective dimension suffused all aspects of artisanal evaluative culture.[10] Measurement of craft labour, appraisal of a building, or evaluation of a workshop product were understood to be fundamentally collaborative exercises, undertaken by craftsmen with weighty accumulated experiential knowledge and invested with civic authority.

The volume's novel emphasis upon the spatial and material dimensions of institutional craft cultures has situated company halls as important sites of metropolitan epistemological culture. In these multifunctional spaces, artisans engaged with knowledge cultures in a variety of different ways. Guild buildings could be active testing sites in which substances, materials, and objects were evaluated by groups of experts. Halls might also operate as ceremonial workshops in which masterpieces were produced or displayed. More broadly, the gifting of tools and objects for exhibition and ceremony, within and outside company buildings, worked to elevate the cultural significance of the craft mystery and its practitioners. Livery halls were not simply sites of craft regulation, though this was undoubtably one of their significant facets; they were also spaces of epistemological exchange.

This brings us to the central theme of identities. Early chapters established the significance of participation with institutions and networks in formulating and understanding personal identities in this period. And, through close examination of the remodelling of institutional artisanal buildings and the everyday and ritualised practices located within, we have observed 'the social self', that is, the individual artisan in relation to his craft community, and how this was shaped by his placement and movement within the artisanal company hall.[11] In short, the built environment and material cultures were central in the understanding, construction, and enactment of artisanal identities in early modern London. The various degrees of political and social privilege and responsibility which constituted the hierarchical body of the guild – from apprentices to master of the company – were experienced, performed, and reinforced through access to, or exclusion from, prestigious routes, chambers, and precious things. Attainment of full civic manhood, with its associations of householder status, economic independence, and participation in craft governance, was both reproduced and strengthened through experiential practices within company halls. Many mature adult guildsmen were denied these spatial and status privileges for a time, or permanently (at Pewterers' Hall, for instance, only the company assistants might freely enjoy the adjoining bowling alley for their recreations).[12] This spatial ordering of masculine honour and hierarchy was not new in the mid-sixteenth century, but the relationship between identity and space intensified as halls grew and diversified, and as guild populations expanded. It might also have proved problematic. Indeed, looking forward to the increasingly politically charged atmosphere of 1640s London, it does not seem too far a stretch to suggest that the spatial embeddedness and experience of exclusion within livery halls, particularly for the yeomanry, contributed to intensified 'demands for wider participation' in company governance.[13]

Repeatedly in the preceding chapters we have seen how institutional artisanal spaces and material cultures worked to bolster the masculine nature of artisanal identity. Certainly, women were not absent from guild buildings. Women might be resident in artisanal halls and carry out valuable (though low-status) work tasks, such as cleaning linen after civic dinners, preparing food, and tending to corporate gardens. The presence of women in these institutional built environments was, however, highly regulated. They were not welcome in or granted access to spaces associated with civic governance, trade regulation, or record management, such as parlours, treasuries, or galleries: these were the exclusive domain of mature adult men. Even the company and movement of wealthy guild widows were closely monitored within guild halls. During feasts, women frequently sat at separate tables (sometimes in entirely separate rooms) and were denied access to or the ability to touch the most treasured material possessions, such as election cups and crowns. Evidently these materially and spatially exclusionary practices, rooted in gender difference, consolidated the status of artisanal masculinity. The association between civic masculinity and political authority was also affirmed through material gifts and furnishings in craft halls. Only male donors presented high-status objects associated with governance and regulation (such as wooden tables inscribed with historic ordinances, or chests for the storage of archives). Notably, prominent male artisans also gave gifts which reinforced the symbolic capital of skill and independence,[14] including tools for display in institutional spaces (such as the armourer William Seger, who gave 'to the Hall a great Biccorne [an anvil] and a pair of great sheires') and objects inscribed with a personal craft mark (for example a silver gilt spoon donated by pewterer Walter Walshe 'grauyn on the ende his marke').[15] Female benefactors did not give such showpieces. Textile gifts might embody feminine accomplishments in needlework, but they did not relate to the particular embodied skills of the craft mystery, or the independent status of a workshop householder.

By 1640 London's craft company halls were highly significant, multi-functional, and architecturally complex spaces. Livery halls were centres of artisanal regulation, politics, sociability, and culture, densely interconnected to workshops and retail spaces across the metropolis. These built environments had also become fundamental to a collective institutionalised sense of artisanal legacy and craft history. We can no longer speak of early modern London's diverse network of sites and spaces of economic, cultural, civic, or social import without including company halls as a fundamental element of this dynamic urban environment. As flames lapped across the City of London in September 1666, this rich built heritage, the work of generations of craftsmen, was largely reduced to piles of rubble and ash.[16] As he walked through the smouldering remains of the City, Samuel Pepys picked up in Cheapside 'a piece of glass of Mercer's chapel in the street, where much more was, so melted and buckled with the heat of the fire, like parchment'.[17] And yet, following concerted programmes of reconstruction on the original sites, in under a decade the great majority of these institutional buildings were to re-emerge once again within the metropolitan landscape.[18]

Notes

1 GHA, WA/CM, R2, fo. 243.
2 Glanville, *Silver in England*, p. 42; Marian Campbell, 'The table and feasting', in Richard Marks and Paul Williamson (eds), *Gothic: Art for England 1400–1547* (London: V&A, 2003), pp. 309–11, at p. 311.
3 GHA, WA/CM, R2, fo. 243.
4 TNA, PROB 11/192/524. See also *Records of London's Livery Companies Online*. http://londonroll.org/about [accessed 27 July 2020].
5 For objects as 'sites for a dialogue between architecture and the other arts', see Alina Payne, 'Materiality, crafting and scale in Renaissance architecture', *Oxford Art Journal*, 32:3 (2009), 365–86, at p. 373. On the historic 'nexus between architecture and goldsmithing', see François Bucher, 'Micro-architecture as the "idea" of Gothic theory and style', *Gesta*, 15:1/2 (1976), 71–89, at p. 73.
6 On civic culture see Berlin, 'Civic ceremony in early modern London'; Hill, *Pageantry and Power*, ch. 1.
7 Munday, *Chruso-Thriambos*, sigs. B1v, C2r.
8 Barry, 'Civility and civic culture', pp. 193–5; Withington, *The Politics of Commonwealth*, ch. 6; Tittler, *The Face of the City*, ch. 5.
9 Ashton, *The City and the Court*, p. 176.
10 Smith, 'Making and knowing in a sixteenth-century goldsmith's workshop', p. 37.
11 On the 'social self' see Martin, *Myths of Renaissance Individualism*, p. 22.
12 Welch, *History of the Pewterers' Company*, II, p. 8.

13 Norah Carlin, 'Liberty and fraternities in the English Revolution: the politics of London artisans' protests, 1635–59', *International Review of Social History*, 39:2 (1994), 223–54, at pp. 229–31.
14 Karras, *From Boys to Men*, p. 118, 'tools of the trade ... which could be worth a substantial amount but also symbolized independence'.
15 GL, MSS 12105, fo. 11r; 7110, fo. 2r.
16 Reddaway, *The Rebuilding of London*, p. 26. An estimated forty-four out of sixty livery company halls were destroyed.
17 Wednesday 5 September 1666. *The Diary of Samuel Pepys: A Selection*. Selected and ed. by Robert Latham from *The Diary of Samuel Pepys, a New and Complete Transcription* ed. by Robert Latham and Matthew Williams (London: Penguin Books, 2003), p. 666.
18 Lucas and Russell, *The Livery Halls of the City of London*, p. 242, 'three-quarters [of the City's destroyed livery halls] were structurally complete by 1673'.

Select bibliography

Manuscript sources

British Library

Additional MS 34307
Harley MS 38
Harley MS 541
Sloane MS 1423

Drapers' Company Archive, London

DB1 'Dinner Book', 1564–1602

Goldsmiths' Hall Archive, London

WA/CM [Wardens Accounts and Court Minutes], C-T (1509–1639)
C II.2.1 H. Gamon, *The Gouldesmythes' Storehowse. Wherein is layde up many hidden secrets of that Ingenious Misterie* (1604).
2524 The Book of Ordinances and Statutes, 1478.

Guildhall Library, City of London

Armourers' and Brasiers' Company

12071/1 Court Minutes, 1413–1559
12071/2 Court Minutes, 1559–1621
12073 Yeomanry Court Minutes, 1552–1604
12085 Livery Quarterage Book, 1604–65
12065/1 Wardens' Accounts, 1497–1563
12065/2 Wardens' Accounts, 1563–1616
12065/3 Wardens' Accounts, 1616–63
12079/2 Yeomanry Quarterly Supper Expenses Accounts, 1604–16

12157	List of armourers working at Greenwich, *c.* 1630
12105	Benefactions book, 1660–1877
12106	Extracts from wills (1551–1826), 1848
12104	Plans and Surveys of Hall and Estates, 1679
12107	Inventories, 1663–1791

Bakers' Company

5177/1	Court Minutes, 1537–61
5177/2	Court Minutes, 1561–92
5174/3	Wardens' Accounts, 1586–1625
5201	Inventories, 1604–26

Blacksmiths' Company

2883/1	Memorandum book

Carpenters' Company

4329/1	Court Minutes, 1533–73
4329/2	Court Minutes, 1573–94
4329/3	Court Minutes, 1600–18
4326/2	Wardens' Accounts, 1546–73
4326/5	Wardens' Accounts, 1593–1613
4326/6	Wardens' Accounts, 1592–1622
4329A	Inventories, 1627–59
4332	Register of Leases, 1477–1835

Clockmakers' Company

2710/1	Court Minutes, 1632–80
2710/2	Court Minutes, 1680/1–99

Cooks' Company

MS 3115	Benefaction Book, 1617
MS 9999	Inventories, 1752–68

Coopers' Company

5618/1	Benefactors Lists, 1718–85
5618/2	Benefactors Lists, 1718–85
5621	Inventories, 1673–1726

Cordwainers' Company

7351/1	Wardens' Accounts, 1595–1636

Curriers' Company

14357	Hall Inventory (fragment), 1558

Cutlers' Company

7164	Inventories, 1586–1664

Founders' Company

6335	Court Orders, 1603–38
6330/1	Wardens' Accounts, 1497–1576
6330/2	Wardens' Accounts, 1576–1681
6353/1	'Some Account of the Worshipful Company of Founders', 1800? –1867?
6353/2	'Some Account of the Worshipful Company of Founders', 1800? –1867?

Girdlers' Company

5817	Benefactions Book, 1431–1638

Haberdashers' Company

15868	Yeomanry Wardens' Accounts, 1601–61
15874	'The State of the Charities, 1597'

Ironmongers' Company

16967/1	Court Minutes, 1555–1603
16988/2	Wardens' Accounts, 1539–92
16988/3	Wardens' Accounts, 1593–1616
16988/4	Wardens' Accounts, 1616–34
16988/5	Wardens' Accounts, 1634–51
16960	Will Book, 1471–1799
17155	Surveyor's Reports and Plans, 1613–14

Parish Clerks' Company

4890	Receipt Book, 1583–1657

Pewterers' Company

7090/1	Court Minutes, 1551–61
7090/2	Court Minutes, 1561–89
7090/3	Court Minutes, 1589–1611
7090/4	Court Minutes, 1611–43
22181	Yeomanry Wardens' Accounts, 1608–19
22191	Wardens' Accounts – expenditure on dinners, 1637–53
7110	Inventories, 1490–1756

Plumbers' Company

MS 2208/1	Court Minutes, 1621–47

Tallow Chandlers' Company

6152/1	Court Minutes, 1534–77
6153/1	Court Minutes, 1607–48

6163/1 Papers concerning entertainments and ceremonies, 1624–39, 1662–75
6155/1 Yeomanry Wardens' Accounts, 1519–49
6155/2 Yeomanry Wardens' Accounts, 1550–1627

Tylers' and Bricklayers' Company

3043/1 Court Minutes, 1580–1667

Weavers' Company

4646 Wardens' Accounts, 1588–1732

London Metropolitan Archive

LMA, COL/CA/01/01/030 Repertory of the Court of Aldermen, 1605–7
LMA, COL/CA/01/01/033 Repertory of the Court of Aldermen, 1610–12
LMA, COL/CA/01/01/038 Repertory of the Court of Aldermen, 1618–20
LMA, COL/CA/01/01/039 Repertory of the Court of Aldermen, 1620–21
COL/SJ/27/465 Viewers' Reports, 1623–36

The National Archive, Kew

Probate Records:
PROB 11/46/67
PROB 11/53/33
PROB 11/203/300
PROB 11/61/343
PROB 11/132/202
PROB 11/192/524

Sir John Soane's Museum, London

MS 22 The Account Book of Nicholas Stone
MS 23 The Note Book of Nicholas Stone

Published sources

Primary sources

Agricola, Georgius, *De Re Metallica*, trans. by Herbert Hoover and Lou Hoover (New York, 1950).

The Annals of the Barber-Surgeons of London, compiled from their records and other sources, by Sidney Young (London: Blades, East & Blades, 1890).

B., W., *A touch-stone for gold and silver wares; or, a manual for goldsmiths and all other persons, whether buyers, sellers, or wearers of any manner of goldsmiths work* (London, 1677).

Bacon, Francis, *Novum Organum: with other parts of the great instauration*, trans. and ed. by Peter Urbach and John Gibson (Chicago, IL: Open Court, 1994).

Calendar of Wills Proved and Enrolled in the Court of Husting, London, A.D. 1258–A.D. 1688, ed. by Reginald R. Sharpe, 2 vols (London: John C. Francis, 1889–90).

The Diary of Samuel Pepys: A Selection. Selected and ed. by Robert Latham from *The Diary of Samuel Pepys, a New and Complete Transcription*, ed. by Robert Latham and Matthew Williams (London: Penguin Books, 2003).

The De Moneta of Nicolas Oresme and English Mint Documents, trans. by C. Johnson (London; New York: Nelson 1956).

Dee, John, *The Mathematicall Preface to the Elements of Geometrie of Euclid of Megara* (London, 1570).

Digges, Leonard, *A boke named tectonicon briefelye shewynge the exacte measurynge, and speady rekenynge all maner lande, squared timber, stone, steaples, pyllers, globes* (London, 1556).

The Dinner Book of the London Drapers' Company, 1564–1602, ed. by Sarah Milne (Woodbridge: The Boydell Press, 2019).

Ercker, Lazarus, *Treatise on Ores and Assaying*, trans. by Anneliese Grünhaldt Sisco and Cyril Stanley Smith (Chicago, IL: University of Chicago Press, 1951).

Gerhold, Dorian, *London Plotted: Plans of London Buildings c. 1450–1720* (London: London Topographical Society, 2016).

Harrison, William, *The description of England*, ed. by George Edelen (Washington, DC: Folger Shakespeare Library, and Dover; London: Constable, 1994).

The London Surveys of Ralph Treswell, ed. by John Schofield (London: London Topographical Society, 1987).

London Viewers and their Certificates, 1508–1558: Certificates of the Sworn Viewers of the City of London, ed. by Janet Senderowitz Loengard (London: London Record Society, 1989).

Machyn, Henry, *The Diary of Henry Machyn, Citizen and Merchant-Taylor of London, from A.D. 1550 to A.D. 1563*, ed. by John Gough (London, 1848).

Memorials of the Guild of Merchant Taylors of the Fraternity of St. John the Baptist, in the City of London; and of its Associated Charities and Institutions, compiled and selected by Charles M. Clode (London: Harrison & Sons, 1875).

Milles, Thomas, *The custumers alphabet and primer* (London, 1608).

Monconys, Balthasar de, *Journal des Voyages*, 2 vols (Lyon, 1665–66).

More, Richard, *The carpenters rule; or, a book shewing many plain waies, truly to measure ordinarie timber* (London, 1602).

Moxon, Joseph, *Mechanick exercises: or, the doctrine of handy-works* (London, 1677).

Munday, Anthony, *Chruso-Thriambos: The Triumphes of Golde* (London, 1611).

The Notebooks of Nehemiah Wallington, 1618–1654, ed. by David Booy (Aldershot: Ashgate, 2007).

Prideaux, Walter Sherburne, *Memorials of the Goldsmiths' Company*, 2 vols (London: Eyre and Spottiswoode, 1896–97).

Records of the Worshipful Company of Carpenters, ed. by B. Marsh, J. Ainsworth, and A. M. Millard, 7 vols (Oxford: Oxford University Press, 1914–68).

Records of the Worshipful Company of Tallow Chandlers, ed. by M. F. Monier-Williams, 2 vols (London, 1897–98).

Spiers, Walter Lewis, 'The note-book and account book of Nicholas Stone', *The Volume of the Walpole Society*, 7 (1918–19), pp. 1–200.

Stuart Royal Proclamations, ed. by James F. Larkin and Paul L. Hughes, 2 vols (Oxford: Clarendon Press, 1973–).

A Survey of Documentary Sources for Property Holding before the Great Fire, ed. by Derek Keene and Vanessa Harding (London, 1985), British History Online, www.british-history.ac.uk/london-record-soc/vol22 [accessed 14 July 2020].

A Survey of London by John Stow; Reprinted from the Text of 1603, with Introduction and Notes by Charles Lethbridge Kingsford, 2 vols (Oxford: Clarendon Press, 1908).

Wardens' Accounts of the Worshipful Company of Founders of the City of London, 1497–1681. Transcribed, calendared, and edited by Guy Parsloe (London: Athlone Press, 1964).

Wotton, Henry, *The Elements of Architecture, collected by Henry Wotton Knight, from the Best Authors and Examples* (London, 1624).

Secondary sources

Alford, B. and Barker, T. C., *A History of the Carpenters' Company* (London: Allen and Unwin, 1968).

Amelang, James S., *The Flight of Icarus: Artisan Autobiography in Early Modern Europe* (Stanford, CA: Stanford University Press, 1998).

Anderson, Christy, *Inigo Jones and the Classical Tradition* (Cambridge: Cambridge University Press, 2007).

Anderson, Christy, 'Live words and experience in early modern architecture', in Nebahat Avcioglu and Allison Sherman (eds), *Artistic Practices and Cultural Transfer in Early Modern Italy: Essays in Honour of Deborah Howard* (Farnham: Ashgate, 2015), pp. 77–87.

Appadurai, Arjun, 'Introduction: commodities and the politics of value', in Appadurai (ed.), *The Social Life of Things: Commodities in Cultural Perspective* (Cambridge: Cambridge University Press, 1986), pp. 3–63.

Archer, Ian, *The Pursuit of Stability: Social Relations in Elizabethan London* (Cambridge: Cambridge University Press, 1991).

Archer, Ian, 'The arts and acts of memorialisation in early modern London', in J. F. Merritt (ed.), *Imagining Early Modern London: Perceptions and Portrayals of the City from Stow to Strype, 1598–1720* (Cambridge: Cambridge University Press, 2001), pp. 89–113.

Archer, Ian, 'The livery companies and charity in the sixteenth and seventeenth centuries', in Ian Anders Gadd and Patrick Wallis (eds), *Guilds, Society and Economy in London 1450–1800* (London: Centre for Metropolitan History, Institute of Historical Research in association with Guildhall Library, 2002), pp. 15–28.

Archer, Ian, 'Discourses of history in Elizabethan and early Stuart London', *Huntingdon Library Quarterly*, 68: 1–2 (2005), 205–26.

Archer, Jayne E., Goldring, Elizabeth, and Knight, Sarah (eds), *The Intellectual and Cultural World of the Early Modern Inns of Court* (Manchester; New York: Manchester University Press, 2011).

Arnade, Peter, Howell, Martha, and Simons, Walter, 'Fertile spaces: the productivity of urban space in northern Europe', *The Journal of Interdisciplinary History*, 32:4 (2002), 515–48.

Ash, Eric, *Power, Knowledge and Expertise in Elizabethan England* (Baltimore, MD; London: Johns Hopkins University Press, 2004).

Ash, Eric (ed.), *Expertise: Practical Knowledge and the Early Modern State* (Chicago, IL: University of Chicago Press, 2010).

Ashton, Robert, *The City and the Court, 1603–1643* (Cambridge: Cambridge University Press, 1979).

Barron, Caroline, *London in the Later Middle Ages: Government and People, 1200–1500* (Oxford: Oxford University Press, 2004).

Barry, Jonathan, 'Bourgeois collectivism? Urban association and the middling sort', in Jonathan Barry and Christopher Brooks (eds), *The Middling Sort of People: Culture, Society and Politics in England, 1550–1800* (London: Macmillan, 1994), pp. 84–112.

Ben-Amos, Ilana Krausman, *The Culture of Giving: Informal Support and Gift-Exchange in Early Modern England* (Cambridge: Cambridge University Press, 2008).

Bergeron, David M., *English Civic Pageantry, 1558–1642*, rev. edn (Tempe, AZ: Arizona State University, 2003).

Berlin, Michael, 'Civic ceremony in early modern London', *Urban History Yearbook*, 13 (1986), 15–27.

Berlin, Michael, '"Broken all in pieces": artisans and the regulation of workmanship in early modern London', in Geoffrey Crossick (ed.), *The Artisan and the European Town, 1500–1900* (Aldershot: Scolar, 1997), pp. 75–91.

Berlin, Michael, 'Guilds in decline? London livery companies and the rise of a liberal economy, 1600–1800', in S. R. Epstein and Maarten Prak (eds), *Guilds, Innovation and the European Economy, 1400–1800* (Cambridge: Cambridge University Press, 2008), pp. 316–41.

Bertucci, Paola, *Artisanal Enlightenment: Science and the Mechanical Arts in Old Regime France* (New Haven, CT: Yale University Press, 2017).

Bishop, Jennifer, 'The clerk's tale: civic writing in sixteenth-century London', in Liesbeth Corens, Kate Peters, and Alexandra Walsham (eds), *The Social History of the Archive: Record Keeping in Early Modern Europe*, Past and Present Supplement 11 (Oxford, 2016), pp. 112–30.

Branch, Laura, *Faith and Fraternity: London Livery Companies and the Reformation, 1510–1603* (Leiden; Boston, MA: Brill, 2017).

Brigden, Susan, 'Religion and social obligation in early sixteenth-century London', *Past and Present*, 103:1 (1984), 67–112.

Capp, Bernard, *The World of John Taylor the Water-Poet* (Oxford: Clarendon, 1994).

Cavallo, Sandra, *Artisans of the Body in Early Modern Italy* (Manchester: Manchester University Press, 2007).

Cooper, Nicholas, *Houses of the Gentry: 1480–1680* (New Haven, CT; London: Yale University Press, 1999).

Cooper, Nicholas, 'Rank, manners and display: the gentlemanly house, 1500–1750', *Transactions of the Royal Historical Society*, 12 (2002), 291–310.

Cooper, Tarnya, *Citizen Portrait: Portrait Painting and the Urban Elites of Tudor and Jacobean England and Wales* (New Haven, CT; London: Yale University Press, 2012).

Cressy, David, *Literacy and the Social Order: Reading and Writing in Tudor and Stuart England* (Cambridge: Cambridge University Press, 1980).

Davids, Karel, 'Craft secrecy in Europe in the early modern period: a comparative view', *Early Science and Medicine*, 10:3 (2005), 341–8.

Davis, Natalie Zemon, *The Gift in Sixteenth-Century France* (Oxford: Oxford University Press, 2000).

Dillon, Janette, *The Language of Space in Court Performance, 1400–1625* (Cambridge: Cambridge University Press, 2010).

Durning, Louise, 'The Oxford college as household, 1580–1640', in Sandra Cavallo and Silvia Evangelisti (eds), *Domestic Institutional Interiors in Early Modern Europe* (Farnham: Ashgate, 2009), pp. 83–101.

Eamon, William, *Science and the Secrets of Nature: Books of Secrets in Medieval and Early Modern Culture* (Princeton, NJ: Princeton University Press, 1994).

Eamon, William, 'How to read a book of secrets', in Elaine Leong and Alisha Rankin (eds), *Secrets and Knowledge in Medicine and Science, 1500–1800* (Burlington, VT: Ashgate, 2011), pp. 23–46.

Epstein, S. R., 'Craft guilds, apprenticeship and technological change in pre-industrial Europe', *The Journal of Economic History*, 58:3 (1998), 684–713.

Erickson, Amy, 'Eleanor Mosley and other milliners in the City of London companies 1700–1750', *HWJ*, 71:1 (2011), 147–72.

Farr, James R., *Hands of Honor: Artisans and Their World in Dijon, 1550–1650* (Ithaca, NY; London: Cornell University Press, 1988).

Farr, James R., 'On the shop floor: guilds, artisans and the European market economy, 1350–1750', *Journal of Early Modern History*, 1:1 (1997), 24–54.

Farr, James R., *Artisans in Europe, 1300–1914* (Cambridge: Cambridge University Press, 2000).

Flather, Amanda, *Gender and Space in Early Modern England* (Woodbridge: Boydell, 2007).

Fox, Adam, *Oral and Literate Culture in England 1500–1700* (Oxford: Clarendon, 2000).

Friedrich, Markus, *The Birth of the Archive: A History of Knowledge in the Early Modern World*, trans. by John Noël Dillon (Ann Arbor: University of Michigan Press, 2018).

Gadd, Ian Anders and Wallis, Patrick (eds), *Guilds, Society and Economy in London 1450–1800* (London: Centre for Metropolitan History, Institute of Historical Research in association with Guildhall Library, 2002).

Girouard, Mark, *Elizabethan Architecture: Its Rise and Fall, 1540–1640* (New Haven, CT: Yale University Press, 2009).

Gerbino, Anthony and Johnston, Stephen, *Compass and Rule: Architecture as Mathematical Practice in England, 1500–1750* (New Haven, CT; London: Yale University Press, 2009).

Giles, Katherine, 'The "familiar" fraternity: the appropriation and consumption of medieval guildhalls in early modern York', in Sarah Tarlow and Susie West (eds), *The Familiar Past? Archaeologies of Later Historical Britain* (London; New York, Routledge, 1999), pp. 87–102.

Giles, Katherine, *An Archaeology of Social Identity: Guildhalls in York, c.1350–1630* (Oxford: J. and E. Hedges, 2000).

Gordon, Andrew, *Writing Early Modern London: Memory, Text and Community* (New York: Palgrave Macmillan, 2013).

Gowing, Laura, '"The freedom of the streets": women and social space, 1560–1640', in Paul Griffiths and Mark Jenner (eds), *Londinopolis: Essays in the Social and Cultural History of Early Modern London* (Manchester: Manchester University Press, 2000), pp. 130–51.

Gowing, Laura, 'Girls on forms: apprenticing young women in seventeenth-century London', *Journal of British Studies*, 55:3 (2016), 447–73.

Grassby, Richard, 'Material culture and cultural history', *The Journal of Interdisciplinary History*, 35:4 (2005), 591–603.

Griffiths, Paul, 'Secrecy and authority in late sixteenth- and seventeenth-century London', *The Historical Journal*, 40 (1997), 925–51.

Griffiths, Paul, 'Politics made visible: order, residence and uniformity in Cheapside, 1558–1645', in Paul Griffiths and Mark Jenner (eds), *Londinopolis: Essays in the Social and Cultural History of Early Modern London* (Manchester: Manchester University Press, 2000), pp. 176–96.

Hamling, Tara and Richardson, Catherine, *A Day at Home in Early Modern England: Material Culture and Domestic Life, 1500–1700* (New Haven, CT: Yale University Press, 2017).

Hanawalt, Barbara A., *Ceremony and Civility: Civic Culture in Late Medieval London* (New York: Oxford University Press, 2017).

Harding, Vanessa, 'The population of London, 1550–1700: a review of the published evidence', *The London Journal*, 15:2 (1990), 111–28.

Harding, Vanessa, 'Space, property, and propriety in urban England', *The Journal of Interdisciplinary History*, 32: 4 (2002), 549–69.

Harding, Vanessa, 'Cheapside: commerce and commemoration', *Huntingdon Library Quarterly*, 71:1 (2008), 77–96.

Harkness, Deborah E., *The Jewel House: Elizabethan London and the Scientific Revolution* (New Haven, CT; London: Yale University Press, 2007).

Harris, Eileen, *British Architectural Books and Writers 1556–1785* (Cambridge: Cambridge University Press, 1990).

Heal, Felicity, *Hospitality in Early Modern England* (Oxford: Clarendon Press, 1990).

Heal, Felicity, *The Power of Gifts: Gift-Exchange in Early Modern England* (Oxford: Oxford University Press, 2014).

Herbert, William, *The History of the Great Twelve Livery Companies of London*, 2 vols (London, 1837).

Hill, Tracey, *Pageantry and Power: A Cultural History of the Early Modern Lord Mayor's Show, 1585–1639* (Manchester: Manchester University Press, 2010).

Hills, Helen, 'Theorizing the relationship between architecture and gender in early modern Europe', in H. Hills (ed.), *Architecture and the Politics of Gender in Early Modern Europe* (Aldershot: Ashgate, 2003), pp. 3–22.

Howard, Maurice, 'Classicism and civic architecture in Renaissance England', in Lucy Gent (ed.), *Albion's Classicism: The Visual Arts in Britain, 1550–1660* (New Haven, CT; London: Yale University Press, 1995), pp. 29–49.

Hubbard, Eleanor, *City Women: Money, Sex, and the Social Order in Early Modern London* (Oxford: Oxford University Press, 2012).

Jacobi, Lauren, *The Architecture of Banking in Renaissance Italy: Constructing the Spaces of Money* (Cambridge: Cambridge University Press, 2019).

Johnson, Matthew, 'Meanings of polite architecture in sixteenth-century England', *Historical Archaeology*, 26:3 (1992), 45–56.

Johnson, Matthew, *Housing Culture: Traditional Architecture in an English Landscape* (London: UCL Press, 1993).

Johnson, Matthew, *English Houses, 1300–1800: Vernacular Architecture, Social Life* (Harlow: Longman, 2010).

Johnston, Stephen, 'Mathematical practitioners and instruments in Elizabethan England', *Annals of Science*, 48:4 (1991), 319–44.

Jupp, Edward Basil, *An Historical Account of the Worshipful Company of Carpenters of the City of London: Chiefly Compiled from Records in their Possession* (London: W. Pickering, 1848).

Jütte, Daniel, *The Age of Secrecy: Jews, Christians, and the Economy of Secrets, 1400–1800*, trans. by Jeremiah Riemer (New Haven, CT: Yale University Press, 2015).

Jütte, Daniel, *The Strait Gate: Thresholds and Power in Western History* (New Haven, CT: Yale University Press, 2015).

Karras, Ruth Mazo, *From Boys to Men: Formations of Masculinity in Late Medieval Europe* (Philadelphia, PA: University of Pennsylvania Press, 2003).

Kilburn-Toppin, Jasmine, 'Gifting cultures and artisanal guilds in sixteenth- and early seventeenth-century London', *The Historical Journal*, 60:4 (2017), 865–87.

Kilburn-Toppin, Jasmine, '"A place of great trust to be supplied by men of skill and integrity": assayers and knowledge cultures in late sixteenth- and seventeenth-century London', *The British Journal for the History of Science*, 52:2 (2019), 197–223.

King, Chris, 'The interpretation of urban buildings: power, memory and appropriation in Norwich merchants' houses, c. 1400–1660', *World Archaeology*, 41:3 (2009), 471–88.

Laitinen, Riitta and Cohen, Thomas V. (eds), *Cultural History of Early Modern Streets* (Leiden; Boston, MA: Brill, 2009).

Lancashire, Anne, *London Civic Theatre: City Drama and Pageantry from Roman times to 1558* (Cambridge: Cambridge University Press, 2002).

Lefebvre, Henri, *The Production of Space*, trans. by Donald Nicholson-Smith (Oxford: Blackwell Publishing, 1991).

Long, Pamela O., 'The openness of knowledge: an ideal and its context in sixteenth-century writings on mining and metallurgy', *Technology and Culture*, 32:2 (1991), 318–55.

Long, Pamela O., *Openness, Secrecy, Authorship: Technical Arts and the Culture of Knowledge from Antiquity to the Renaissance* (Baltimore, MD: Johns Hopkins University Press, 2001).

Long, Pamela O., *Artisan/Practitioners and the Rise of the New Sciences, 1400–1600* (Corvallis, OR: Oregon State University Press, 2011).

Luu, Lien Bich, *Immigrants and the Industries of London* (Aldershot; Burlington, VT: Ashgate, 2005).

Mann, Emily, 'In defence of the City: the gates of London and Temple Bar in the seventeenth century', *Architectural History*, 49 (2006), 75–99.

Marsh, Christopher, 'Order and place in England, 1580–1640: the view from the pew', *Journal of British Studies*, 44:1 (2005), 3–26.

Martin, John Jeffries, *Myths of Renaissance Individualism* (Basingstoke: Palgrave Macmillan, 2004).

Mauss, Marcel, *The Gift: The Form and Reason for Exchange in Archaic Societies*, trans. by W. D. Halls (London: Routledge, 1990).

Mitchell, David (ed.), *Goldsmiths, Silversmiths and Bankers: Innovation and the Transfer of Skill, 1550 to 1750* (Stroud: A. Sutton, 1995).

Mitchell, David, *Silversmiths in Elizabethan and Stuart London: Their Lives and their Marks* (Woodbridge: The Boydell Press, 2017).

Mukerji, Chandra, *Impossible Engineering: Technology and Territoriality on the Canal du Midi* (Princeton, NJ; Oxford: Princeton University Press, 2009).

De Munck, Bert, 'Artisans, products and gifts: rethinking the history of material culture in early modern Europe', *Past and Present*, 224:1 (2014), 39–74.

De Munck, Burt, Kaplan, Steven L., and Soly, Hugo (eds), *Learning on the Shop Floor: Historical Perspectives on Apprenticeship* (New York; Oxford: Berghahn Books, 2007).

Nevola, Fabrizio, 'Street life in early modern Europe', *Renaissance Quarterly*, 66:4 (2013), 1332–45.

Newman, John, 'Nicholas Stone's Goldsmiths' Hall: design and practice in the 1630s', *Architectural History*, 14 (1971), 30–9.

Newman, John, 'Inigo Jones and the politics of architecture', in Kevin Sharpe and Peter Lake (eds), *Culture and Politics in Early Stuart England* (Stanford, CA: Stanford University Press, 1993), pp. 229–56.

Ogilvie, Sheilagh, *The European Guilds: An Economic Analysis* (Princeton, NJ: Princeton University Press, 2019).

Orlin, Lena Cowen (ed.), *Material London, ca. 1600* (Philadelphia, PA: University of Pennsylvania Press, 2000).

Orlin, Lena Cowen, *Locating Privacy in Tudor London* (Oxford: Oxford University Press, 2007).

Overton, Mark, *et al.*, *Production and Consumption in English Households, 1600–1750* (London: Routledge, 2004).

Pappano, Margaret A. and Rice, Nicole R., 'Medieval and early modern artisan culture', *The Journal of Medieval and Early Modern Studies*, 43:3 (2013), 473–85.

Peck, Linda Levy, *Consuming Splendor: Society and Culture in Seventeenth-Century England* (Cambridge: Cambridge University Press, 2005).

Pollmann, Judith, *Memory in Early Modern Europe, 1500–1800* (Oxford: Oxford University Press, 2017).

Prak, Maarten and Wallis, Patrick (eds), *Apprenticeship in Early Modern Europe* (Cambridge: Cambridge University Press, 2020).

Rappaport, Steve, *Worlds within Worlds: Structures of Life in Sixteenth-Century London* (Cambridge: Cambridge University Press, 1989).

Reddaway, Thomas F., *The Rebuilding of London after the Great Fire* (London: Arnold, 1951).

Reddaway, Thomas F., 'Elizabethan London – Goldsmiths' Row in Cheapside, 1558–1645', *Guildhall Miscellany*, 2 (1963), 181–206.

Reddaway, Thomas and Walker, Lorna, *The Early History of the Goldsmiths' Company, 1327–1509* (London: Arnold, 1975).

Rice, Nicole R. and Pappano, Margaret A., *The Civic Cycles: Artisan Drama and Identity in Premodern England* (Notre Dame, IN: University of Notre Dame Press, 2015).

Rosser, Gervase, 'Going to the fraternity feast: commensality and social relations in late medieval England', *Journal of British Studies*, 33:4 (1994), 430–46.

Rosser, Gervase, 'Crafts, guilds and the negotiation of work in the medieval town', *Past and Present*, 154:1 (1997), 3–31.

Rosser, Gervase, *The Art of Solidarity in the Middle Ages: Guilds in England 1250–1550* (Oxford: Oxford University Press, 2015).

Schofield, John, *Medieval London Houses* (New Haven, CT; London: Yale University Press for the Paul Mellon Centre for Studies in British Art, 1995).

Schofield, John, *The Building of London: From the Conquest to the Great Fire*, 3rd rev. edn (Stroud: Sutton, 1999).

Seaver, Paul S., *Wallington's World: A Puritan Artisan in Seventeenth-Century London* (Stanford, CA: Stanford University Press, 1985).

Selwood, Jacob, *Diversity and Difference in Early Modern London* (Farnham: Ashgate, 2010).

Shapin, Steven, *A Social History of Truth: Civility and Science in Seventeenth-Century England* (Chicago, IL: University of Chicago Press, 1994).

Shepard, Alexandra, *Meanings of Manhood in Early Modern England* (Cambridge: Cambridge University Press, 2003).

Shepard, Alexandra, *Accounting for Oneself: Worth, Status, and the Social Order in Early Modern England* (Oxford: Oxford University Press, 2015).
Shepard, Alexandra and Withington, Phil (eds), *Communities in Early Modern England* (Manchester: Manchester University Press, 2000).
Smith, Pamela H., *The Body of the Artisan: Art and Experience in the Scientific Revolution* (Chicago, IL: Chicago University Press, 2004).
Smith, Pamela H., 'Making and knowing in a sixteenth-century goldsmith's workshop', in L. Roberts, S. Shaffer, and P. Dear (eds), *The Mindful Hand: Inquiry and Invention from the Late Renaissance to Early Industrialisation* (Amsterdam: Koninkliijke Nederlandse Akademie van Wetenschappen, 2007), pp. 33–57.
Smith, Pamela H., 'Why write a book? From lived experience to the written word in early modern Europe', *West 86th: A Journal of Decorative Arts, Design History, and Material Culture*, 19 (2012), 25–50.
Smith, Pamela H. and Schmidt, Benjamin (eds), *Making Knowledge in Early Modern Europe: Practices, Objects, and Texts, 1400–1800* (Chicago, IL; London: University of Chicago Press, 2007).
Smyth, Adam, *Autobiography in Early Modern England* (Cambridge: Cambridge University Press, 2010).
Spaeth, Donald, '"Orderly made": re-appraising household inventories in seventeenth-century England', *Social History*, 41:4 (2016), 417–35.
Spufford, Margaret, 'The limitations of the probate inventory', in Joan Chartres and David Hey (eds), *English Rural Society, 1500–1800: Essays in Honour of Joan Thirsk* (Cambridge: Cambridge University press, 1990), pp. 139–74.
Stevenson, Christine, *The City and the King: Architecture and Politics in Restoration London* (New Haven, CT: Yale University Press, 2013).
Thrupp, Sylvia L., *The Merchant Class of Medieval London, 1300–1500* (Chicago, IL: University of Chicago Press, 1948).
Tittler, Robert, *Architecture and Power: The Town Hall and the English Urban Community c. 1500–1640* (Oxford: Clarendon Press, 1991).
Tittler, Robert, 'Reformation, civic culture and collective memory in English provincial towns', *Urban History*, 24:3 (1997), 283–300.
Tittler, Robert, *The Reformation and the Towns in England: Politics and Political Culture, c.1540–1640* (Oxford: Clarendon, 1998).
Tittler, Robert, *The Face of the City: Civic Portraiture and Civic Identity in Early Modern England* (Manchester: Manchester University Press, 2007).
Tittler, Robert, 'Portraiture, precedence and politics amongst the London liveries, c. 1540–1640', *Urban History*, 35:3 (2008), 349–62.
Unwin, George, *The Gilds and Companies of London*, 4th edn (London: Cass, 1963).
Walker, Matthew, *Architects and Intellectual Culture in Post-Restoration England* (Oxford: Oxford University Press, 2017).
Wallis, Patrick, 'Controlling commodities: search and reconciliation in the early modern livery companies', in Ian Anders Gadd and Patrick Wallis (eds), *Guilds, Society and Economy in London 1450–1800* (London: Centre for Metropolitan History, Institute of Historical Research in association with Guildhall Library, 2002), pp. 85–100.
Wallis, Patrick, 'Apprenticeship and training in premodern England', *The Journal of Economic History*, 68:3 (2008), 832–61.
Wallis, Patrick and Wright, Catherine, 'Evidence, artisan experience, and authority in early modern England', in Pamela H. Smith, Amy R. W. Meyers, and Harold

J. Cook (eds), *Ways of Making and Knowing: The Material Culture of Empirical Knowledge* (Ann Arbor: The University of Michigan Press, 2014), pp. 138–63.

Ward, Joseph, *Metropolitan Communities: Trade Guilds, Identity, and Change in Early Modern London* (Stanford, CA: Stanford University Press, 1997).

Welch, Charles, *History of the Worshipful Company of Pewterers: Based Upon Their Own Records*, 2 vols (London: Blades, East & Blades, 1902).

Welch, Charles, *History of the Cutlers' Company of London and of Minor Cutlery Crafts*, 2 vols (London: Privately printed for the Cutlers' Company, 1916–22).

White, Adam, 'A biographical dictionary of London tomb sculptors *c.* 1560–*c.* 1660', *The Volume of the Walpole Society*, 61 (1999), pp. 1–162.

Whittle, Jane, 'A critique of approaches to "domestic work": women, work and the pre-industrial economy', *Past and Present*, 243:1 (2019), 35–70.

Withington, Phil, 'Two renaissances: urban political culture in post-Reformation England reconsidered', *Historical Journal*, 44:1 (2001), 239–67.

Withington, Phil, *The Politics of Commonwealth: Citizens and Freemen in Early Modern England* (Cambridge: Cambridge University Press, 2005).

Withington, Phil, 'Company and sociability in early modern England', *Social History*, 32:3 (2007), pp. 291–307.

Withington, Phil, *Society in Early Modern England: The Vernacular Origins of Some Powerful Ideas* (Cambridge: Polity, 2010).

Wood, Andy, *The Memory of the People: Custom and Popular Senses of the Past in Early Modern England* (Cambridge: Cambridge University Press, 2013).

Wrightson, Keith, *English Society, 1580–1680* (London: Routledge, 2003).

Zilsel, Edgar, 'The sociological roots of science', *The American Journal of Sociology*, 47:4 (1942), 544–62.

Index

Literary works can be found under authors' names. Page numbers followed by 'n.' and a number refer to a note on that page. Page numbers in italics refer to illustrations.